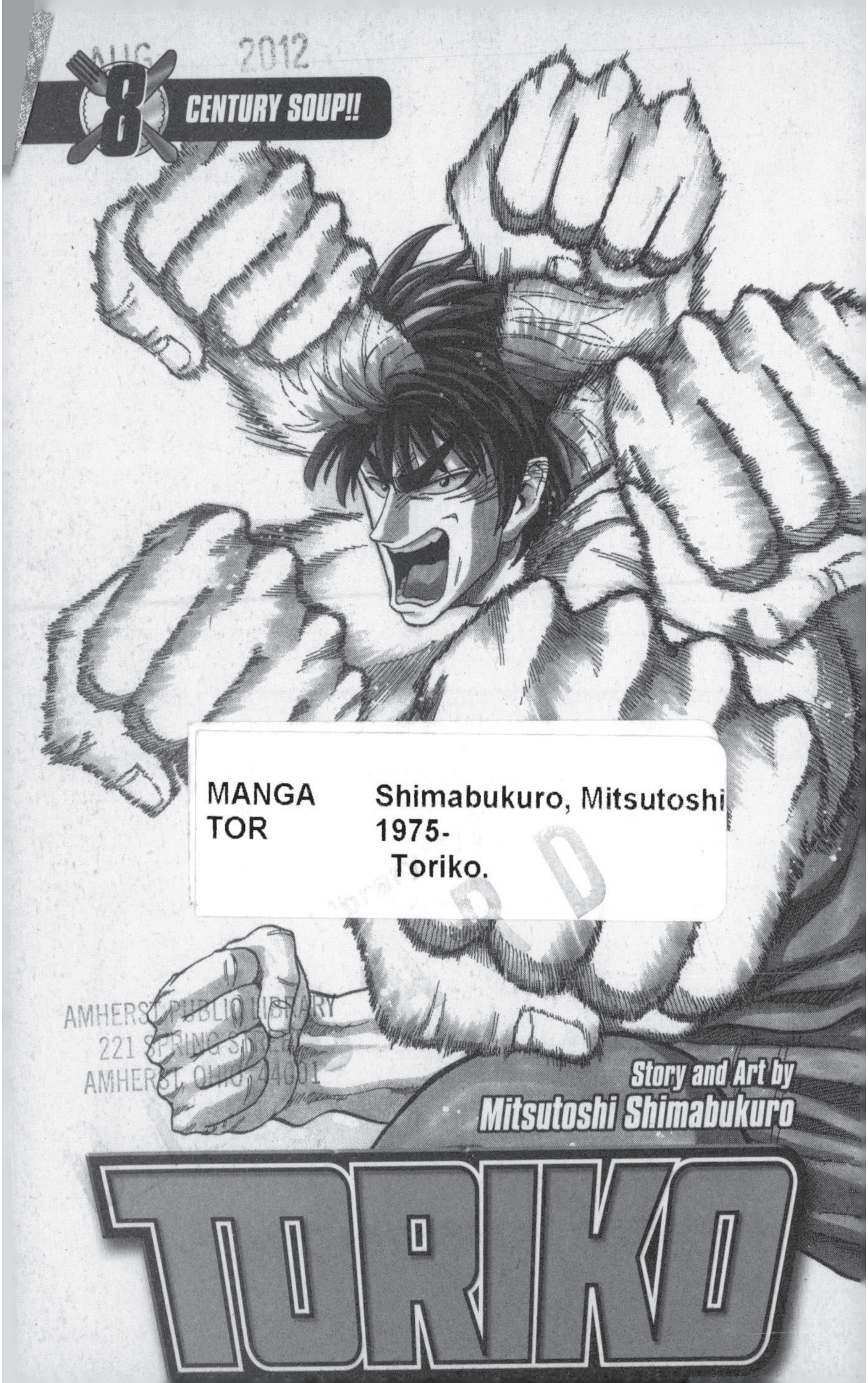
8
CENTURY SOUP!!
Story and Art by
Mitsutoshi Shimabukuro
TORIKO

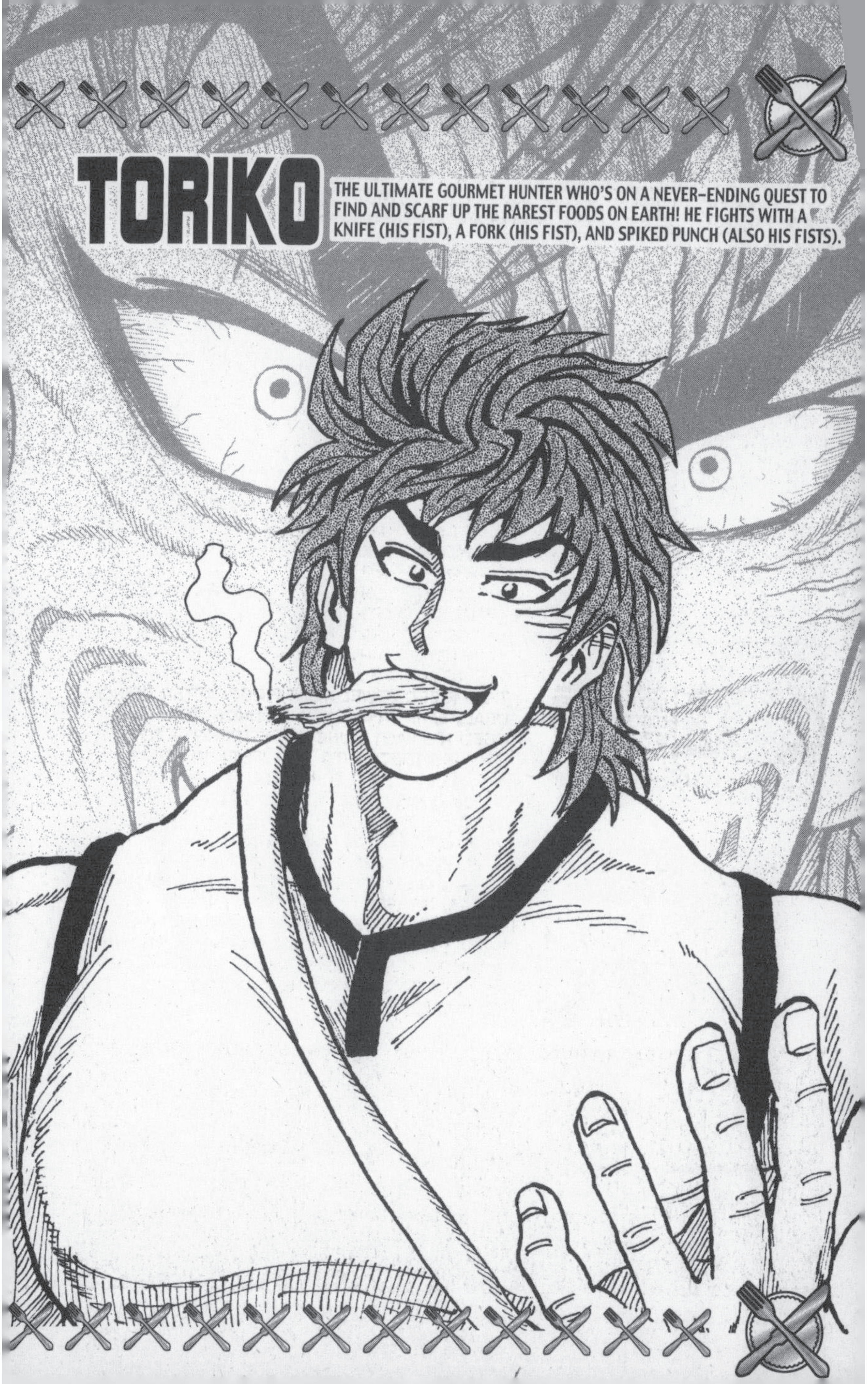
TORIKO
THE ULTIMATE GOURMET HUNTER WHO'S ON A NEVER-ENDING QUEST TO FIND AND SCARF UP THE RAREST FOODS ON EARTH! HE FIGHTS WITH A KNIFE (HIS FIST), A FORK (HIS FIST), AND SPIKED PUNCH (ALSO HIS FISTS).

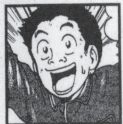

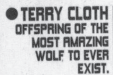

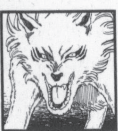

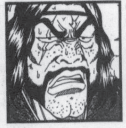

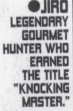

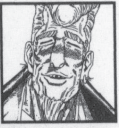

WHAT'S FOR DINNER

IT'S THE AGE OF GOURMET! KOMATSU, THE HEAD CHEF AT THE HOTEL OWNED BY THE IGO (INTERNATIONAL GOURMET ORGANIZATION), BECAME FAST FRIENDS WITH THE LEGENDARY GOURMET HUNTER TORIKO WHILE GATOR HUNTING. NOW KOMATSU ACCOMPANIES TORIKO ON HIS LIFELONG QUEST TO CREATE THE PERFECT FULL-COURSE MEAL.

ONE DAY, HE AND TORIKO ENCOUNTERED A GT ROBOT, A MACHINE DISPATCHED BY THE IGO'S RIVAL ORGANIZATION, "GOURMET CORP." SENSING A FOUL PLOT AFOOT, THE IGO MADE AN EMERGENCY SUMMONS OF THE FOUR KINGS--THE TOP GOURMET HUNTERS IN THE WORLD. THEY ASKED THE FOUR KINGS TO TAKE ON GOURMET CORP.'S GT ROBOTS IN AN ULTIMATE SHOWDOWN OVER THE ANCIENT REGAL MAMMOTH!

TORIKO'S GROUP AND THE GT ROBOTS WENT HEAD TO HEAD OUTSIDE AND INSIDE THE REGAL MAMMOTH, FIGHTING TO REACH THE PRIZED JEWEL MEAT FIRST. AFTER BEING DEALT SWIFT AND FATAL WOUNDS, TORIKO USED HIS LAST OUNCE OF STRENGTH TO SINK HIS TEETH INTO THE JEWEL MEAT. AS THE FLESH COURSED THROUGH HIS SYSTEM, TORIKO WAS MIRACULOUSLY REBORN...AS A STRONGER MAN, ABLE TO SMASH IN THE HEAD ROBOT'S FACE WITH HIS BRAND-NEW 10-FOLD SPIKED PUNCH!

SHORTLY AFTER, TORIKO SOJOURNED TO THE WU JUNGLE IN SEARCH OF BB CORN FOR HIS WOLF PAL, TERRY. BUT NO SOONER WERE THEIR BELLIES FULL AND BB CORN ADDED TO TORIKO'S FULL-COURSE MEAL THAN A WONKY NEW FOE SHOWED UP TO TEST TORIKO'S "EVOLVED" POWERS!

●KOMATSU
IGO HOTEL CHEF AND TORIKO'S #1 FAN

●TERRY CLOTH
OFFSPRING OF THE MOST AMAZING WOLF TO EVER EXIST.

●ZONGEH
SELF-PROCLAIMED SUPER-AWESOME GOURMET HUNTER. LOOKS TOUGH, BUT IS PASSIONATE AND HAS LOYAL FOLLOWERS.

●JIRO
LEGENDARY GOURMET HUNTER WHO EARNED THE TITLE "KNOCKING MASTER."

GOURMET CORP.

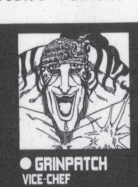

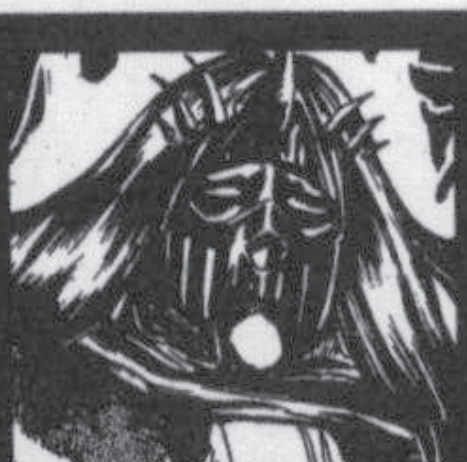

●STARJUN
VICE-CHEF

●GRINPATCH
VICE-CHEF

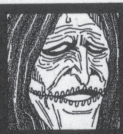

●JOE JOE
GT ROBOT MECHANIC

Contents

TORIKO

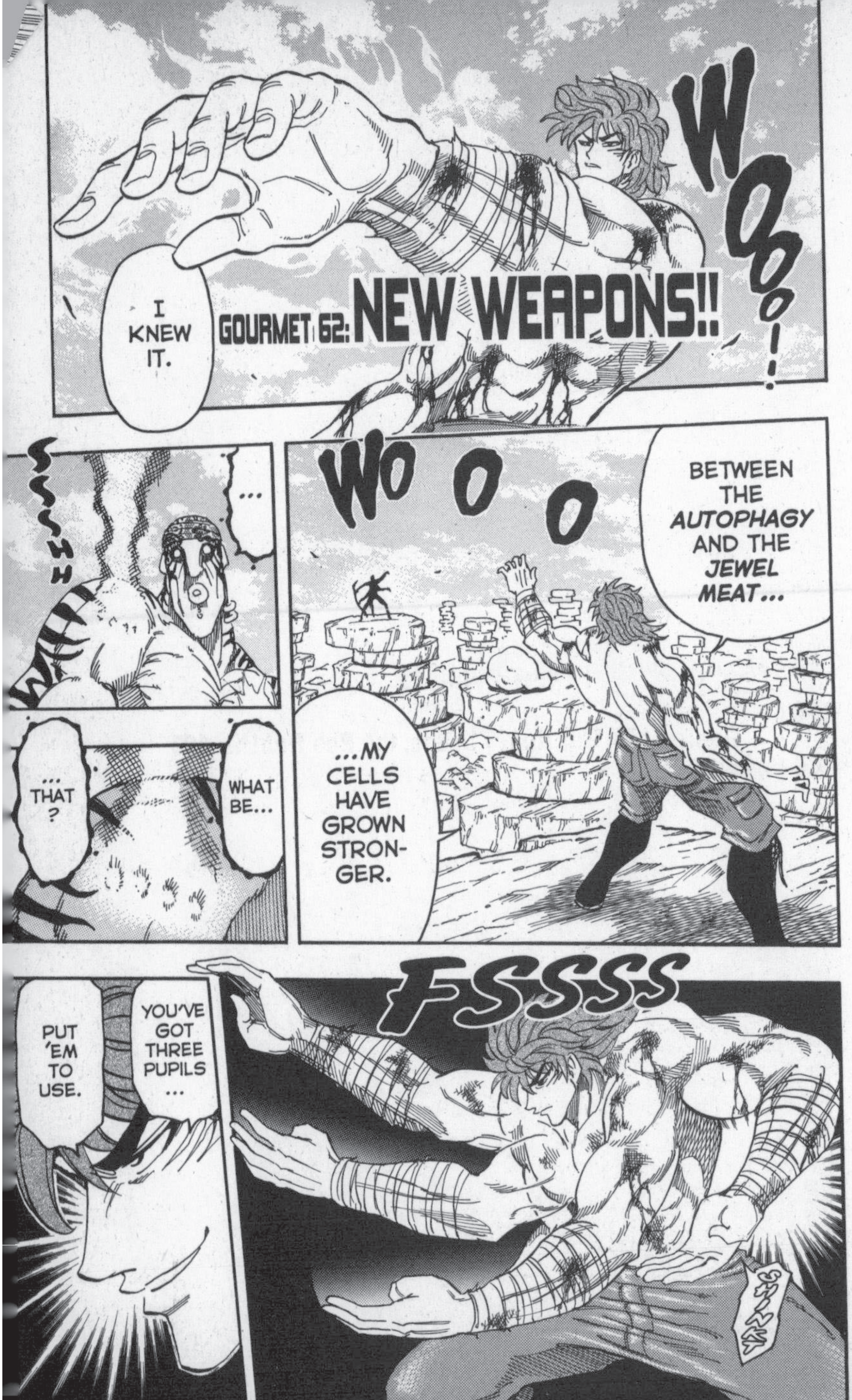
WOOO!!
GOURMET 62: NEW WEAPONS!!
I KNEW IT.
BETWEEN THE *AUTOPHAGY* AND THE *JEWEL MEAT*...
WO O O
...MY CELLS HAVE GROWN STRONGER.
...
SSSHH
WHAT BE...
...THAT?
FSSSS
YOU'VE GOT THREE PUPILS...
PUT 'EM TO USE.

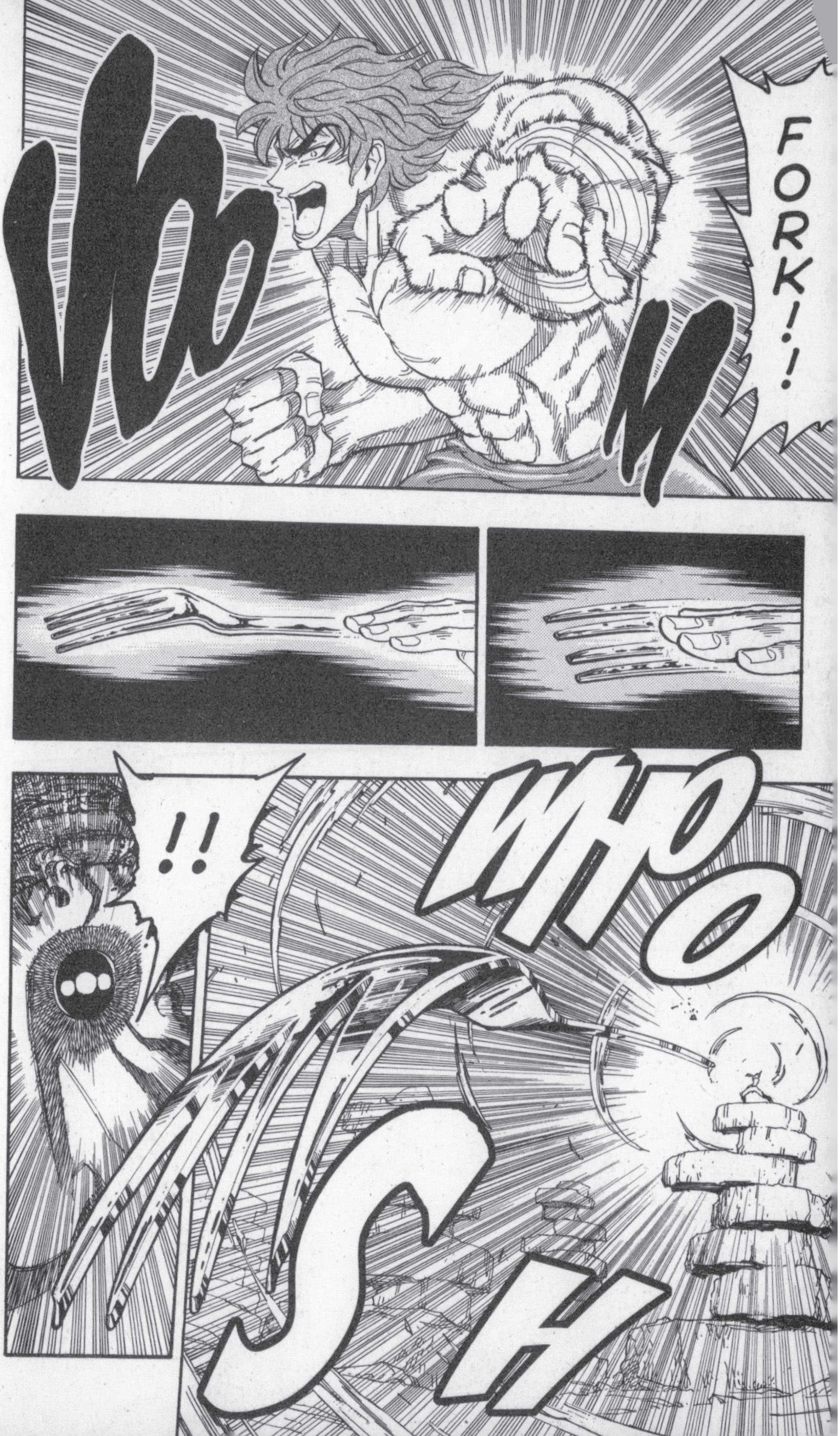
FORK!!!
VOOM
WHOOSH
!!

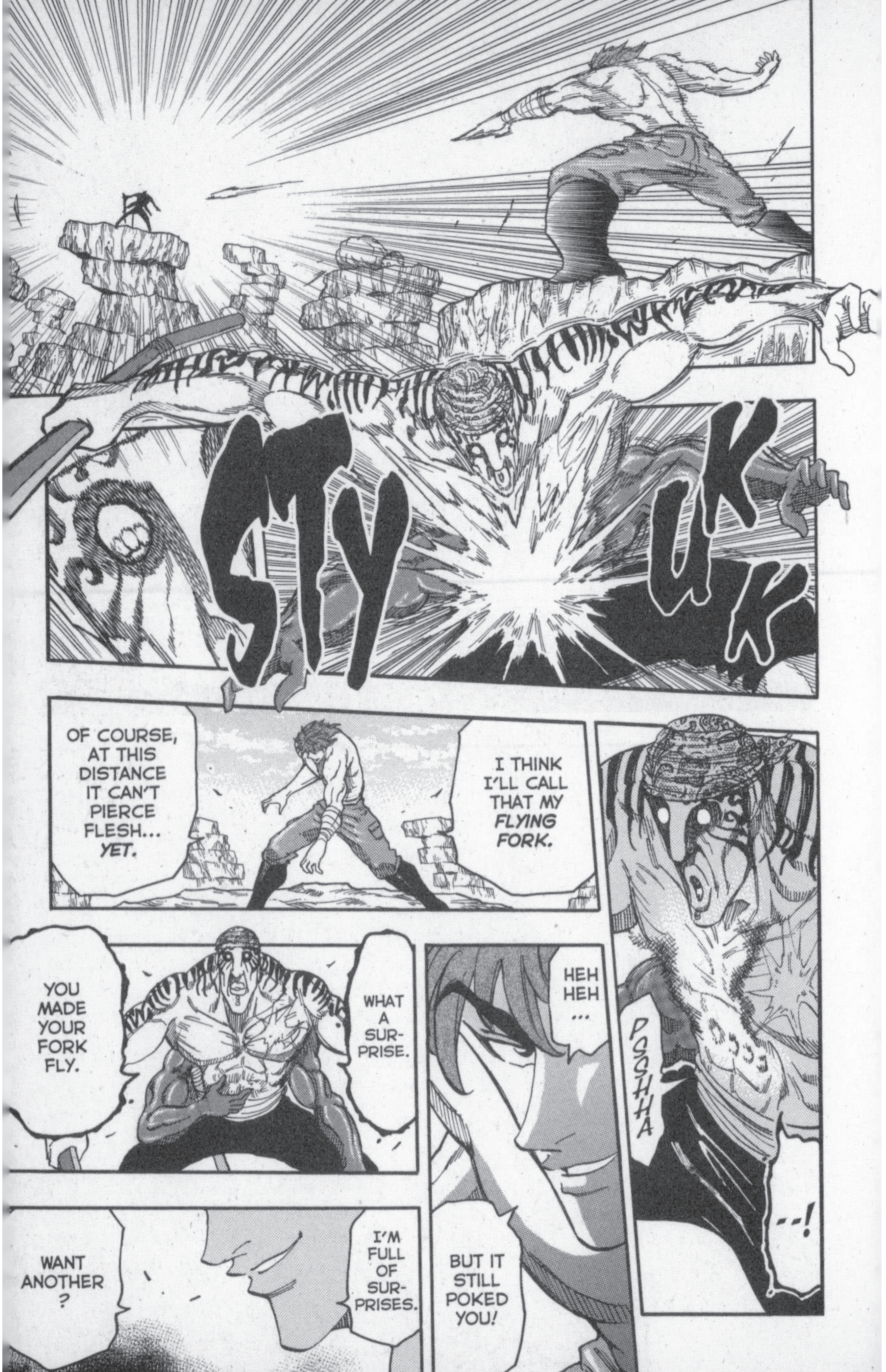
STYUKK
PSCHHA
--!
I THINK I'LL CALL THAT MY *FLYING FORK.*
OF COURSE, AT THIS DISTANCE IT CAN'T PIERCE FLESH... *YET.*
HEH HEH ...
BUT IT STILL POKED YOU!
WHAT A SURPRISE.
YOU MADE YOUR FORK FLY.
I'M FULL OF SURPRISES.
WANT ANOTHER ?

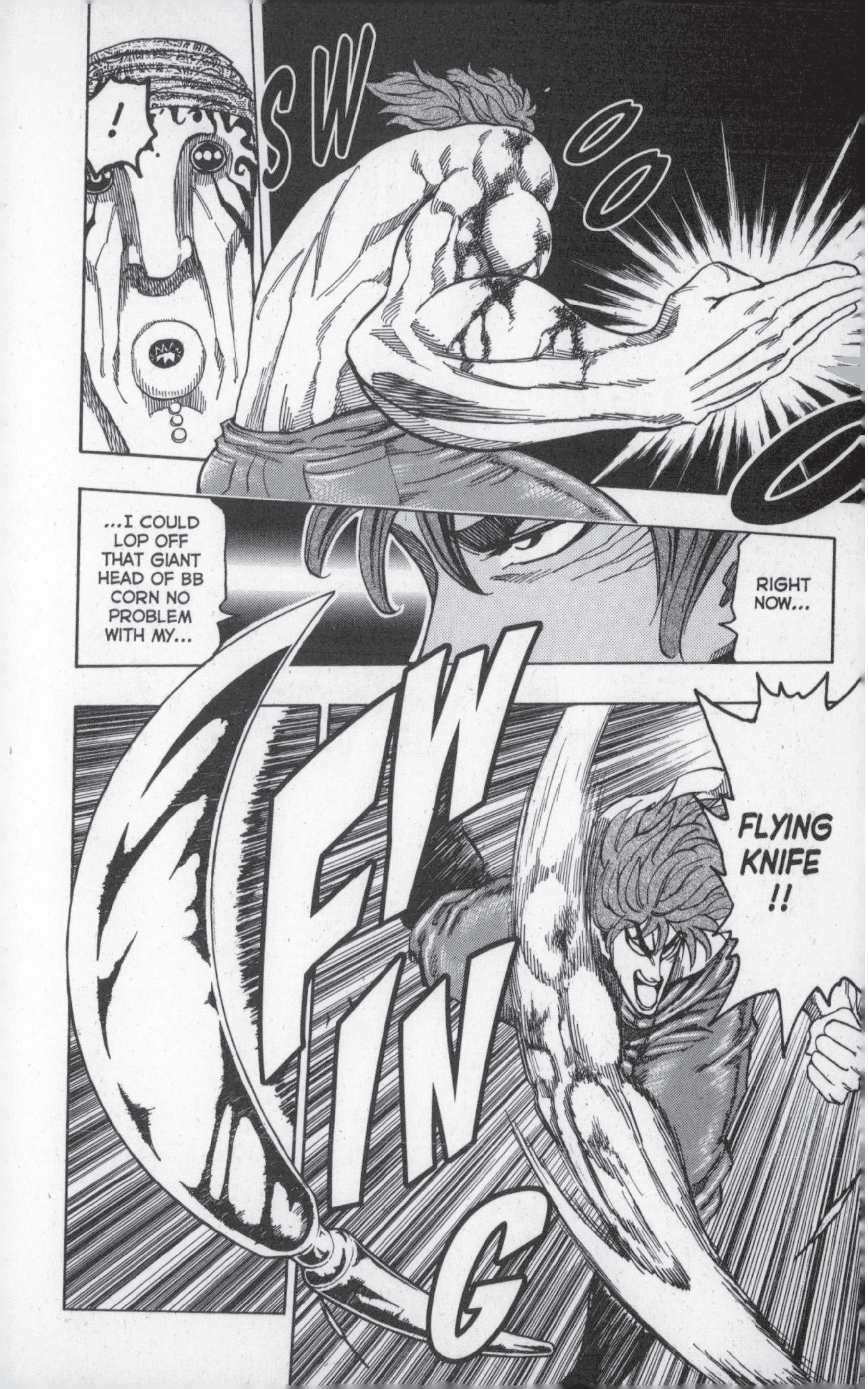
!
RIGHT NOW...
...I COULD LOP OFF THAT GIANT HEAD OF BB CORN NO PROBLEM WITH MY...
FLYING KNIFE !!

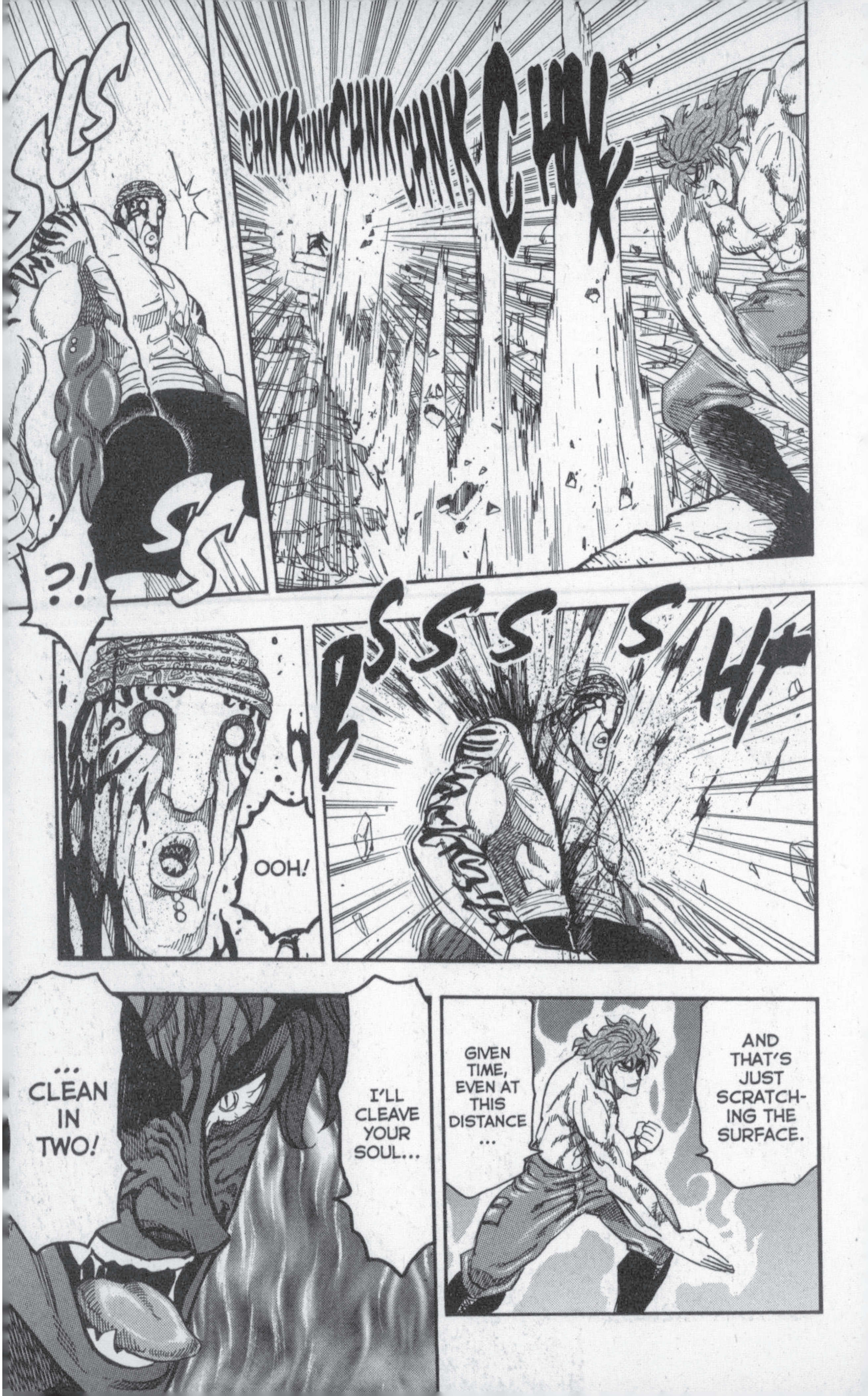
CHNKCHNKCHNKCHNKCHNK
SS
SS
?!
BSSSSSHT
OOH!
AND THAT'S JUST SCRATCHING THE SURFACE.
GIVEN TIME, EVEN AT THIS DISTANCE...
I'LL CLEAVE YOUR SOUL...
...CLEAN IN TWO!

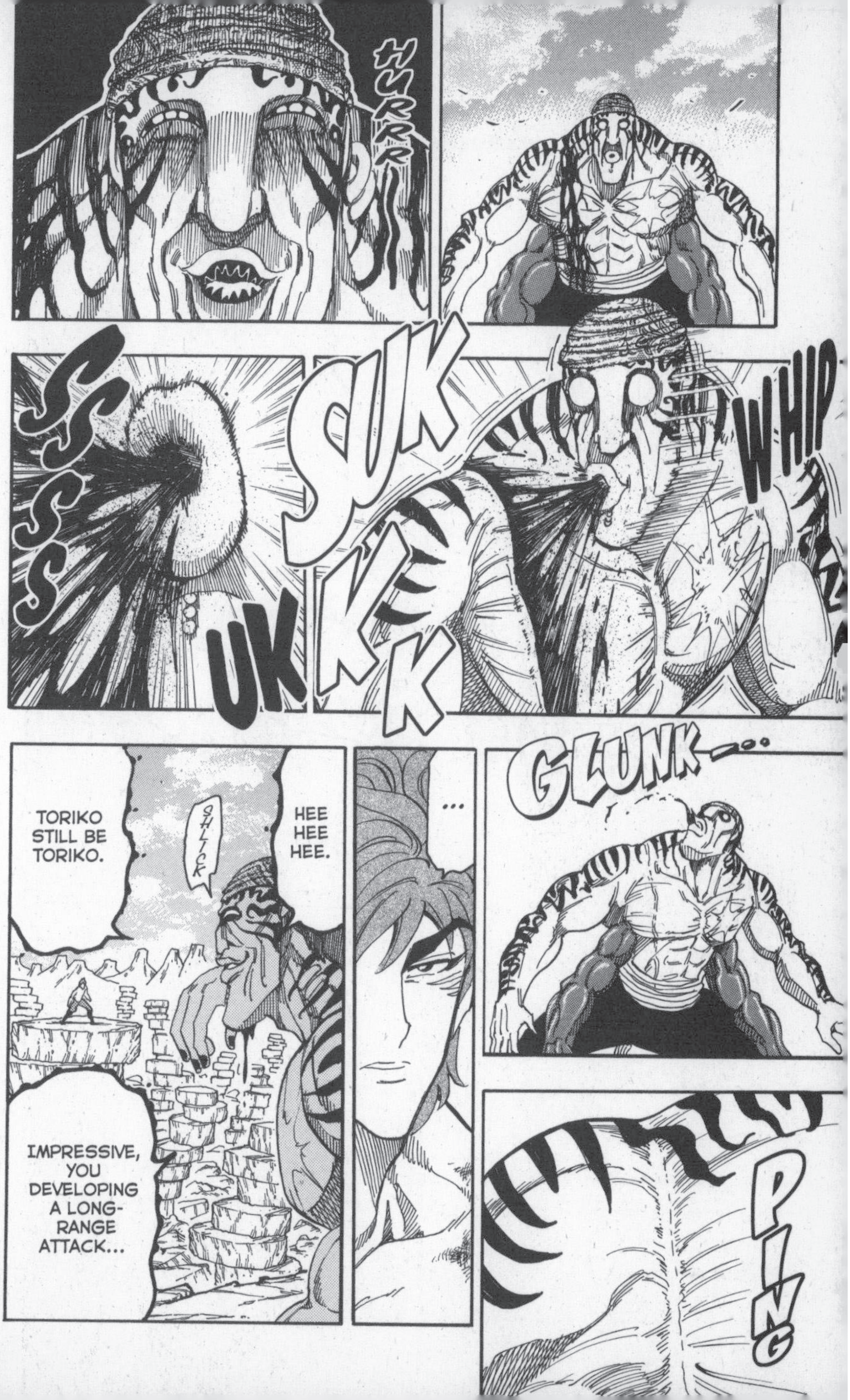

HURRRR
WHIP
SUK
K K
UK
SSSSS
GLUNK...
PING
...
HEE HEE HEE.
SHLICK
TORIKO STILL BE TORIKO.
IMPRESSIVE, YOU DEVELOPING A LONG-RANGE ATTACK...

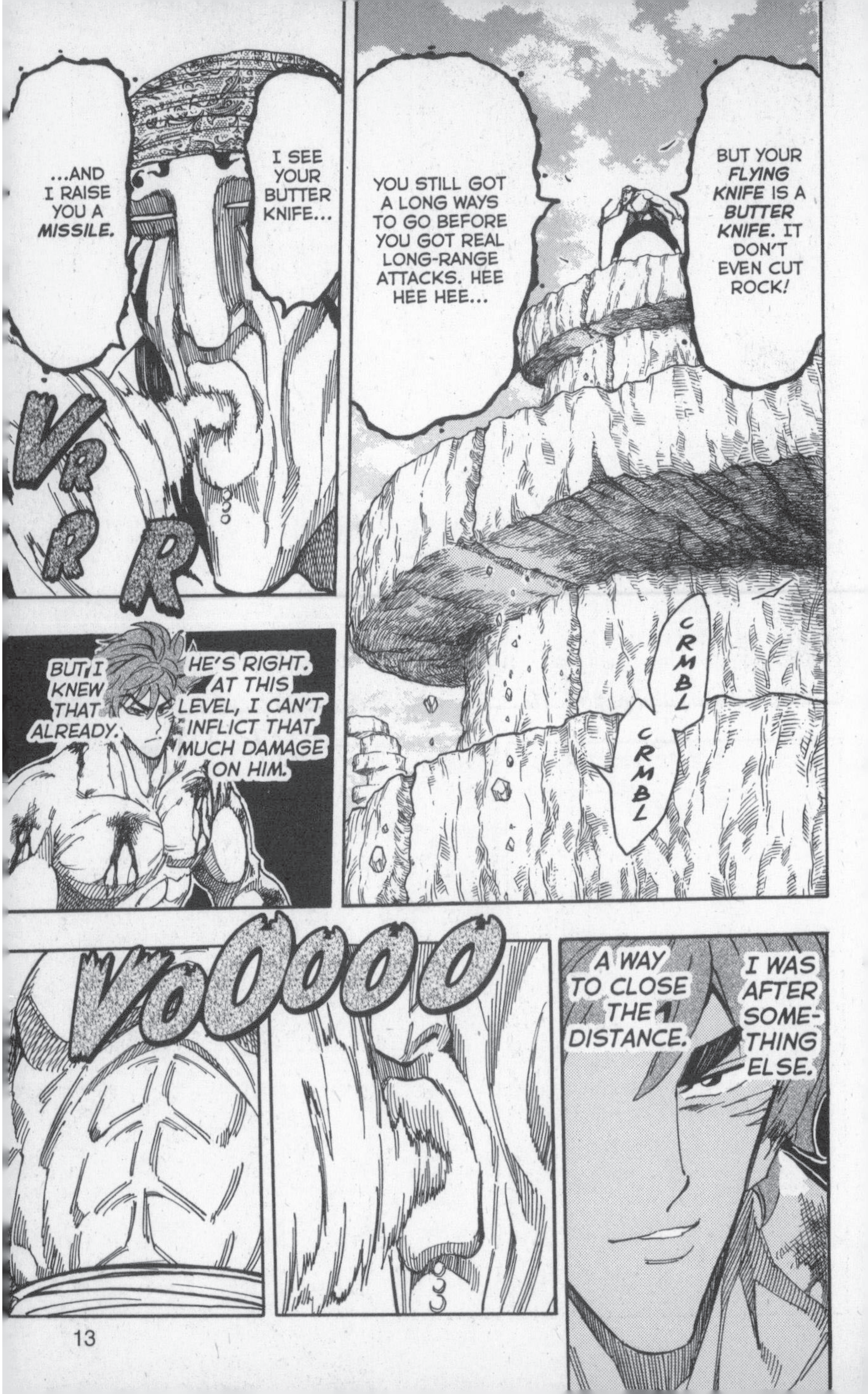
BUT YOUR *FLYING KNIFE* IS A *BUTTER KNIFE*. IT DON'T EVEN CUT ROCK!
YOU STILL GOT A LONG WAYS TO GO BEFORE YOU GOT REAL LONG-RANGE ATTACKS. HEE HEE HEE...
CRMBL CRMBL
I SEE YOUR BUTTER KNIFE...
...AND I RAISE YOU A *MISSILE.*
VRRR
HE'S RIGHT. AT THIS LEVEL, I CAN'T INFLICT THAT MUCH DAMAGE ON HIM.
BUT I KNEW THAT ALREADY.
I WAS AFTER SOME-THING ELSE.
A WAY TO CLOSE THE DISTANCE.
VOOOOO

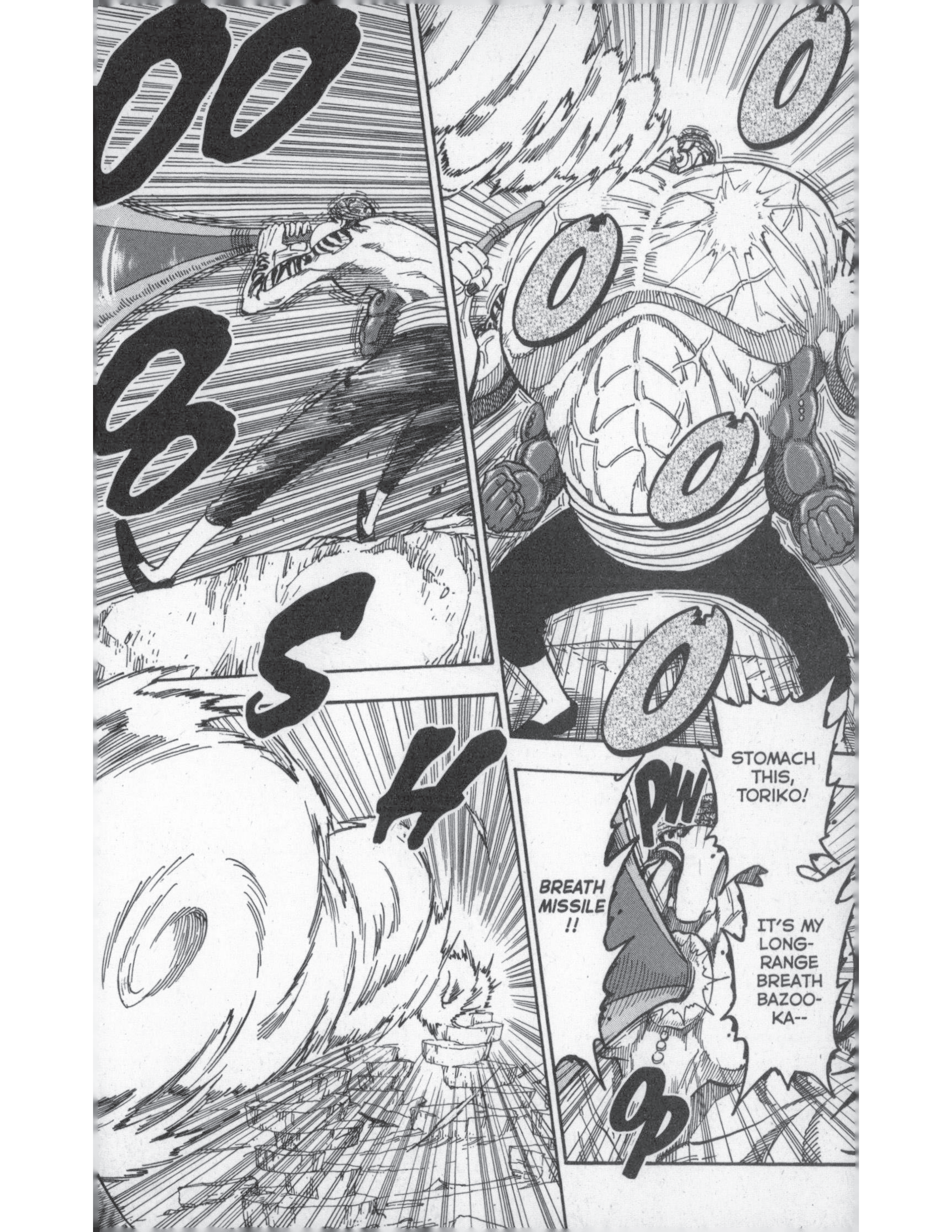
STOMACH THIS, TORIKO!
BREATH MISSILE !!
IT'S MY LONG-RANGE BREATH BAZOO-KA--

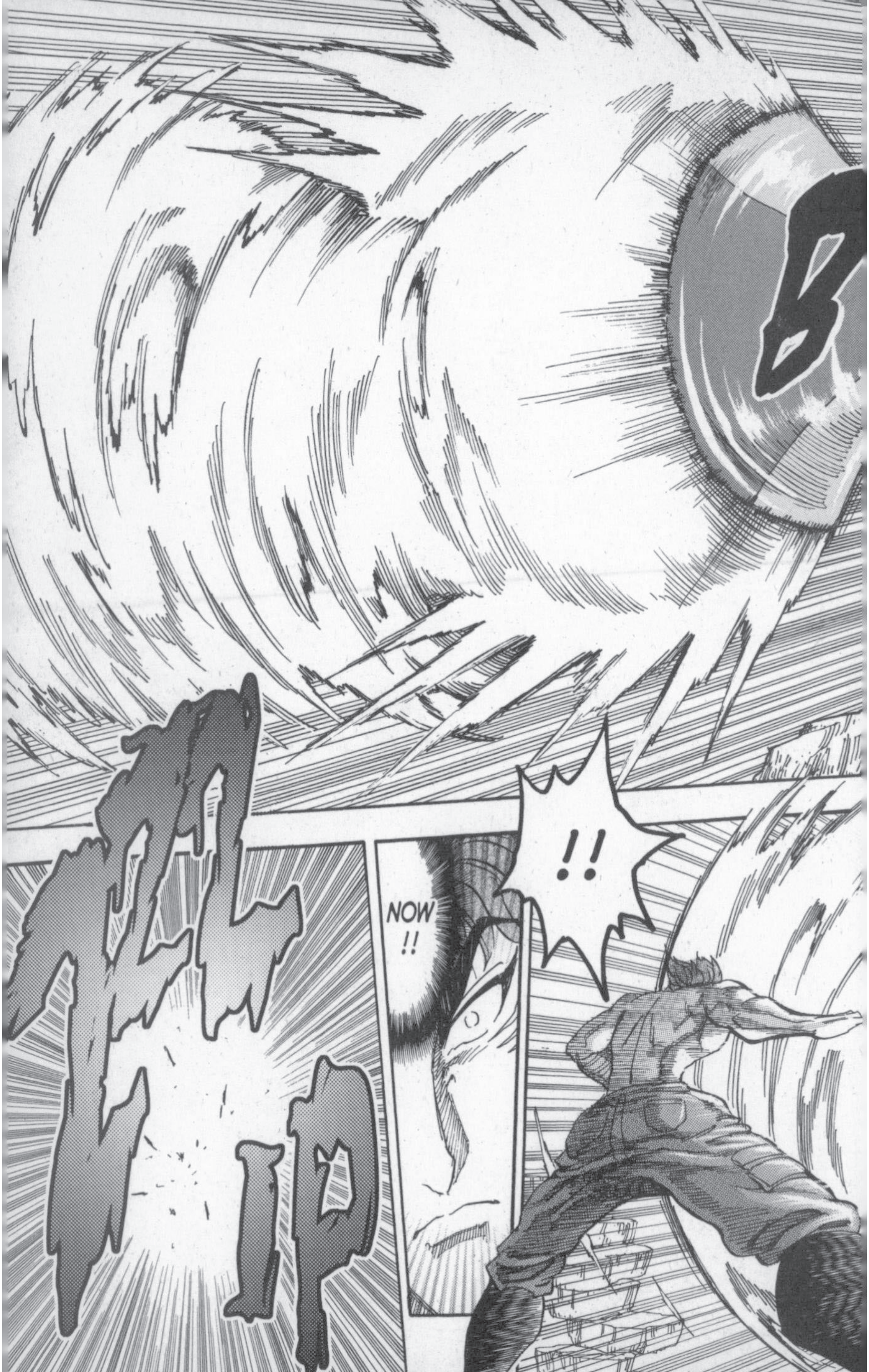

!!
NOW !!

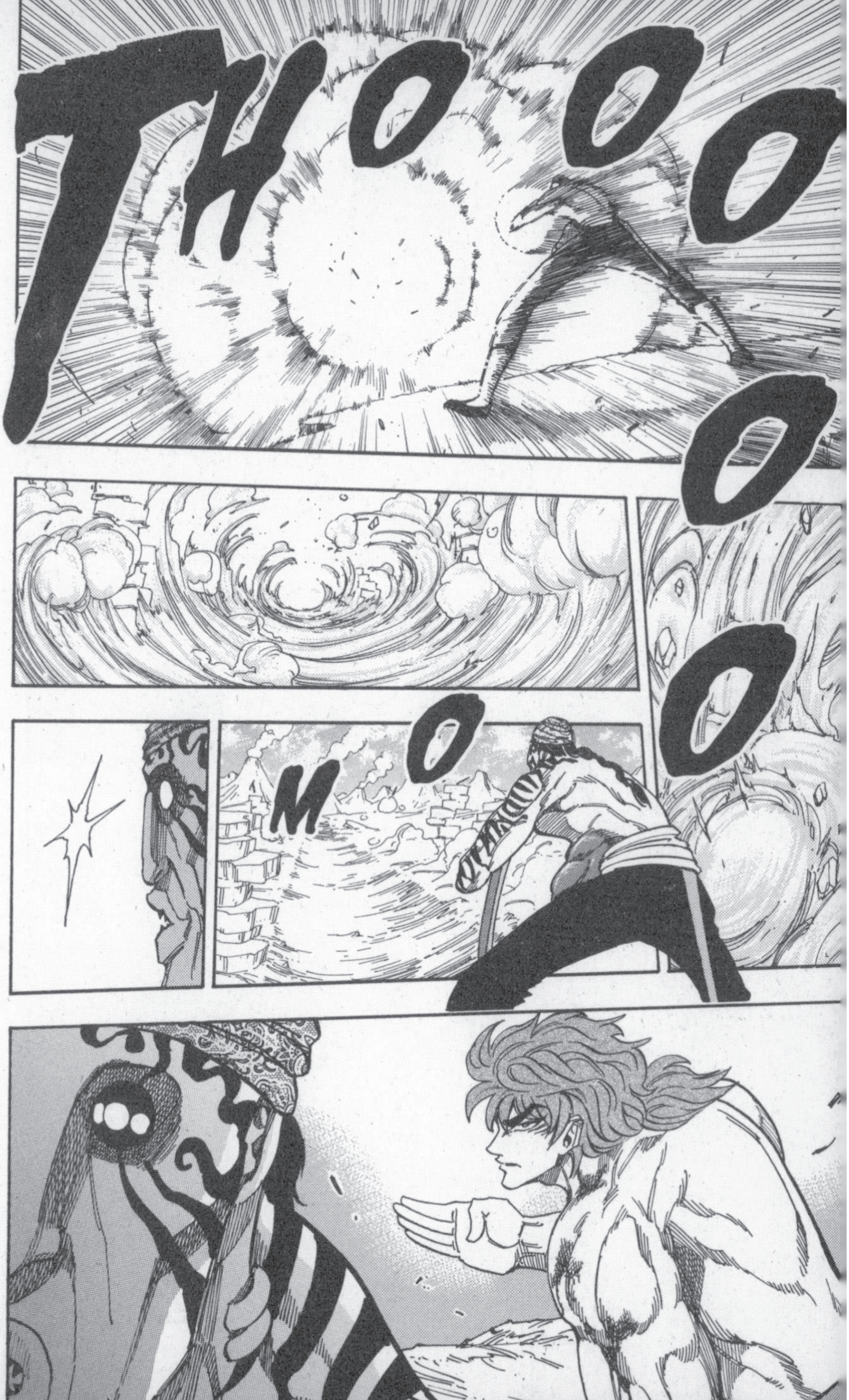
THOOOOOOM

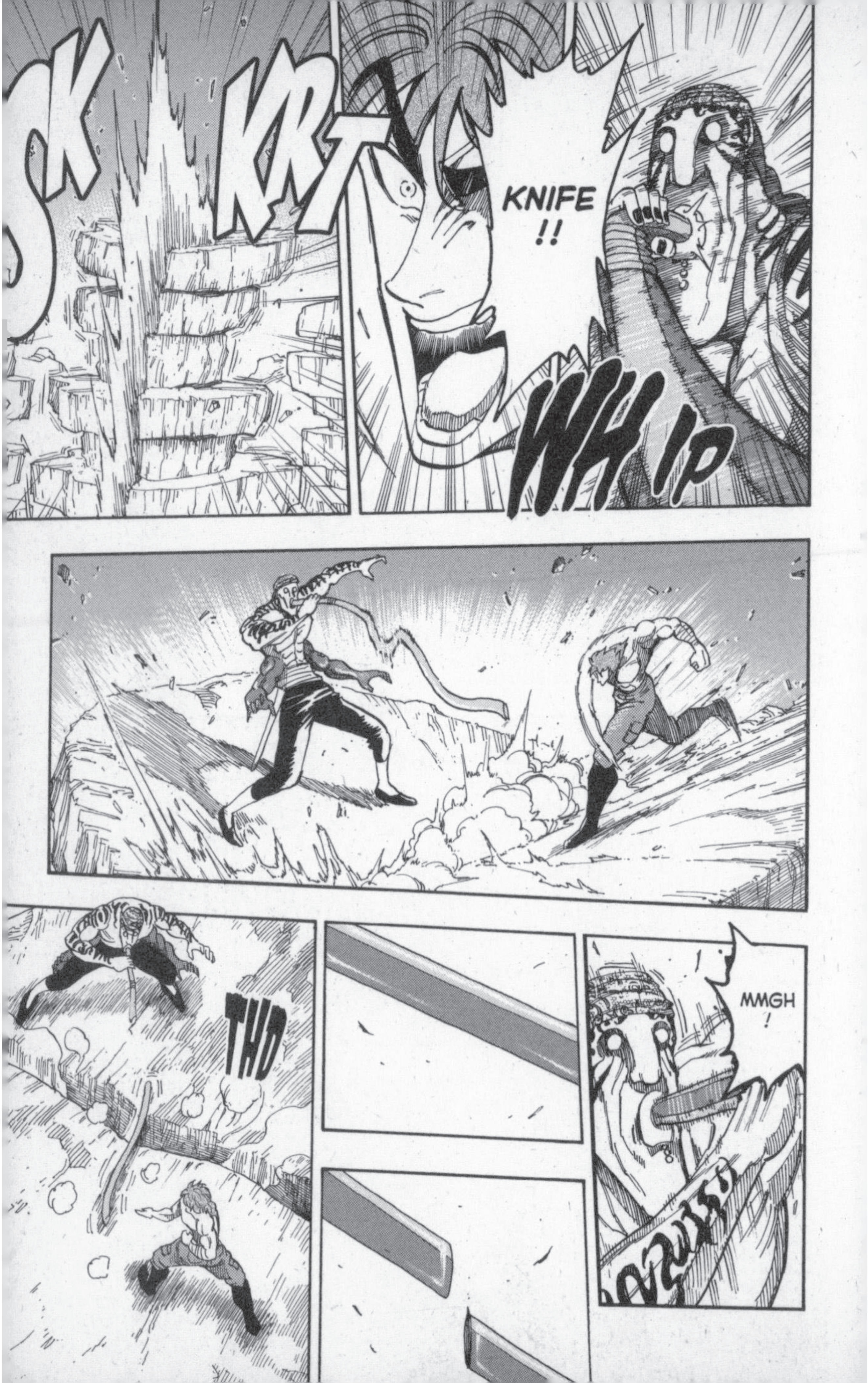
KNIFE !!
KRT
SK
WHIP
MMGH !
THD

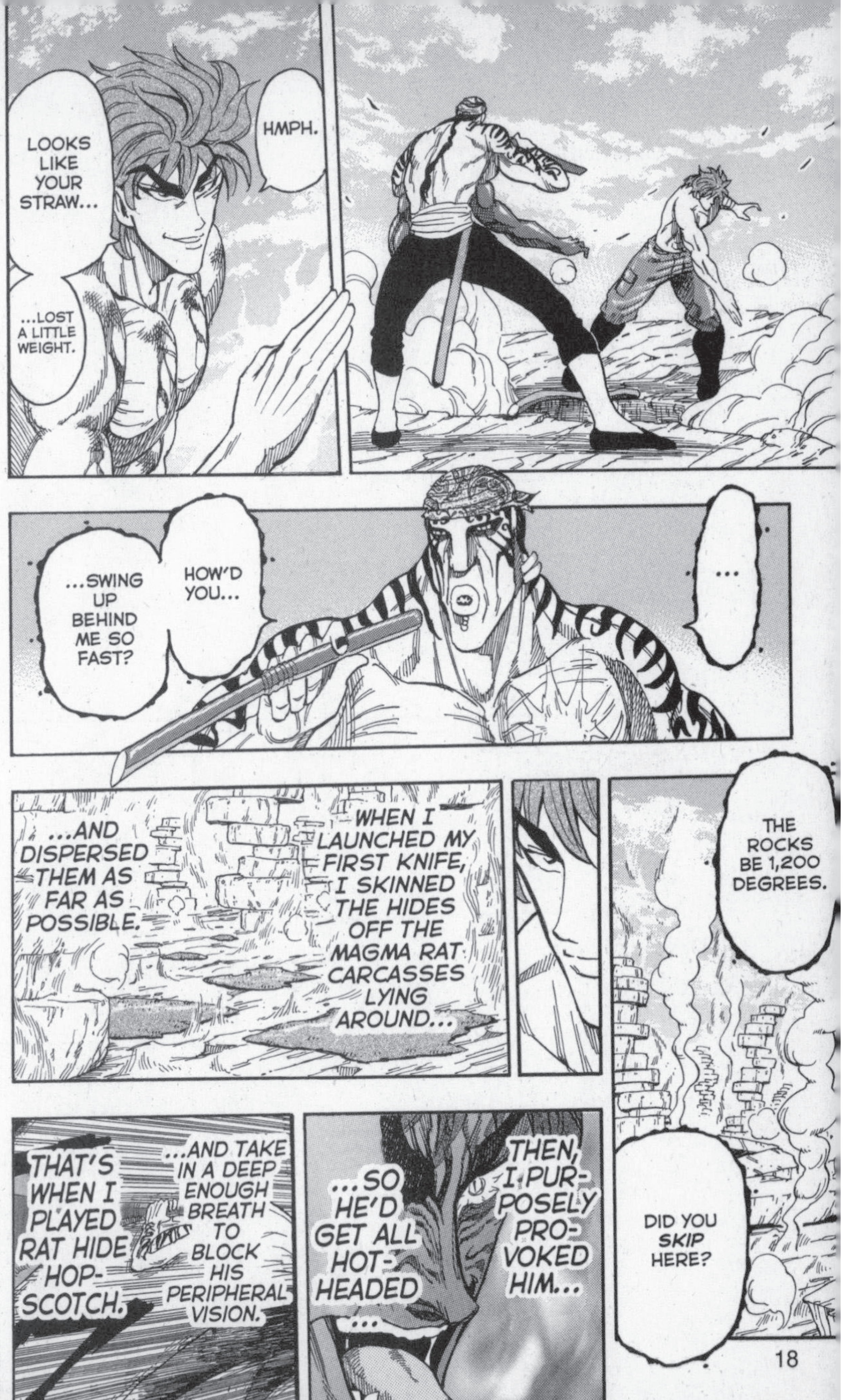
HMPH.
LOOKS LIKE YOUR STRAW...
...LOST A LITTLE WEIGHT.
...
HOW'D YOU...
...SWING UP BEHIND ME SO FAST?
THE ROCKS BE 1,200 DEGREES.
DID YOU SKIP HERE?
WHEN I LAUNCHED MY FIRST KNIFE, I SKINNED THE HIDES OFF THE MAGMA RAT CARCASSES LYING AROUND...
...AND DISPERSED THEM AS FAR AS POSSIBLE.
THEN, I PUR-POSELY PRO-VOKED HIM...
...SO HE'D GET ALL HOT-HEADED...
...AND TAKE IN A DEEP ENOUGH BREATH TO BLOCK HIS PERIPHERAL VISION.
THAT'S WHEN I PLAYED RAT HIDE HOP-SCOTCH.

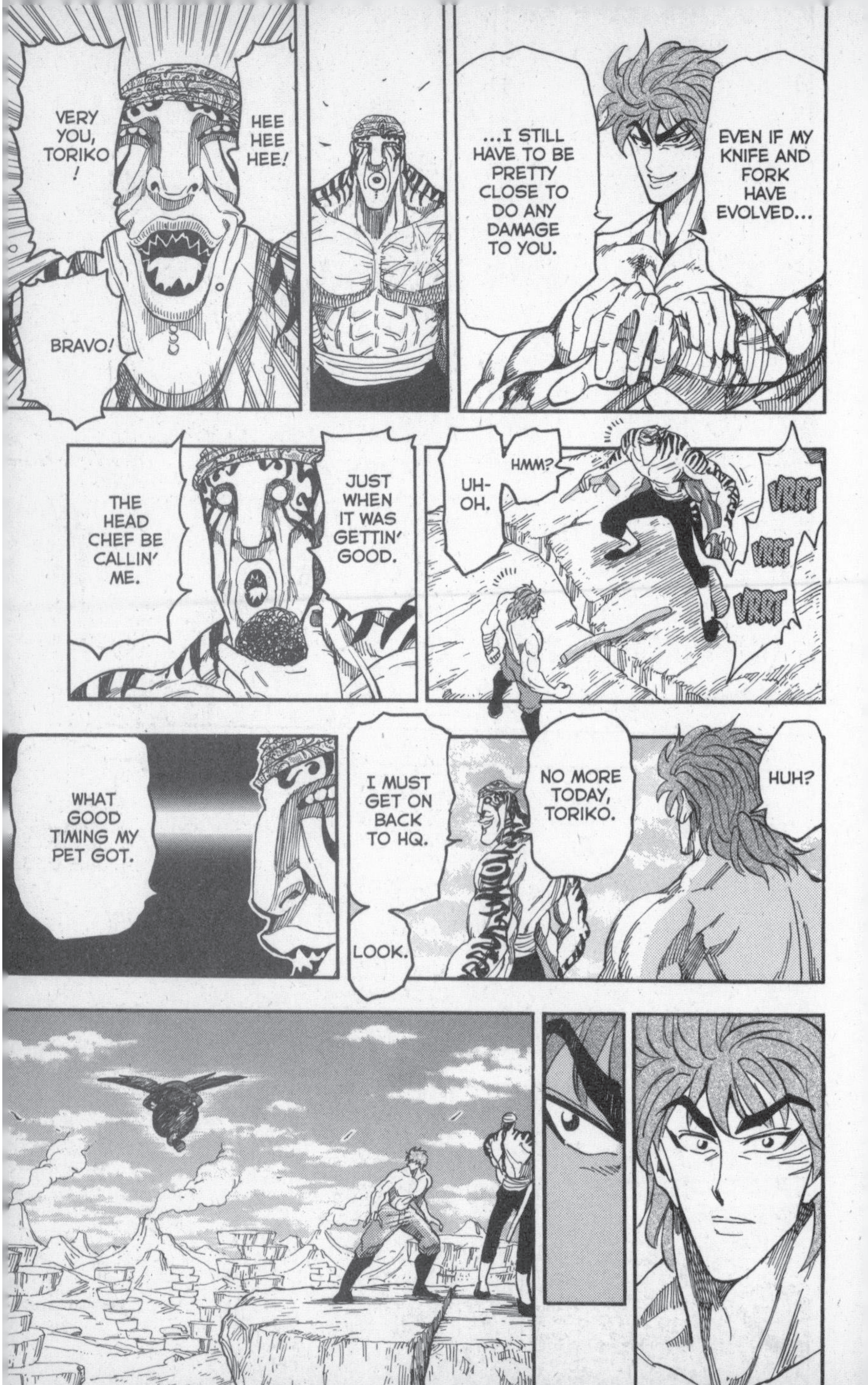
EVEN IF MY KNIFE AND FORK HAVE EVOLVED...
...I STILL HAVE TO BE PRETTY CLOSE TO DO ANY DAMAGE TO YOU.
HEE HEE HEE!
VERY YOU, TORIKO!
BRAVO!
VRRT
VRRT
VRRT
HMM?
UH-OH.
JUST WHEN IT WAS GETTIN' GOOD.
THE HEAD CHEF BE CALLIN' ME.
HUH?
NO MORE TODAY, TORIKO.
I MUST GET ON BACK TO HQ.
LOOK.
WHAT GOOD TIMING MY PET GOT.

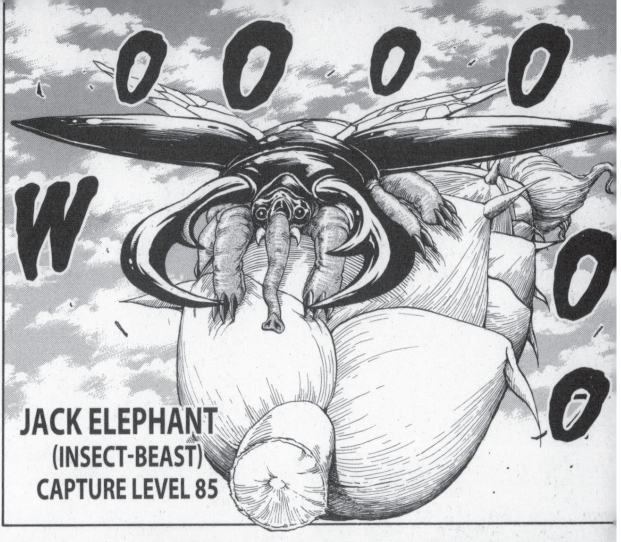

JACK ELEPHANT
(INSECT-BEAST)
CAPTURE LEVEL 85

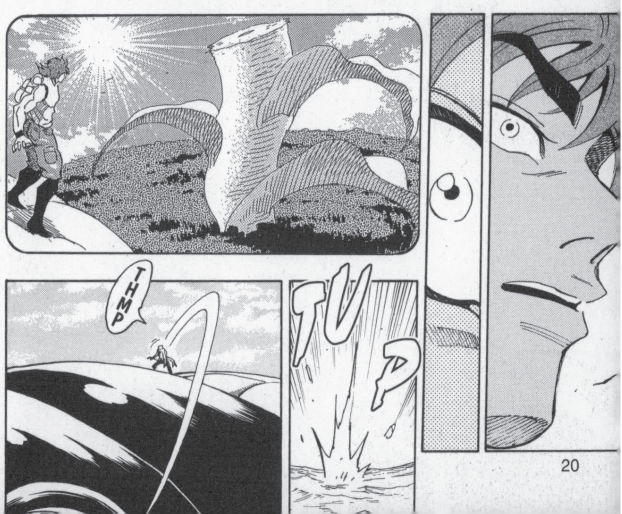

20

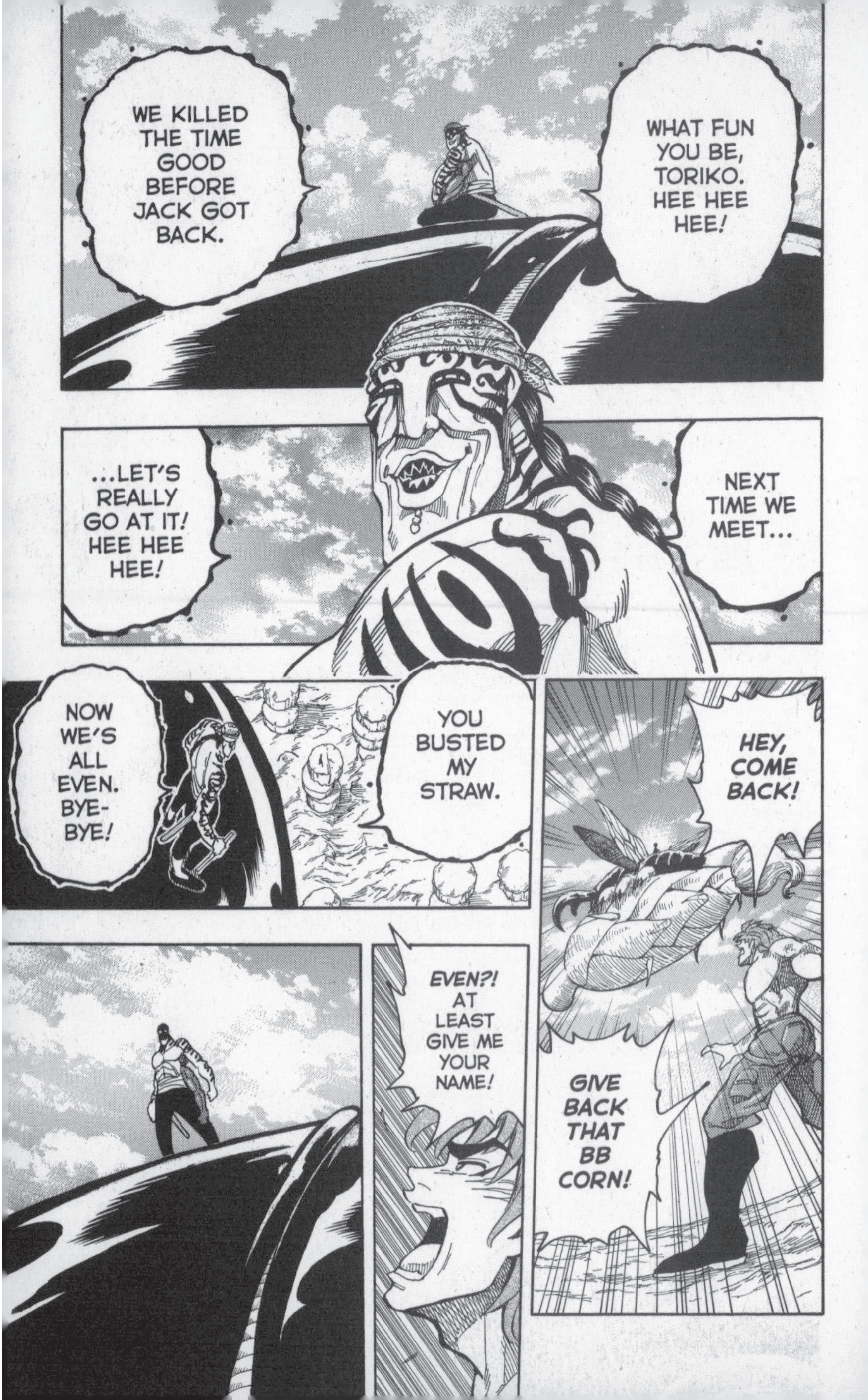
WHAT FUN YOU BE, TORIKO. HEE HEE HEE!
WE KILLED THE TIME GOOD BEFORE JACK GOT BACK.
NEXT TIME WE MEET...
...LET'S REALLY GO AT IT! HEE HEE HEE!
HEY, COME BACK!
GIVE BACK THAT BB CORN!
YOU BUSTED MY STRAW.
NOW WE'S ALL EVEN. BYE-BYE!
EVEN?! AT LEAST GIVE ME YOUR NAME!

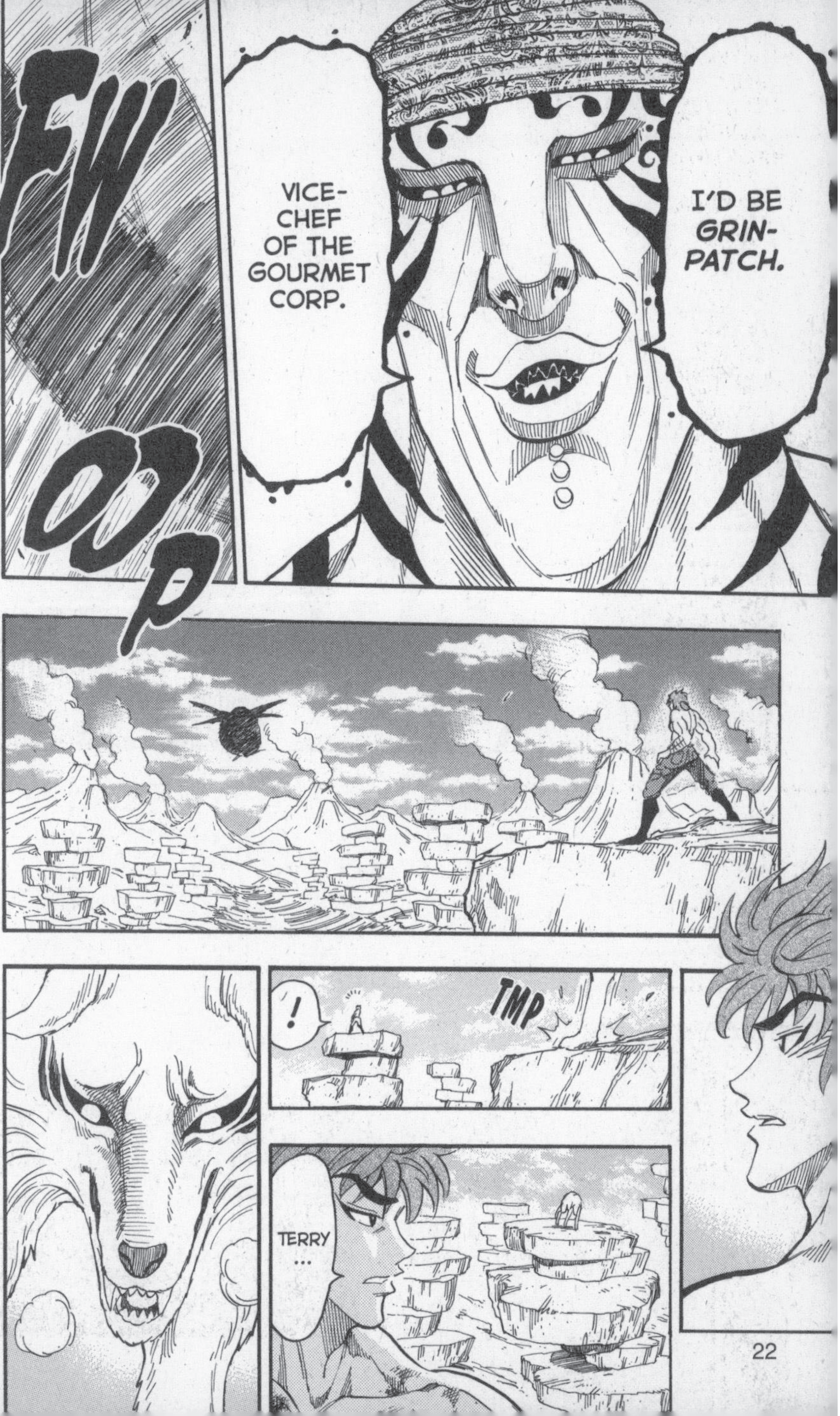
I'D BE GRIN-PATCH.
VICE-CHEF OF THE GOURMET CORP.
FWOOP
TMP
!
TERRY...

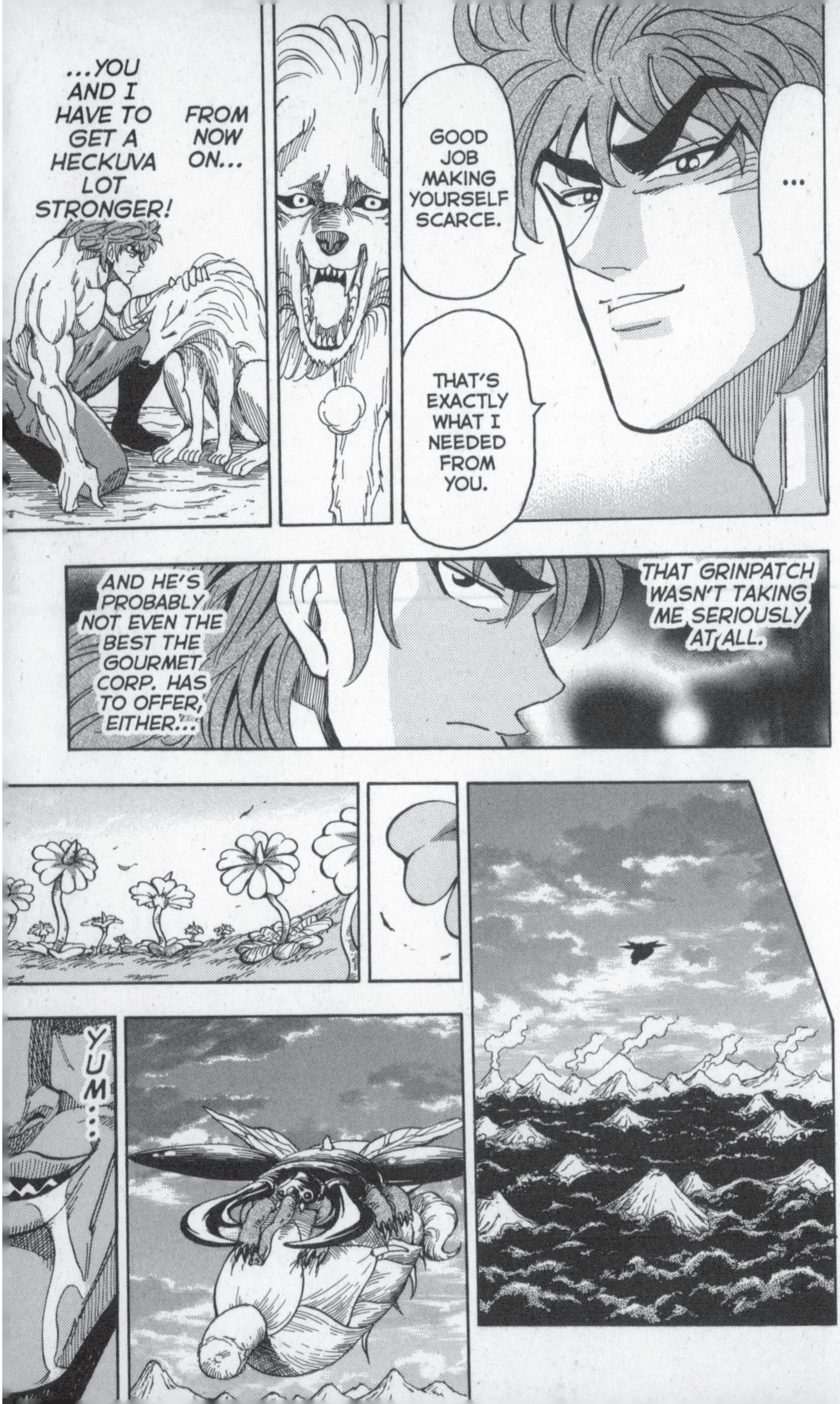
...
GOOD JOB MAKING YOURSELF SCARCE.
THAT'S EXACTLY WHAT I NEEDED FROM YOU.
FROM NOW ON...
...YOU AND I HAVE TO GET A HECKUVA LOT STRONGER!
THAT GRINPATCH WASN'T TAKING ME SERIOUSLY AT ALL.
AND HE'S PROBABLY NOT EVEN THE BEST THE GOURMET CORP. HAS TO OFFER, EITHER...
YUM...

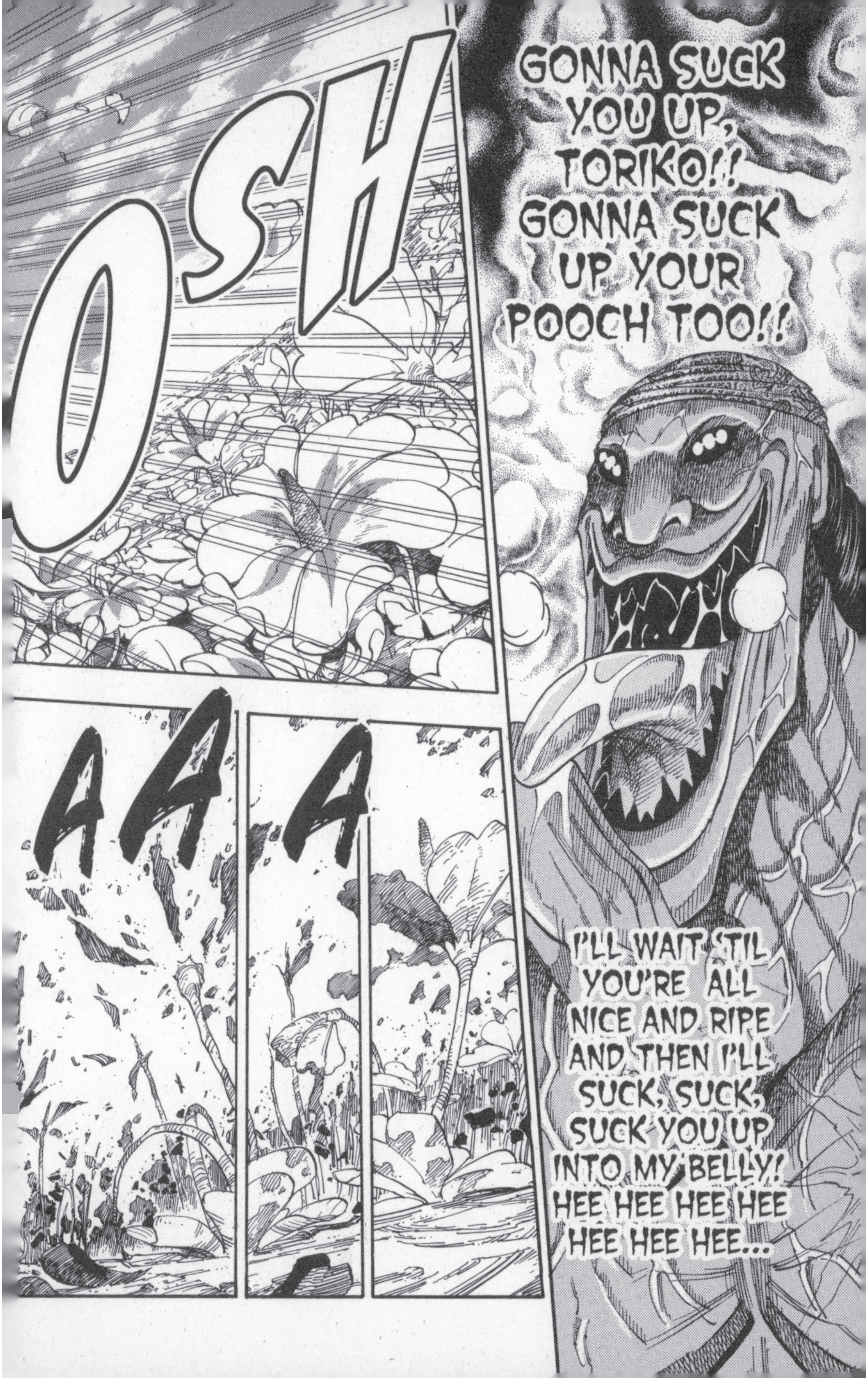

GONNA SUCK YOU UP, TORIKO!! GONNA SUCK UP YOUR POOCH TOO!!
I'LL WAIT 'TIL YOU'RE ALL NICE AND RIPE AND THEN I'LL SUCK, SUCK, SUCK YOU UP INTO MY BELLY! HEE HEE HEE HEE HEE HEE HEE...
OSH
A
AA

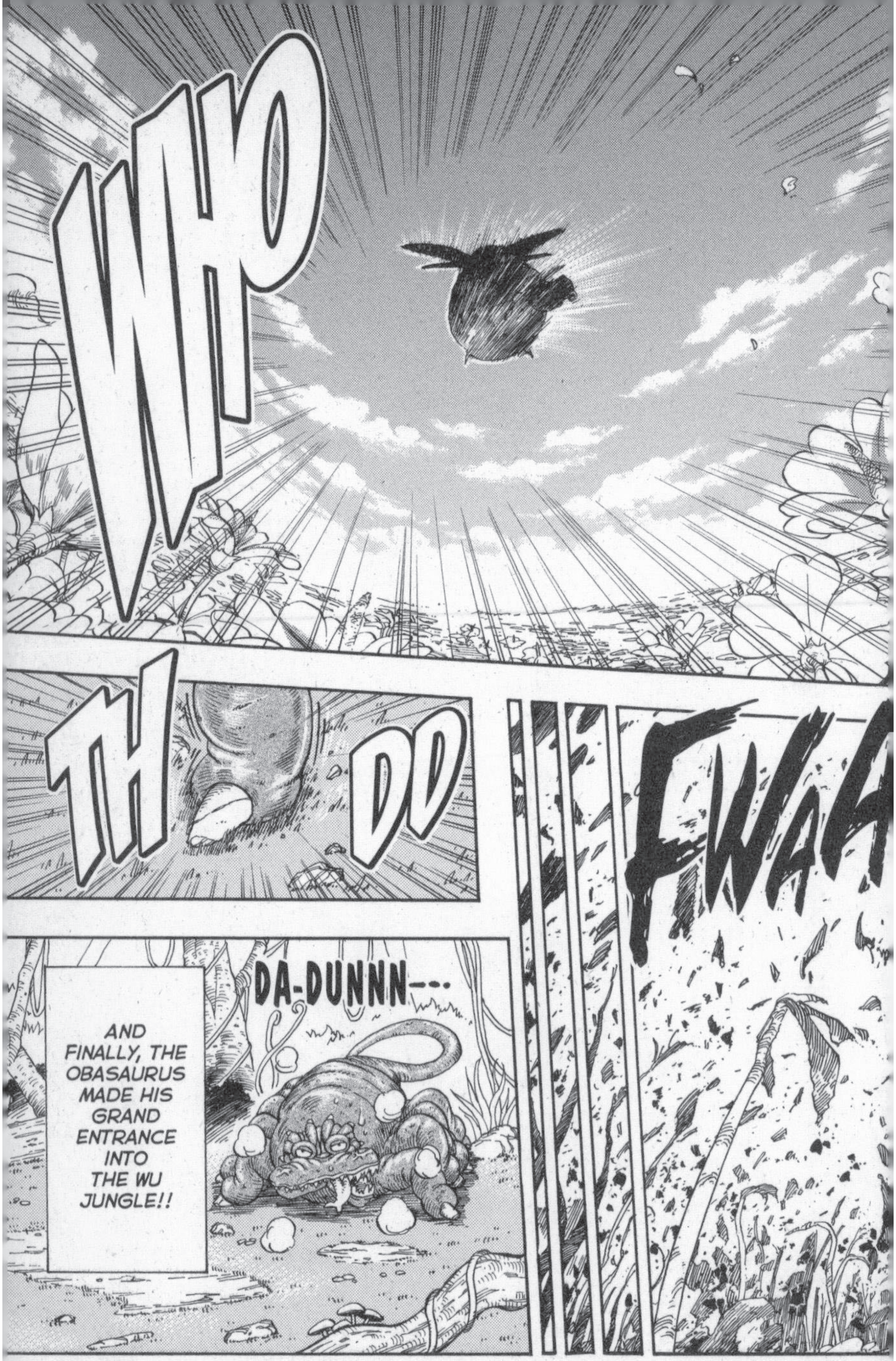
WHO
FWAA
TH
DD
DA-DUNNN---
AND FINALLY, THE OBASAURUS MADE HIS GRAND ENTRANCE INTO THE WU JUNGLE!!

TORIKO

GOURMET CHECKLIST

Vol. 049

DOM
(MAMMAL)

CAPTURE LEVEL: 19

HABITAT: REGAL ISLE (WHITE FOREST)

LENGTH: 10 METERS

HEIGHT: 3.5 METERS

WEIGHT: 16 TONS

PRICE: 100 G / 5,200 YEN

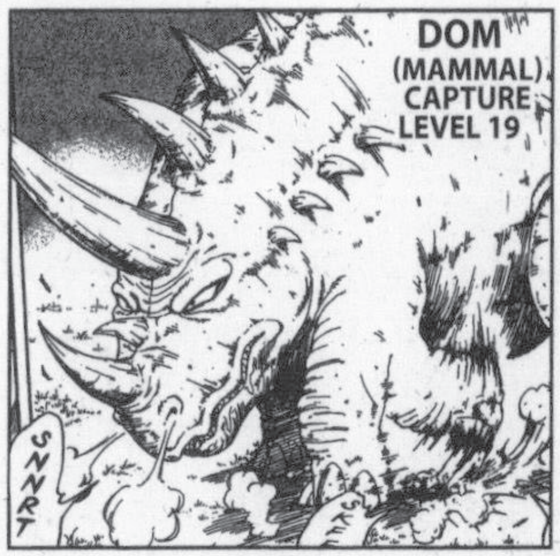
DOM (MAMMAL) CAPTURE LEVEL 19
SNNRT

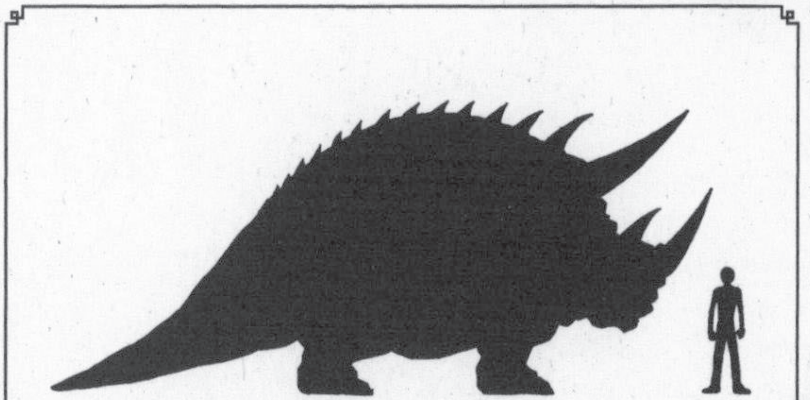

SCALE

THREE TO FIVE TIMES LARGER AND HEAVIER THAN A RHINOCEROS, NOT TO MENTION FESTOONED WITH SHARP HORNS, THIS BEAST CHARGES ITS PREY AND IMPALES THEM ON ITS HORNS. THE FORCE OF A DOM'S CHARGE COULD EASILY TOPPLE A FIVE-STORY BUILDING.

GOURMET 63: ZENITH OF EVOLUTION...!!

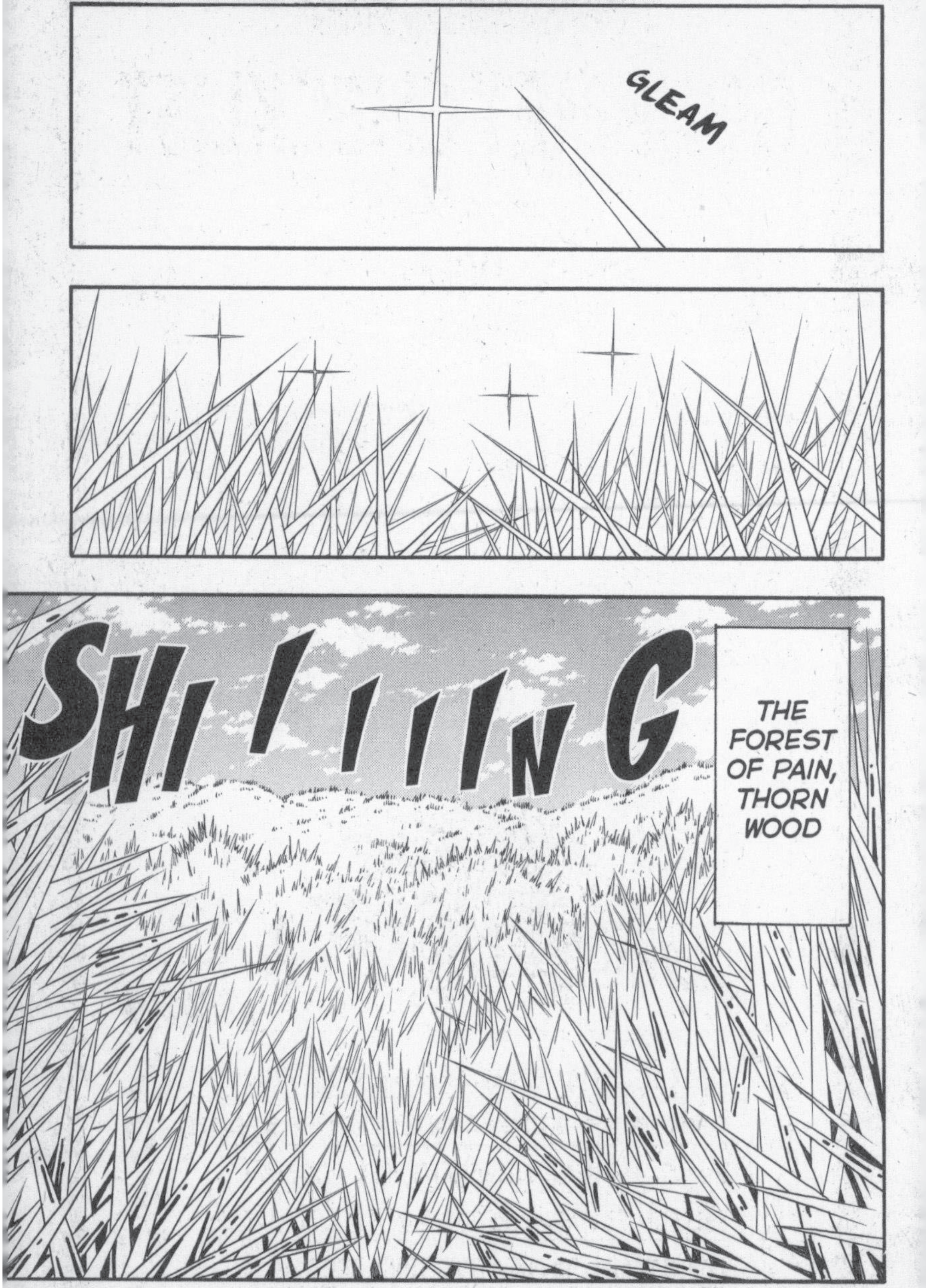
GLEAM
THE FOREST OF PAIN, THORN WOOD
SHIIIING

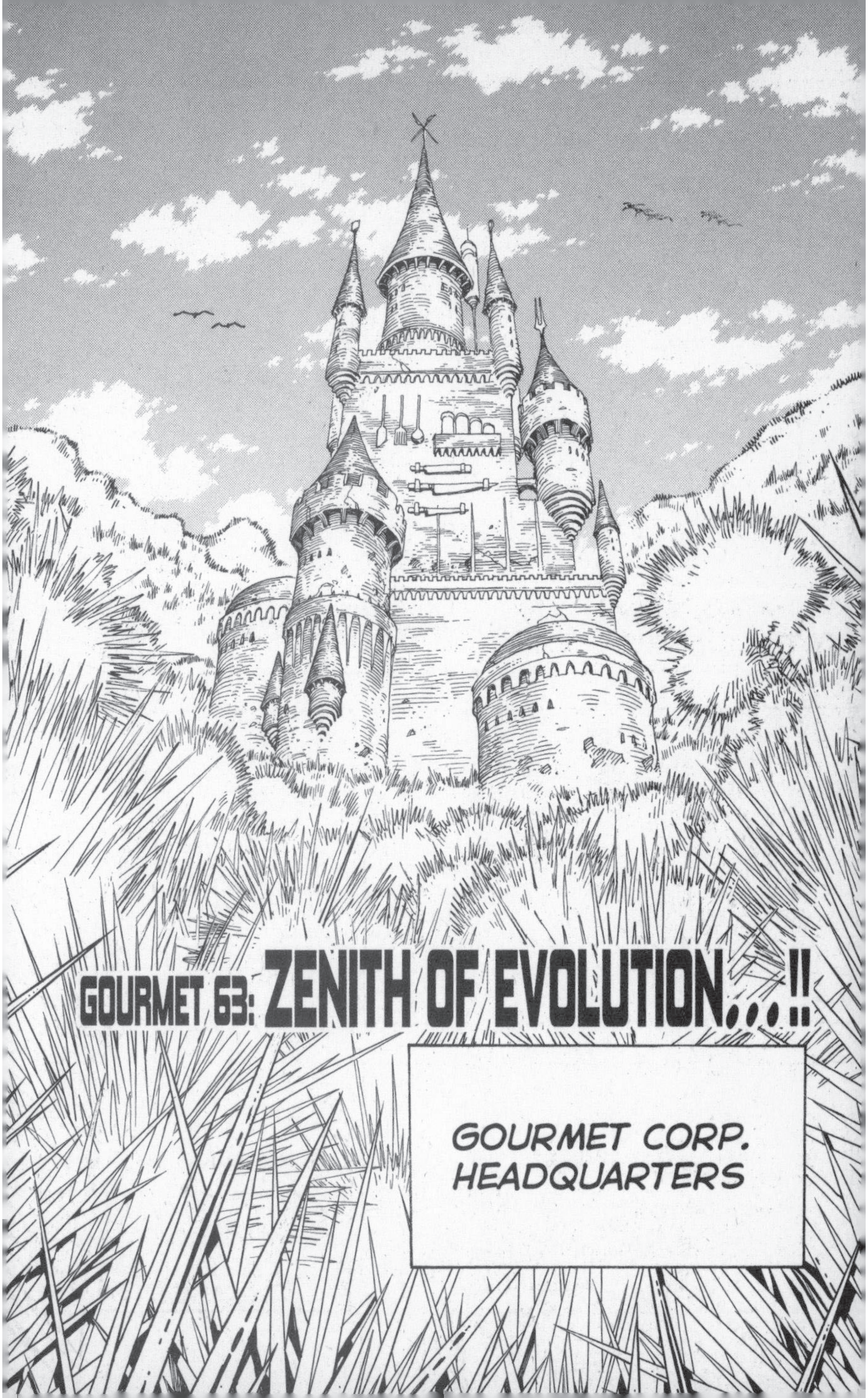
GOURMET 63: ZENITH OF EVOLUTION...!!
GOURMET CORP. HEADQUARTERS

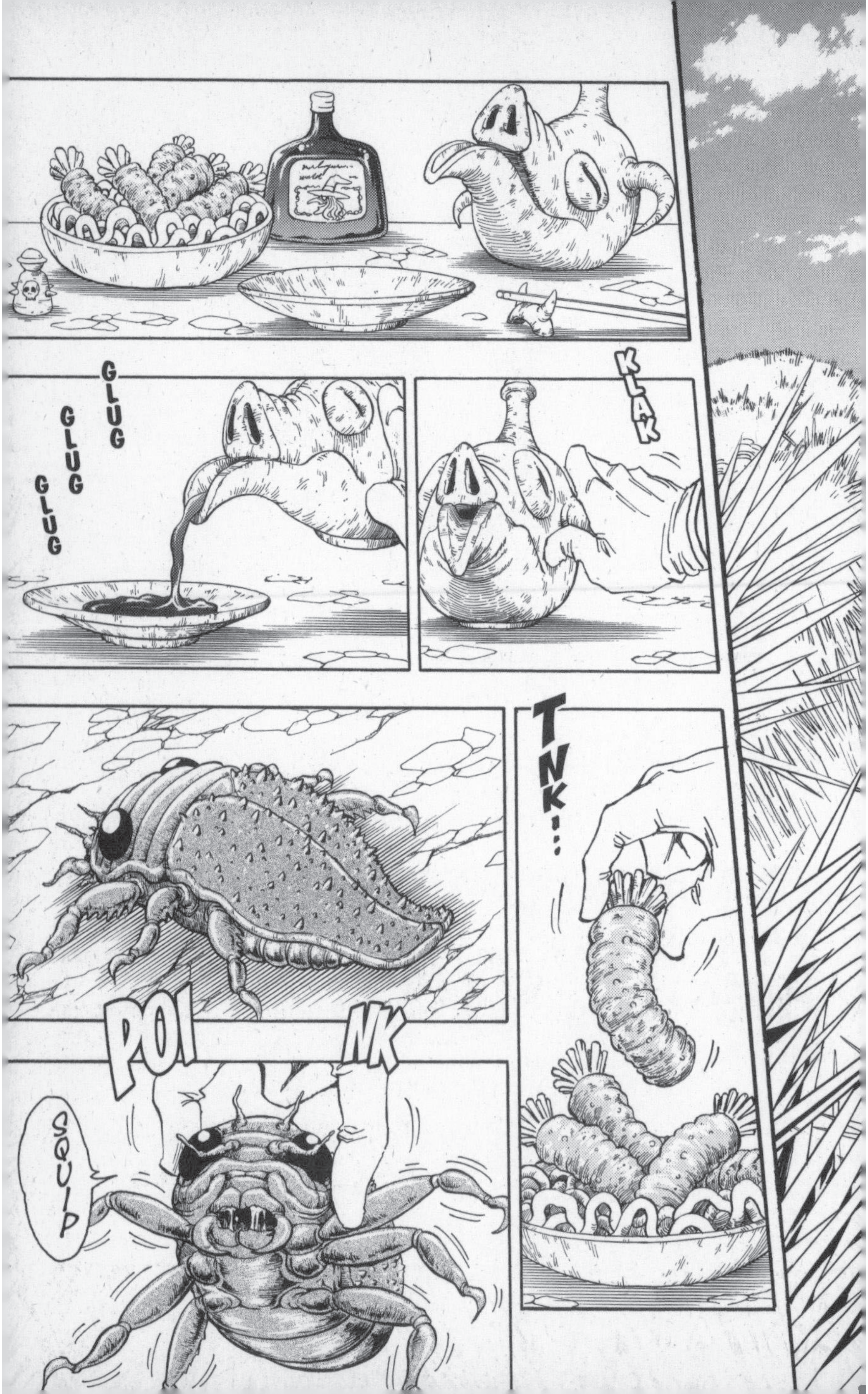
KLAK
GLUG
GLUG
GLUG
TNK!!
POINK
SQUIP

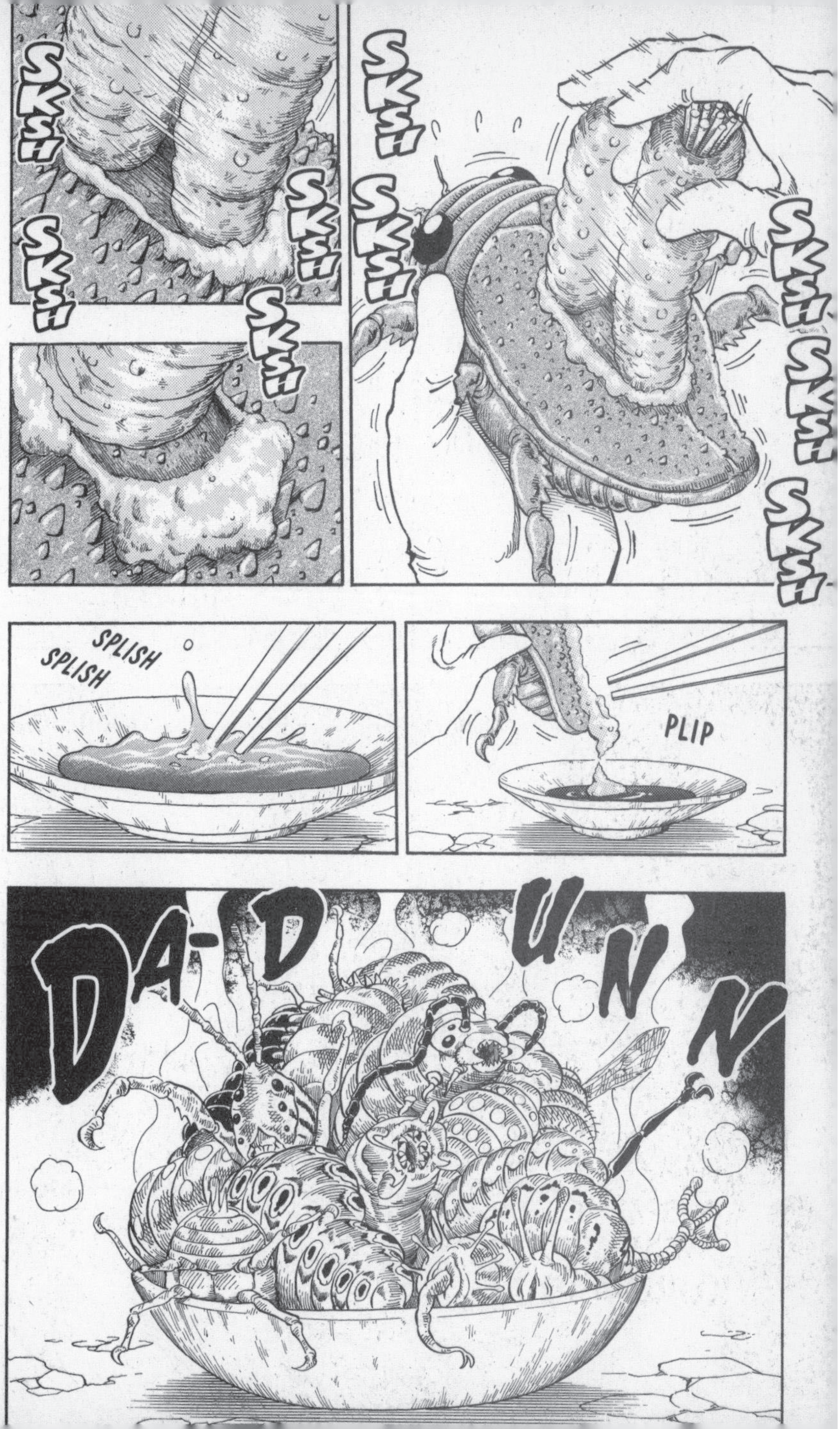
SKSH SKSH SKSH SKSH
SKSH SKSH
SKSH SKSH SKSH
PLIP
SPLISH SPLISH
DA-DUNN

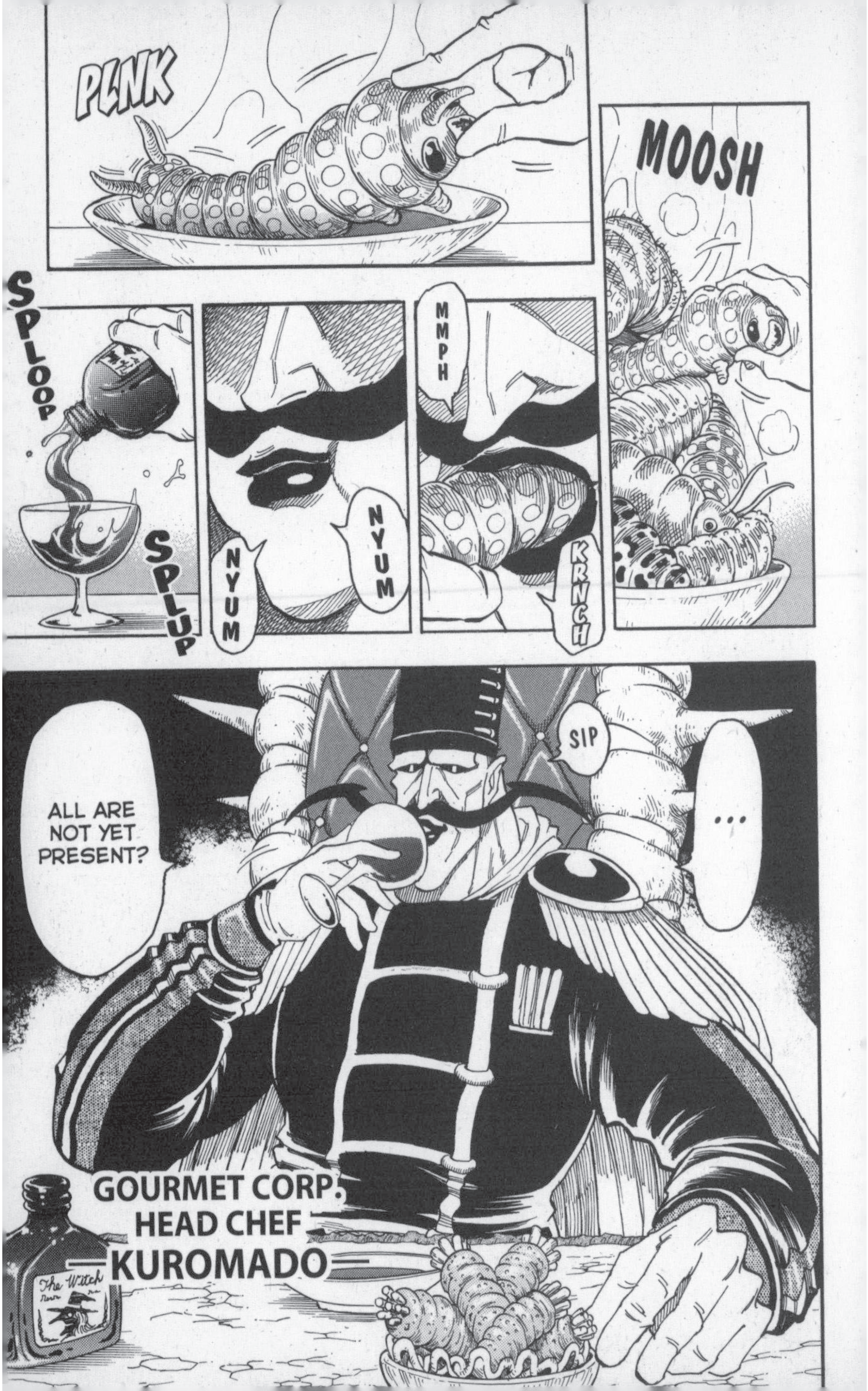

MOOSH
PLNK
MMPH
KRNCH
NYUM
NYUM
SPLOOP
SPLUP
SIP
...
ALL ARE NOT YET PRESENT?
GOURMET CORP. HEAD CHEF KUROMADO
The Witch

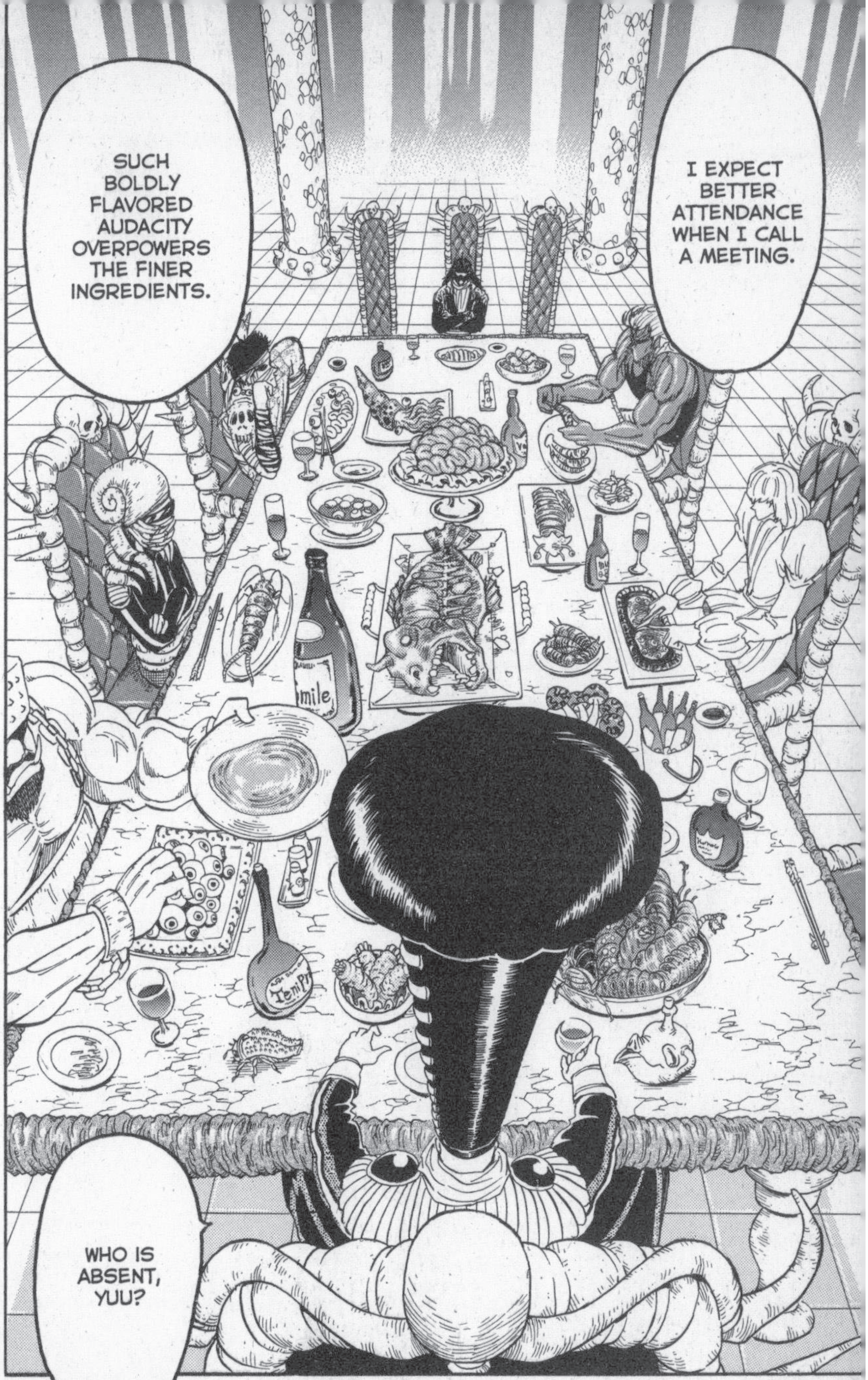
I EXPECT BETTER ATTENDANCE WHEN I CALL A MEETING.
SUCH BOLDLY FLAVORED AUDACITY OVERPOWERS THE FINER INGREDIENTS.
WHO IS ABSENT, YUU?

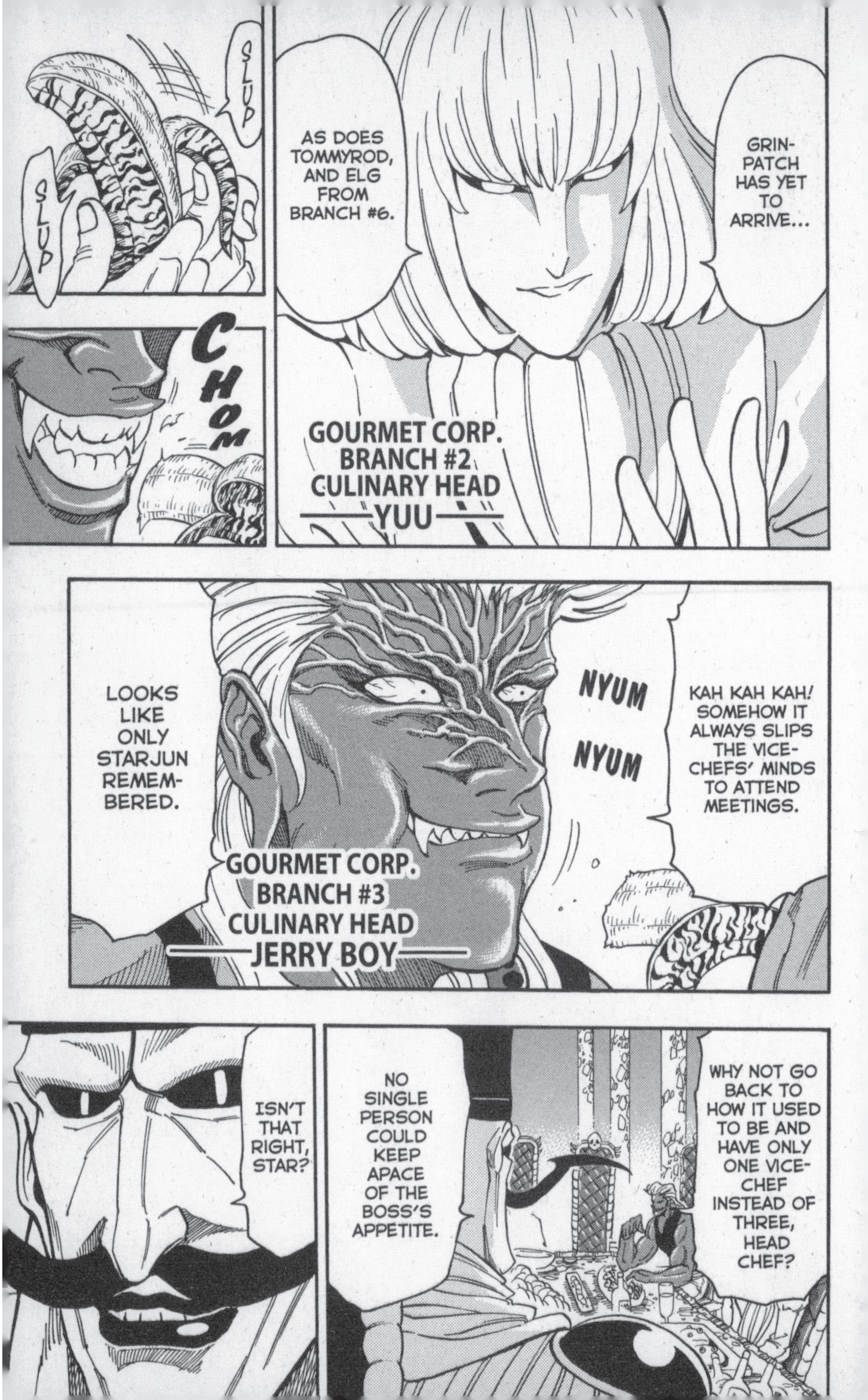
GRIN-PATCH HAS YET TO ARRIVE...
AS DOES TOMMYROD, AND ELG FROM BRANCH #6.
GOURMET CORP. BRANCH #2 CULINARY HEAD —YUU—
SLUP
SLUP
CHOM
KAH KAH KAH! SOMEHOW IT ALWAYS SLIPS THE VICE-CHEFS' MINDS TO ATTEND MEETINGS.
NYUM
NYUM
LOOKS LIKE ONLY STARJUN REMEMBERED.
GOURMET CORP. BRANCH #3 CULINARY HEAD —JERRY BOY—
WHY NOT GO BACK TO HOW IT USED TO BE AND HAVE ONLY ONE VICE-CHEF INSTEAD OF THREE, HEAD CHEF?
NO SINGLE PERSON COULD KEEP APACE OF THE BOSS'S APPETITE.
ISN'T THAT RIGHT, STAR?

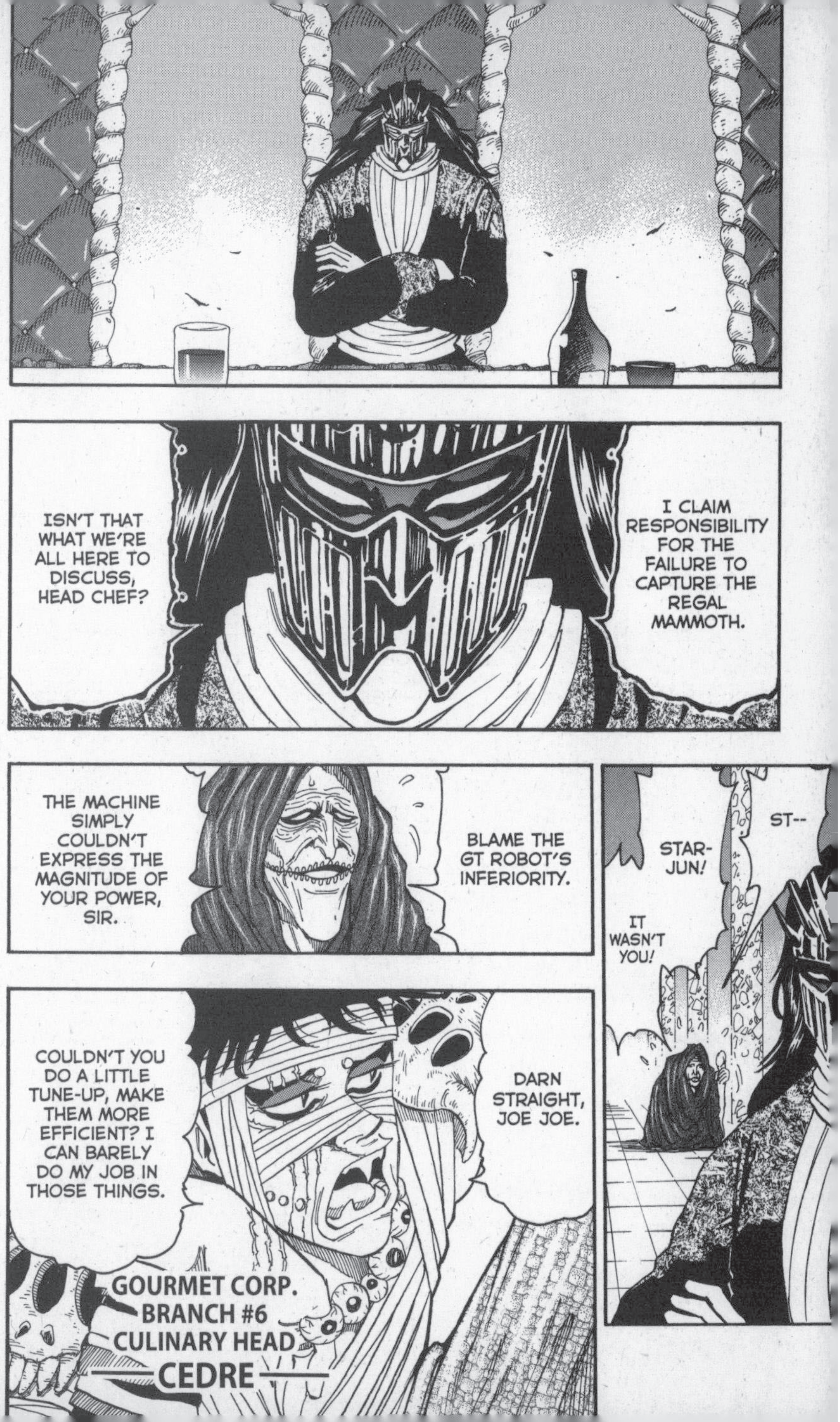

I CLAIM RESPONSIBILITY FOR THE FAILURE TO CAPTURE THE REGAL MAMMOTH.
ISN'T THAT WHAT WE'RE ALL HERE TO DISCUSS, HEAD CHEF?
ST--
STAR-JUN!
IT WASN'T YOU!
BLAME THE GT ROBOT'S INFERIORITY.
THE MACHINE SIMPLY COULDN'T EXPRESS THE MAGNITUDE OF YOUR POWER, SIR.
DARN STRAIGHT, JOE JOE.
COULDN'T YOU DO A LITTLE TUNE-UP, MAKE THEM MORE EFFICIENT? I CAN BARELY DO MY JOB IN THOSE THINGS.
GOURMET CORP. BRANCH #6 CULINARY HEAD
CEDRE

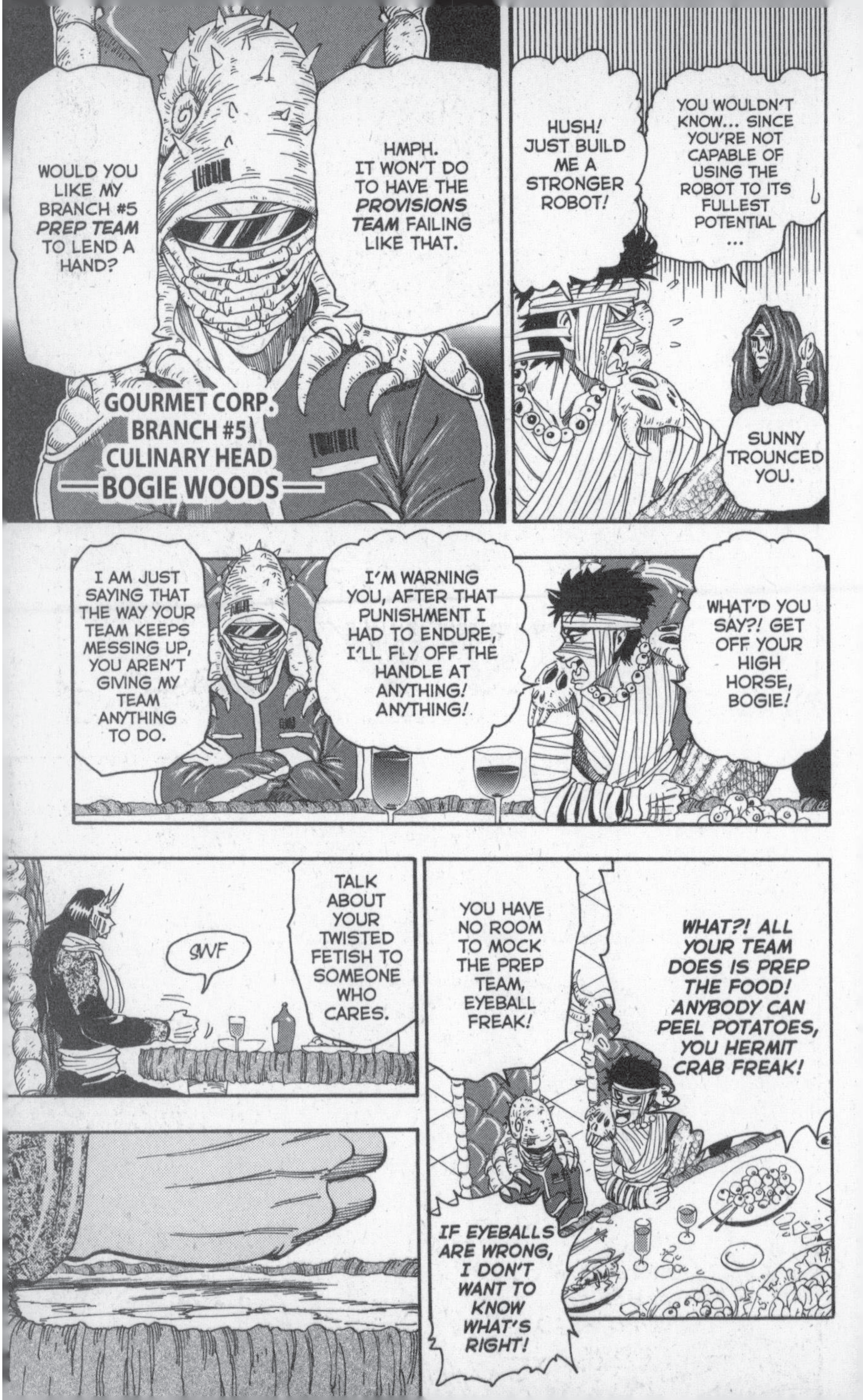

YOU WOULDN'T KNOW... SINCE YOU'RE NOT CAPABLE OF USING THE ROBOT TO ITS FULLEST POTENTIAL ...
HUSH! JUST BUILD ME A STRONGER ROBOT!
SUNNY TROUNCED YOU.
HMPH. IT WON'T DO TO HAVE THE *PROVISIONS TEAM* FAILING LIKE THAT.
WOULD YOU LIKE MY BRANCH #5 *PREP TEAM* TO LEND A HAND?
GOURMET CORP. BRANCH #5 CULINARY HEAD —BOGIE WOODS—
WHAT'D YOU SAY?! GET OFF YOUR HIGH HORSE, BOGIE!
I'M WARNING YOU, AFTER THAT PUNISHMENT I HAD TO ENDURE, I'LL FLY OFF THE HANDLE AT ANYTHING! ANYTHING!
I AM JUST SAYING THAT THE WAY YOUR TEAM KEEPS MESSING UP, YOU AREN'T GIVING MY TEAM ANYTHING TO DO.
WHAT?! ALL YOUR TEAM DOES IS PREP THE FOOD! ANYBODY CAN PEEL POTATOES, YOU HERMIT CRAB FREAK!
YOU HAVE NO ROOM TO MOCK THE PREP TEAM, EYEBALL FREAK!
IF EYEBALLS ARE WRONG, I DON'T WANT TO KNOW WHAT'S RIGHT!
TALK ABOUT YOUR TWISTED FETISH TO SOMEONE WHO CARES.
SNIF

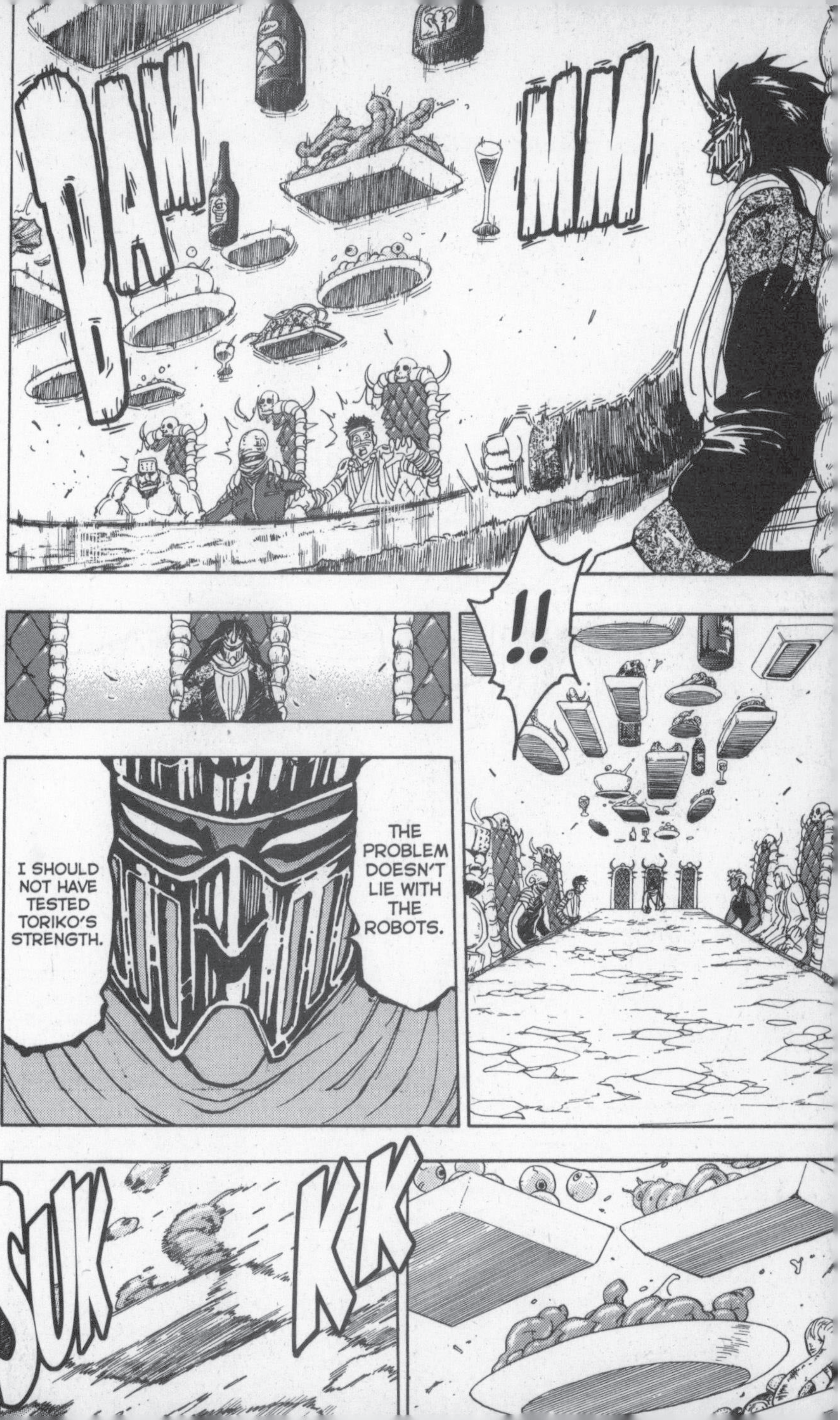
DAH
MM
!!
THE PROBLEM DOESN'T LIE WITH THE ROBOTS.
I SHOULD NOT HAVE TESTED TORIKO'S STRENGTH.
SUK
KK

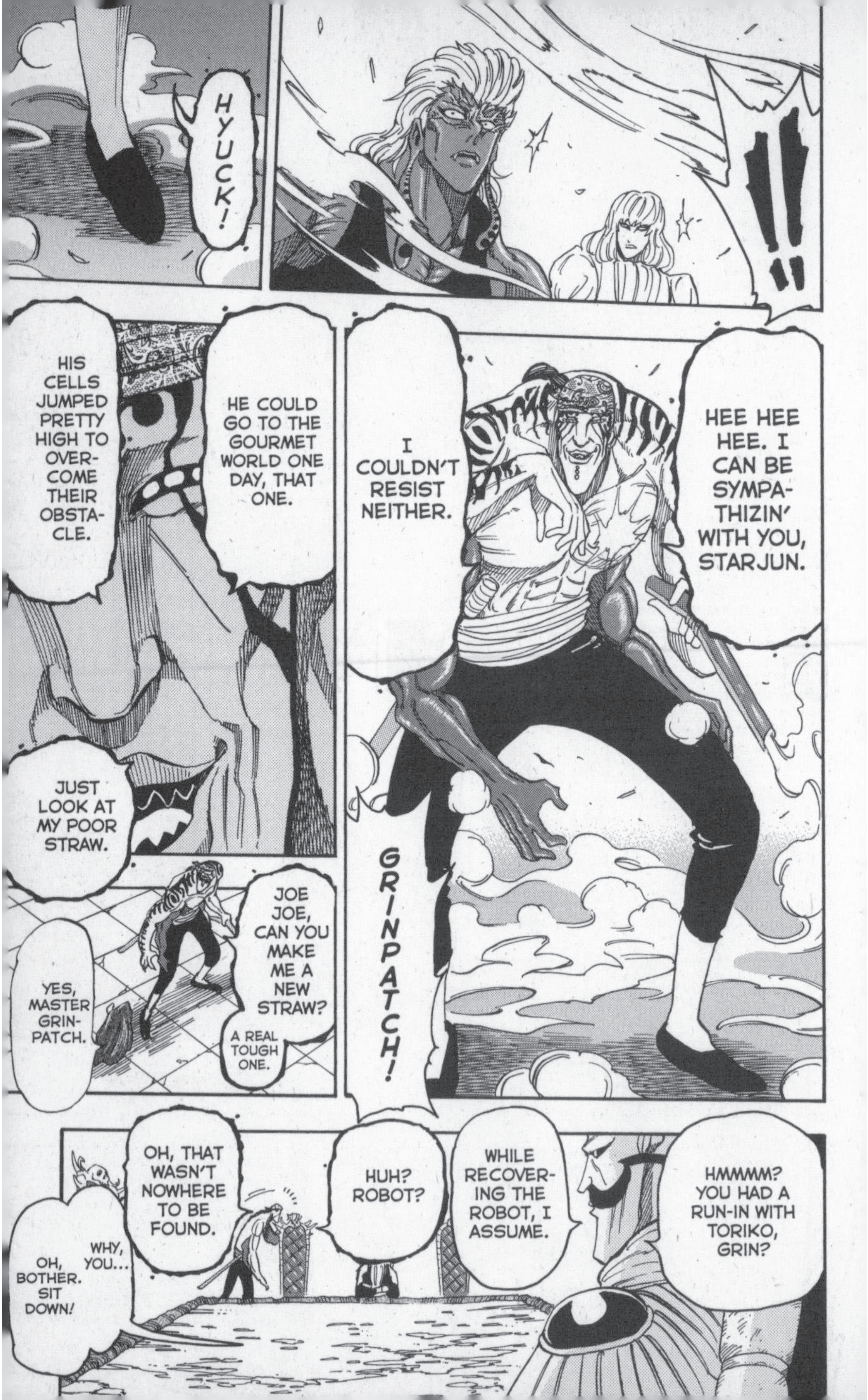
!!
HYUCK!
HEE HEE HEE. I CAN BE SYMPA-THIZIN' WITH YOU, STARJUN.
I COULDN'T RESIST NEITHER.
GRINPATCH!
HE COULD GO TO THE GOURMET WORLD ONE DAY, THAT ONE.
HIS CELLS JUMPED PRETTY HIGH TO OVER-COME THEIR OBSTA-CLE.
JUST LOOK AT MY POOR STRAW.
JOE JOE, CAN YOU MAKE ME A NEW STRAW?
A REAL TOUGH ONE.
YES, MASTER GRIN-PATCH.
HMMMM? YOU HAD A RUN-IN WITH TORIKO, GRIN?
WHILE RECOVER-ING THE ROBOT, I ASSUME.
HUH? ROBOT?
OH, THAT WASN'T NOWHERE TO BE FOUND.
WHY, YOU...
OH, BOTHER. SIT DOWN!

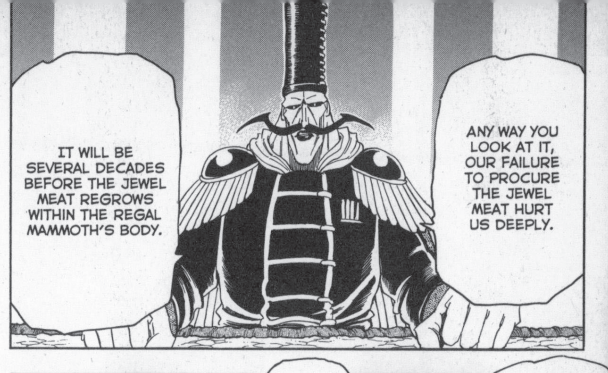

ANY WAY YOU LOOK AT IT, OUR FAILURE TO PROCURE THE JEWEL MEAT HURT US DEEPLY.
IT WILL BE SEVERAL DECADES BEFORE THE JEWEL MEAT REGROWS WITHIN THE REGAL MAMMOTH'S BODY.
THE GOURMET CELLS WITHIN OUR BODIES INEVITABLY HIT A WALL AFTER THEY MATURE A CERTAIN EXTENT.
THAT WALL IS AN OBSTACLE TO FURTHER DEVELOPMENT...
WALL
START
...BUT ALSO A DOOR TO IT, IF THE RIGHT STIMULANTS ARE ADDED.
THE FOOD STIMULANT NEEDED TO OVERCOME THOSE WALLS DIFFERS FROM PERSON TO PERSON.
WALL (4)
WALL (3)
WALL (2)
WALL (1)
START
THESE ARE LIKE CHECKPOINTS.
EVOLUTION IS THE OUTCOME OF CELLS BREAKING THROUGH THEIR WALLS.
(EVOLVE)
WALL
THE JEWEL MEAT WAS A FACILITATIVE FOOD FOR EVOLUTION.
ONE THAT WOULD HAVE OBLITERATED THE WALLS WE ALL, INCLUDING THE BOSS, ARE RUNNING UP AGAINST RIGHT NOW.

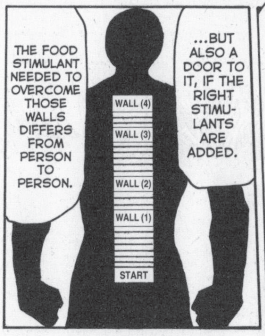

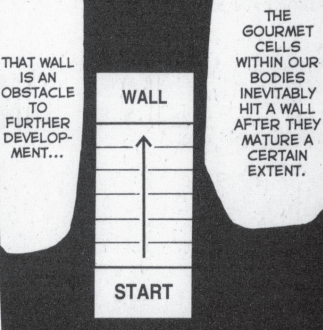

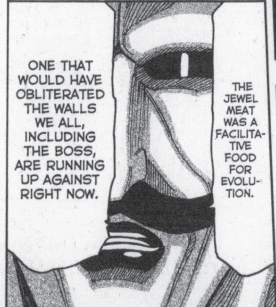

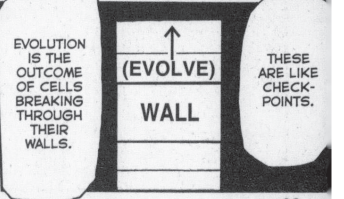

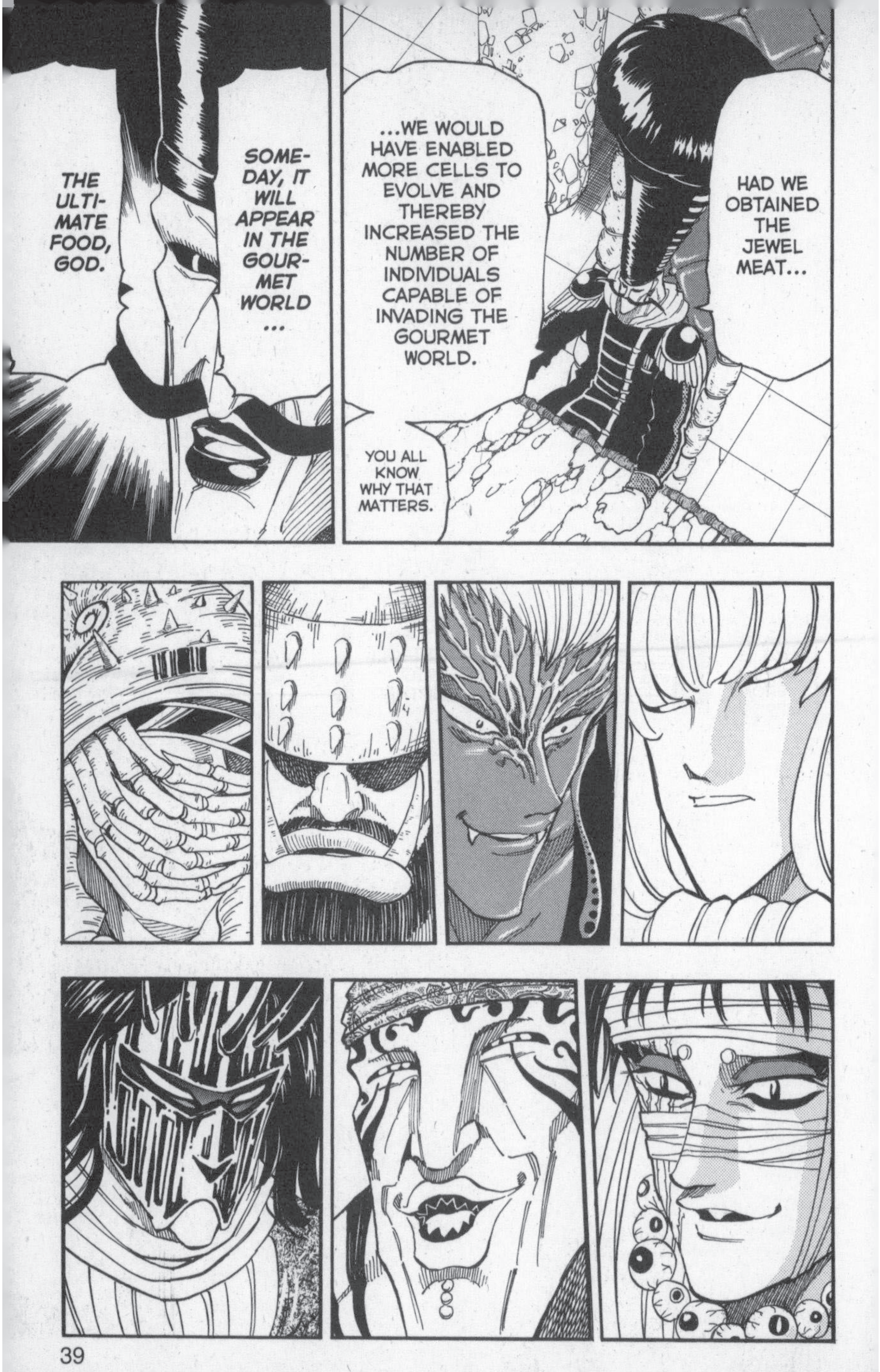
HAD WE OBTAINED THE JEWEL MEAT...
...WE WOULD HAVE ENABLED MORE CELLS TO EVOLVE AND THEREBY INCREASED THE NUMBER OF INDIVIDUALS CAPABLE OF INVADING THE GOURMET WORLD.
YOU ALL KNOW WHY THAT MATTERS.
SOME-DAY, IT WILL APPEAR IN THE GOUR-MET WORLD ...
THE ULTI-MATE FOOD, GOD.

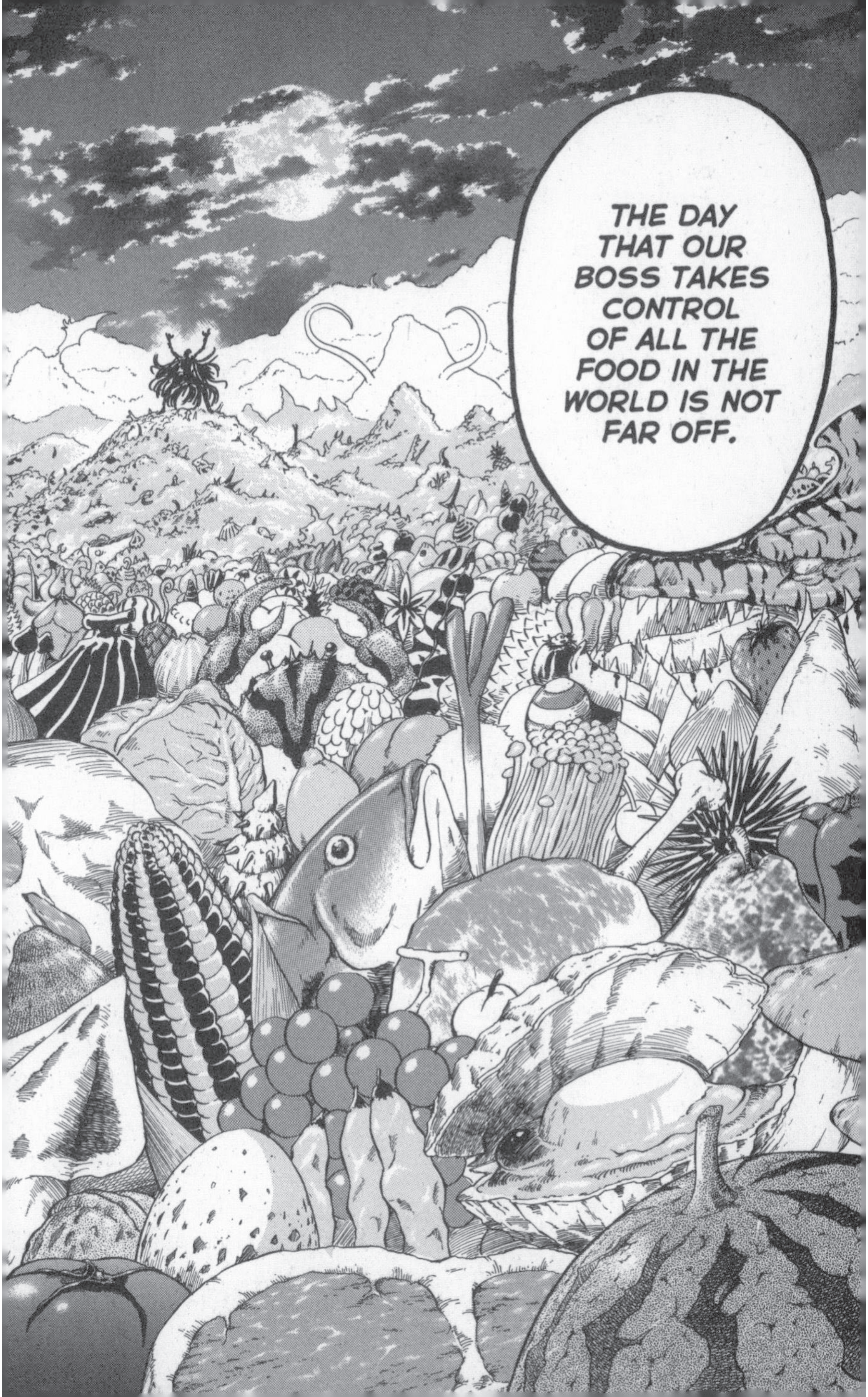
THE DAY THAT OUR BOSS TAKES CONTROL OF ALL THE FOOD IN THE WORLD IS NOT FAR OFF.

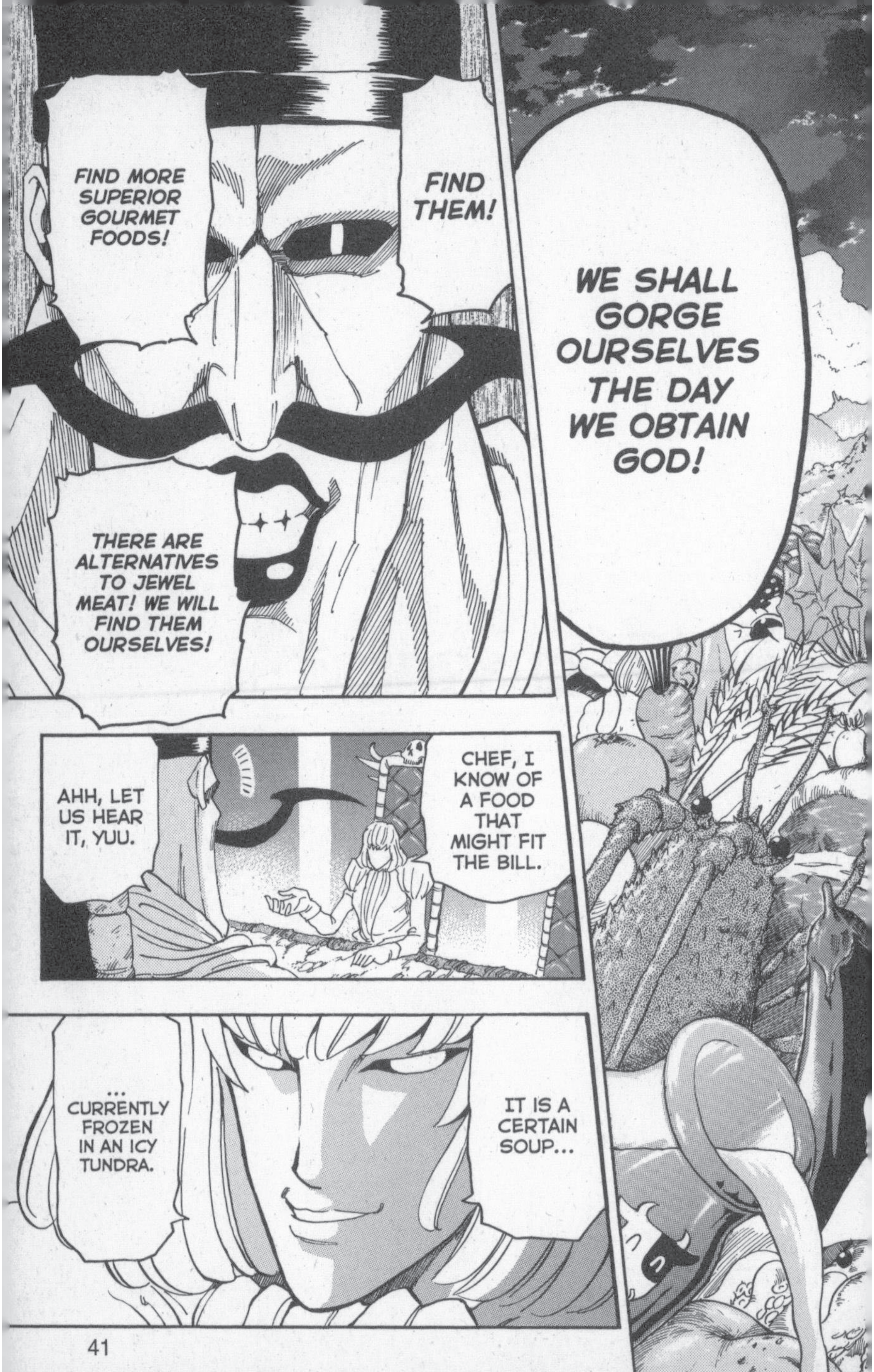
WE SHALL GORGE OURSELVES THE DAY WE OBTAIN GOD!
FIND THEM!
FIND MORE SUPERIOR GOURMET FOODS!
THERE ARE ALTERNATIVES TO JEWEL MEAT! WE WILL FIND THEM OURSELVES!
CHEF, I KNOW OF A FOOD THAT MIGHT FIT THE BILL.
AHH, LET US HEAR IT, YUU.
IT IS A CERTAIN SOUP...
...CURRENTLY FROZEN IN AN ICY TUNDRA.

IGO'S HOTEL GOURMET

FUM

FUM

PENTHOUSE RESTAURANT ON THE 97TH FLOOR

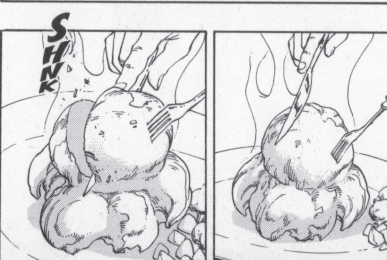

SHNK

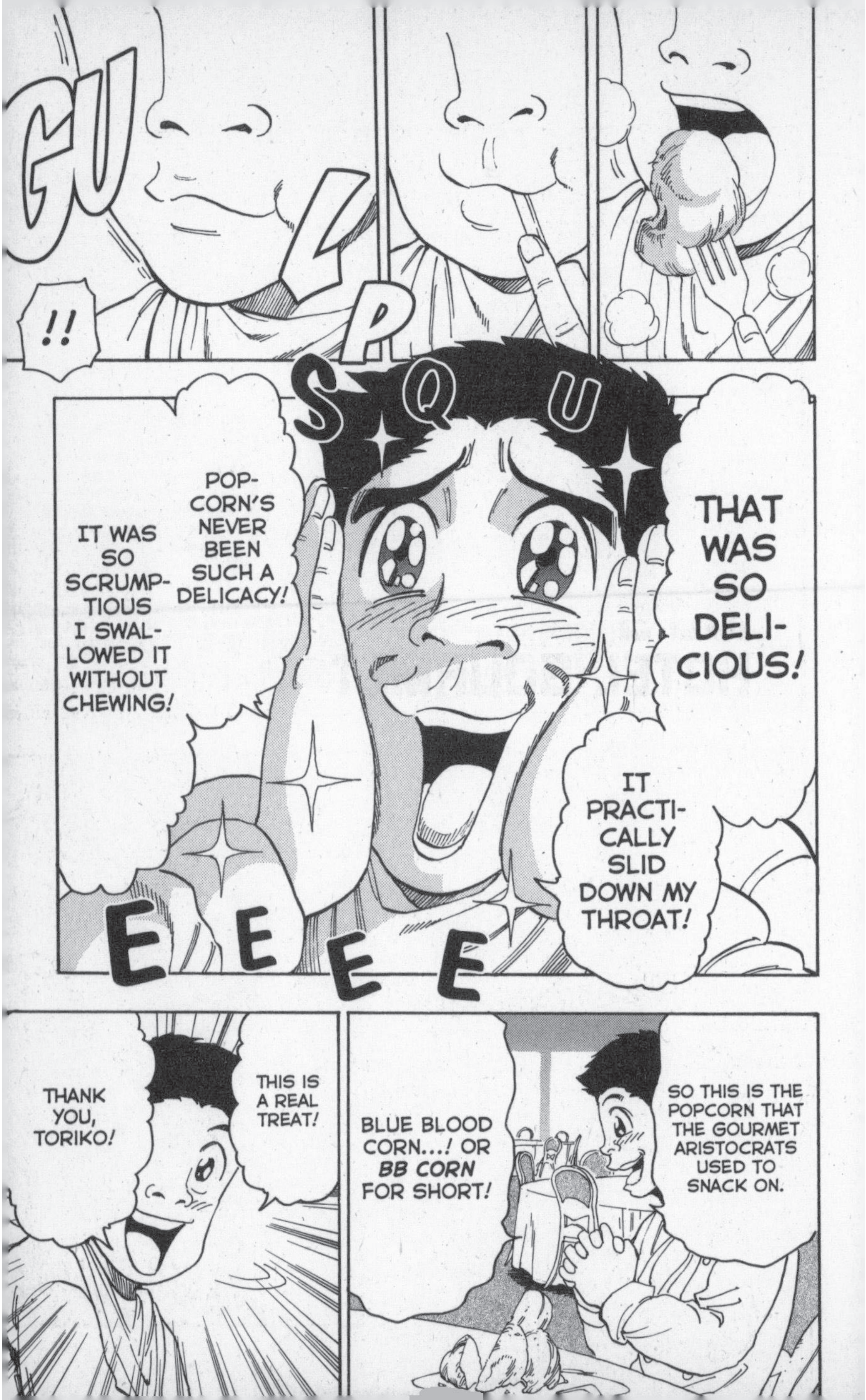
GULP
!!
SQUEEEE
THAT WAS SO DELICIOUS!
IT PRACTICALLY SLID DOWN MY THROAT!
POPCORN'S NEVER BEEN SUCH A DELICACY!
IT WAS SO SCRUMPTIOUS I SWALLOWED IT WITHOUT CHEWING!
SO THIS IS THE POPCORN THAT THE GOURMET ARISTOCRATS USED TO SNACK ON.
BLUE BLOOD CORN...! OR *BB CORN* FOR SHORT!
THIS IS A REAL TREAT!
THANK YOU, TORIKO!

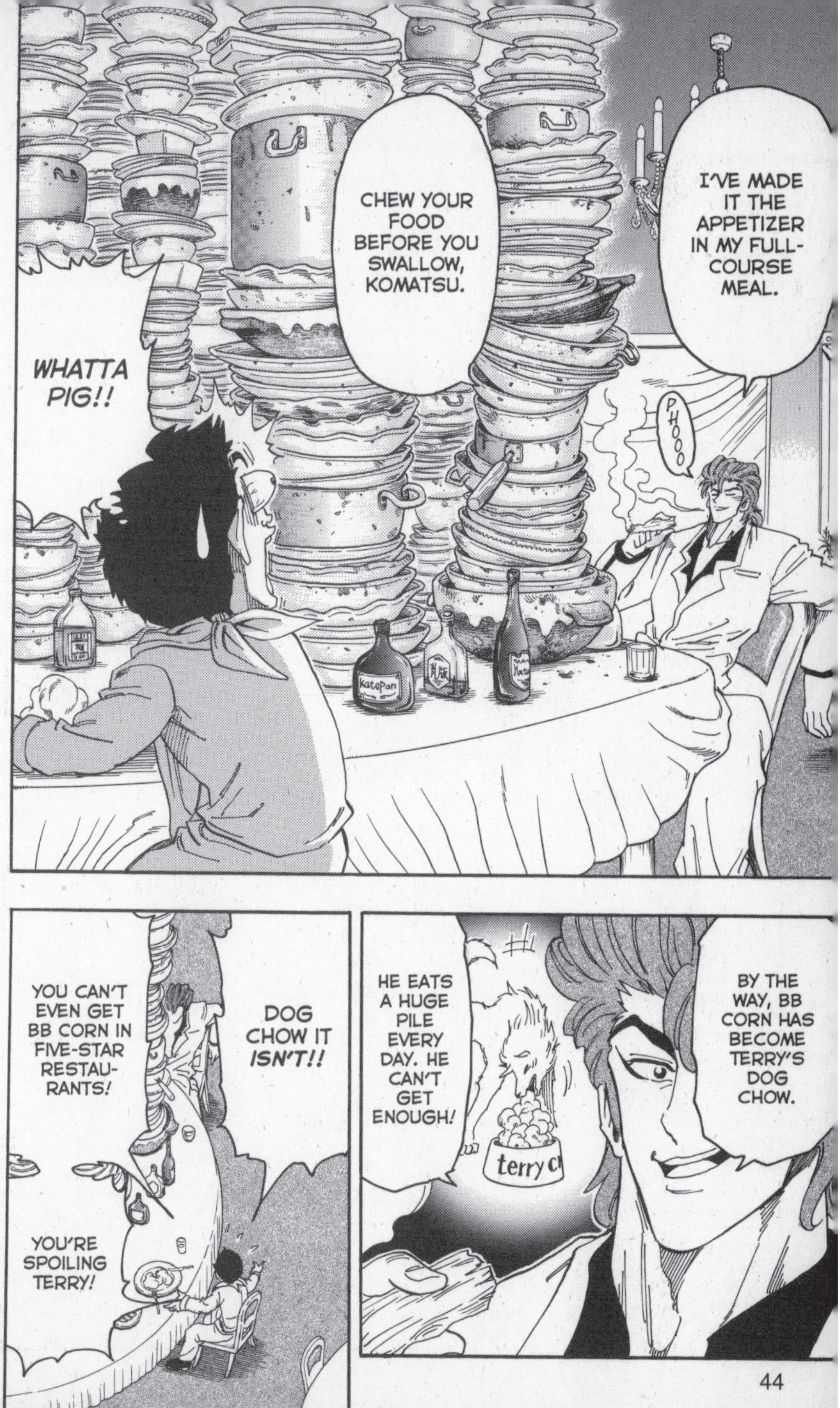
I'VE MADE IT THE APPETIZER IN MY FULL-COURSE MEAL.
PHOOO
CHEW YOUR FOOD BEFORE YOU SWALLOW, KOMATSU.
WHATTA PIG!!
BY THE WAY, BB CORN HAS BECOME TERRY'S DOG CHOW.
HE EATS A HUGE PILE EVERY DAY. HE CAN'T GET ENOUGH!
terry
DOG CHOW IT *ISN'T!!*
YOU CAN'T EVEN GET BB CORN IN FIVE-STAR RESTAURANTS!
YOU'RE SPOILING TERRY!

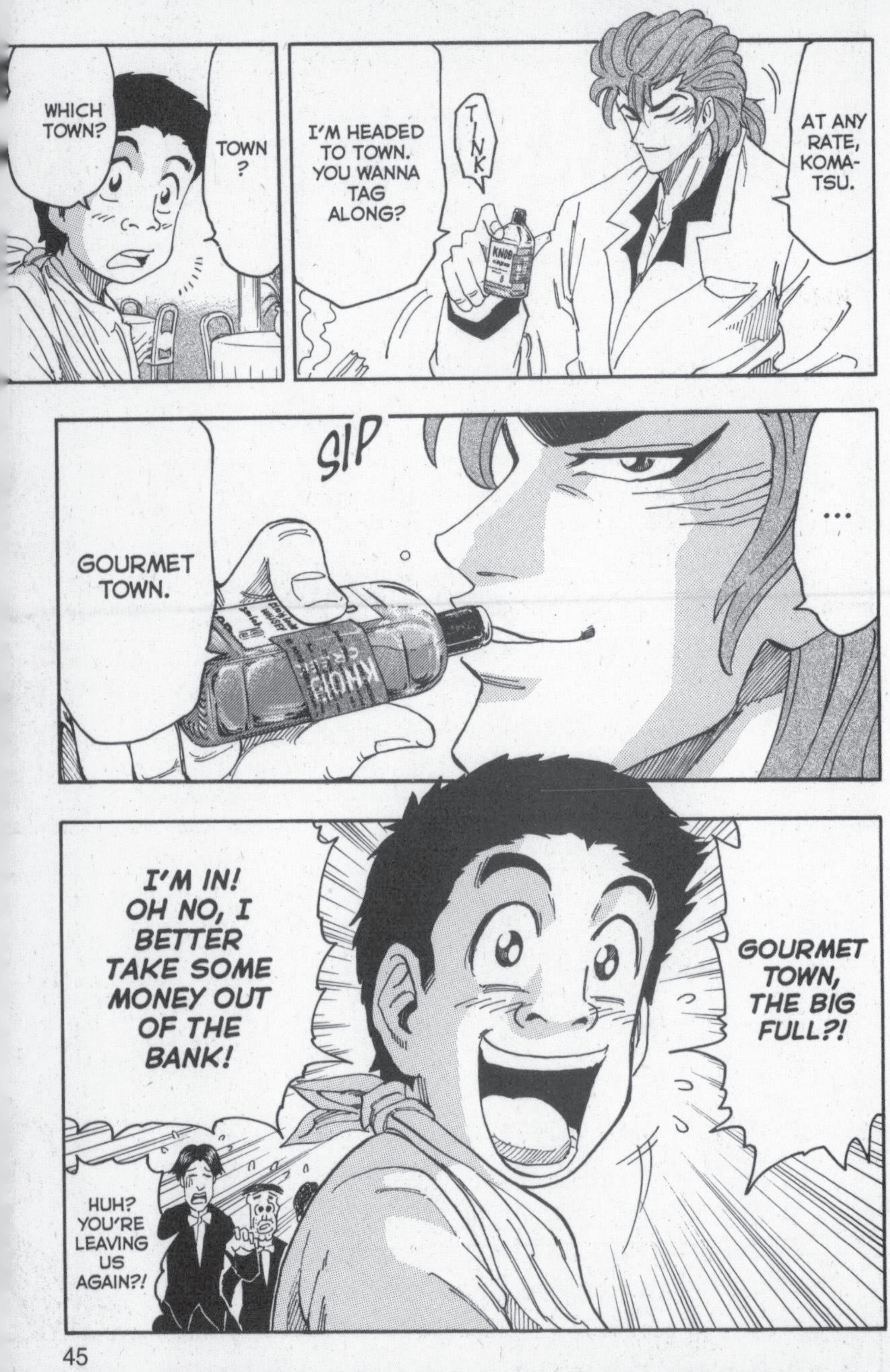
AT ANY RATE, KOMATSU.
TINK
I'M HEADED TO TOWN. YOU WANNA TAG ALONG?
TOWN?
WHICH TOWN?
...
SIP
GOURMET TOWN.
GOURMET TOWN, THE BIG FULL?!
I'M IN! OH NO, I BETTER TAKE SOME MONEY OUT OF THE BANK!
HUH? YOU'RE LEAVING US AGAIN?!

TORIKO

GOURMET CHECKLIST

Vol. 050

BEAR PIG

(MAMMAL)

CAPTURE LEVEL: 14

HABITAT: REGAL ISLE (WHITE FOREST)

LENGTH: 5 METERS

HEIGHT: 2.4 METERS

WEIGHT: 6 TONS

PRICE: 100 G / 8,000 YEN

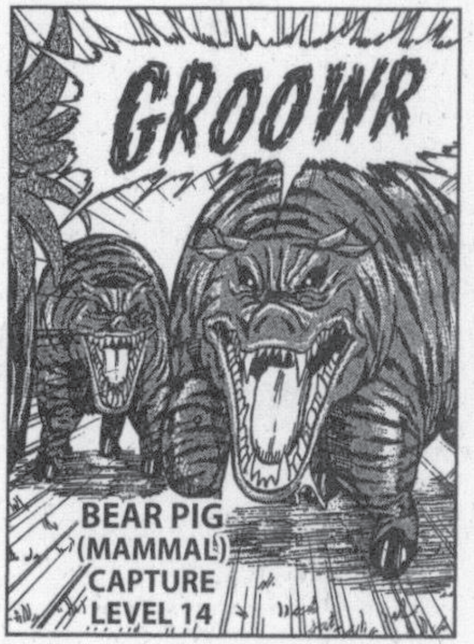
GROOWR
BEAR PIG (MAMMAL) CAPTURE LEVEL 14

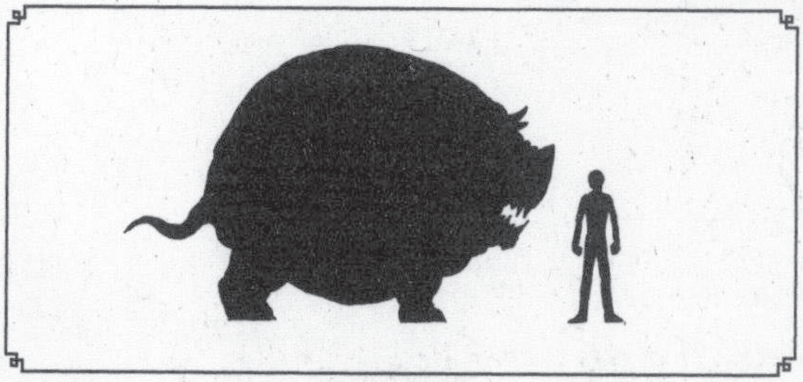

SCALE

THIS PIG IS A REAL BOOR! THE BEAR PIG EATS CLOSE TO 10 TIMES ITS WEIGHT IN FOOD EVERY DAY. IT WILL SOMETIMES RESORT TO CANNIBALISM TO SATISFY ITS VORACIOUS APPETITE. ITS MEAT IS NOT OVERLY FATTY AND IS PACKED FULL OF PROTEIN, MAKING BEAR PIG A POPULAR PORK SUBSTITUTE IN ANY MEAL.

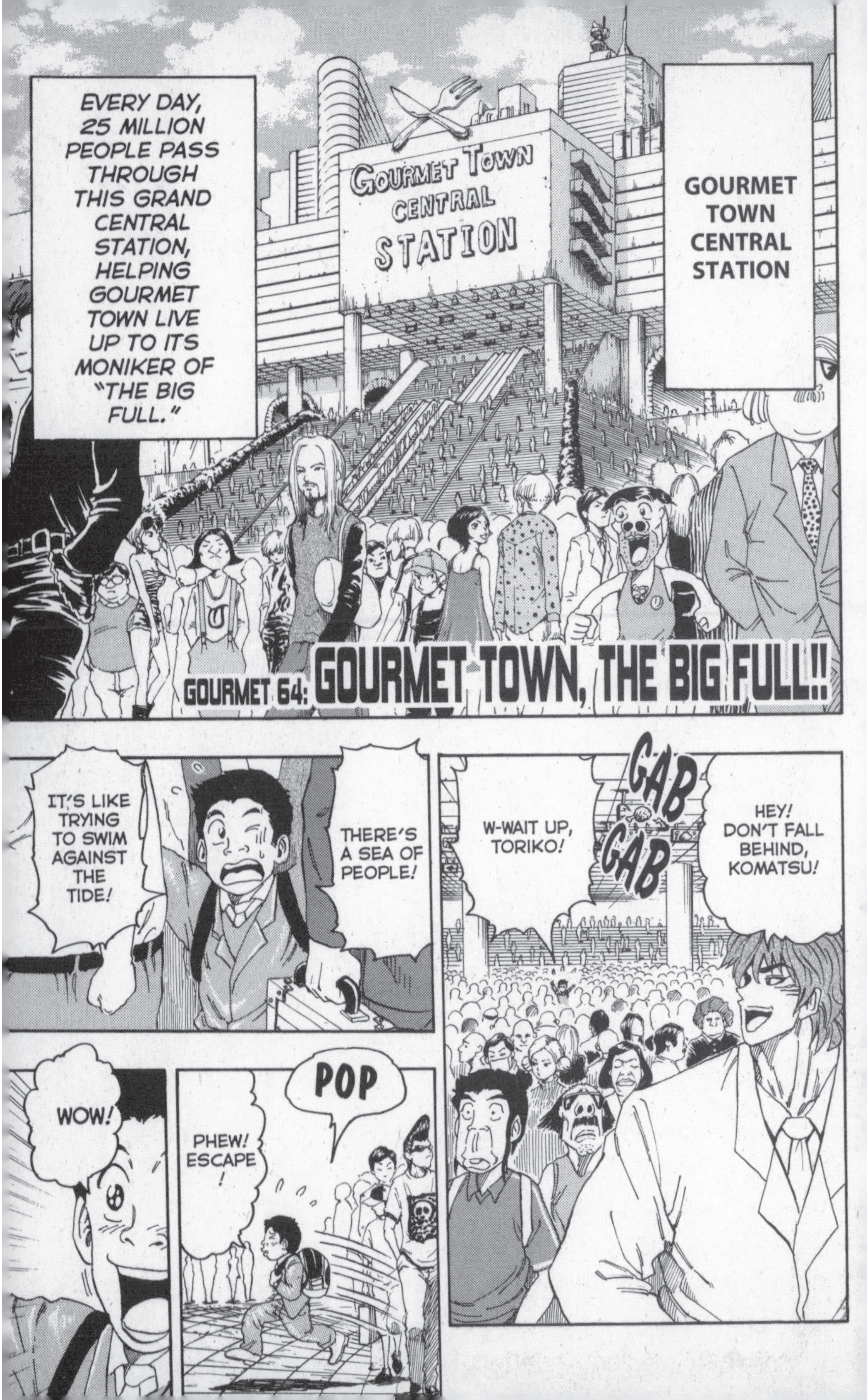
GOURMET TOWN CENTRAL STATION
EVERY DAY, 25 MILLION PEOPLE PASS THROUGH THIS GRAND CENTRAL STATION, HELPING GOURMET TOWN LIVE UP TO ITS MONIKER OF "THE BIG FULL."
GOURMET TOWN CENTRAL STATION
GOURMET 64: GOURMET TOWN, THE BIG FULL!!
HEY! DON'T FALL BEHIND, KOMATSU!
GAB GAB
W-WAIT UP, TORIKO!
THERE'S A SEA OF PEOPLE!
IT'S LIKE TRYING TO SWIM AGAINST THE TIDE!
POP
PHEW! ESCAPE!
WOW!

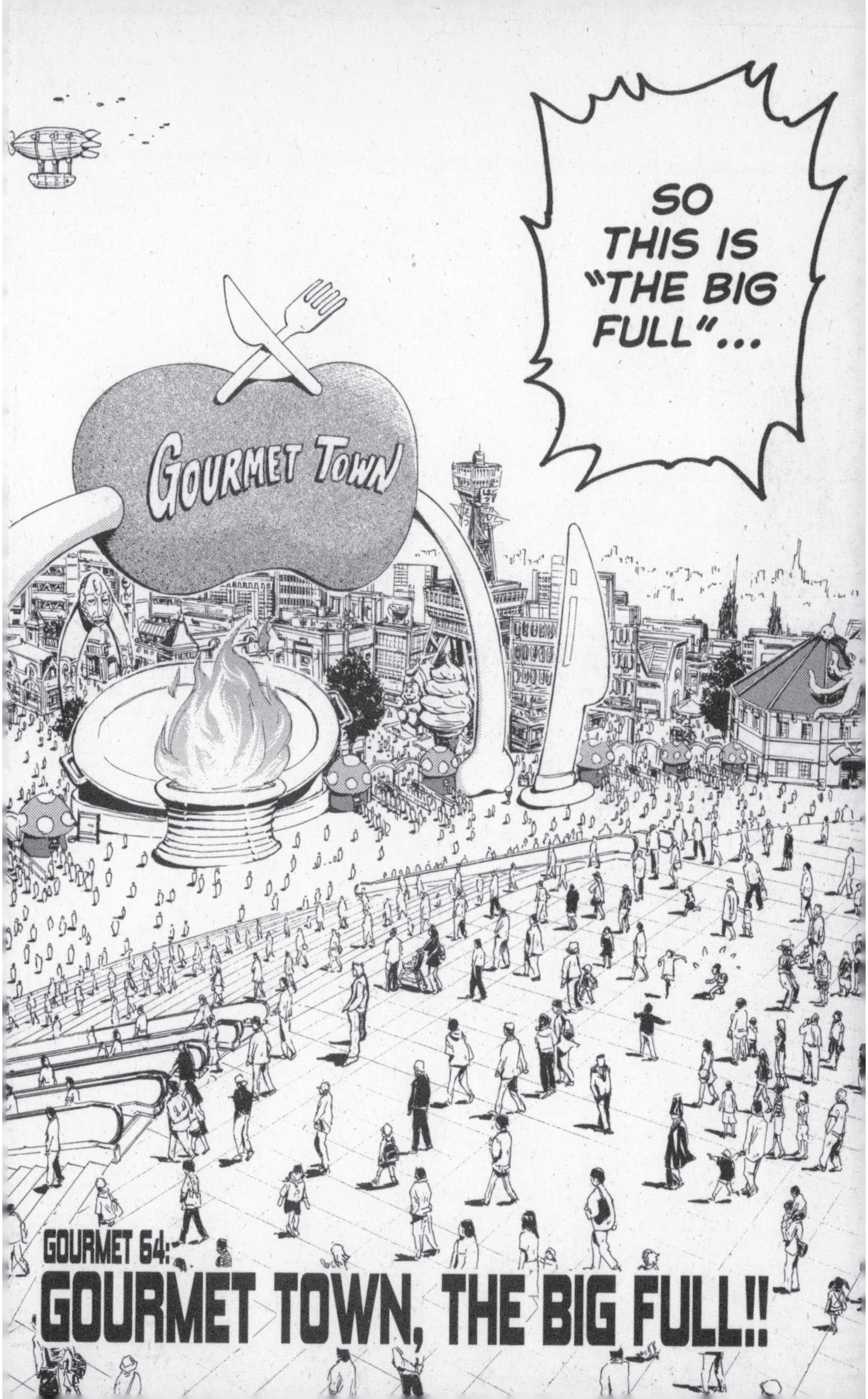
SO THIS IS "THE BIG FULL"...
GOURMET TOWN
GOURMET 64:
GOURMET TOWN, THE BIG FULL!!

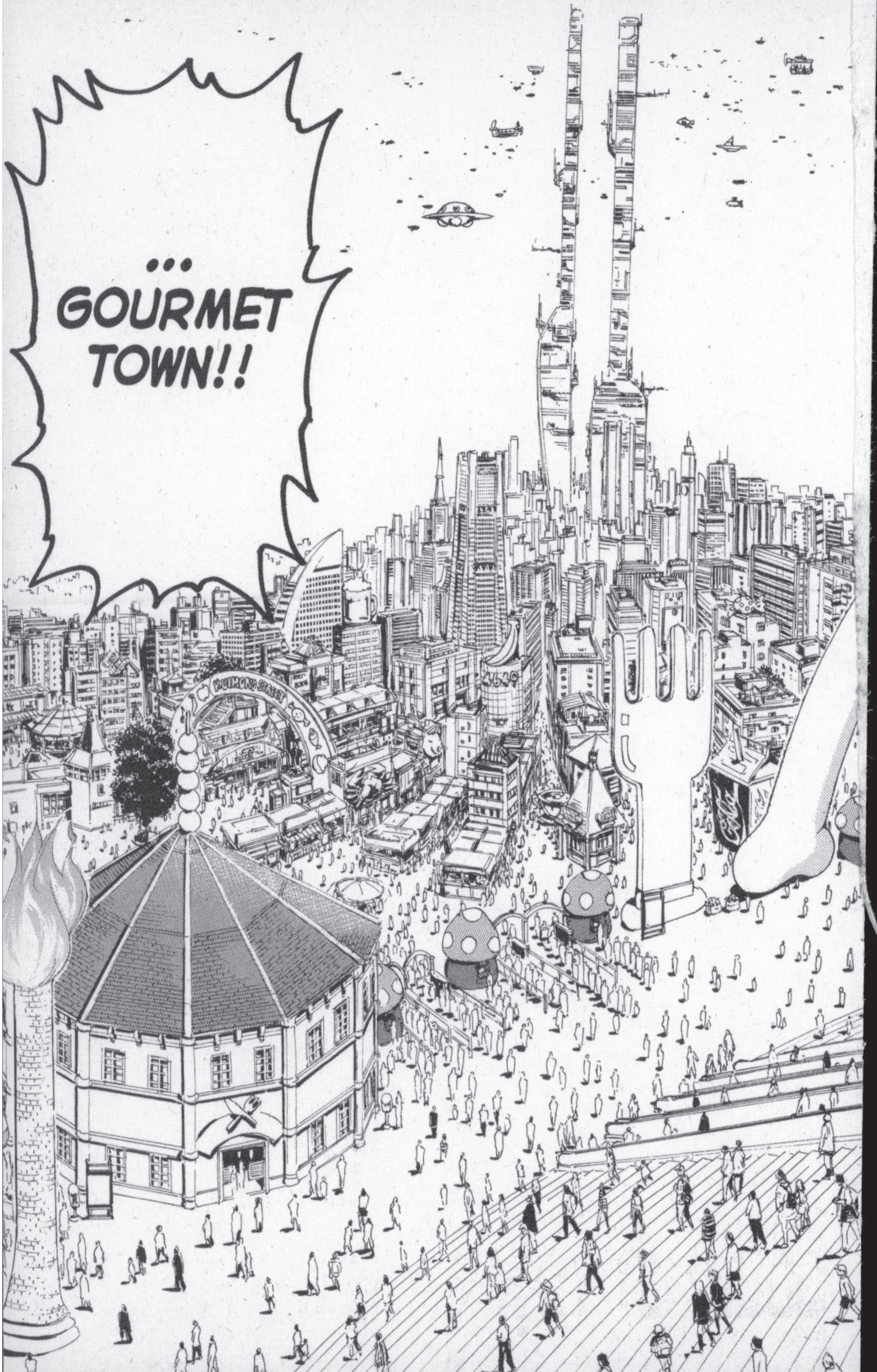
...GOURMET TOWN!!

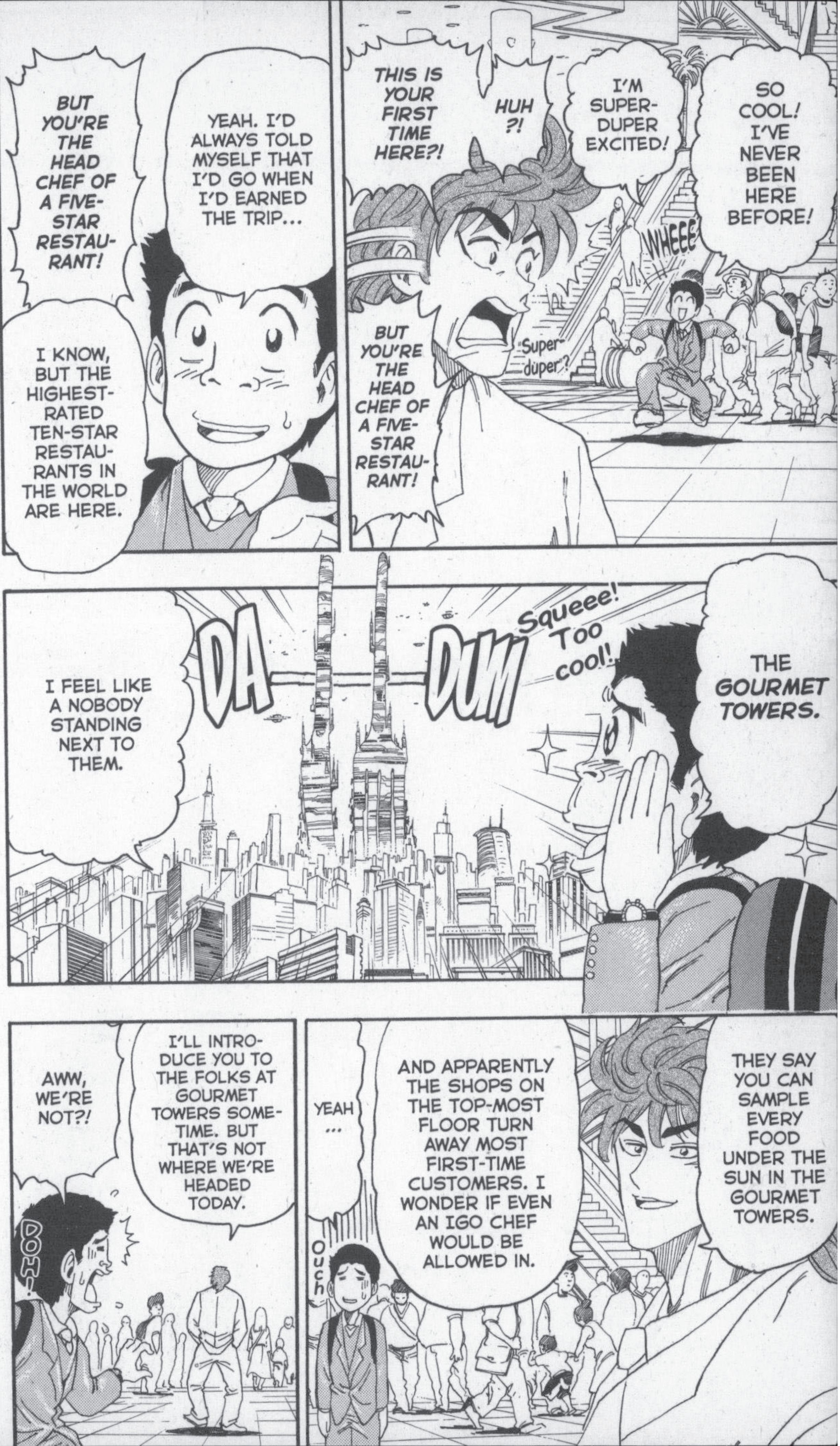
SO COOL! I'VE NEVER BEEN HERE BEFORE!
I'M SUPER-DUPER EXCITED!
WHEEEE
HUH ?!
THIS IS YOUR FIRST TIME HERE?!
"Super-duper"?
BUT YOU'RE THE HEAD CHEF OF A FIVE-STAR RESTAURANT!
YEAH. I'D ALWAYS TOLD MYSELF THAT I'D GO WHEN I'D EARNED THE TRIP...
BUT YOU'RE THE HEAD CHEF OF A FIVE-STAR RESTAURANT!
I KNOW, BUT THE HIGHEST-RATED TEN-STAR RESTAURANTS IN THE WORLD ARE HERE.
THE GOURMET TOWERS.
Squeee! Too cool!
DA
DUM
I FEEL LIKE A NOBODY STANDING NEXT TO THEM.
THEY SAY YOU CAN SAMPLE EVERY FOOD UNDER THE SUN IN THE GOURMET TOWERS.
AND APPARENTLY THE SHOPS ON THE TOP-MOST FLOOR TURN AWAY MOST FIRST-TIME CUSTOMERS. I WONDER IF EVEN AN IGO CHEF WOULD BE ALLOWED IN.
YEAH ...
Ouch
I'LL INTRODUCE YOU TO THE FOLKS AT GOURMET TOWERS SOMETIME. BUT THAT'S NOT WHERE WE'RE HEADED TODAY.
AWW, WE'RE NOT?!
DOH!

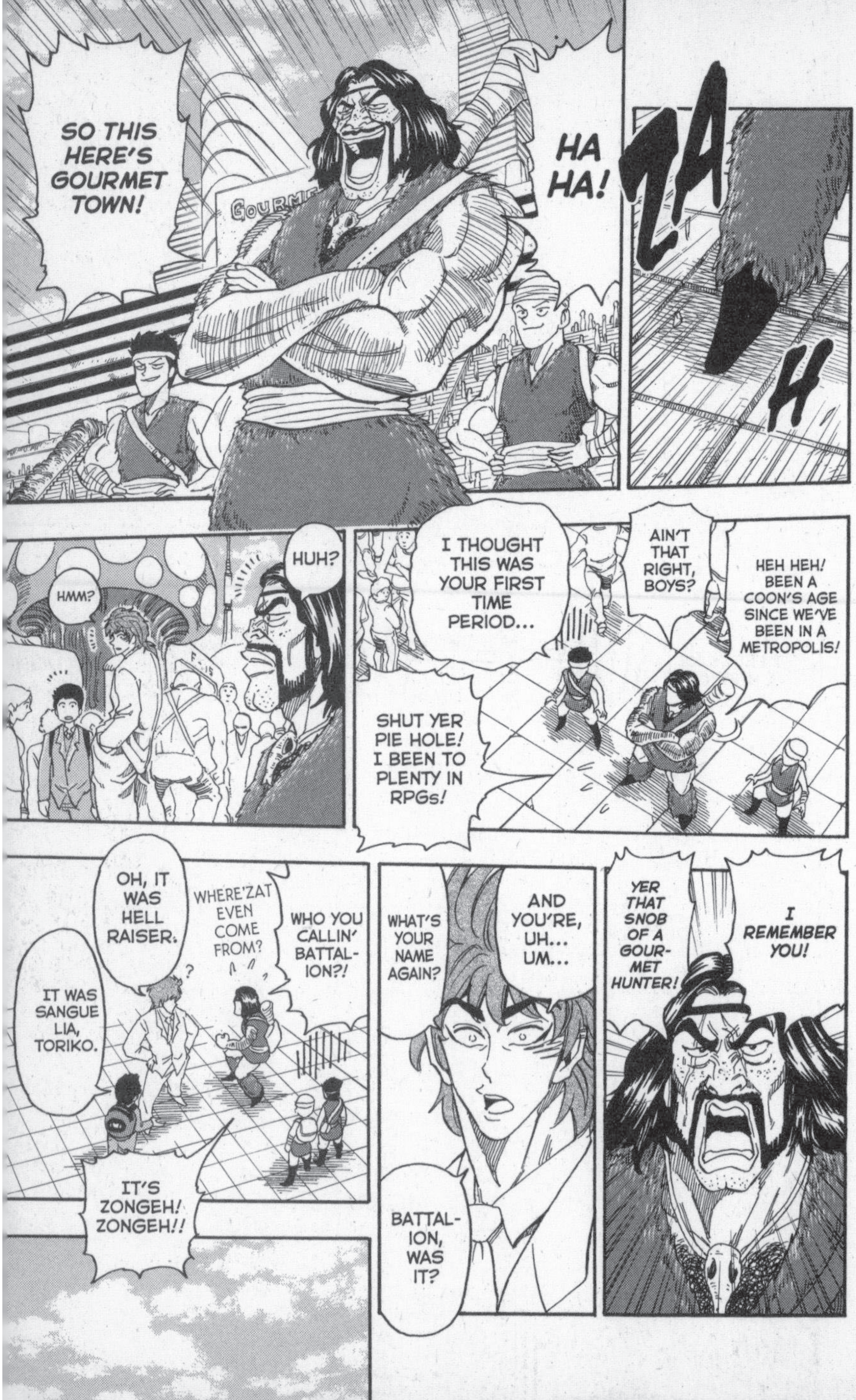
ZAH
HA HA!
SO THIS HERE'S GOURMET TOWN!
HEH HEH! BEEN A COON'S AGE SINCE WE'VE BEEN IN A METROPOLIS!
AIN'T THAT RIGHT, BOYS?
I THOUGHT THIS WAS YOUR FIRST TIME PERIOD...
SHUT YER PIE HOLE! I BEEN TO PLENTY IN RPGs!
HUH?
HMM?
I REMEMBER YOU!
YER THAT SNOB OF A GOURMET HUNTER!
AND YOU'RE, UH... UM...
WHAT'S YOUR NAME AGAIN?
BATTALION, WAS IT?
WHO YOU CALLIN' BATTALION?!
WHERE'ZAT EVEN COME FROM?
OH, IT WAS HELL RAISER.
IT WAS SANGUE LIA, TORIKO.
IT'S ZONGEH! ZONGEH!!

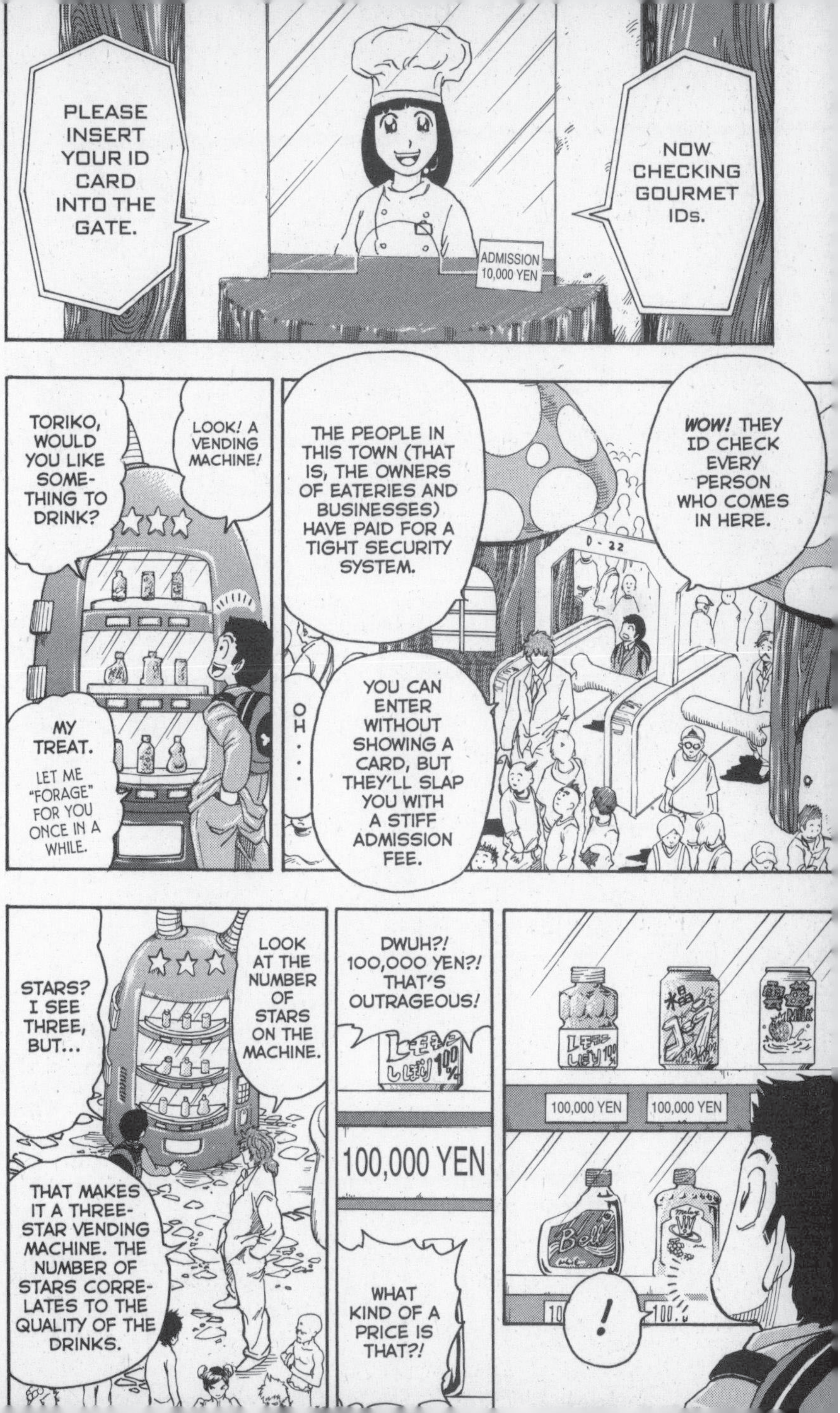
NOW CHECKING GOURMET IDs.
ADMISSION 10,000 YEN
PLEASE INSERT YOUR ID CARD INTO THE GATE.
WOW! THEY ID CHECK EVERY PERSON WHO COMES IN HERE.
THE PEOPLE IN THIS TOWN (THAT IS, THE OWNERS OF EATERIES AND BUSINESSES) HAVE PAID FOR A TIGHT SECURITY SYSTEM.
D-22
YOU CAN ENTER WITHOUT SHOWING A CARD, BUT THEY'LL SLAP YOU WITH A STIFF ADMISSION FEE.
OH...
LOOK! A VENDING MACHINE!
TORIKO, WOULD YOU LIKE SOME-THING TO DRINK?
MY TREAT.
LET ME "FORAGE" FOR YOU ONCE IN A WHILE.
100,000 YEN
100,000 YEN
!
DWUH?! 100,000 YEN?! THAT'S OUTRAGEOUS!
100,000 YEN
WHAT KIND OF A PRICE IS THAT?!
LOOK AT THE NUMBER OF STARS ON THE MACHINE.
STARS? I SEE THREE, BUT...
THAT MAKES IT A THREE-STAR VENDING MACHINE. THE NUMBER OF STARS CORRE-LATES TO THE QUALITY OF THE DRINKS.

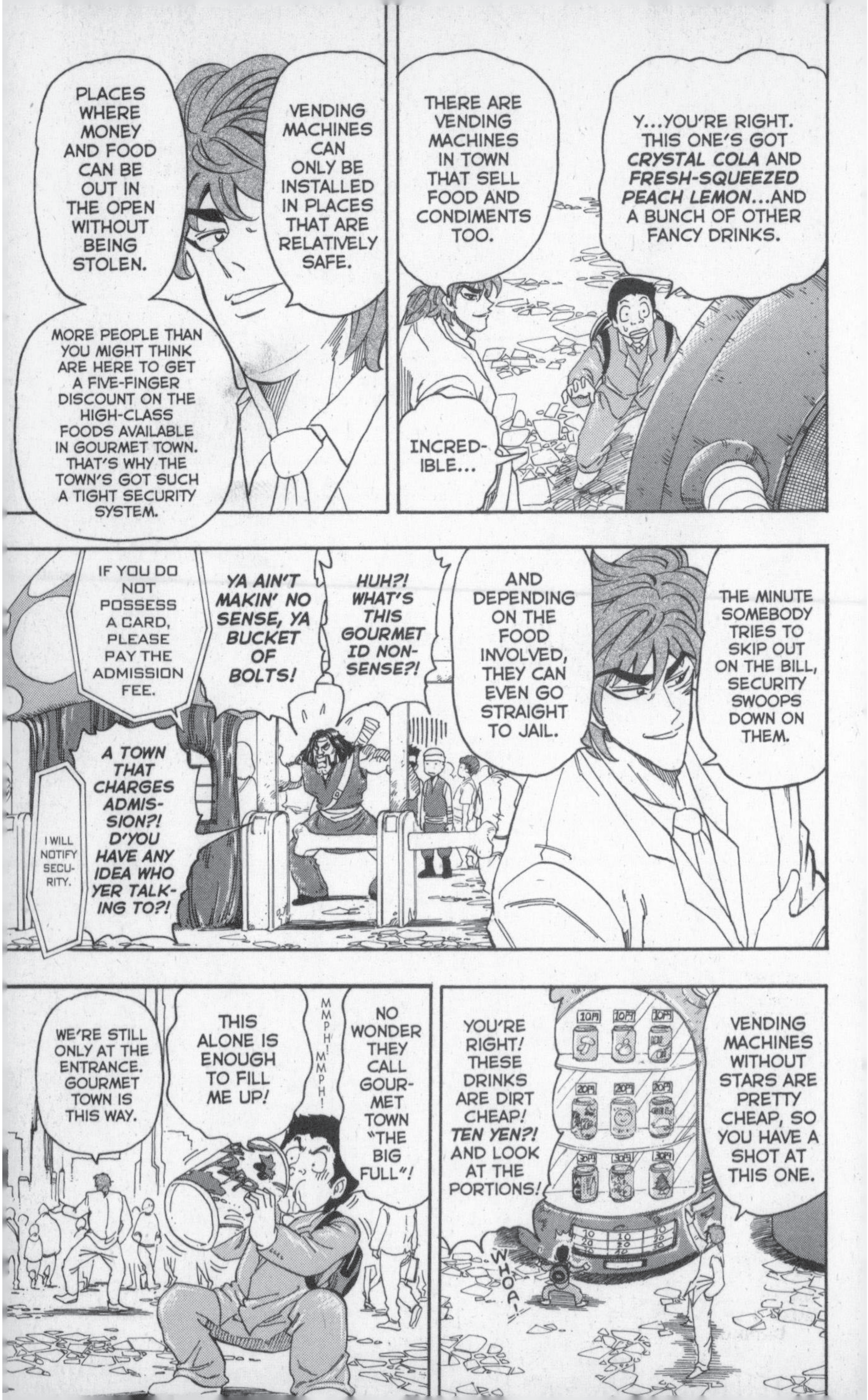
Y...YOU'RE RIGHT. THIS ONE'S GOT *CRYSTAL COLA* AND *FRESH-SQUEEZED PEACH LEMON*...AND A BUNCH OF OTHER FANCY DRINKS.
THERE ARE VENDING MACHINES IN TOWN THAT SELL FOOD AND CONDIMENTS TOO.
INCRED-IBLE...
VENDING MACHINES CAN ONLY BE INSTALLED IN PLACES THAT ARE RELATIVELY SAFE.
PLACES WHERE MONEY AND FOOD CAN BE OUT IN THE OPEN WITHOUT BEING STOLEN.
MORE PEOPLE THAN YOU MIGHT THINK ARE HERE TO GET A FIVE-FINGER DISCOUNT ON THE HIGH-CLASS FOODS AVAILABLE IN GOURMET TOWN. THAT'S WHY THE TOWN'S GOT SUCH A TIGHT SECURITY SYSTEM.
THE MINUTE SOMEBODY TRIES TO SKIP OUT ON THE BILL, SECURITY SWOOPS DOWN ON THEM.
AND DEPENDING ON THE FOOD INVOLVED, THEY CAN EVEN GO STRAIGHT TO JAIL.
HUH?! WHAT'S THIS GOURMET ID NON-SENSE?!
YA AIN'T MAKIN' NO SENSE, YA BUCKET OF BOLTS!
IF YOU DO NOT POSSESS A CARD, PLEASE PAY THE ADMISSION FEE.
A TOWN THAT CHARGES ADMIS-SION?! D'YOU HAVE ANY IDEA WHO YER TALK-ING TO?!
I WILL NOTIFY SECU-RITY.
VENDING MACHINES WITHOUT STARS ARE PRETTY CHEAP, SO YOU HAVE A SHOT AT THIS ONE.
YOU'RE RIGHT! THESE DRINKS ARE DIRT CHEAP! *TEN YEN?!* AND LOOK AT THE PORTIONS!
WHOA!
NO WONDER THEY CALL GOUR-MET TOWN "THE BIG FULL"!
MMPH! MMPH!
THIS ALONE IS ENOUGH TO FILL ME UP!
WE'RE STILL ONLY AT THE ENTRANCE. GOURMET TOWN IS THIS WAY.

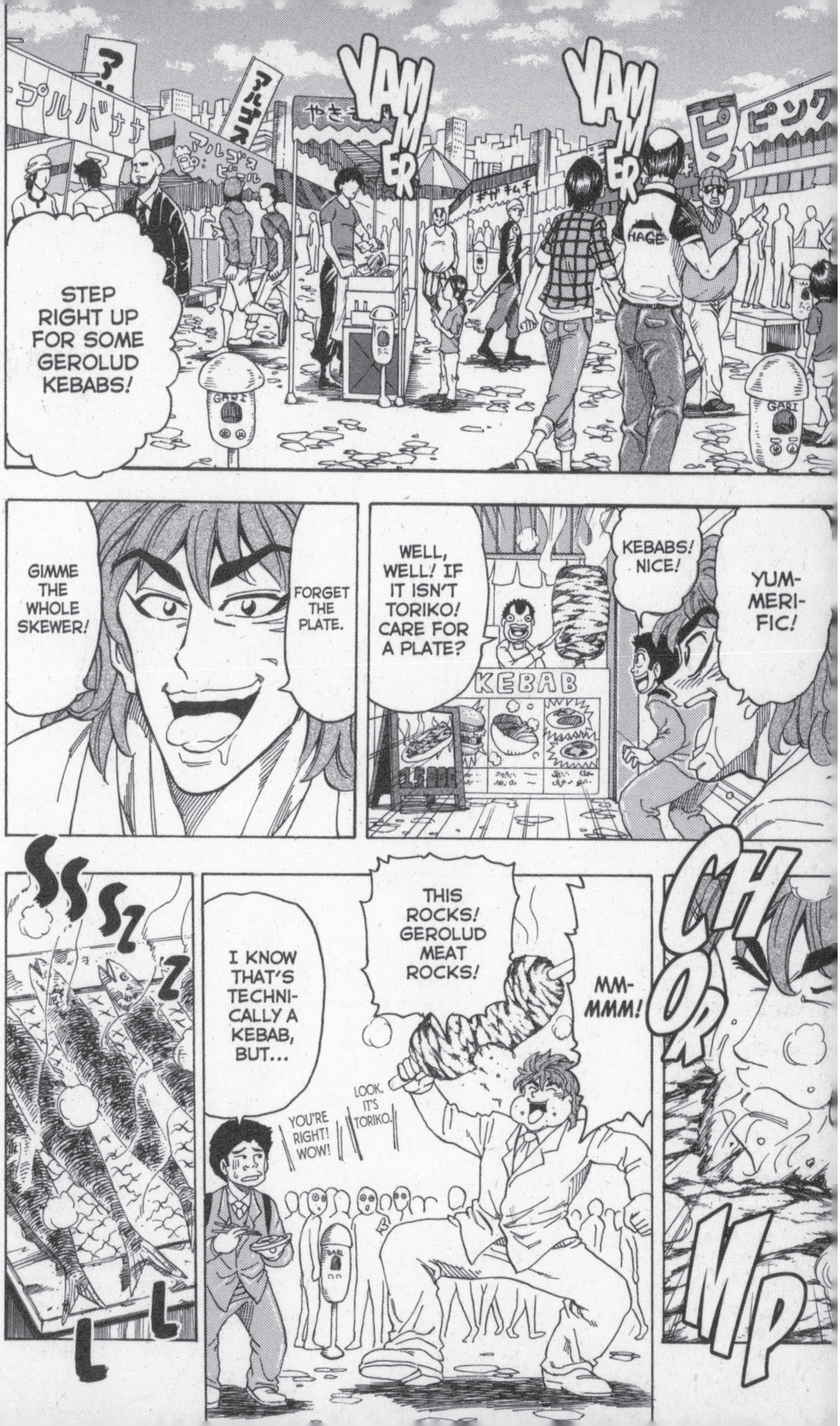
YAMMER
YAMMER
STEP RIGHT UP FOR SOME GEROLUD KEBABS!
HAGE
GARI
YUMMERIFIC!
KEBABS! NICE!
WELL, WELL! IF IT ISN'T TORIKO! CARE FOR A PLATE?
KEBAB
FORGET THE PLATE.
GIMME THE WHOLE SKEWER!
CHOMP
MM-MMM!
THIS ROCKS! GEROLUD MEAT ROCKS!
LOOK, IT'S TORIKO.
YOU'RE RIGHT! WOW!
I KNOW THAT'S TECHNICALLY A KEBAB, BUT...
SSSZZZLLL

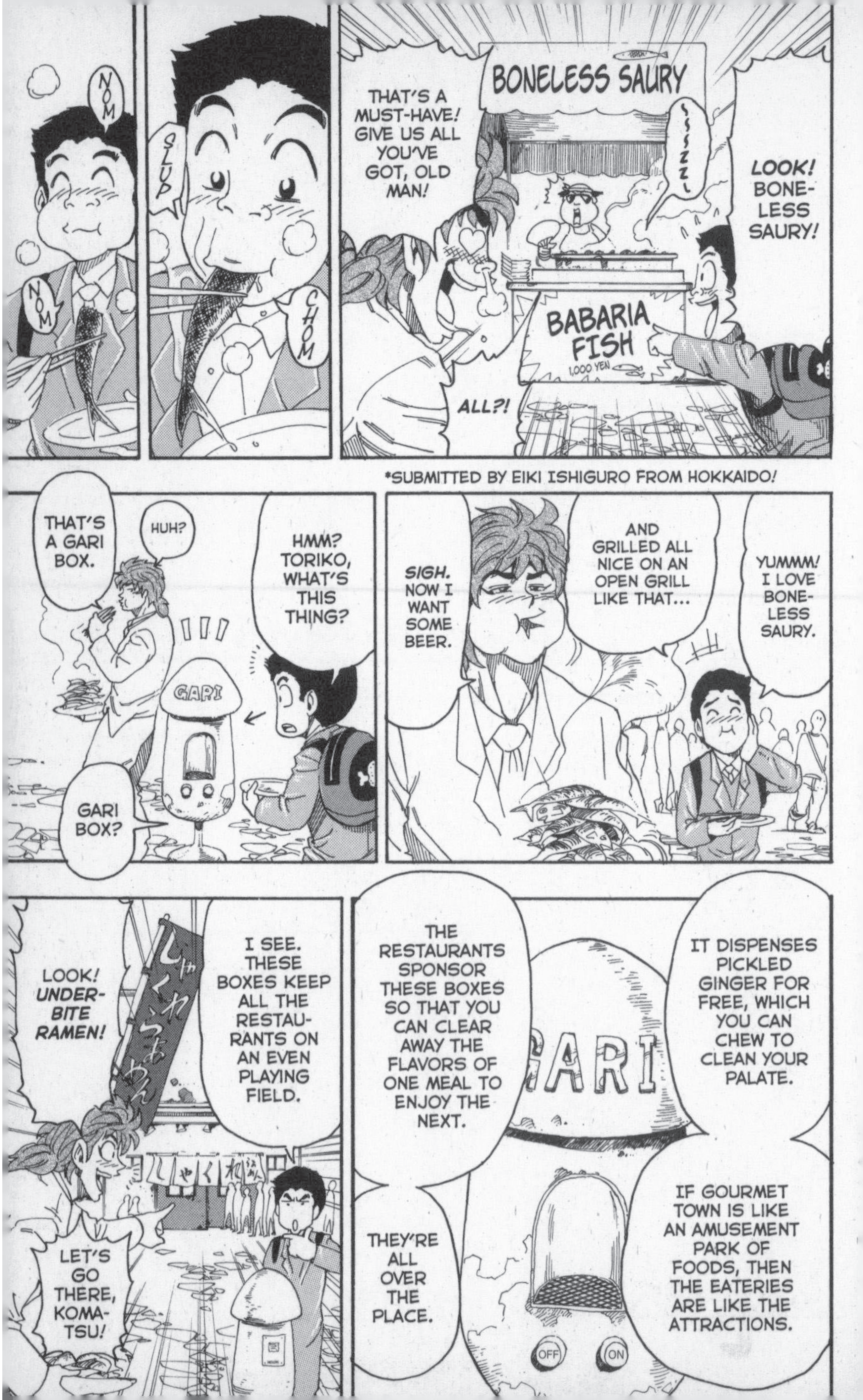
BONELESS SAURY
LOOK! BONELESS SAURY!
SSSZZL
THAT'S A MUST-HAVE! GIVE US ALL YOU'VE GOT, OLD MAN!
BABARIA FISH
1,000 YEN
ALL?!
SLUP
CHOM
NOM
NOM
*SUBMITTED BY EIKI ISHIGURO FROM HOKKAIDO!
YUMMM! I LOVE BONELESS SAURY.
AND GRILLED ALL NICE ON AN OPEN GRILL LIKE THAT...
SIGH. NOW I WANT SOME BEER.
HMM? TORIKO, WHAT'S THIS THING?
GARI
HUH?
THAT'S A GARI BOX.
GARI BOX?
IT DISPENSES PICKLED GINGER FOR FREE, WHICH YOU CAN CHEW TO CLEAN YOUR PALATE.
THE RESTAURANTS SPONSOR THESE BOXES SO THAT YOU CAN CLEAR AWAY THE FLAVORS OF ONE MEAL TO ENJOY THE NEXT.
GARI
IF GOURMET TOWN IS LIKE AN AMUSEMENT PARK OF FOODS, THEN THE EATERIES ARE LIKE THE ATTRACTIONS.
THEY'RE ALL OVER THE PLACE.
OFF
ON
I SEE. THESE BOXES KEEP ALL THE RESTAURANTS ON AN EVEN PLAYING FIELD.
LOOK! UNDERBITE RAMEN!
LET'S GO THERE, KOMATSU!

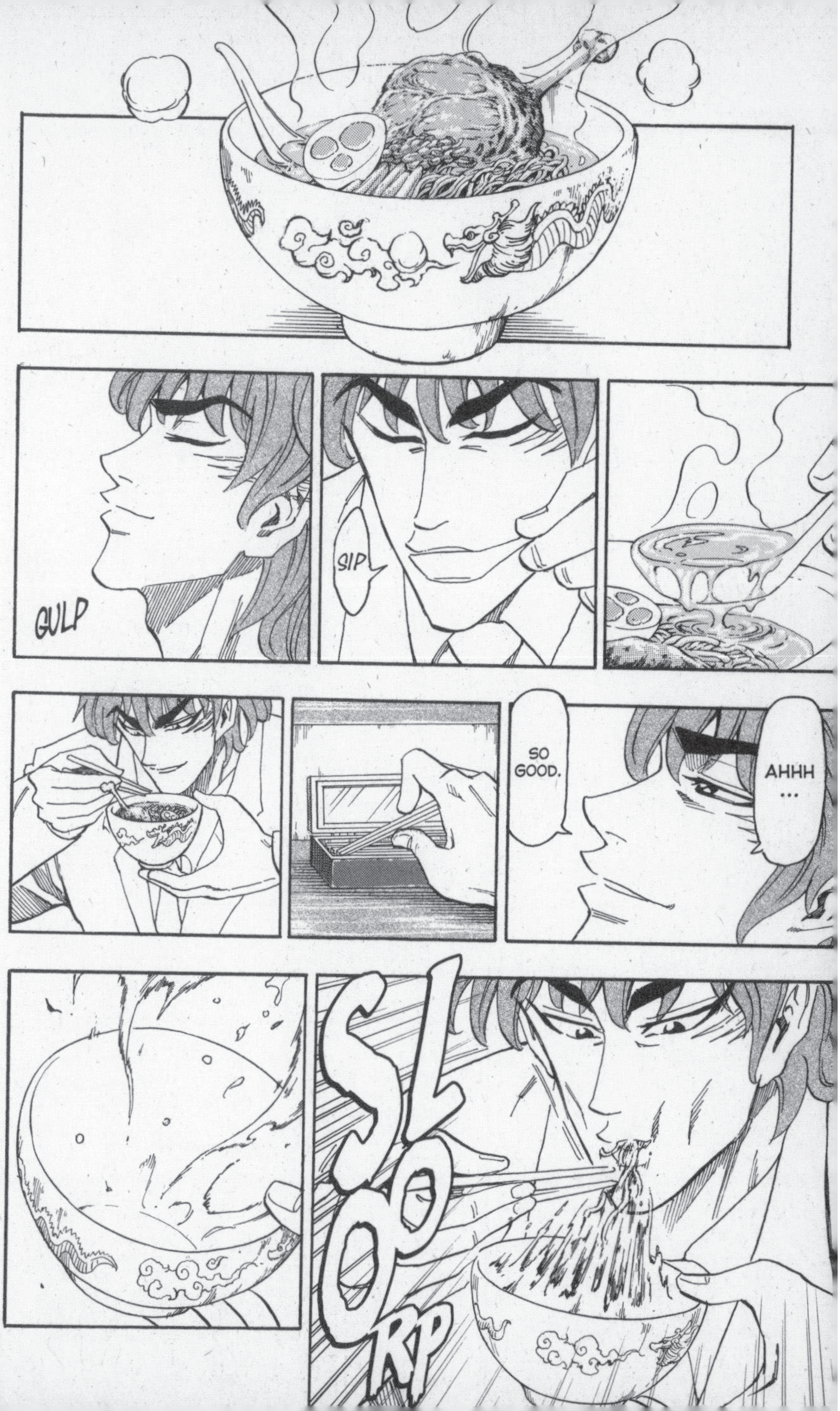
SIP
GULP
AHHH ...
SO GOOD.
SLOORP

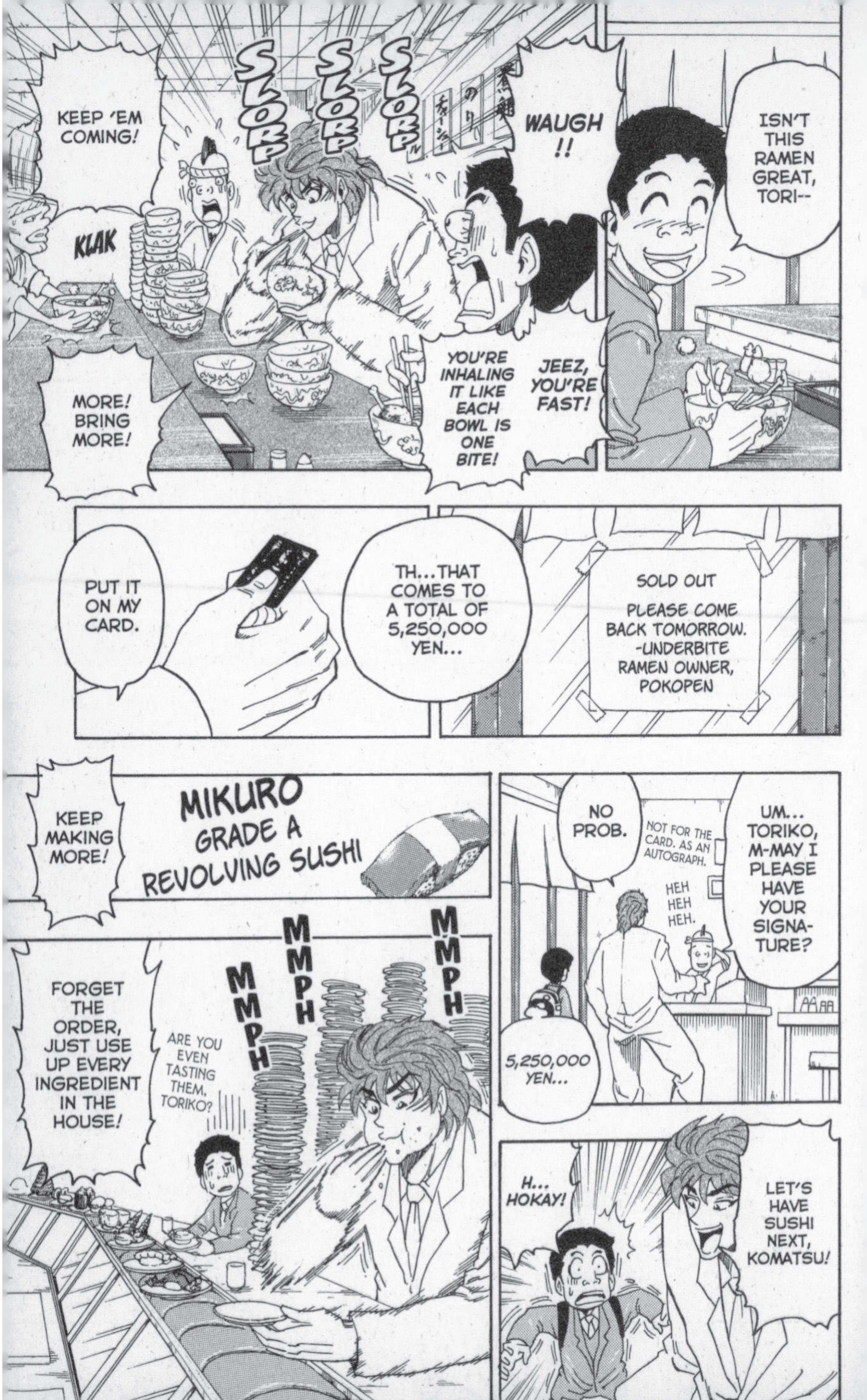
ISN'T THIS RAMEN GREAT, TORI--
WAUGH !!
SLORP
SLORP
SLORP
KEEP 'EM COMING!
KLAK
JEEZ, YOU'RE FAST!
YOU'RE INHALING IT LIKE EACH BOWL IS ONE BITE!
MORE! BRING MORE!
SOLD OUT
PLEASE COME BACK TOMORROW.
-UNDERBITE RAMEN OWNER, POKOPEN
TH...THAT COMES TO A TOTAL OF 5,250,000 YEN...
PUT IT ON MY CARD.
UM... TORIKO, M-MAY I PLEASE HAVE YOUR SIGNA-TURE?
NO PROB.
NOT FOR THE CARD. AS AN AUTOGRAPH.
HEH HEH HEH.
5,250,000 YEN...
LET'S HAVE SUSHI NEXT, KOMATSU!
H... HOKAY!
KEEP MAKING MORE!
MIKURO GRADE A REVOLVING SUSHI
MMPH
MMPH
MMPH
FORGET THE ORDER, JUST USE UP EVERY INGREDIENT IN THE HOUSE!
ARE YOU EVEN TASTING THEM, TORIKO?

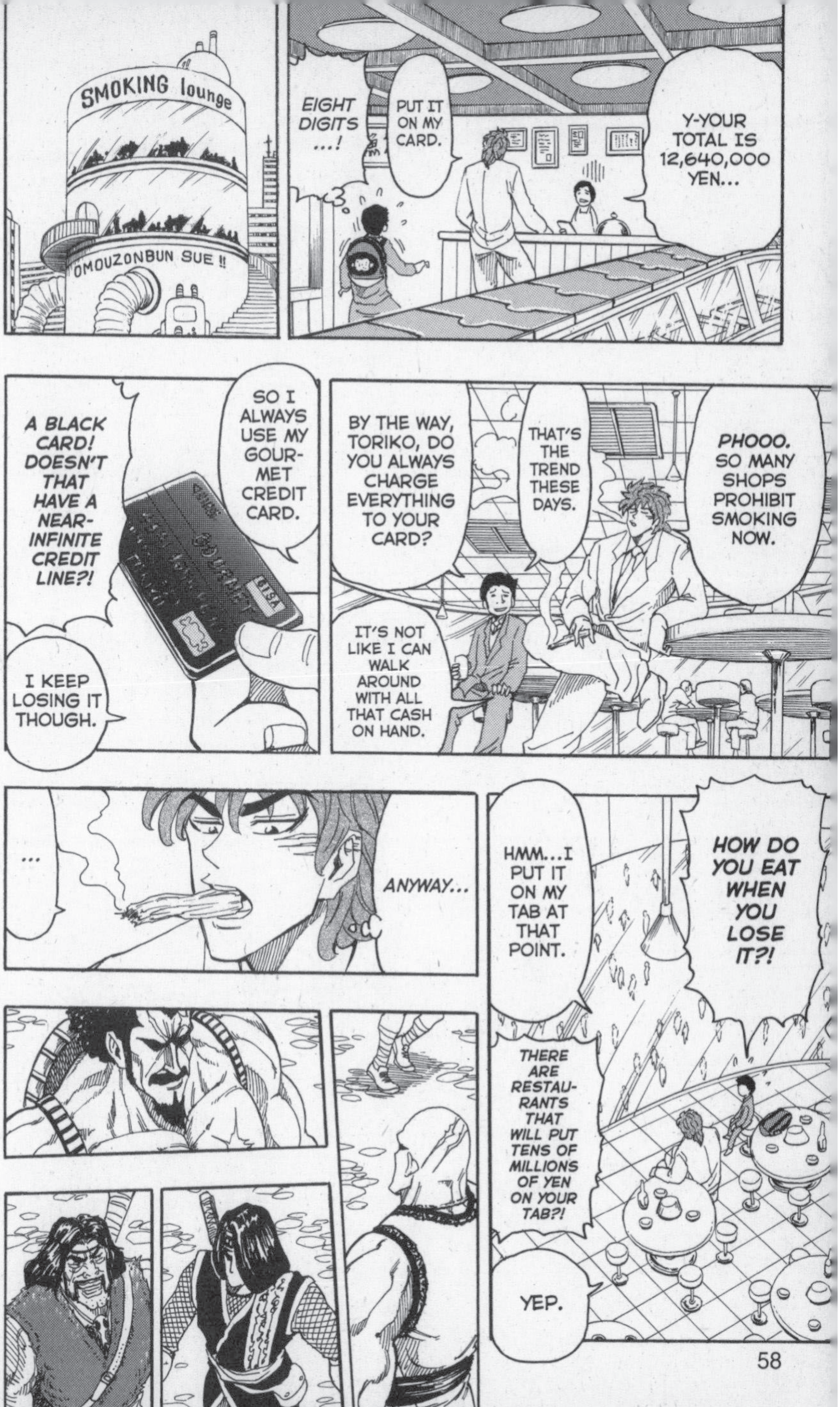
Y-YOUR TOTAL IS 12,640,000 YEN...
PUT IT ON MY CARD.
EIGHT DIGITS ...!
SMOKING lounge
OMOUZONBUN SUE !!
PHOOO. SO MANY SHOPS PROHIBIT SMOKING NOW.
THAT'S THE TREND THESE DAYS.
BY THE WAY, TORIKO, DO YOU ALWAYS CHARGE EVERYTHING TO YOUR CARD?
IT'S NOT LIKE I CAN WALK AROUND WITH ALL THAT CASH ON HAND.
SO I ALWAYS USE MY GOURMET CREDIT CARD.
A BLACK CARD! DOESN'T THAT HAVE A NEAR-INFINITE CREDIT LINE?!
I KEEP LOSING IT THOUGH.
HOW DO YOU EAT WHEN YOU LOSE IT?!
HMM...I PUT IT ON MY TAB AT THAT POINT.
THERE ARE RESTAURANTS THAT WILL PUT TENS OF MILLIONS OF YEN ON YOUR TAB?!
YEP.
ANYWAY...
...

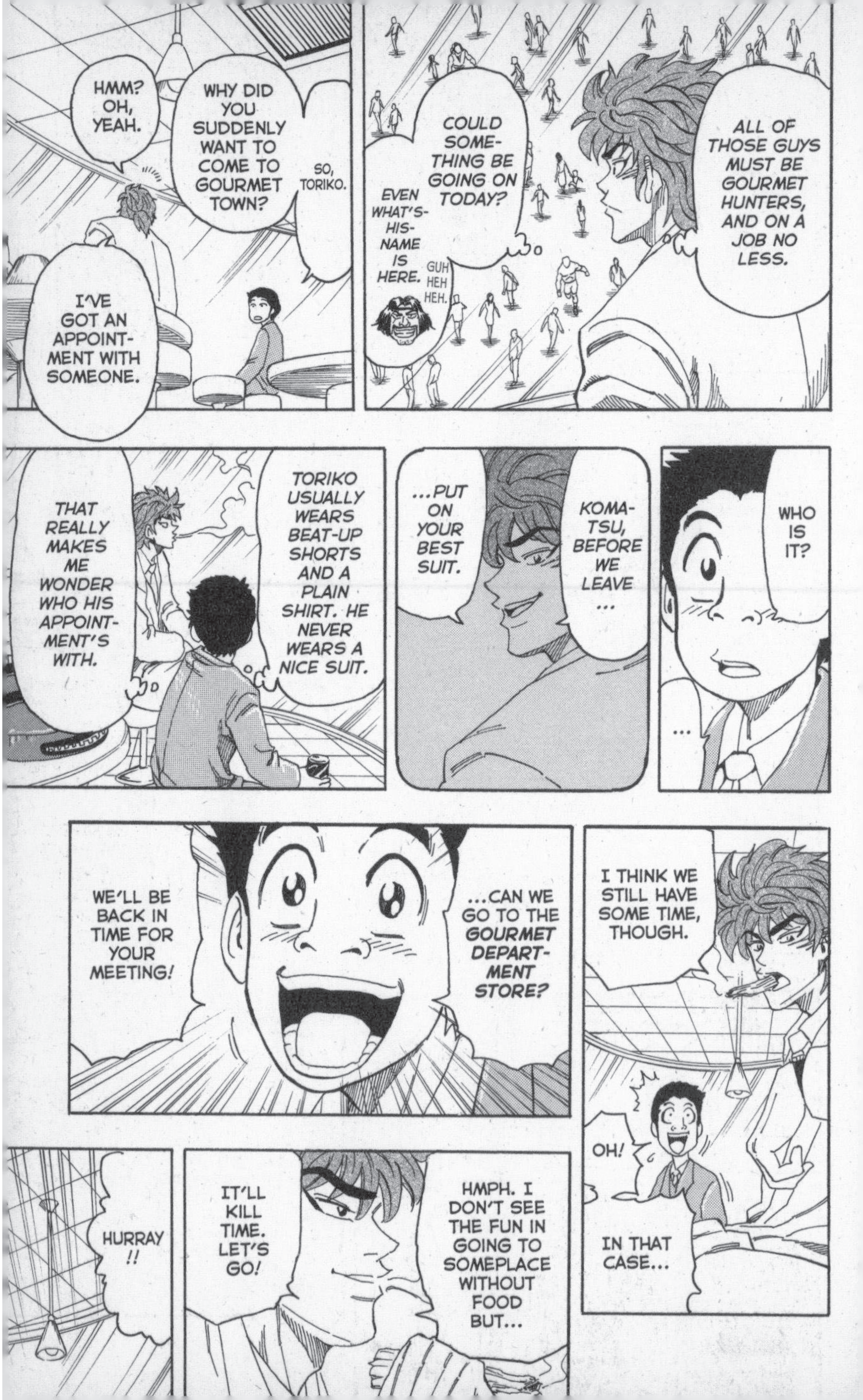
ALL OF THOSE GUYS MUST BE GOURMET HUNTERS, AND ON A JOB NO LESS.
COULD SOME-THING BE GOING ON TODAY?
EVEN WHAT'S-HIS-NAME IS HERE.
GUH HEH HEH.
SO, TORIKO.
WHY DID YOU SUDDENLY WANT TO COME TO GOURMET TOWN?
HMM? OH, YEAH.
I'VE GOT AN APPOINT-MENT WITH SOMEONE.
WHO IS IT?
...
KOMA-TSU, BEFORE WE LEAVE...
...PUT ON YOUR BEST SUIT.
TORIKO USUALLY WEARS BEAT-UP SHORTS AND A PLAIN SHIRT. HE NEVER WEARS A NICE SUIT.
THAT REALLY MAKES ME WONDER WHO HIS APPOINT-MENT'S WITH.
I THINK WE STILL HAVE SOME TIME, THOUGH.
OH!
IN THAT CASE...
...CAN WE GO TO THE *GOURMET DEPART-MENT STORE?*
WE'LL BE BACK IN TIME FOR YOUR MEETING!
HMPH. I DON'T SEE THE FUN IN GOING TO SOMEPLACE WITHOUT FOOD BUT...
IT'LL KILL TIME. LET'S GO!
HURRAY!!

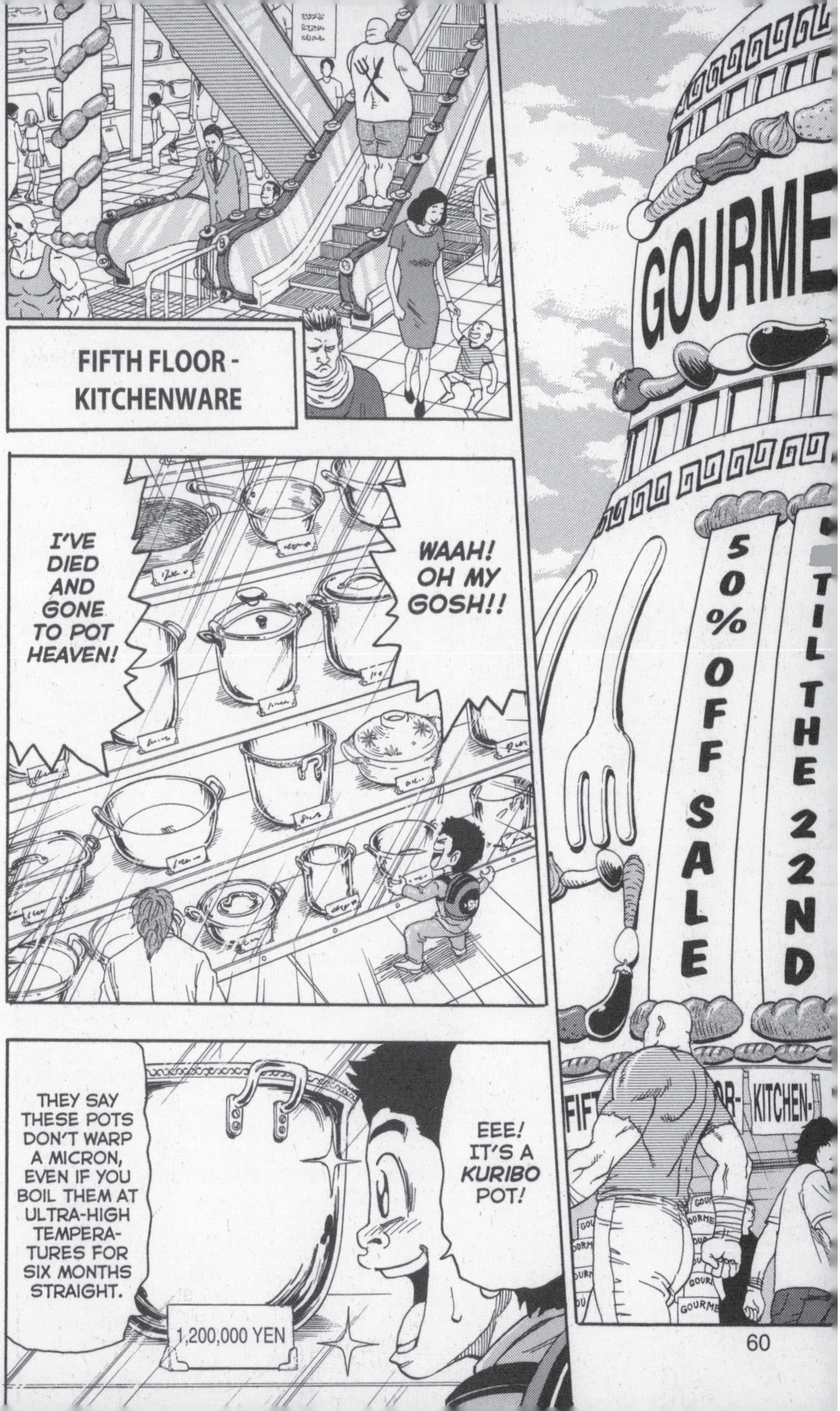
GOURME
50% OFF SALE
TIL THE 22ND
FIFT
OR- KITCHEN-
FIFTH FLOOR - KITCHENWARE
WAAH! OH MY GOSH!!
I'VE DIED AND GONE TO POT HEAVEN!
EEE! IT'S A KURIBO POT!
THEY SAY THESE POTS DON'T WARP A MICRON, EVEN IF YOU BOIL THEM AT ULTRA-HIGH TEMPERA-TURES FOR SIX MONTHS STRAIGHT.
1,200,000 YEN

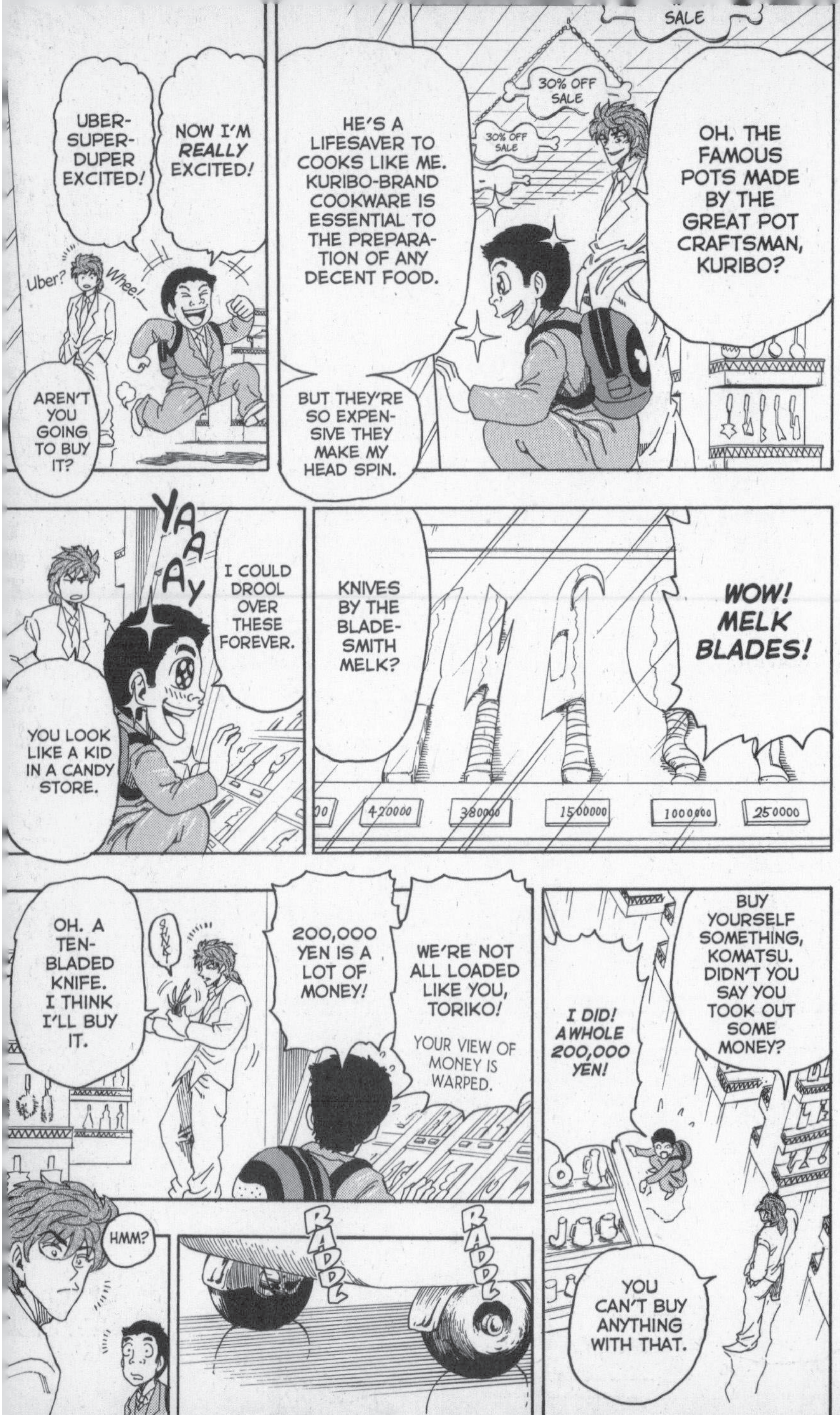
SALE
30% OFF SALE
30% OFF SALE
OH. THE FAMOUS POTS MADE BY THE GREAT POT CRAFTSMAN, KURIBO?
HE'S A LIFESAVER TO COOKS LIKE ME. KURIBO-BRAND COOKWARE IS ESSENTIAL TO THE PREPARATION OF ANY DECENT FOOD.
BUT THEY'RE SO EXPENSIVE THEY MAKE MY HEAD SPIN.
NOW I'M *REALLY* EXCITED!
UBER-SUPER-DUPER EXCITED!
Whee!
Uber?
AREN'T YOU GOING TO BUY IT?
WOW! MELK BLADES!
250000
1000000
1500000
380000
420000
KNIVES BY THE BLADE-SMITH MELK?
YAAAAY
I COULD DROOL OVER THESE FOREVER.
YOU LOOK LIKE A KID IN A CANDY STORE.
BUY YOURSELF SOMETHING, KOMATSU. DIDN'T YOU SAY YOU TOOK OUT SOME MONEY?
I DID! A WHOLE 200,000 YEN!
YOU CAN'T BUY ANYTHING WITH THAT.
WE'RE NOT ALL LOADED LIKE YOU, TORIKO!
200,000 YEN IS A LOT OF MONEY!
YOUR VIEW OF MONEY IS WARPED.
SNKT
OH. A TEN-BLADED KNIFE. I THINK I'LL BUY IT.
RADDL
RADDL
HMM?

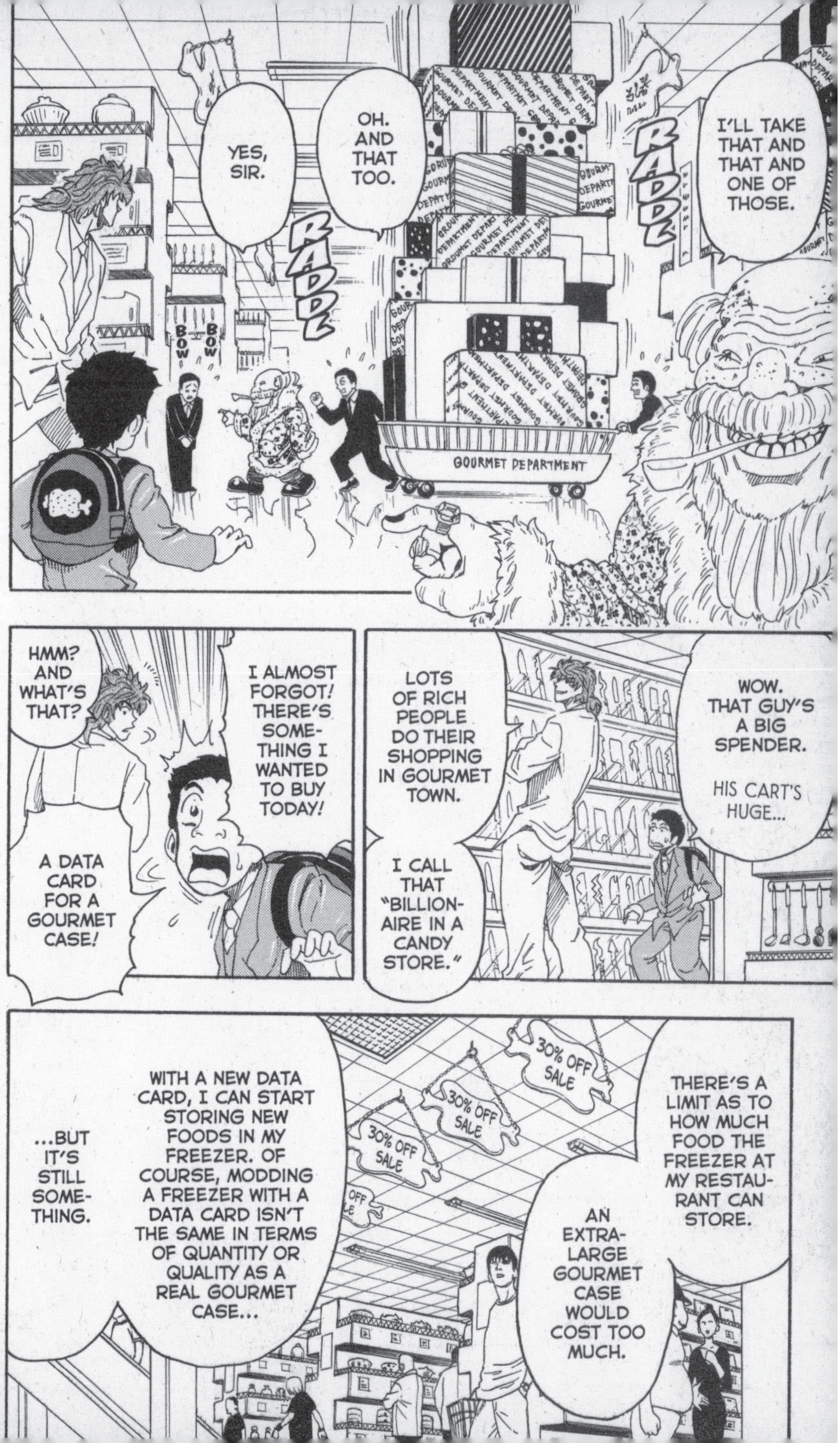
I'LL TAKE THAT AND THAT AND ONE OF THOSE.
RADDE
OH. AND THAT TOO.
RADDE
GOURMET DEPARTMENT
BOW BOW
YES, SIR.
WOW. THAT GUY'S A BIG SPENDER.
HIS CART'S HUGE...
LOTS OF RICH PEOPLE DO THEIR SHOPPING IN GOURMET TOWN.
I CALL THAT "BILLIONAIRE IN A CANDY STORE."
I ALMOST FORGOT! THERE'S SOMETHING I WANTED TO BUY TODAY!
HMM? AND WHAT'S THAT?
A DATA CARD FOR A GOURMET CASE!
THERE'S A LIMIT AS TO HOW MUCH FOOD THE FREEZER AT MY RESTAURANT CAN STORE.
30% OFF SALE
30% OFF SALE
30% OFF SALE
AN EXTRA-LARGE GOURMET CASE WOULD COST TOO MUCH.
WITH A NEW DATA CARD, I CAN START STORING NEW FOODS IN MY FREEZER. OF COURSE, MODDING A FREEZER WITH A DATA CARD ISN'T THE SAME IN TERMS OF QUANTITY OR QUALITY AS A REAL GOURMET CASE...
...BUT IT'S STILL SOMETHING.

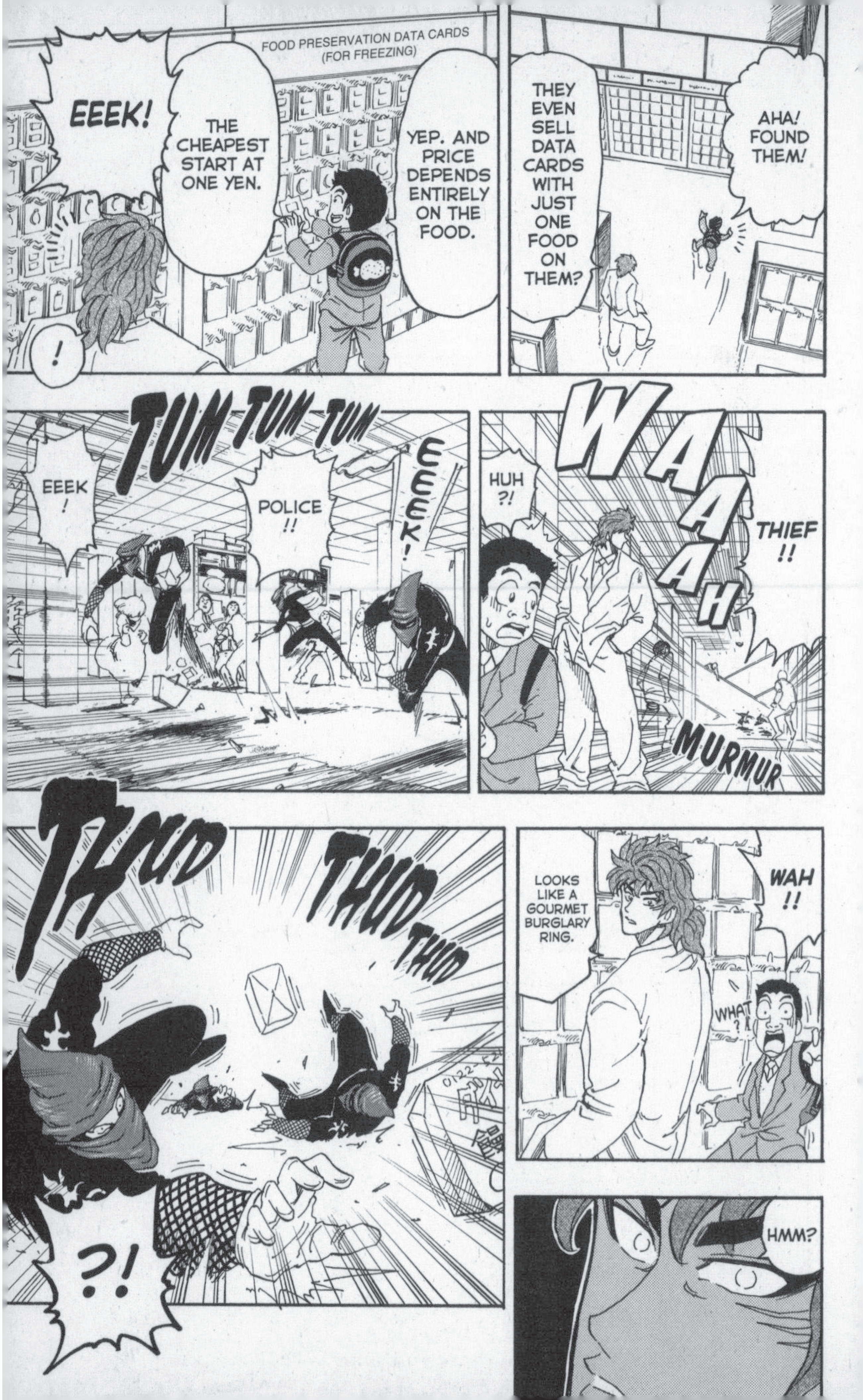
AHA! FOUND THEM!
THEY EVEN SELL DATA CARDS WITH JUST ONE FOOD ON THEM?
FOOD PRESERVATION DATA CARDS (FOR FREEZING)
YEP. AND PRICE DEPENDS ENTIRELY ON THE FOOD.
THE CHEAPEST START AT ONE YEN.
EEEK!
!
WAAAAH
THIEF !!
HUH ?!
MURMUR
TUM TUM TUM
EEEEK!
POLICE !!
EEEK !
WAH !!
LOOKS LIKE A GOURMET BURGLARY RING.
WHAT ?
HMM?
THUD THUD THUD
?!

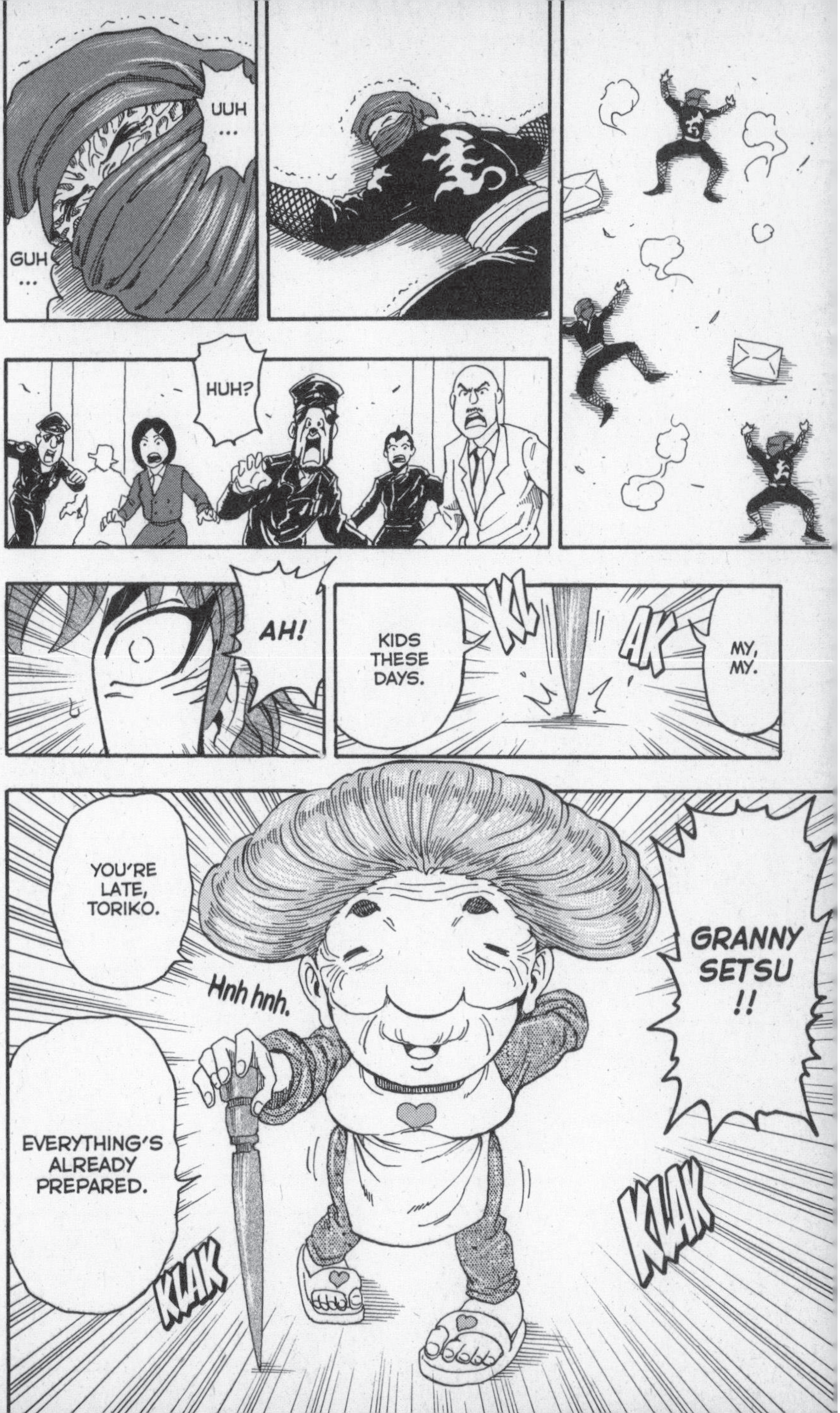
UUH ...
GUH ...
HUH?
MY, MY.
KI
AK
KIDS THESE DAYS.
AH!
GRANNY SETSU !!
YOU'RE LATE, TORIKO.
Hnh hnh.
KLAK
EVERYTHING'S ALREADY PREPARED.
KLAK

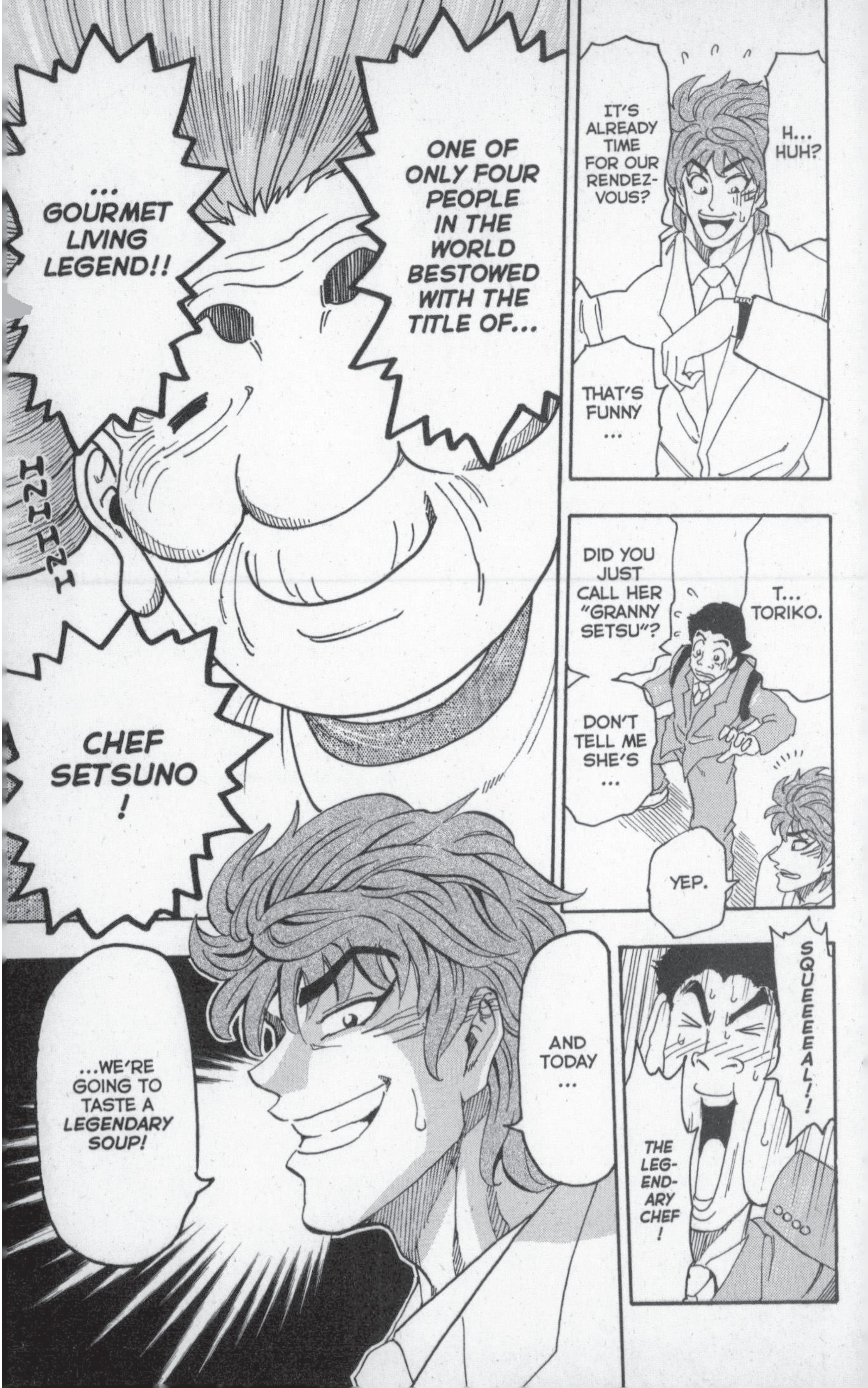
H... HUH?
IT'S ALREADY TIME FOR OUR RENDEZ-VOUS?
THAT'S FUNNY ...
T... TORIKO.
DID YOU JUST CALL HER "GRANNY SETSU"?
DON'T TELL ME SHE'S ...
YEP.
ONE OF ONLY FOUR PEOPLE IN THE WORLD BESTOWED WITH THE TITLE OF...
... GOURMET LIVING LEGEND!!
CHEF SETSUNO !
SQUEEEEEAL!!
THE LEG-END-ARY CHEF !
AND TODAY ...
...WE'RE GOING TO TASTE A LEGENDARY SOUP!

TORIKO
GOURMET CHECKLIST
Vol. 051

BALOGG
(BIRD)

CAPTURE LEVEL: 16

HABITAT: FORESTS AND PLAINS

LENGTH: ---

HEIGHT: 15 METERS

WEIGHT: 9 TONS

PRICE: 100 G / 10,000 YEN;

1 EGG / 600,000 YEN

BALOGG
(BIRD)
CAPTURE LEVEL 16

SCALE

THE LONG LEGS OF THIS AVIAN MONSTER ENABLE IT TO RUN MORE THAN 180 KILOMETERS PER HOUR. IT ALSO LAYS EGGS APPROXIMATELY 1,000 TIMES LARGER THAN THAT OF A TYPICAL CHICKEN, SO GLUTTONS WORLDWIDE FEAST ON BALOGG EGG OMELETS.

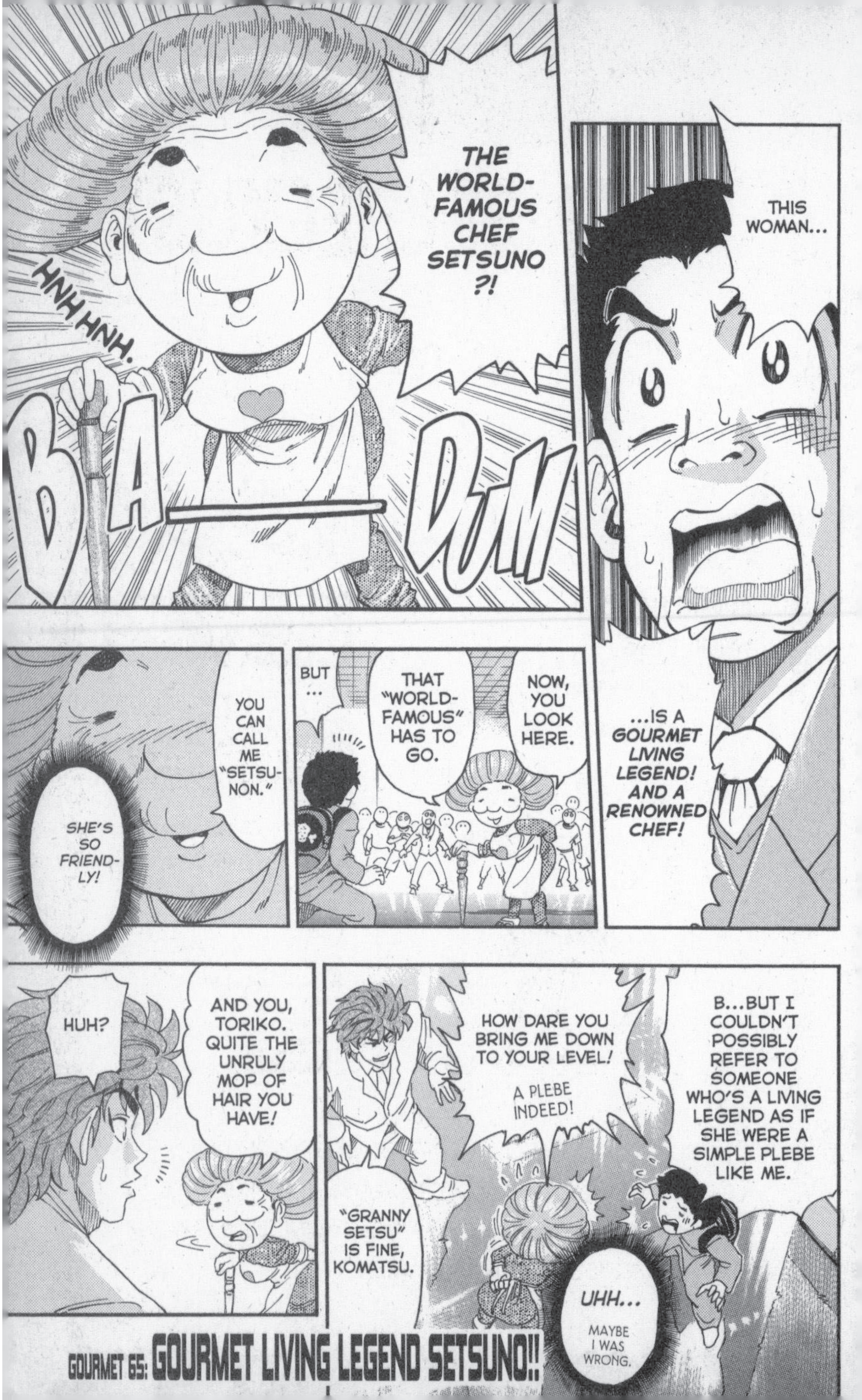
THIS WOMAN...
...IS A GOURMET LIVING LEGEND! AND A RENOWNED CHEF!
THE WORLD-FAMOUS CHEF SETSUNO ?!
HNH HNH.
BA—DUM
NOW, YOU LOOK HERE.
THAT "WORLD-FAMOUS" HAS TO GO.
BUT ...
YOU CAN CALL ME "SETSU-NON."
SHE'S SO FRIEND-LY!
B...BUT I COULDN'T POSSIBLY REFER TO SOMEONE WHO'S A LIVING LEGEND AS IF SHE WERE A SIMPLE PLEBE LIKE ME.
HOW DARE YOU BRING ME DOWN TO YOUR LEVEL!
A PLEBE INDEED!
UHH...
MAYBE I WAS WRONG.
AND YOU, TORIKO. QUITE THE UNRULY MOP OF HAIR YOU HAVE!
HUH?
"GRANNY SETSU" IS FINE, KOMATSU.
GOURMET 65: GOURMET LIVING LEGEND SETSUNO!!

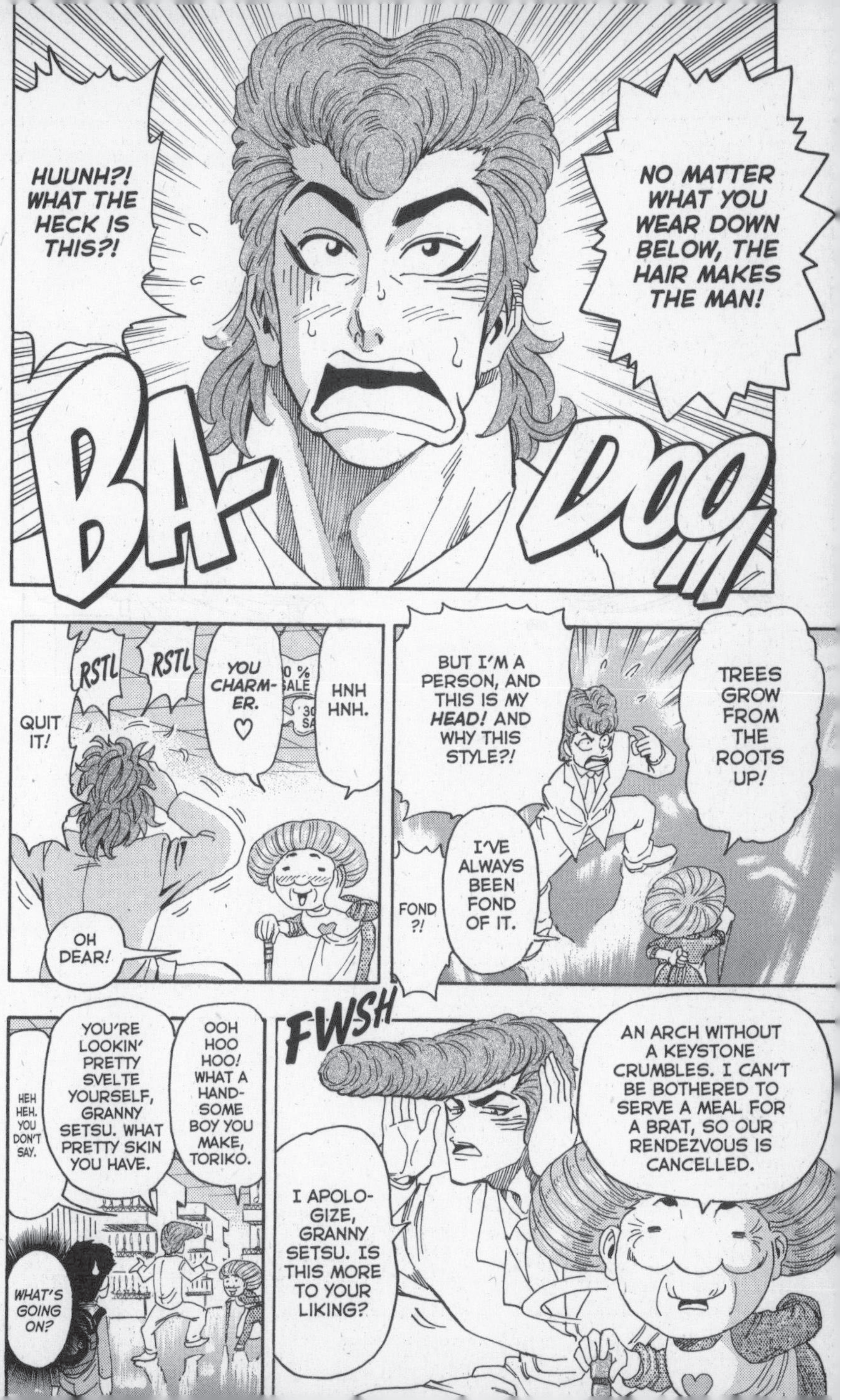
NO MATTER WHAT YOU WEAR DOWN BELOW, THE HAIR MAKES THE MAN!
HUUNH?! WHAT THE HECK IS THIS?!
BA- DOOM
TREES GROW FROM THE ROOTS UP!
BUT I'M A PERSON, AND THIS IS MY *HEAD!* AND WHY THIS STYLE?!
I'VE ALWAYS BEEN FOND OF IT.
FOND?!
HNH HNH.
YOU CHARMER. ♡
RSTL RSTL
QUIT IT!
OH DEAR!
AN ARCH WITHOUT A KEYSTONE CRUMBLES. I CAN'T BE BOTHERED TO SERVE A MEAL FOR A BRAT, SO OUR RENDEZVOUS IS CANCELLED.
FWSH
I APOLOGIZE, GRANNY SETSU. IS THIS MORE TO YOUR LIKING?
OOH HOO HOO! WHAT A HANDSOME BOY YOU MAKE, TORIKO.
YOU'RE LOOKIN' PRETTY SVELTE YOURSELF, GRANNY SETSU. WHAT PRETTY SKIN YOU HAVE.
HEH HEH. YOU DON'T SAY.
WHAT'S GOING ON?

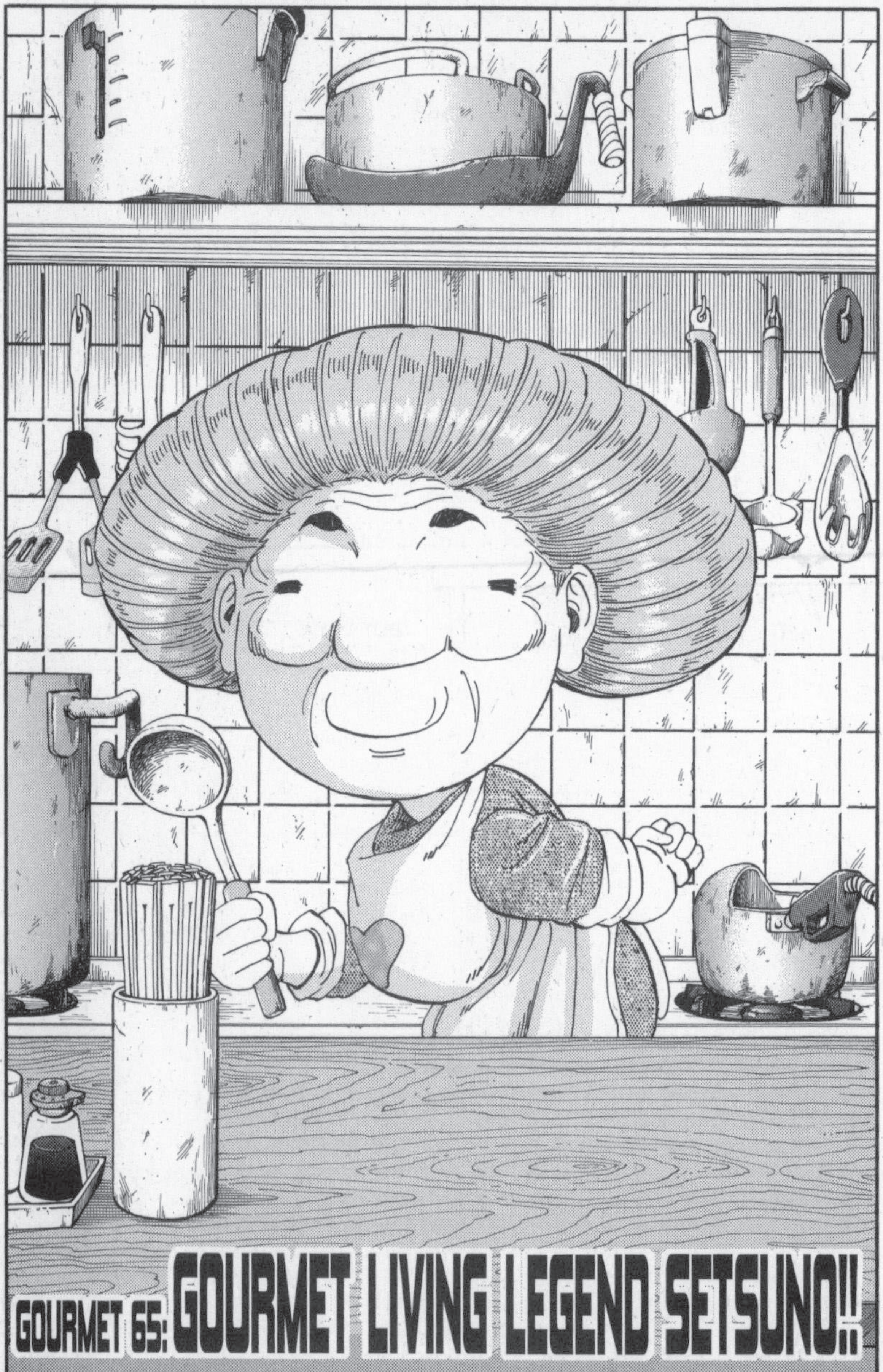
GOURMET 65: GOURMET LIVING LEGEND SETSUNO!!

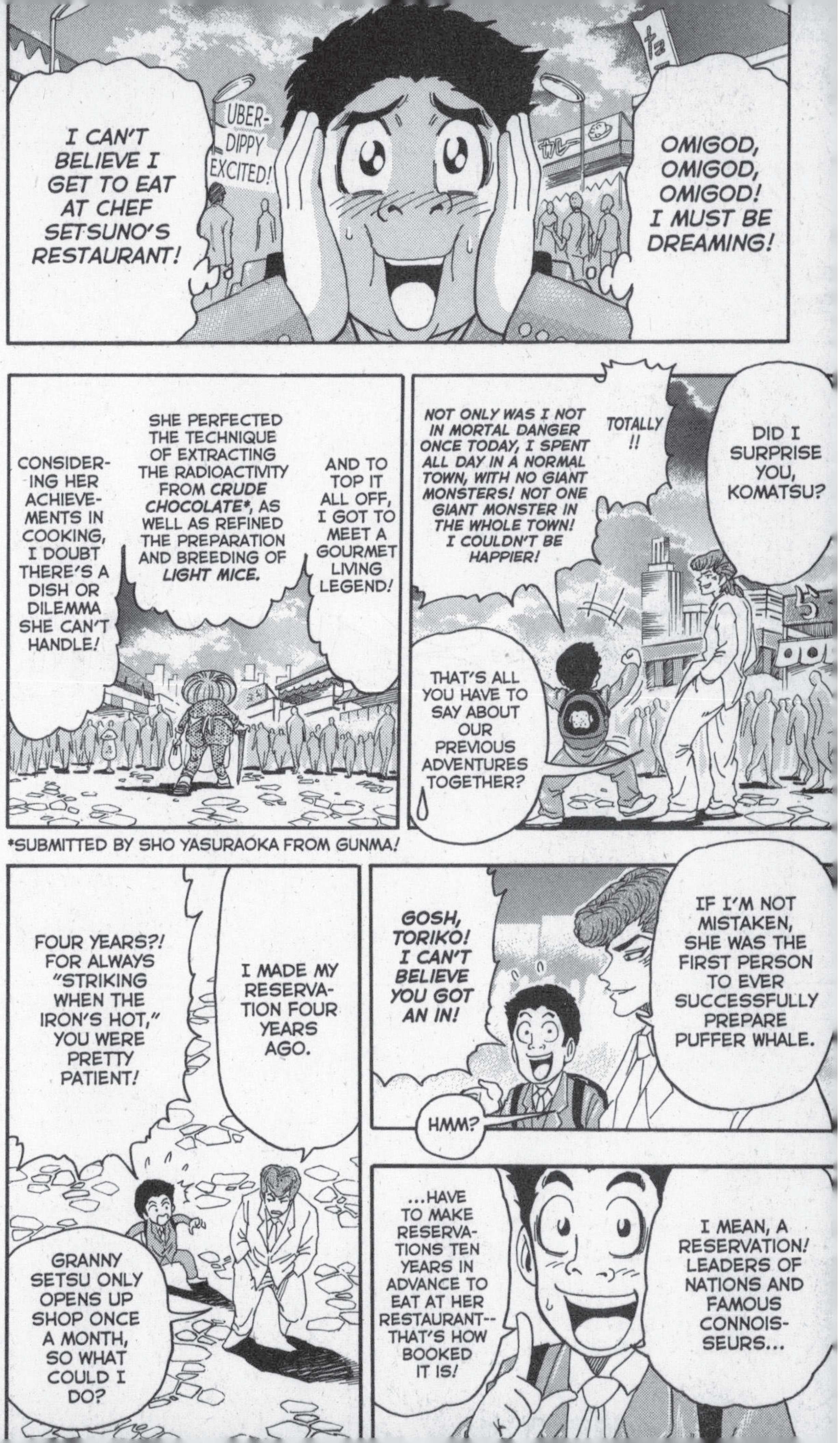
OMIGOD, OMIGOD, OMIGOD! I MUST BE DREAMING!
UBER-DIPPY EXCITED!
I CAN'T BELIEVE I GET TO EAT AT CHEF SETSUNO'S RESTAURANT!
DID I SURPRISE YOU, KOMATSU?
TOTALLY!!
NOT ONLY WAS I NOT IN MORTAL DANGER ONCE TODAY, I SPENT ALL DAY IN A NORMAL TOWN, WITH NO GIANT MONSTERS! NOT ONE GIANT MONSTER IN THE WHOLE TOWN! I COULDN'T BE HAPPIER!
THAT'S ALL YOU HAVE TO SAY ABOUT OUR PREVIOUS ADVENTURES TOGETHER?
AND TO TOP IT ALL OFF, I GOT TO MEET A GOURMET LIVING LEGEND!
SHE PERFECTED THE TECHNIQUE OF EXTRACTING THE RADIOACTIVITY FROM CRUDE CHOCOLATE*, AS WELL AS REFINED THE PREPARATION AND BREEDING OF LIGHT MICE.
CONSIDERING HER ACHIEVEMENTS IN COOKING, I DOUBT THERE'S A DISH OR DILEMMA SHE CAN'T HANDLE!
*SUBMITTED BY SHO YASURAOKA FROM GUNMA!
IF I'M NOT MISTAKEN, SHE WAS THE FIRST PERSON TO EVER SUCCESSFULLY PREPARE PUFFER WHALE.
GOSH, TORIKO! I CAN'T BELIEVE YOU GOT AN IN!
HMM?
I MEAN, A RESERVATION! LEADERS OF NATIONS AND FAMOUS CONNOIS-SEURS...
...HAVE TO MAKE RESERVA-TIONS TEN YEARS IN ADVANCE TO EAT AT HER RESTAURANT-- THAT'S HOW BOOKED IT IS!
I MADE MY RESERVA-TION FOUR YEARS AGO.
FOUR YEARS?! FOR ALWAYS "STRIKING WHEN THE IRON'S HOT," YOU WERE PRETTY PATIENT!
GRANNY SETSU ONLY OPENS UP SHOP ONCE A MONTH, SO WHAT COULD I DO?

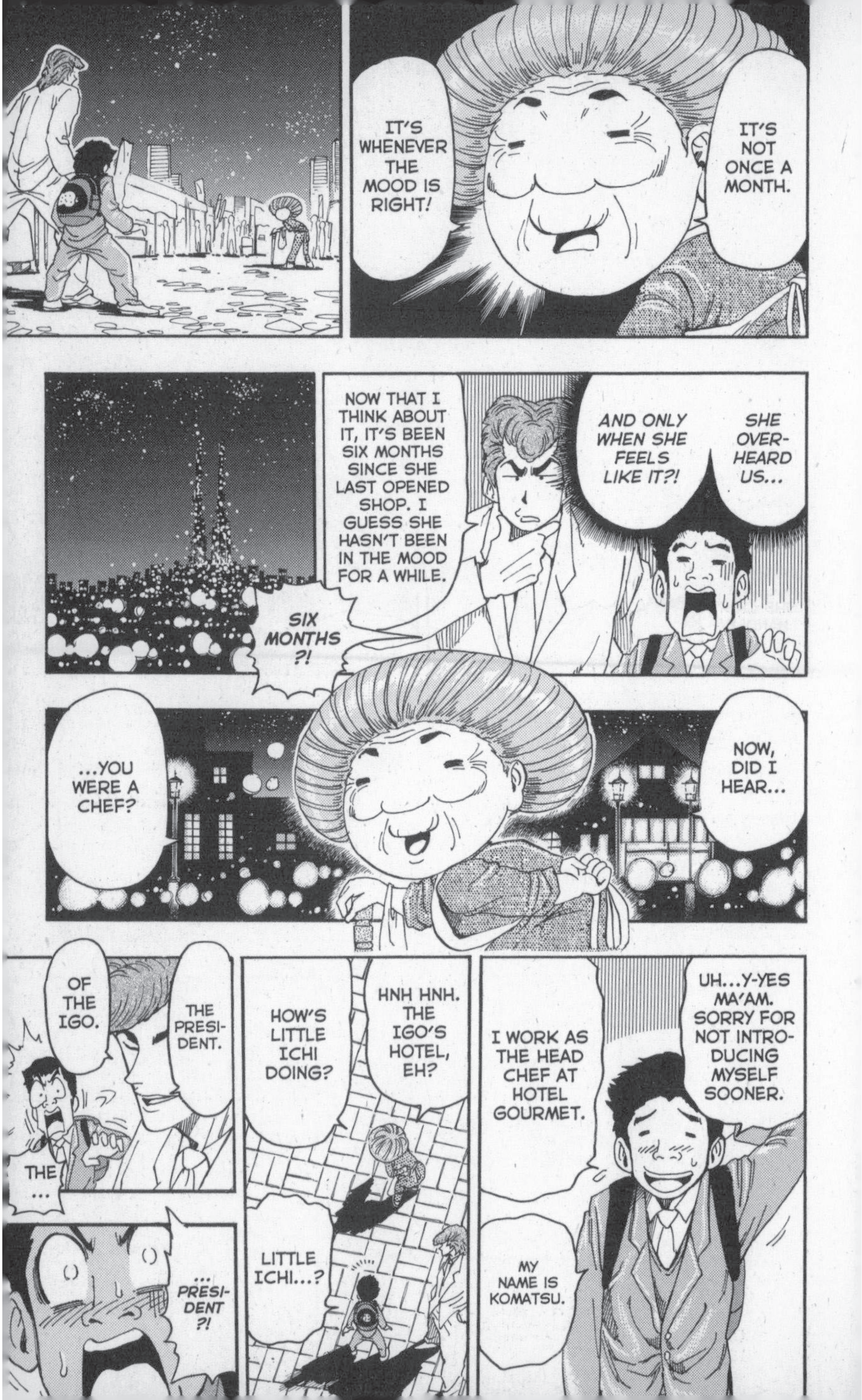
IT'S NOT ONCE A MONTH.
IT'S WHENEVER THE MOOD IS RIGHT!
SHE OVER-HEARD US...
AND ONLY WHEN SHE FEELS LIKE IT?!
NOW THAT I THINK ABOUT IT, IT'S BEEN SIX MONTHS SINCE SHE LAST OPENED SHOP. I GUESS SHE HASN'T BEEN IN THE MOOD FOR A WHILE.
SIX MONTHS ?!
NOW, DID I HEAR...
...YOU WERE A CHEF?
UH...Y-YES MA'AM. SORRY FOR NOT INTRO-DUCING MYSELF SOONER.
I WORK AS THE HEAD CHEF AT HOTEL GOURMET.
MY NAME IS KOMATSU.
HNH HNH. THE IGO'S HOTEL, EH?
HOW'S LITTLE ICHI DOING?
LITTLE ICHI...?
THE PRESI-DENT.
OF THE IGO.
THE ...
... PRESI-DENT ?!

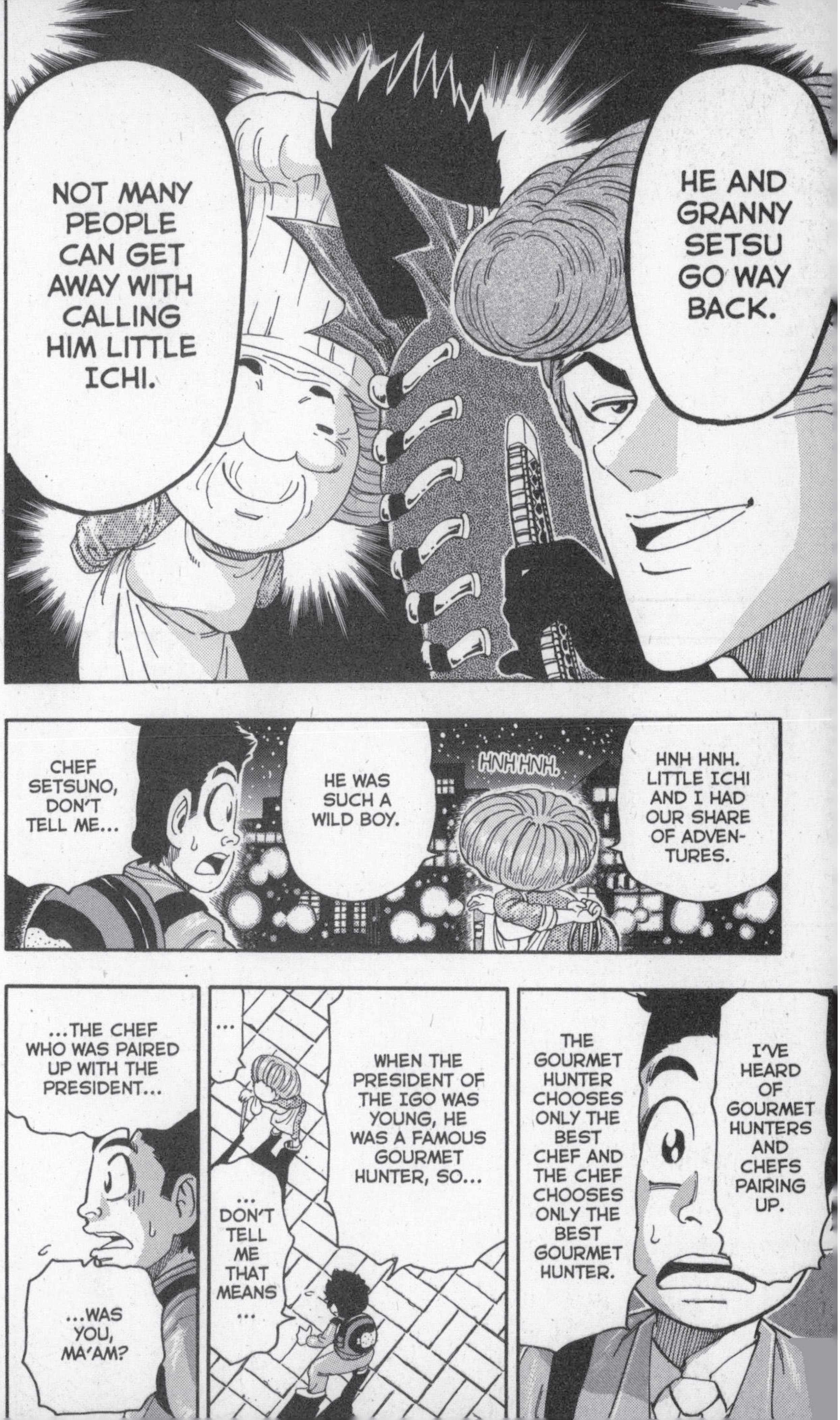

HE AND GRANNY SETSU GO WAY BACK.
NOT MANY PEOPLE CAN GET AWAY WITH CALLING HIM LITTLE ICHI.
HNH HNH. LITTLE ICHI AND I HAD OUR SHARE OF ADVEN-TURES.
HNHHNH.
HE WAS SUCH A WILD BOY.
CHEF SETSUNO, DON'T TELL ME...
I'VE HEARD OF GOURMET HUNTERS AND CHEFS PAIRING UP.
THE GOURMET HUNTER CHOOSES ONLY THE BEST CHEF AND THE CHEF CHOOSES ONLY THE BEST GOURMET HUNTER.
WHEN THE PRESIDENT OF THE IGO WAS YOUNG, HE WAS A FAMOUS GOURMET HUNTER, SO...
...
...DON'T TELL ME THAT MEANS...
...THE CHEF WHO WAS PAIRED UP WITH THE PRESIDENT...
...WAS YOU, MA'AM?

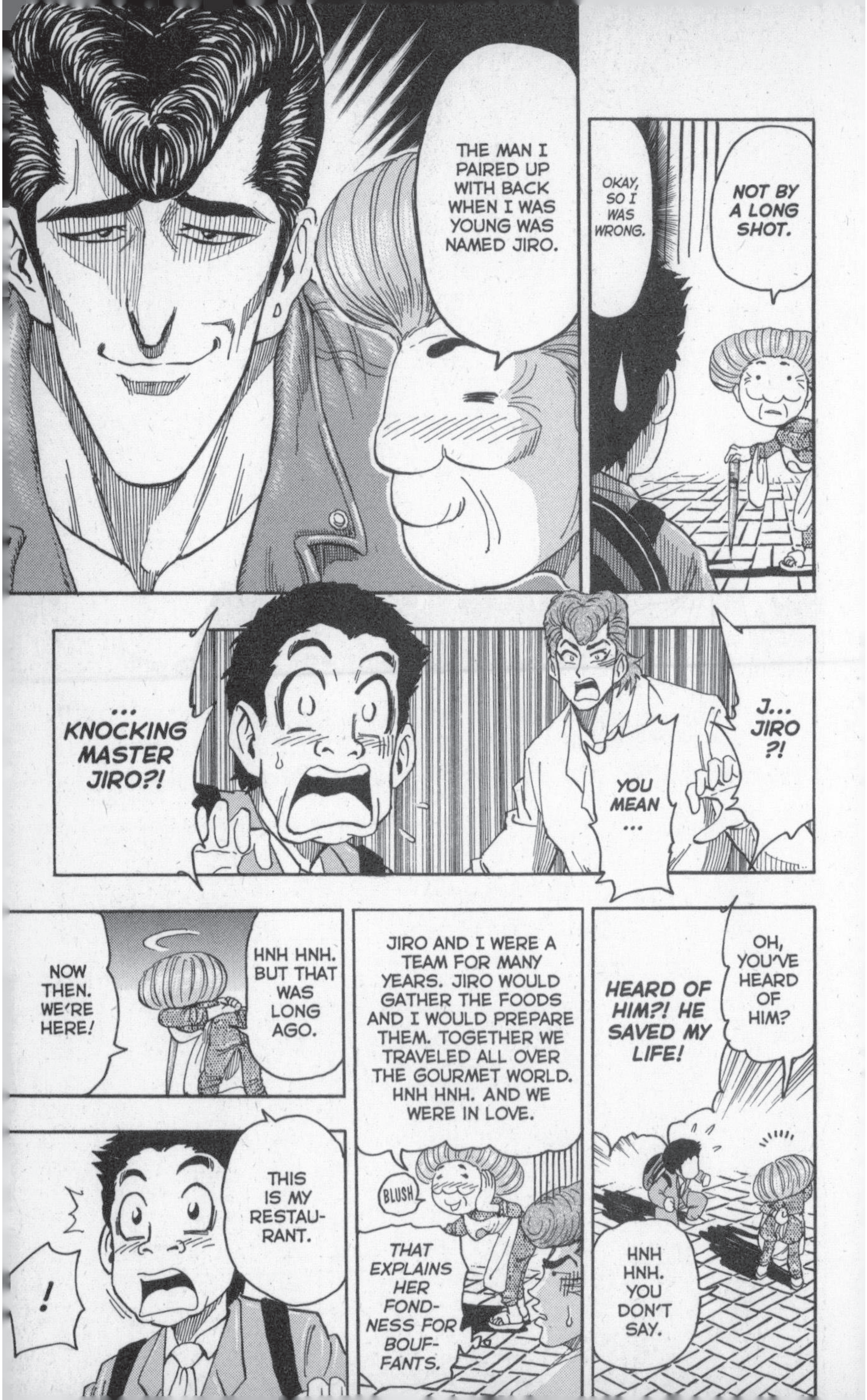

NOT BY A LONG SHOT.
OKAY, SO I WAS WRONG.
THE MAN I PAIRED UP WITH BACK WHEN I WAS YOUNG WAS NAMED JIRO.
J... JIRO?!
YOU MEAN ...
... KNOCKING MASTER JIRO?!
OH, YOU'VE HEARD OF HIM?
HEARD OF HIM?! HE SAVED MY LIFE!
HNH HNH. YOU DON'T SAY.
JIRO AND I WERE A TEAM FOR MANY YEARS. JIRO WOULD GATHER THE FOODS AND I WOULD PREPARE THEM. TOGETHER WE TRAVELED ALL OVER THE GOURMET WORLD. HNH HNH. AND WE WERE IN LOVE.
BLUSH
THAT EXPLAINS HER FONDNESS FOR BOUFFANTS.
HNH HNH. BUT THAT WAS LONG AGO.
NOW THEN. WE'RE HERE!
THIS IS MY RESTAURANT.
!

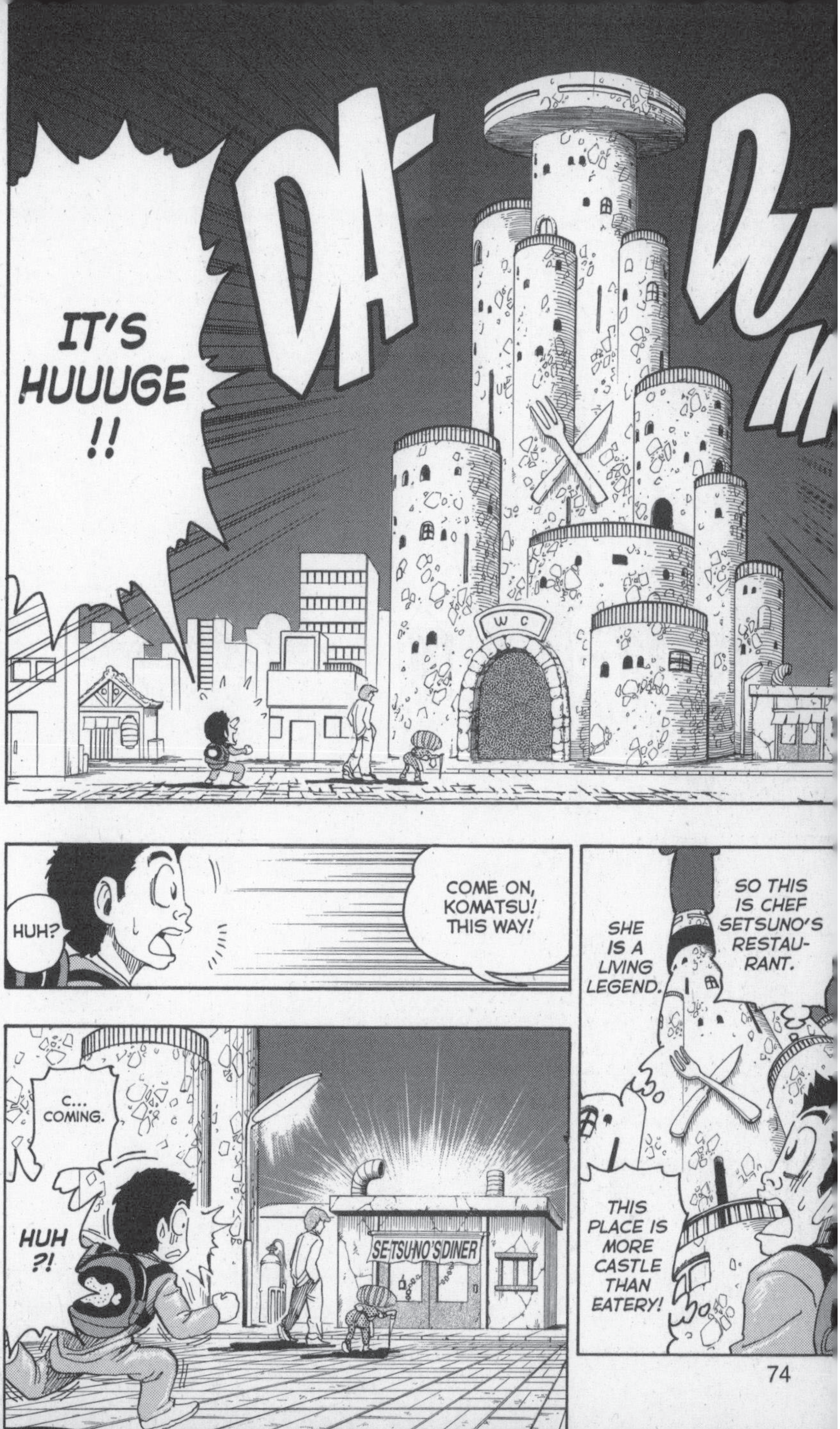
DA-
DUM
IT'S HUUUGE !!
SO THIS IS CHEF SETSUNO'S RESTAURANT.
SHE IS A LIVING LEGEND.
THIS PLACE IS MORE CASTLE THAN EATERY!
COME ON, KOMATSU! THIS WAY!
HUH?
SE-TSUNO'S DINER
C... COMING.
HUH ?!

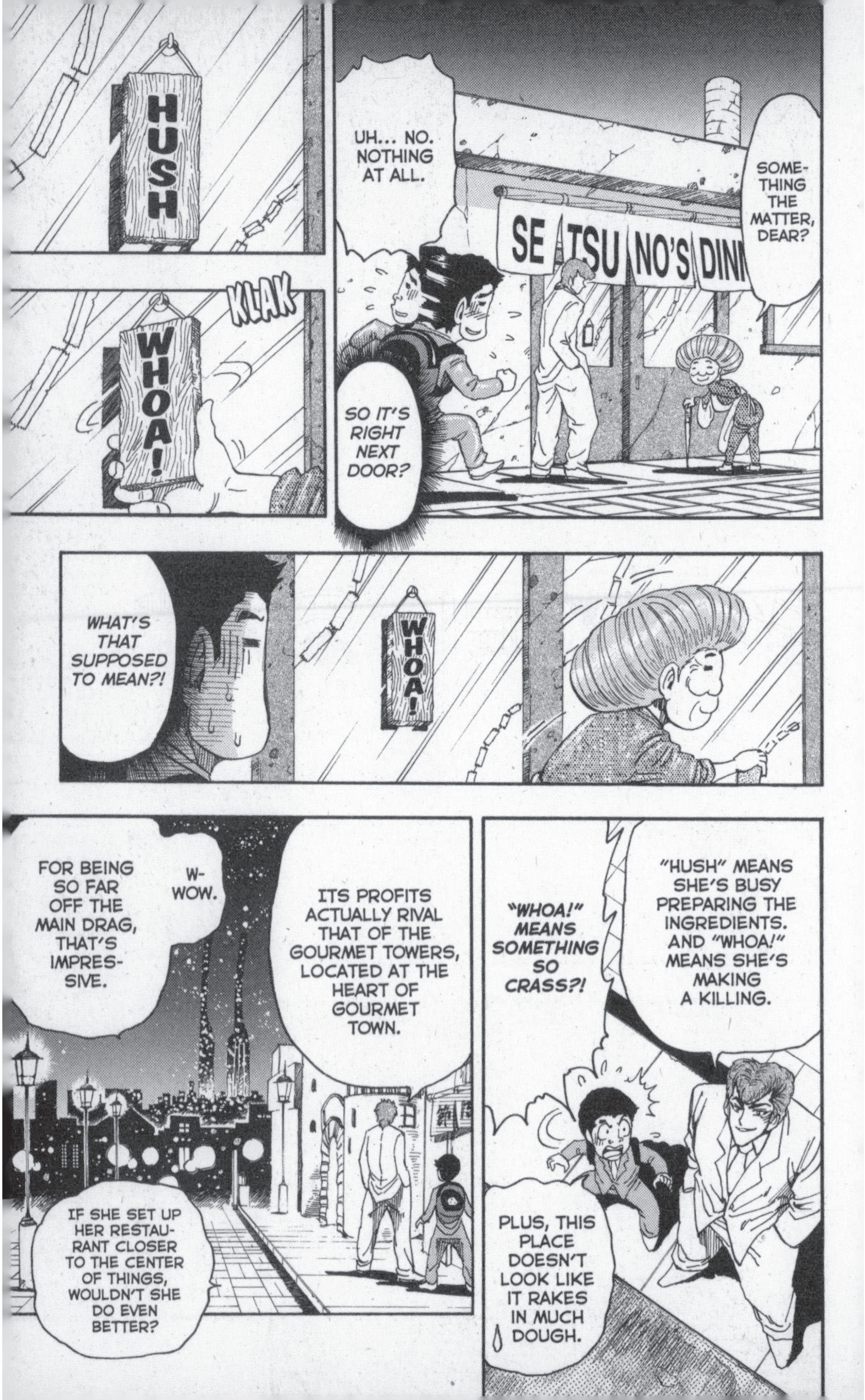
SOMETHING THE MATTER, DEAR?
SE TSU NO'S DINI
UH... NO. NOTHING AT ALL.
SO IT'S RIGHT NEXT DOOR?
HUSH
KLAK
WHOA!
WHOA!
WHAT'S THAT SUPPOSED TO MEAN?!
"HUSH" MEANS SHE'S BUSY PREPARING THE INGREDIENTS. AND "WHOA!" MEANS SHE'S MAKING A KILLING.
"WHOA!" MEANS SOMETHING SO CRASS?!
PLUS, THIS PLACE DOESN'T LOOK LIKE IT RAKES IN MUCH DOUGH.
ITS PROFITS ACTUALLY RIVAL THAT OF THE GOURMET TOWERS, LOCATED AT THE HEART OF GOURMET TOWN.
W-WOW.
FOR BEING SO FAR OFF THE MAIN DRAG, THAT'S IMPRESSIVE.
IF SHE SET UP HER RESTAURANT CLOSER TO THE CENTER OF THINGS, WOULDN'T SHE DO EVEN BETTER?

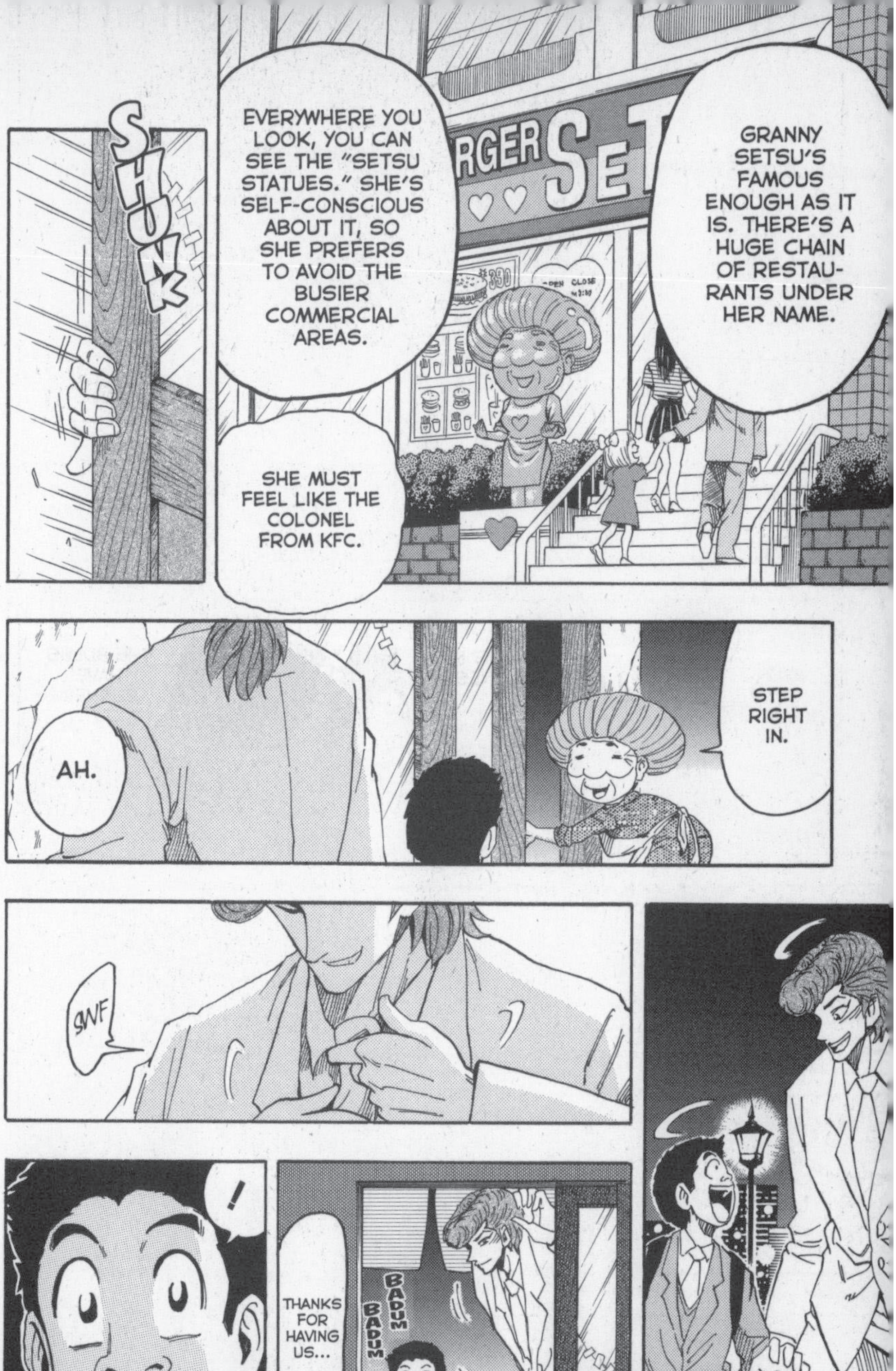
GRANNY SETSU'S FAMOUS ENOUGH AS IT IS. THERE'S A HUGE CHAIN OF RESTAU-RANTS UNDER HER NAME.
EVERYWHERE YOU LOOK, YOU CAN SEE THE "SETSU STATUES." SHE'S SELF-CONSCIOUS ABOUT IT, SO SHE PREFERS TO AVOID THE BUSIER COMMERCIAL AREAS.
SHE MUST FEEL LIKE THE COLONEL FROM KFC.
SHUNK
STEP RIGHT IN.
AH.
SNF
BADUM BADUM
THANKS FOR HAVING US...
!

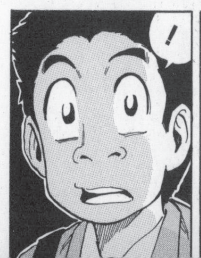

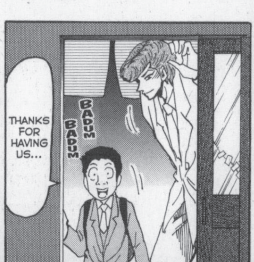

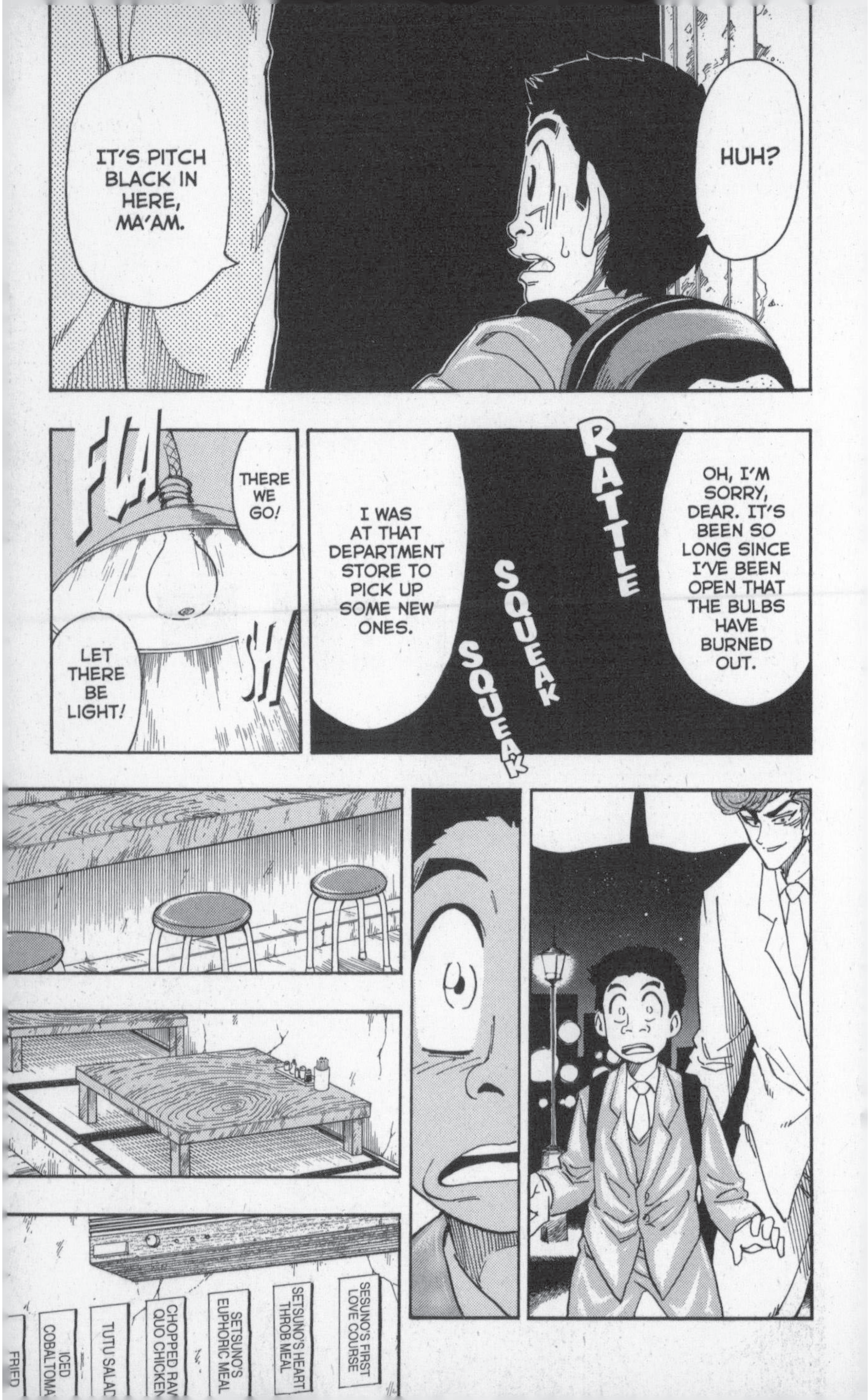
HUH?
IT'S PITCH BLACK IN HERE, MA'AM.
OH, I'M SORRY, DEAR. IT'S BEEN SO LONG SINCE I'VE BEEN OPEN THAT THE BULBS HAVE BURNED OUT.
RATTLE
SQUEAK SQUEAK
I WAS AT THAT DEPARTMENT STORE TO PICK UP SOME NEW ONES.
THERE WE GO!
FLASH
LET THERE BE LIGHT!
SESUNO'S FIRST LOVE COURSE
SETSUNO'S HEART THROB MEAL
SETSUNO'S EUPHORIC MEAL
CHOPPED RAV QUO CHICKEN
TUTU SALAD
ICED COBALTOMA
FRIED

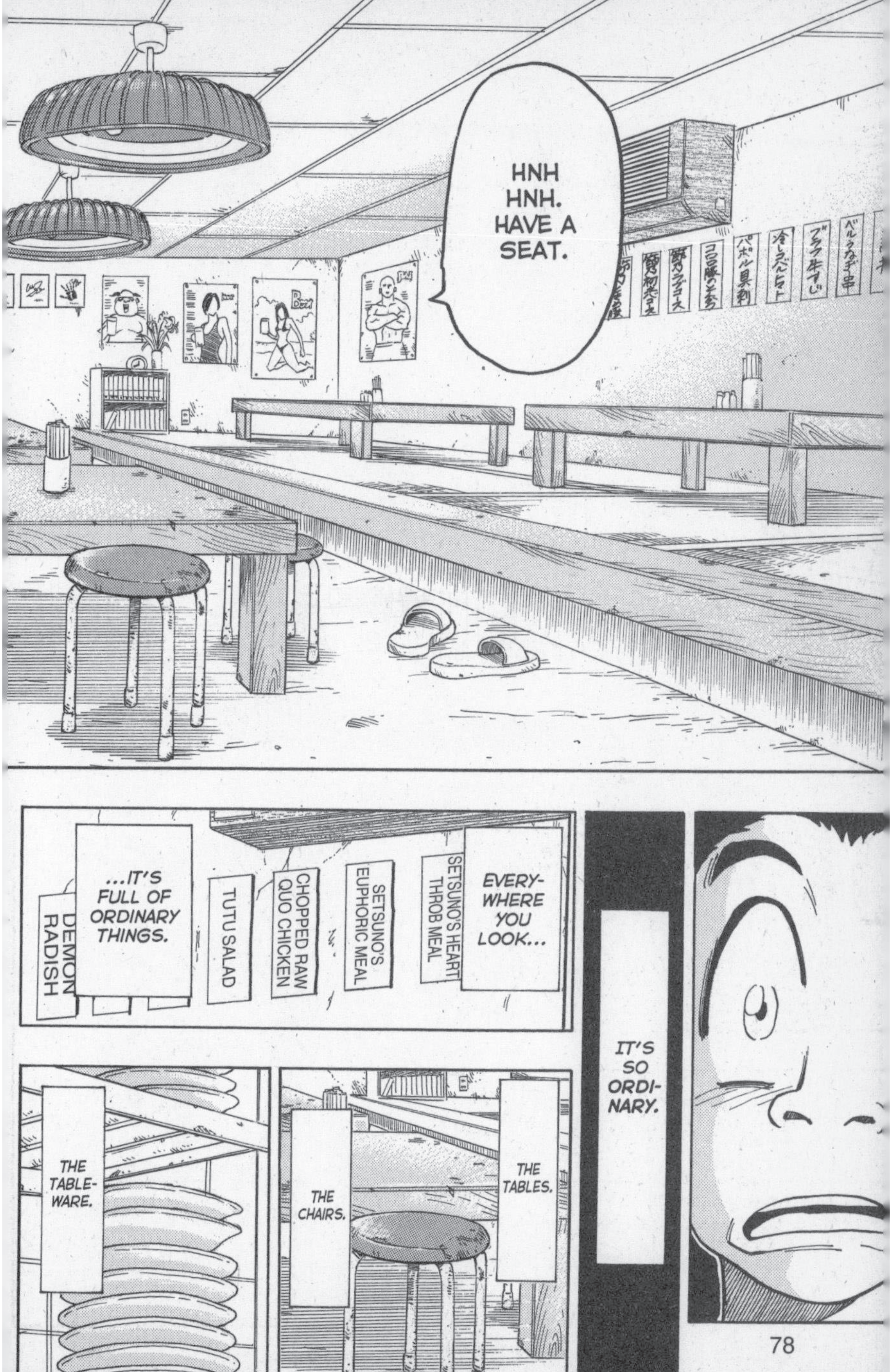
HNH HNH. HAVE A SEAT.
IT'S SO ORDINARY.
EVERY-WHERE YOU LOOK...
SETSUNO'S HEART THROB MEAL
SETSUNO'S EUPHORIC MEAL
CHOPPED RAW QUO CHICKEN
TUTU SALAD
...IT'S FULL OF ORDINARY THINGS.
DEMON RADISH
THE TABLES.
THE CHAIRS.
THE TABLE-WARE.

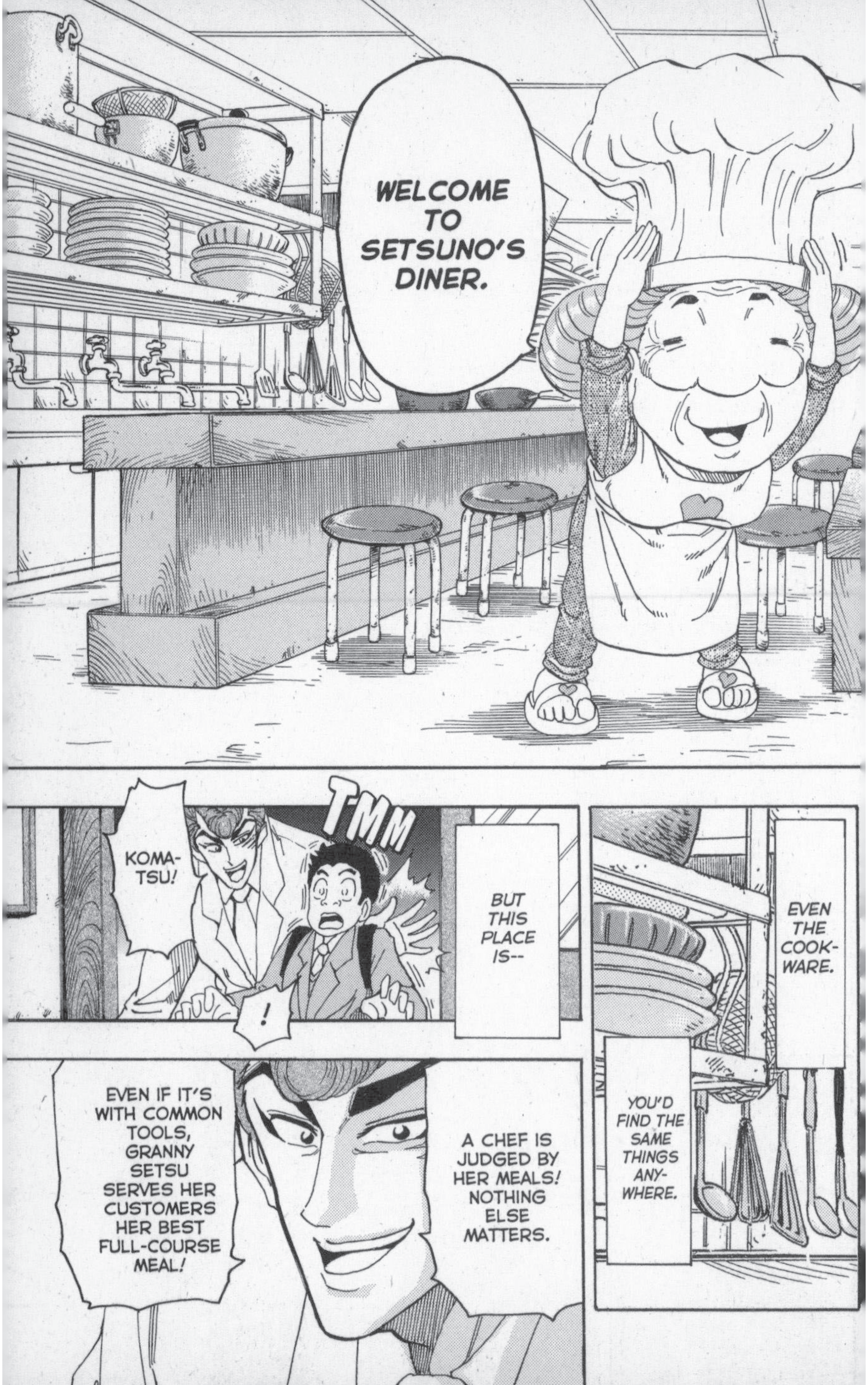
WELCOME TO SETSUNO'S DINER.
EVEN THE COOK-WARE.
YOU'D FIND THE SAME THINGS ANY-WHERE.
TMM
BUT THIS PLACE IS--
KOMA-TSU!
!
A CHEF IS JUDGED BY HER MEALS! NOTHING ELSE MATTERS.
EVEN IF IT'S WITH COMMON TOOLS, GRANNY SETSU SERVES HER CUSTOMERS HER BEST FULL-COURSE MEAL!

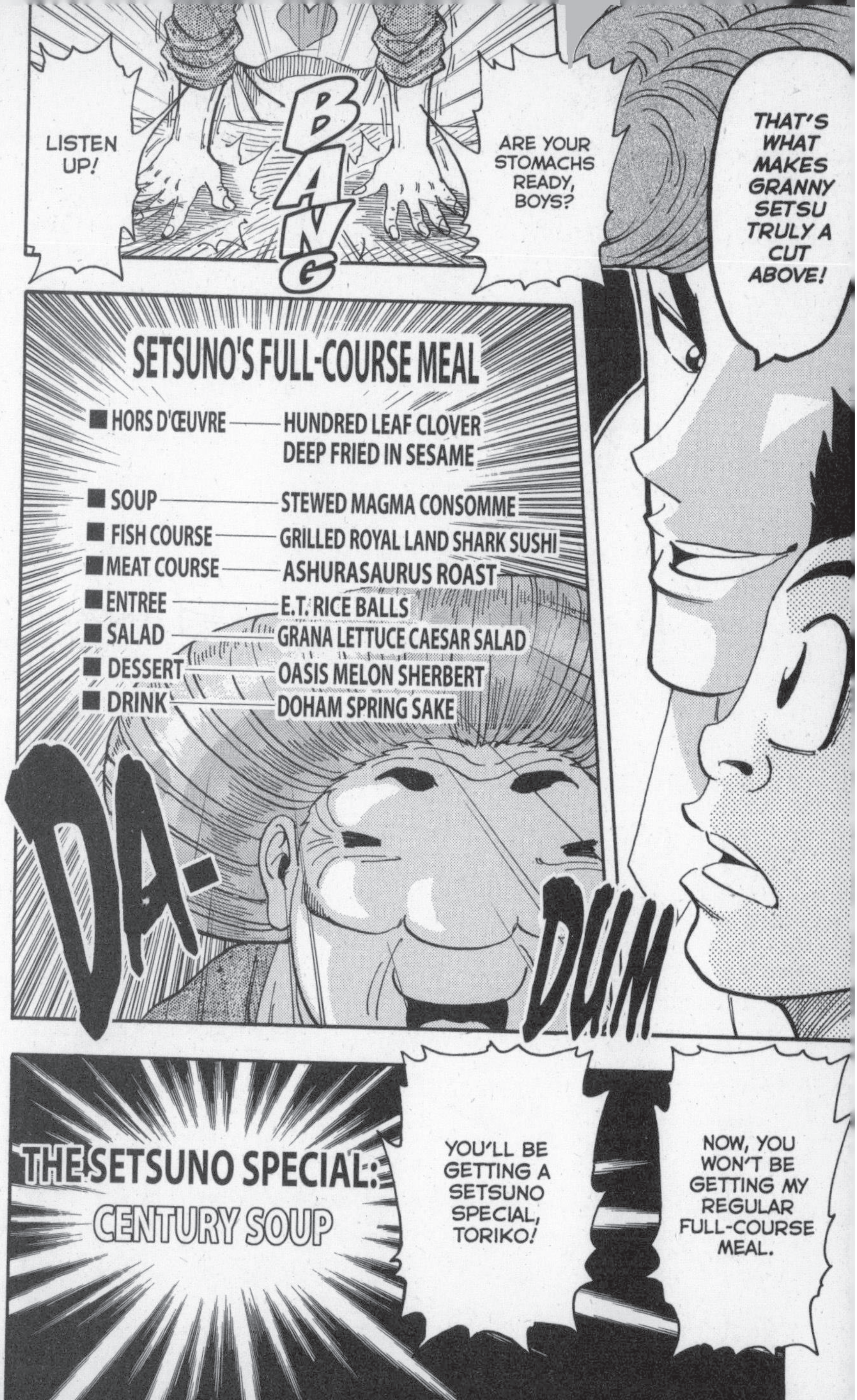

THAT'S WHAT MAKES GRANNY SETSU TRULY A CUT ABOVE!
ARE YOUR STOMACHS READY, BOYS?
BANG
LISTEN UP!
SETSUNO'S FULL-COURSE MEAL
■ HORS D'ŒUVRE — HUNDRED LEAF CLOVER DEEP FRIED IN SESAME
■ SOUP — STEWED MAGMA CONSOMME
■ FISH COURSE — GRILLED ROYAL LAND SHARK SUSHI
■ MEAT COURSE — ASHURASAURUS ROAST
■ ENTREE — E.T. RICE BALLS
■ SALAD — GRANA LETTUCE CAESAR SALAD
■ DESSERT — OASIS MELON SHERBERT
■ DRINK — DOHAM SPRING SAKE
DA-DUM
NOW, YOU WON'T BE GETTING MY REGULAR FULL-COURSE MEAL.
YOU'LL BE GETTING A SETSUNO SPECIAL, TORIKO!
THE SETSUNO SPECIAL:
CENTURY SOUP

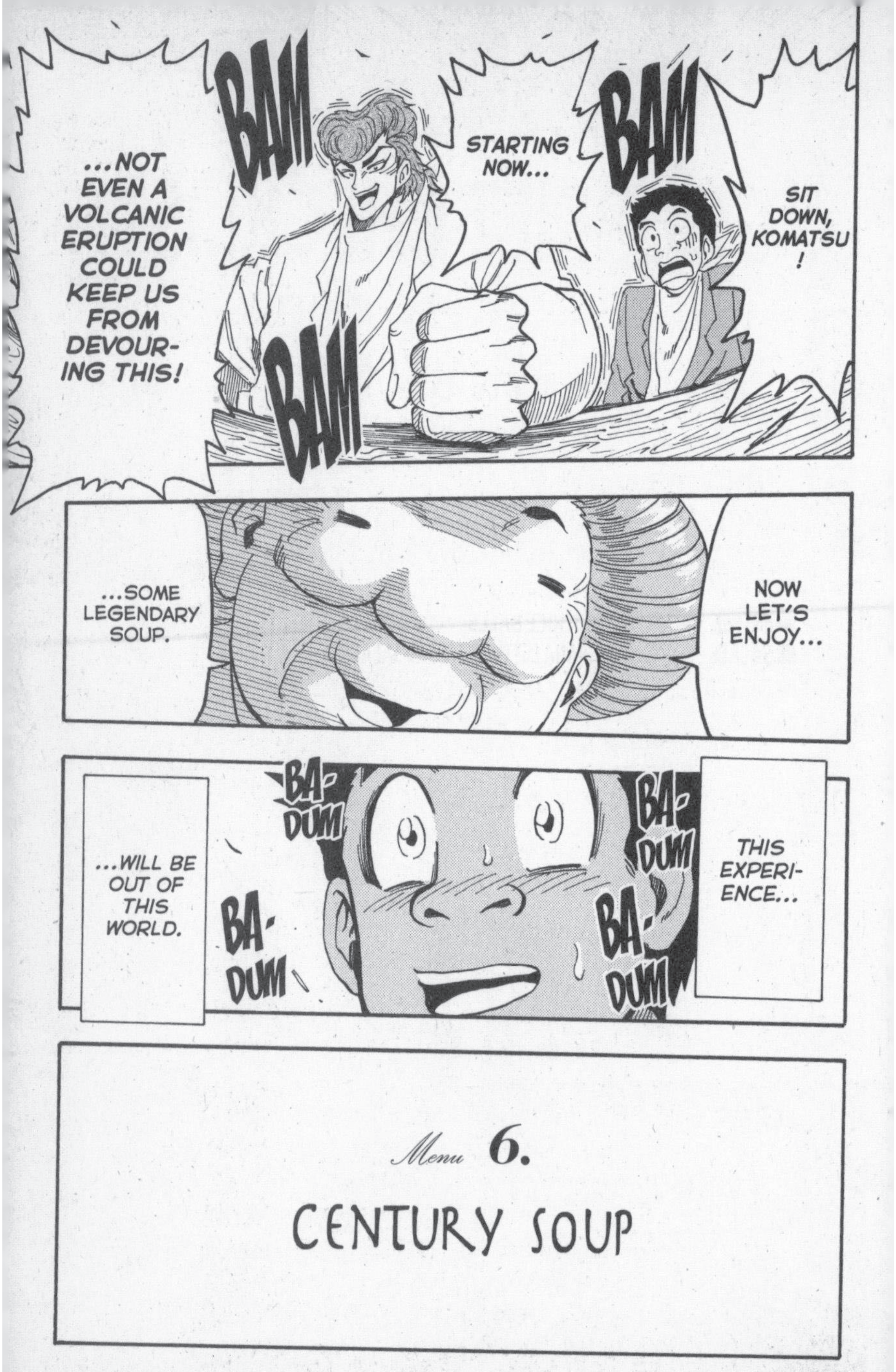
SIT DOWN, KOMATSU!
BAM
STARTING NOW...
BAM
...NOT EVEN A VOLCANIC ERUPTION COULD KEEP US FROM DEVOURING THIS!
BAM
NOW LET'S ENJOY...
...SOME LEGENDARY SOUP.
THIS EXPERIENCE...
BA-DUM
BA-DUM
BA-DUM
BA-DUM
...WILL BE OUT OF THIS WORLD.

Menu 6.

CENTURY SOUP

TORIKO

GOURMET CHECKLIST

Vol. 052

ZEBRA KONG

(MAMMAL)

CAPTURE LEVEL: 9

HABITAT: REGAL ISLE (WHITE FOREST), ETC.

LENGTH: ---

HEIGHT: 6.2 METERS

WEIGHT: 3.5 TONS

PRICE: 1 KG / 900 YEN (MEAT IS EDIBLE, BUT NOT A GOURMET ITEM)

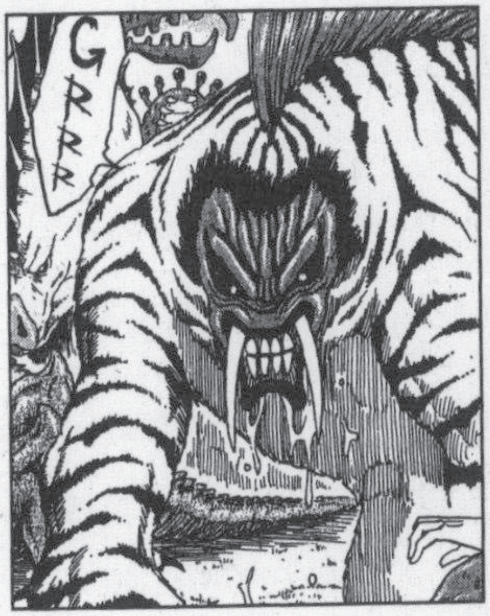
GRRR

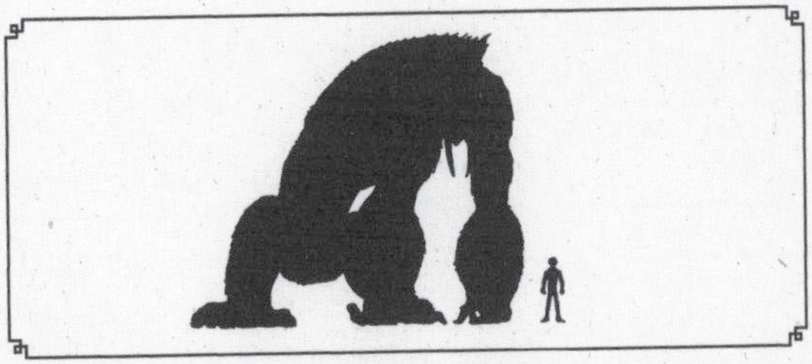

SCALE

THIS GORILLA HAS AN IDENTITY CRISIS. IT'S STRIPED LIKE A ZEBRA WHILE ITS HANDS AND FEET ARE STICKY LIKE A CHAMELEON'S. STILL, IT'S THOSE CLINGY PHALANGES, COMBINED WITH THE ZEBRA KONG'S INCREDIBLE GRIP AND STRENGTH, WHICH MAKE IT A PERFECT ARBOREAL HUNTER, CAPABLE OF SWINGING ITS WAY THROUGH THE CANOPY AT A DIZZYING PACE. THEY LIVE AND HUNT IN GROUPS, SO TRAVELERS SHOULD TAKE CAUTION NOT TO BECOME TARGETED BY A BAND OF ZEBRA KONGS.

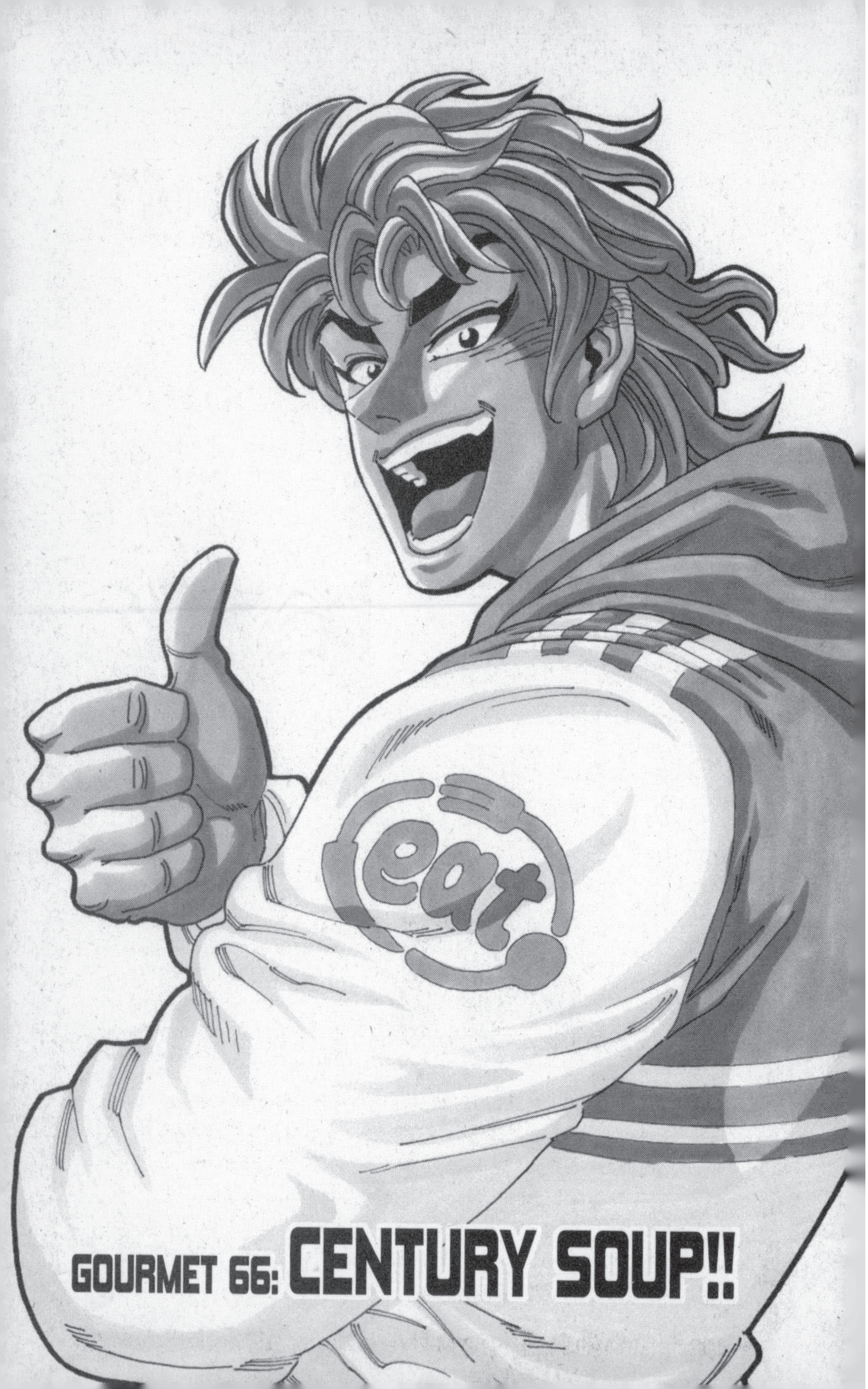
eat

GOURMET 66: CENTURY SOUP!!

TORIKO

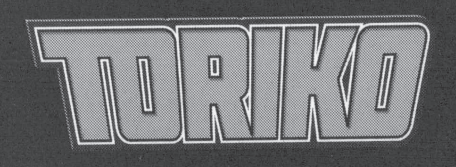

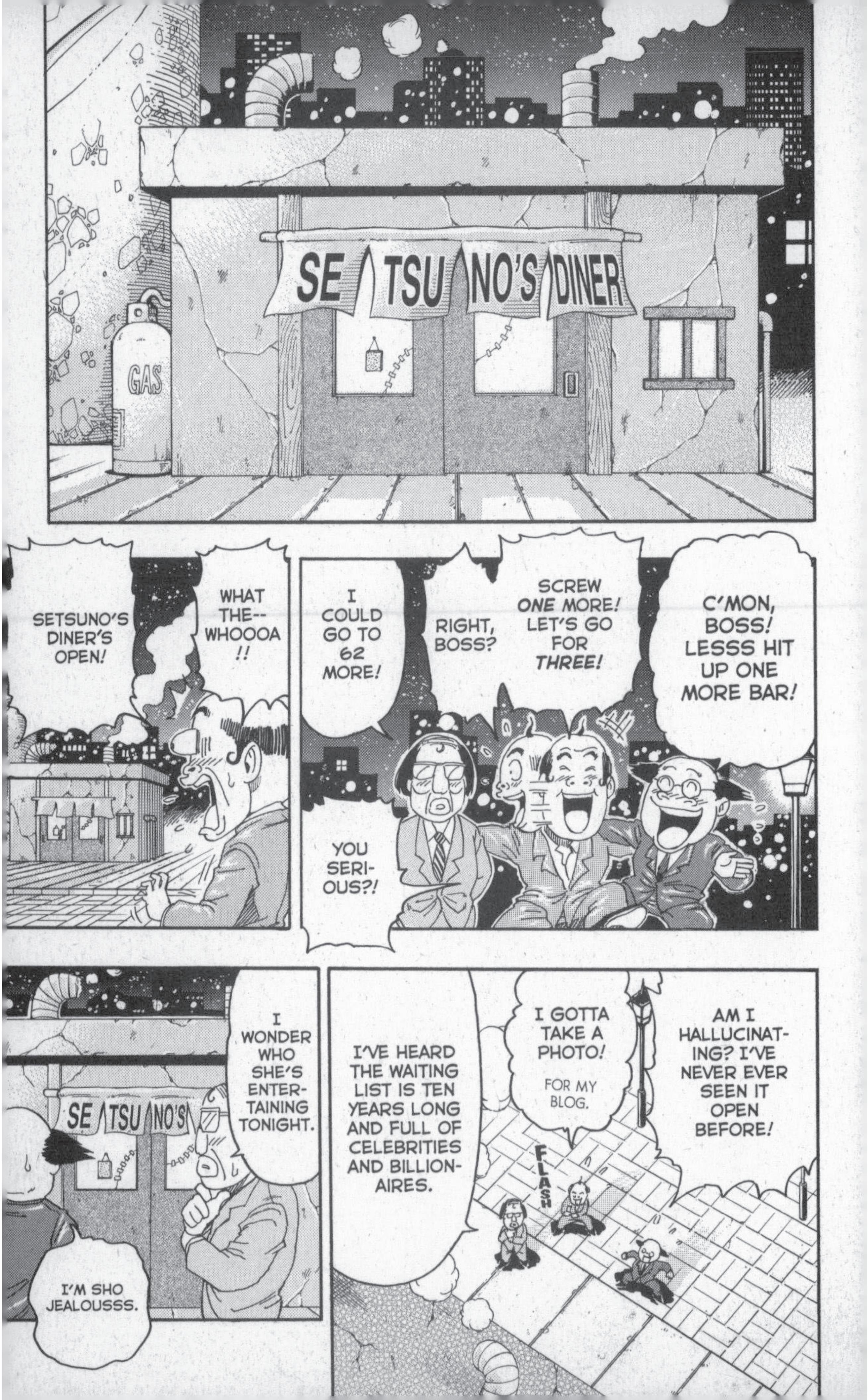

SE TSU NO'S DINER
GAS
C'MON, BOSS! LESSS HIT UP ONE MORE BAR!
SCREW *ONE* MORE! LET'S GO FOR *THREE!*
RIGHT, BOSS?
I COULD GO TO 62 MORE!
YOU SERI-OUS?!
WHAT THE-- WHOOOA!!
SETSUNO'S DINER'S OPEN!
AM I HALLUCINAT-ING? I'VE NEVER EVER SEEN IT OPEN BEFORE!
I GOTTA TAKE A PHOTO!
FOR MY BLOG.
FLASH
I'VE HEARD THE WAITING LIST IS TEN YEARS LONG AND FULL OF CELEBRITIES AND BILLION-AIRES.
I WONDER WHO SHE'S ENTER-TAINING TONIGHT.
SE TSU NO'S
I'M SHO JEALOUSSS.

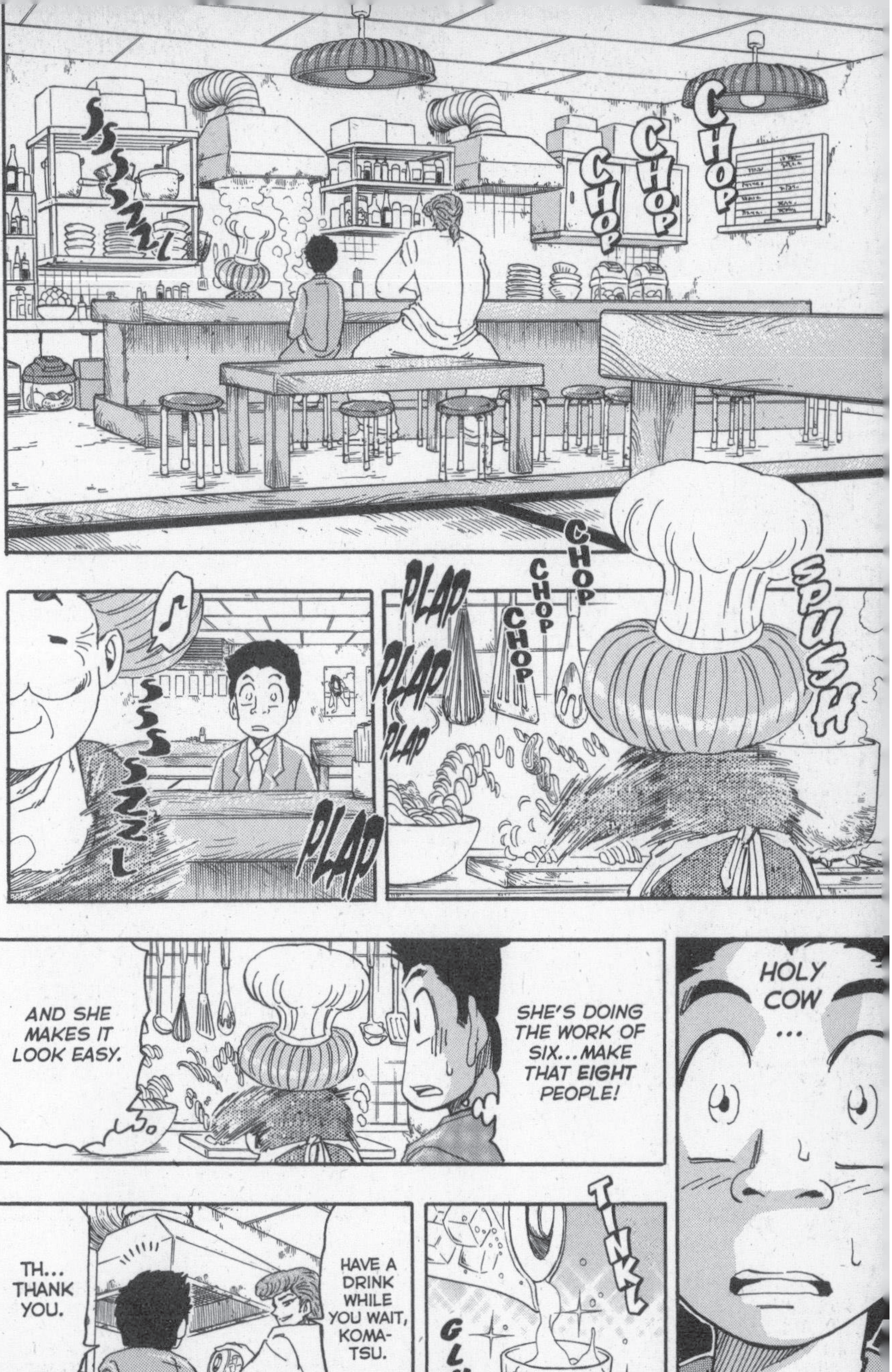
CHOP
CHOP
CHOP
SSSSZZZL
SPUSH
CHOP
CHOP
CHOP
PLAP
PLAP
PLAP
♪
SSSSZZZL
PLAP
HOLY COW ...
SHE'S DOING THE WORK OF SIX...MAKE THAT EIGHT PEOPLE!
AND SHE MAKES IT LOOK EASY.
TINKL
GLUB
HAVE A DRINK WHILE YOU WAIT, KOMA-TSU.
TH... THANK YOU.

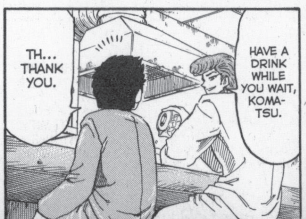

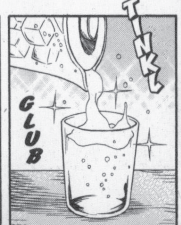

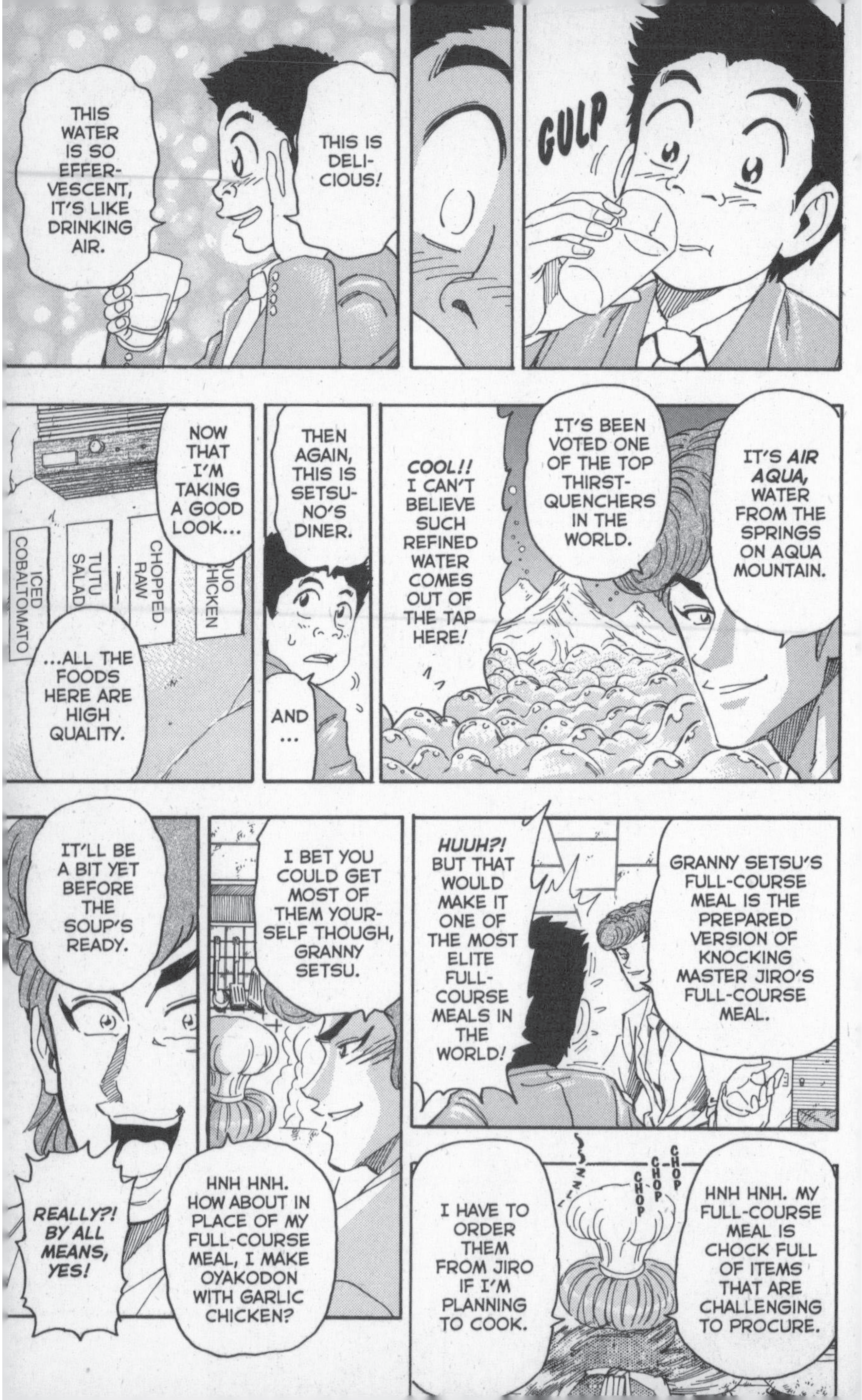
GULP
THIS IS DELI- CIOUS!
THIS WATER IS SO EFFER- VESCENT, IT'S LIKE DRINKING AIR.
IT'S *AIR AQUA*, WATER FROM THE SPRINGS ON AQUA MOUNTAIN.
IT'S BEEN VOTED ONE OF THE TOP THIRST- QUENCHERS IN THE WORLD.
COOL!! I CAN'T BELIEVE SUCH REFINED WATER COMES OUT OF THE TAP HERE!
THEN AGAIN, THIS IS SETSU- NO'S DINER.
AND ...
NOW THAT I'M TAKING A GOOD LOOK...
QUO CHICKEN
CHOPPED RAW
TUTU SALAD
ICED COBALTOMATO
...ALL THE FOODS HERE ARE HIGH QUALITY.
GRANNY SETSU'S FULL-COURSE MEAL IS THE PREPARED VERSION OF KNOCKING MASTER JIRO'S FULL-COURSE MEAL.
HUUH?! BUT THAT WOULD MAKE IT ONE OF THE MOST ELITE FULL- COURSE MEALS IN THE WORLD!
HNH HNH. *MY* FULL-COURSE MEAL IS CHOCK FULL OF ITEMS THAT ARE CHALLENGING TO PROCURE.
CHOP CHOP CHOP
I HAVE TO ORDER THEM FROM JIRO IF I'M PLANNING TO COOK.
I BET YOU COULD GET MOST OF THEM YOUR- SELF THOUGH, GRANNY SETSU.
HNH HNH. HOW ABOUT IN PLACE OF MY FULL-COURSE MEAL, I MAKE OYAKODON WITH GARLIC CHICKEN?
IT'LL BE A BIT YET BEFORE THE SOUP'S READY.
REALLY?! BY ALL MEANS, YES!

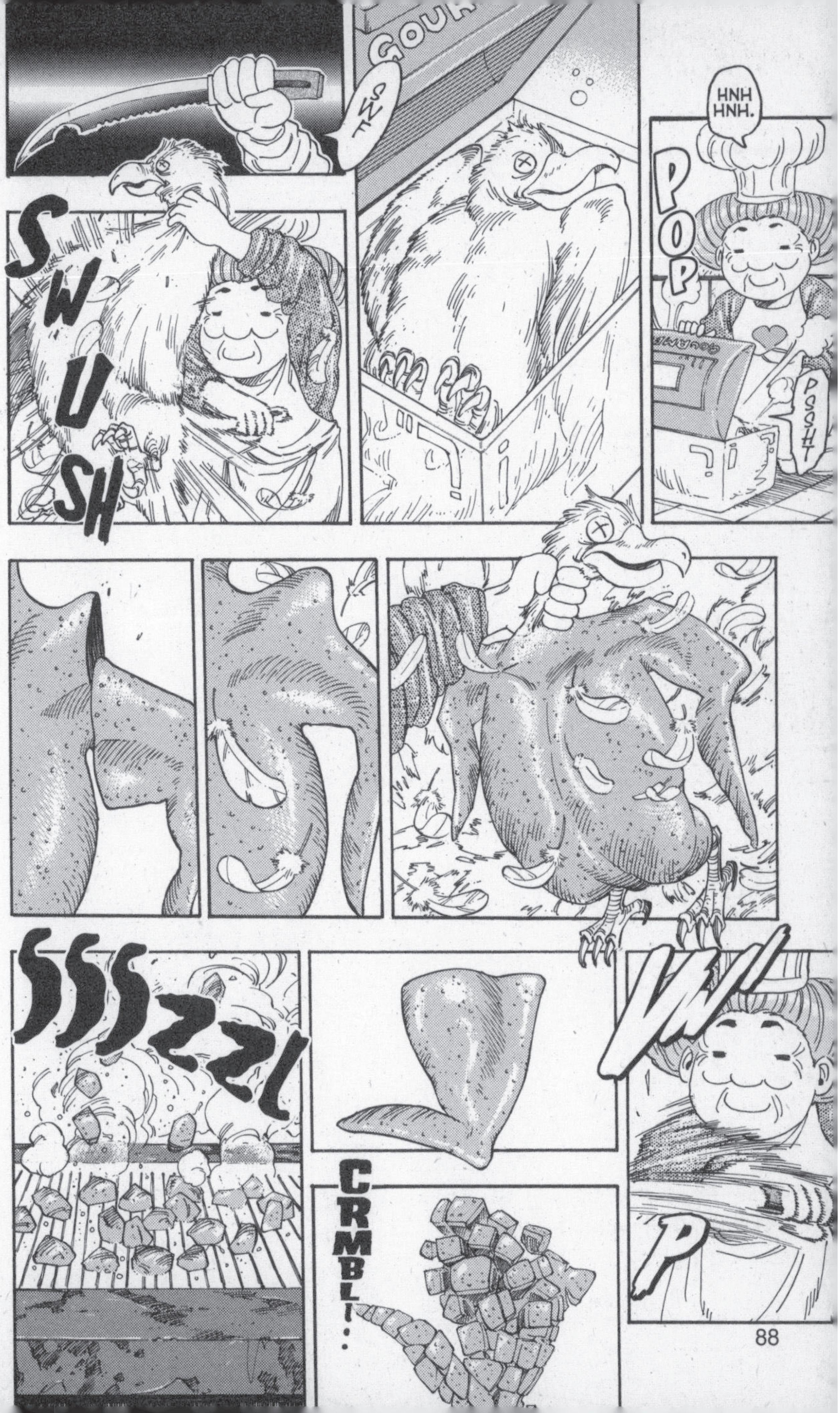
HNH HNH.
POP
PSSHT
GOUR
SWF
SWUSH
VW!
P
CRMBL!..
SSSZZZL

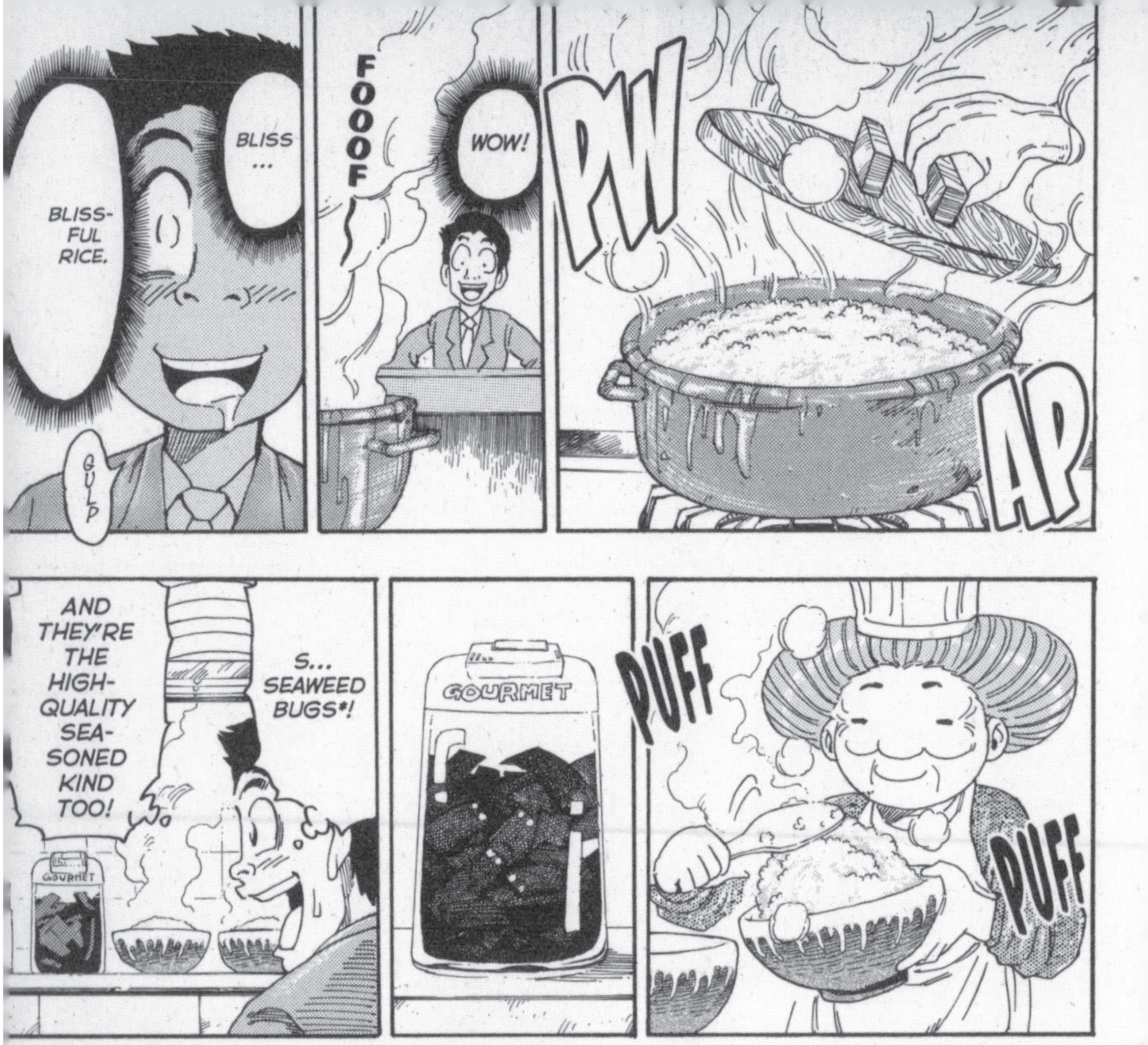
PW
AP
FOOOF
WOW!
BLISS...
BLISS-FUL RICE.
GULP
PUFF
PUFF
GOURMET
S... SEAWEED BUGS*!
AND THEY'RE THE HIGH-QUALITY SEA-SONED KIND TOO!
GOURMET

*SUBMITTED BY SHOSUKE ARIMA FROM FUKUOKA!

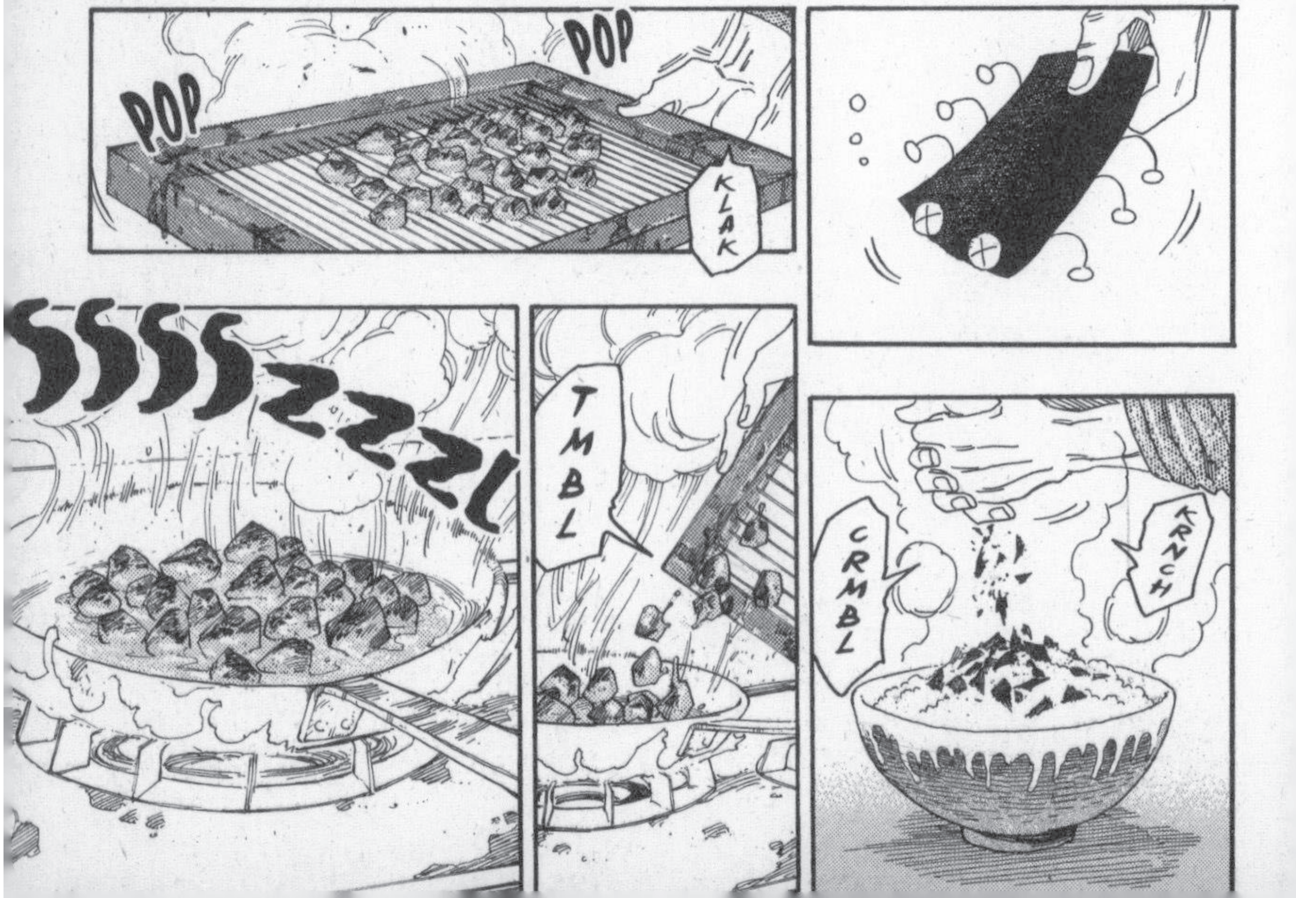
POP
POP
KLAK
KRNCH
CRMBL
TMBL
SSSSSZZZZL

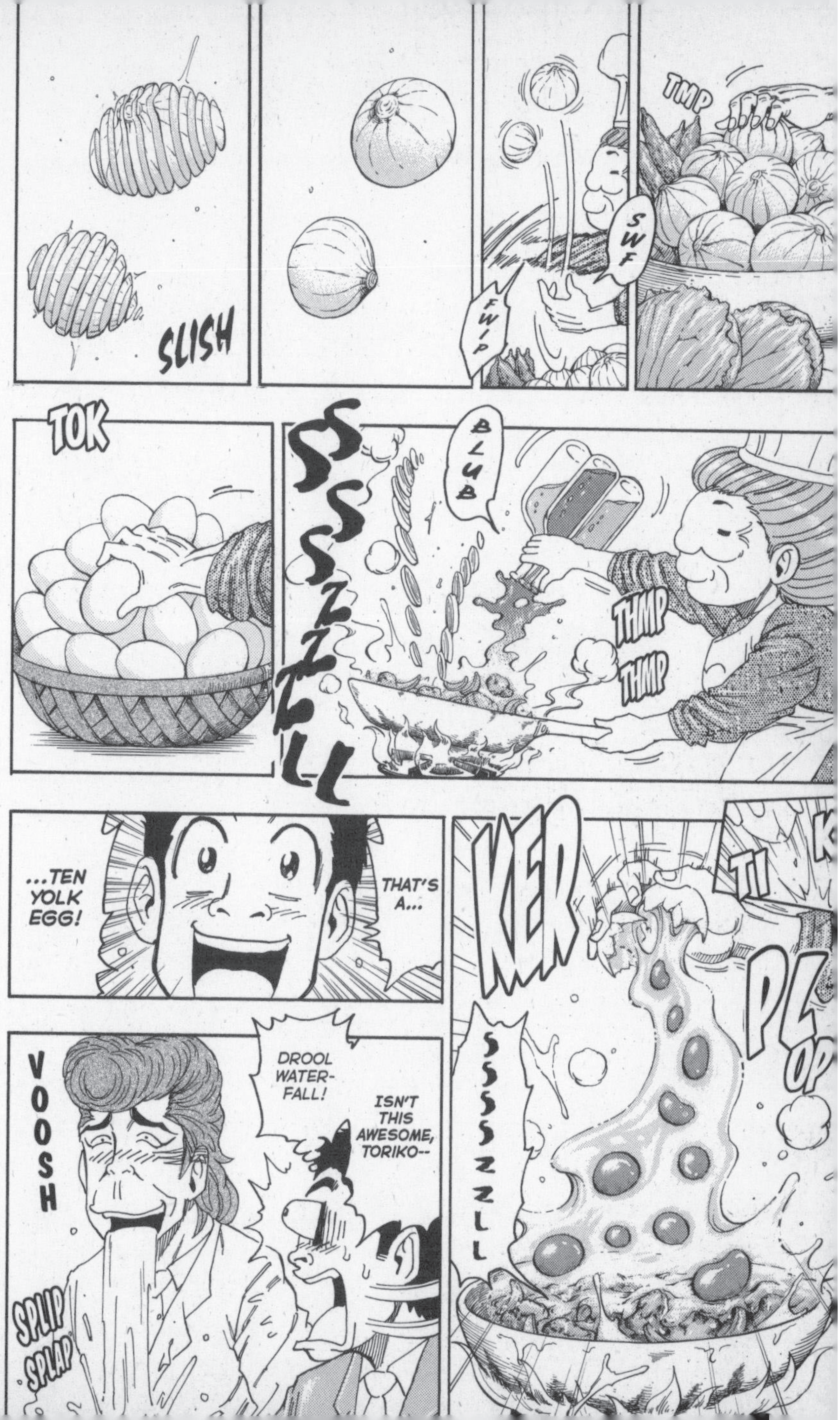
TMP
SWF
FWIP
SLISH
BLUB
SSSZZZLLL
THMP
THMP
TOK
KER
TI
K
PL
OP
SSSSZZLL
THAT'S A...
...TEN YOLK EGG!
DROOL WATER-FALL!
ISN'T THIS AWESOME, TORIKO--
VOOSH
SPLIP
SPLAP

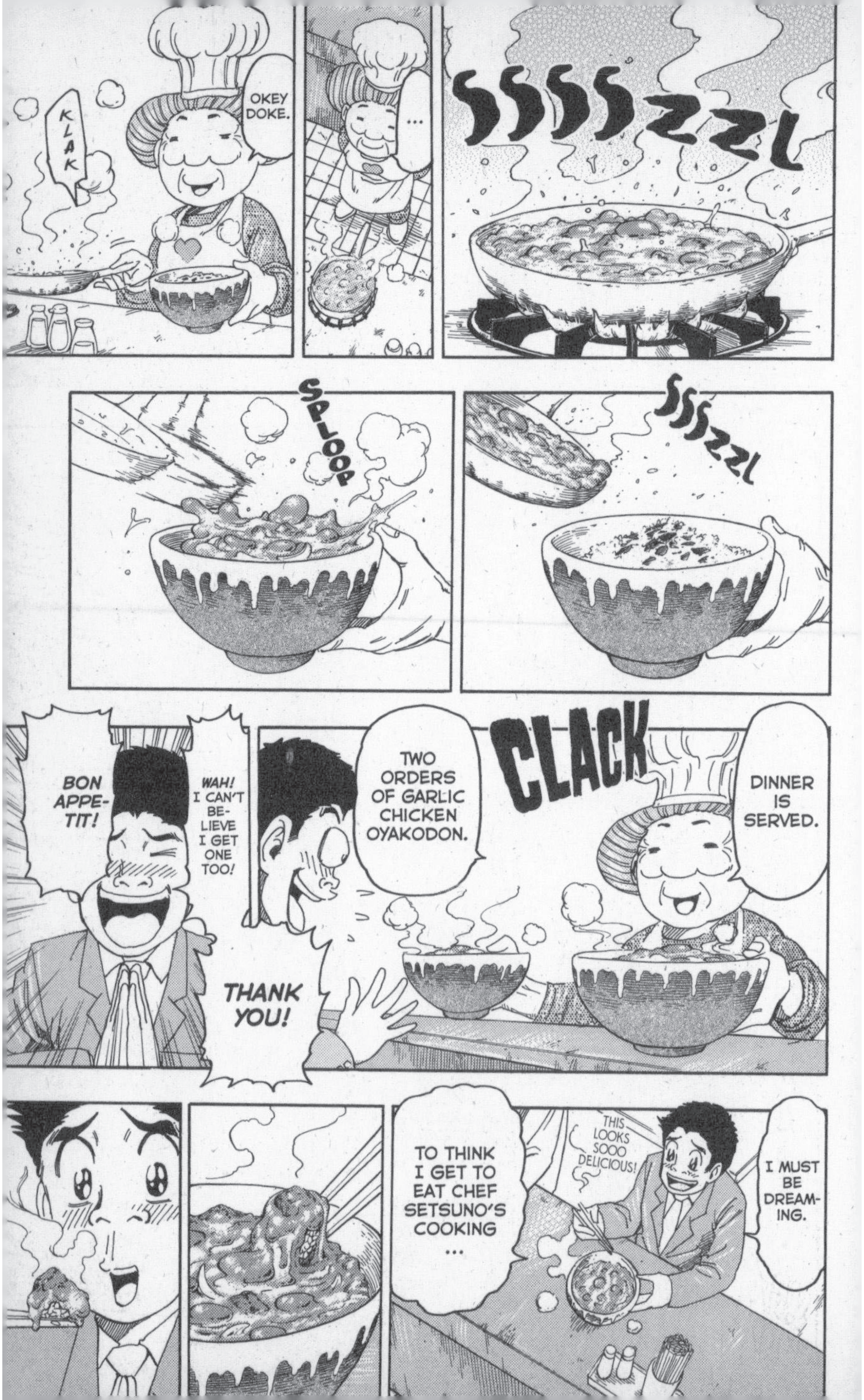
SSSSZZZL
...
OKEY DOKE.
KLAK
SSSZZZL
SPLOOP
CLACK
DINNER IS SERVED.
TWO ORDERS OF GARLIC CHICKEN OYAKODON.
THANK YOU!
WAH! I CAN'T BE-LIEVE I GET ONE TOO!
BON APPE-TIT!
I MUST BE DREAM-ING.
THIS LOOKS SOOO DELICIOUS!
TO THINK I GET TO EAT CHEF SETSUNO'S COOKING ...

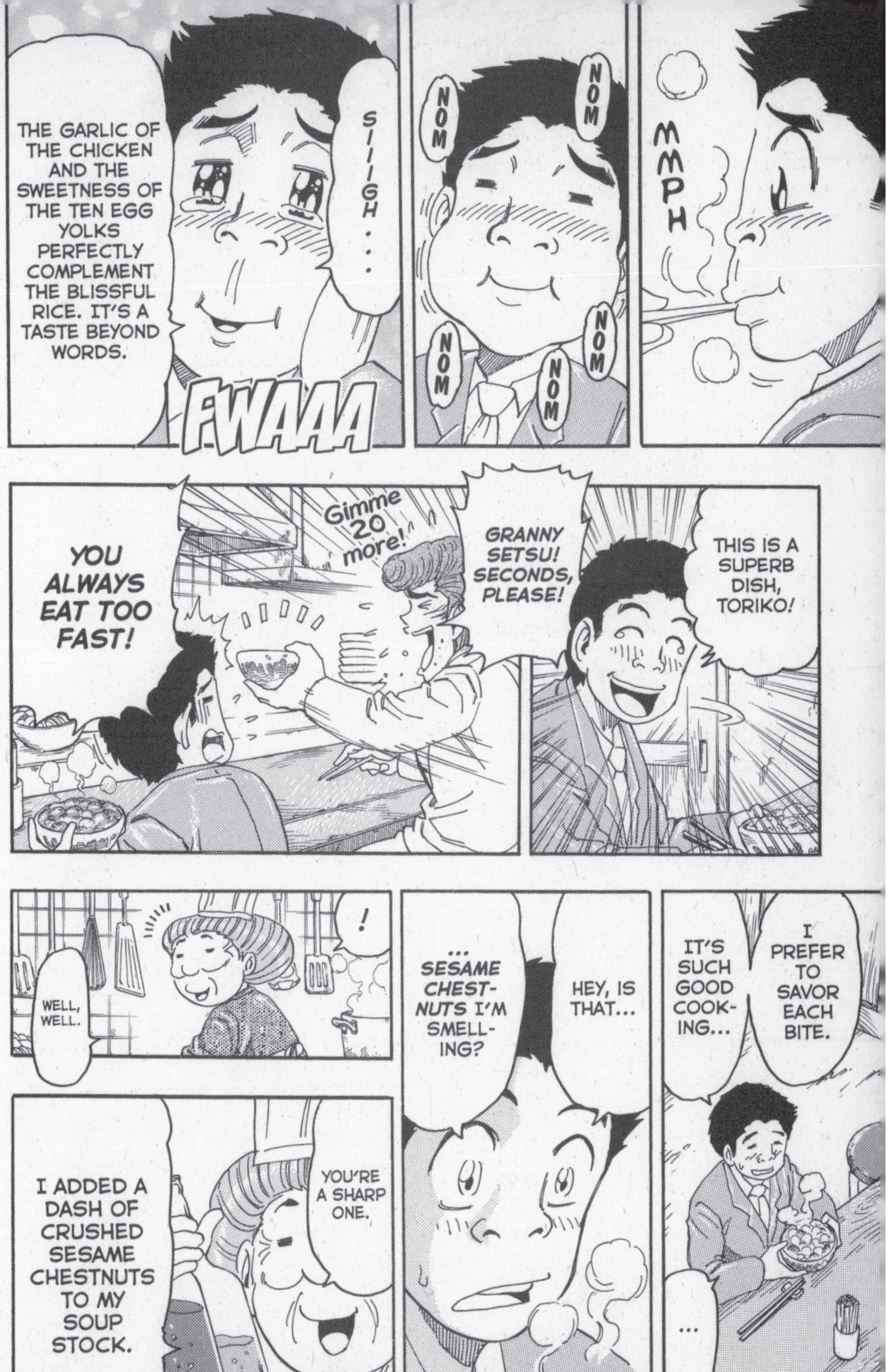
MMPH
NOM NOM NOM
NOM NOM NOM
SIIIGH...
THE GARLIC OF THE CHICKEN AND THE SWEETNESS OF THE TEN EGG YOLKS PERFECTLY COMPLEMENT THE BLISSFUL RICE. IT'S A TASTE BEYOND WORDS.
FWAAA
THIS IS A SUPERB DISH, TORIKO!
GRANNY SETSU! SECONDS, PLEASE!
Gimme 20 more!
YOU ALWAYS EAT TOO FAST!
I PREFER TO SAVOR EACH BITE.
IT'S SUCH GOOD COOKING...
...
HEY, IS THAT...
...SESAME CHESTNUTS I'M SMELLING?
!
WELL, WELL.
YOU'RE A SHARP ONE.
I ADDED A DASH OF CRUSHED SESAME CHESTNUTS TO MY SOUP STOCK.

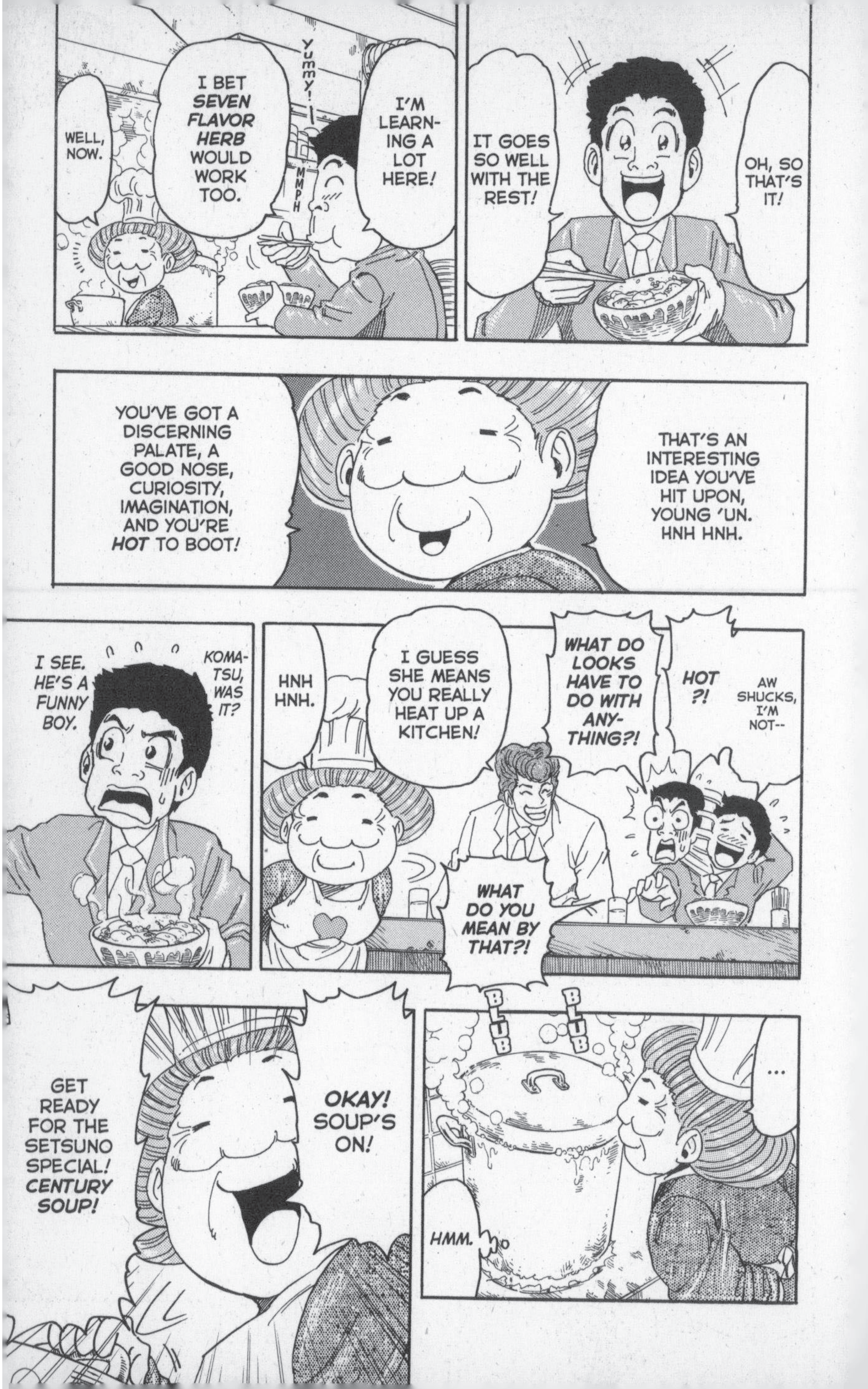
OH, SO THAT'S IT!
IT GOES SO WELL WITH THE REST!
I'M LEARNING A LOT HERE!
YUMMY!
MMPH
I BET SEVEN FLAVOR HERB WOULD WORK TOO.
WELL, NOW.
THAT'S AN INTERESTING IDEA YOU'VE HIT UPON, YOUNG 'UN. HNH HNH.
YOU'VE GOT A DISCERNING PALATE, A GOOD NOSE, CURIOSITY, IMAGINATION, AND YOU'RE HOT TO BOOT!
AW SHUCKS, I'M NOT--
HOT?!
WHAT DO LOOKS HAVE TO DO WITH ANYTHING?!
I GUESS SHE MEANS YOU REALLY HEAT UP A KITCHEN!
HNH HNH.
WHAT DO YOU MEAN BY THAT?!
KOMATSU, WAS IT?
I SEE. HE'S A FUNNY BOY.
BLUB
BLUB
...
HMM.
OKAY! SOUP'S ON!
GET READY FOR THE SETSUNO SPECIAL! CENTURY SOUP!

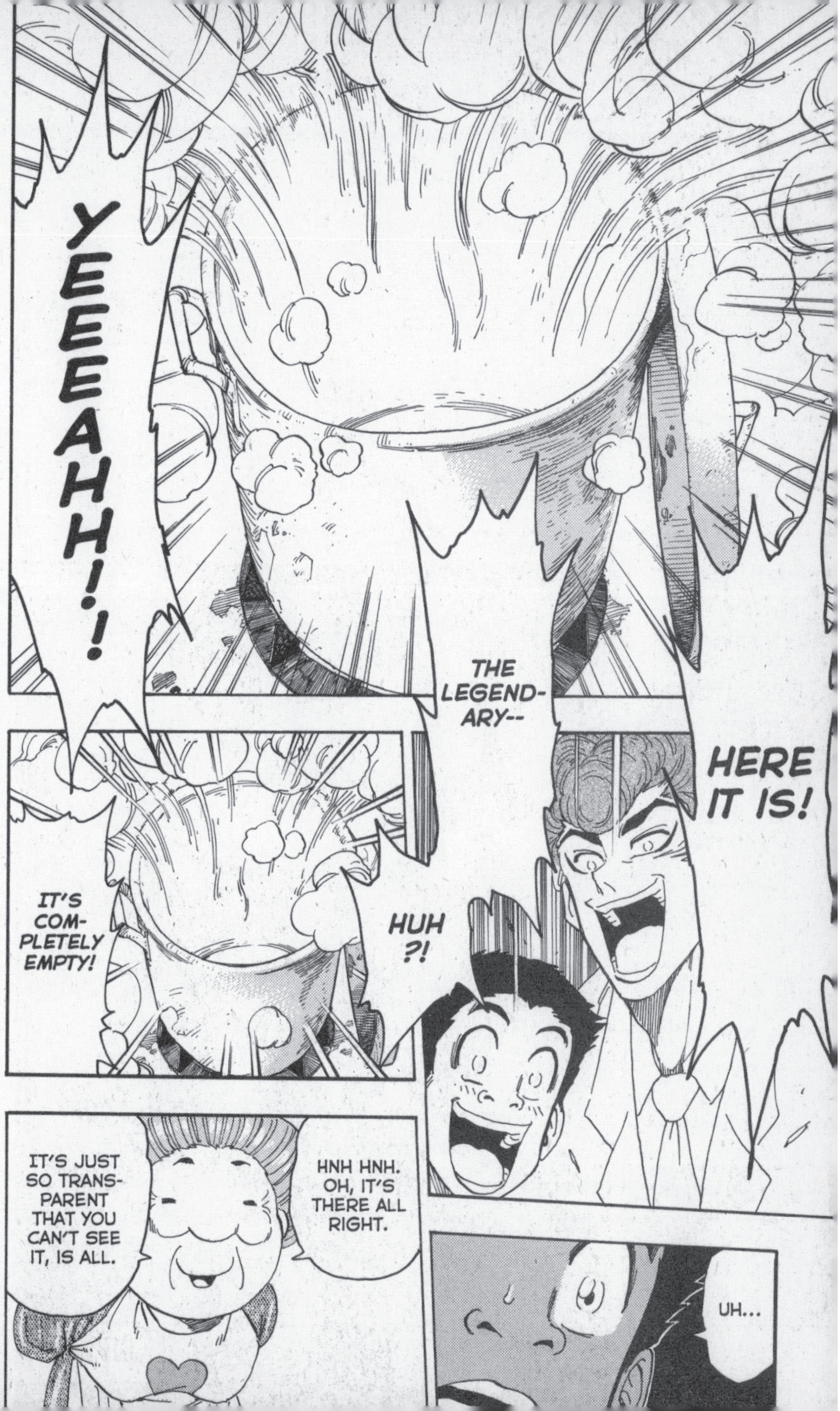
YEEEAHH!!
THE LEGEND-ARY--
HERE IT IS!
HUH ?!
IT'S COM-PLETELY EMPTY!
UH...
HNH HNH. OH, IT'S THERE ALL RIGHT.
IT'S JUST SO TRANS-PARENT THAT YOU CAN'T SEE IT, IS ALL.

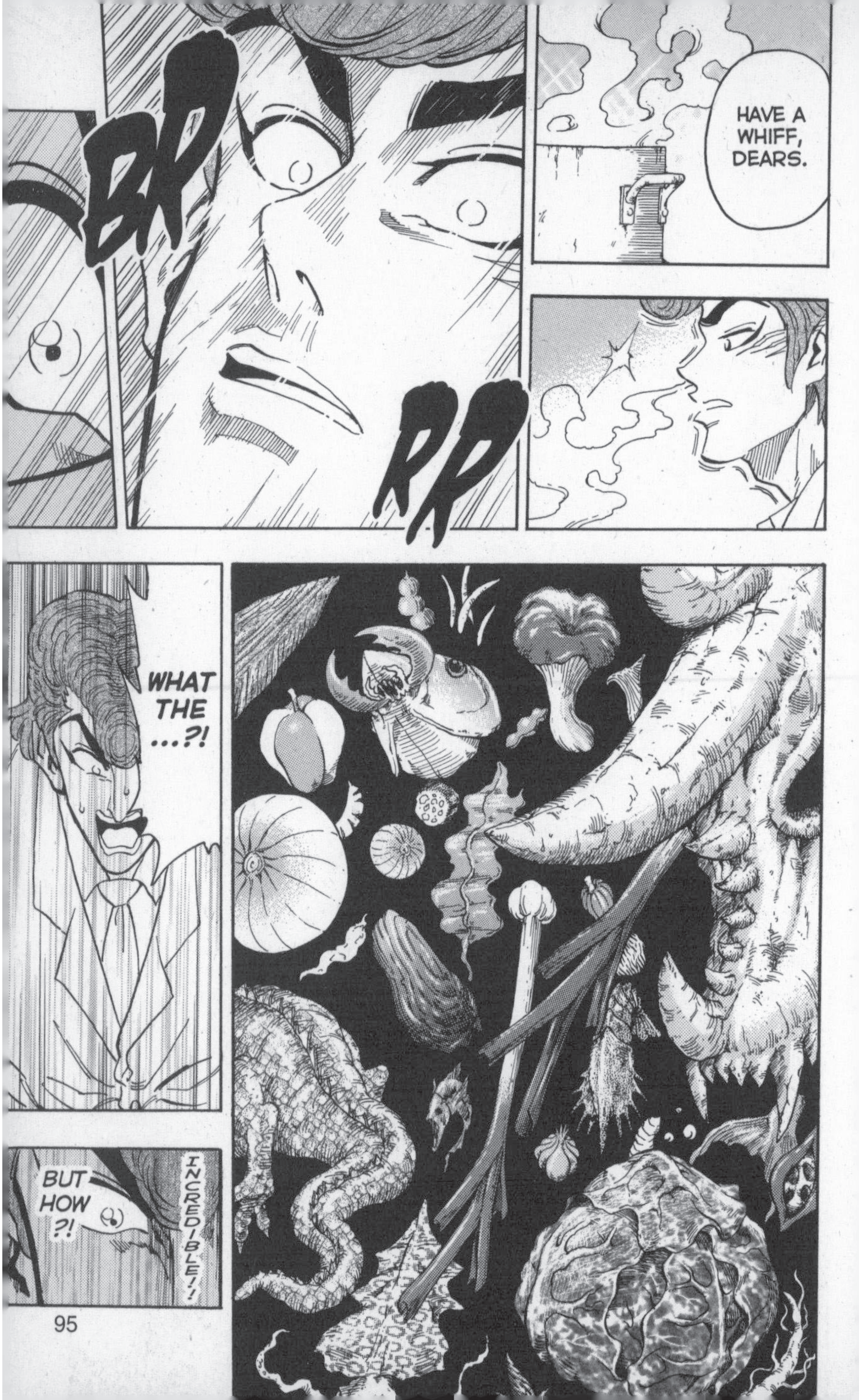

HAVE A WHIFF, DEARS.
BR
RR
WHAT THE ...?!
INCREDIBLE!!
BUT HOW?!

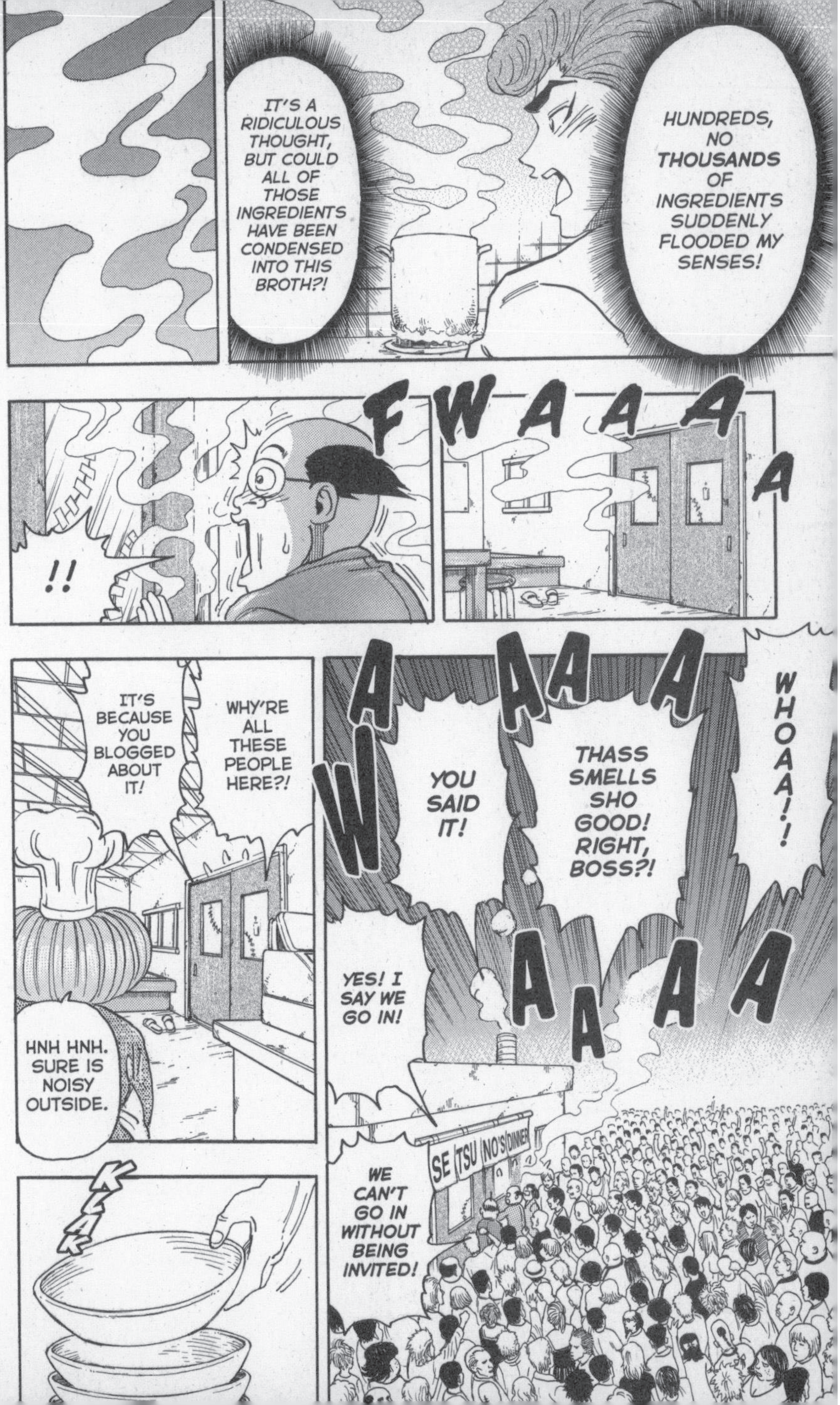
HUNDREDS, NO THOUSANDS OF INGREDIENTS SUDDENLY FLOODED MY SENSES!
IT'S A RIDICULOUS THOUGHT, BUT COULD ALL OF THOSE INGREDIENTS HAVE BEEN CONDENSED INTO THIS BROTH?!
FWAAAAA
!!
WHOAAA!!
THASS SMELLS SHO GOOD! RIGHT, BOSS?!
YOU SAID IT!
WAAAA
AAAAA
YES! I SAY WE GO IN!
SE TSU NO'S DINNER
WE CAN'T GO IN WITHOUT BEING INVITED!
WHY'RE ALL THESE PEOPLE HERE?!
IT'S BECAUSE YOU BLOGGED ABOUT IT!
HNH HNH. SURE IS NOISY OUTSIDE.
KLAK

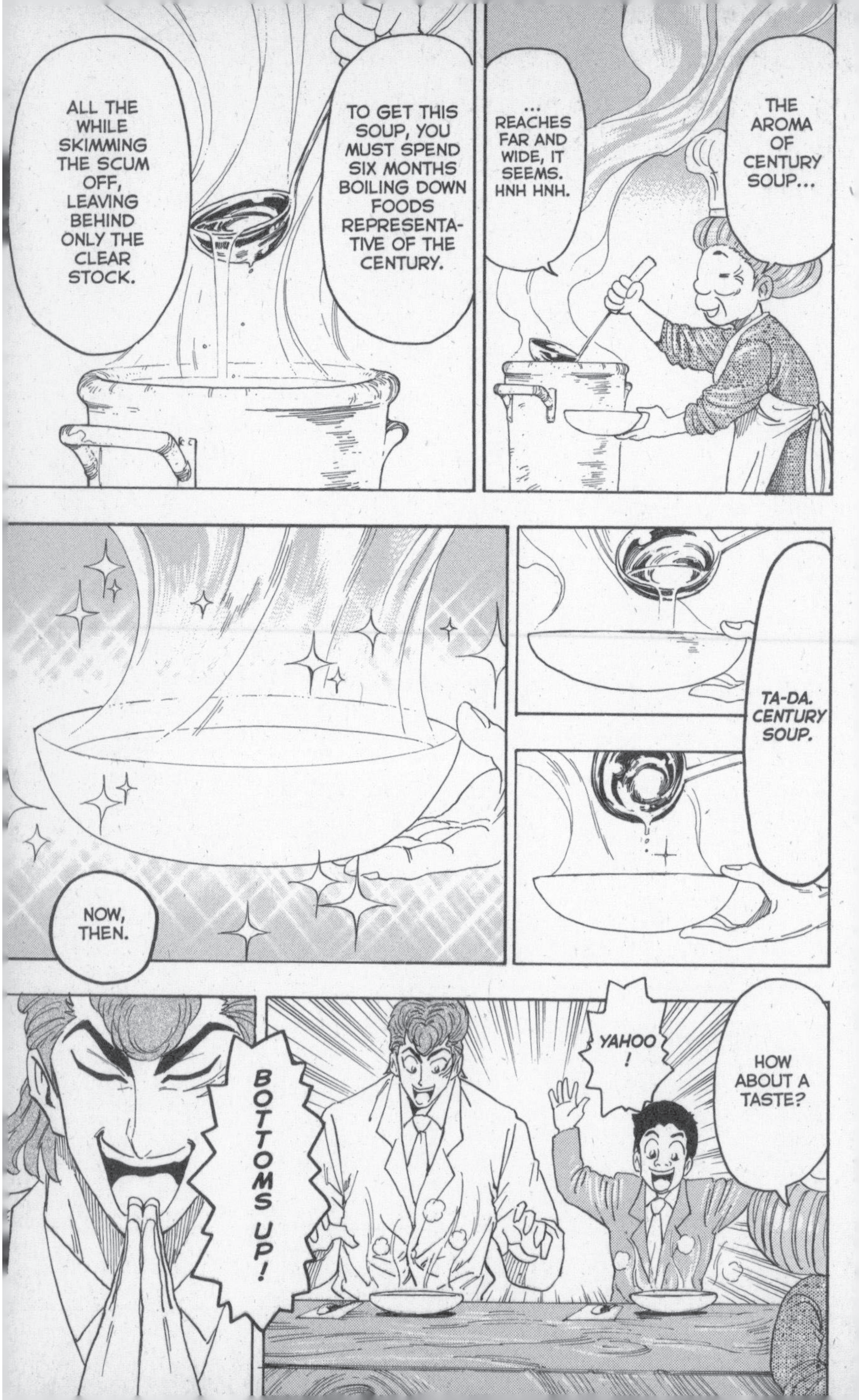
THE AROMA OF CENTURY SOUP...
... REACHES FAR AND WIDE, IT SEEMS. HNH HNH.
TO GET THIS SOUP, YOU MUST SPEND SIX MONTHS BOILING DOWN FOODS REPRESENTATIVE OF THE CENTURY.
ALL THE WHILE SKIMMING THE SCUM OFF, LEAVING BEHIND ONLY THE CLEAR STOCK.
TA-DA. CENTURY SOUP.
NOW, THEN.
HOW ABOUT A TASTE?
YAHOO!
BOTTOMS UP!

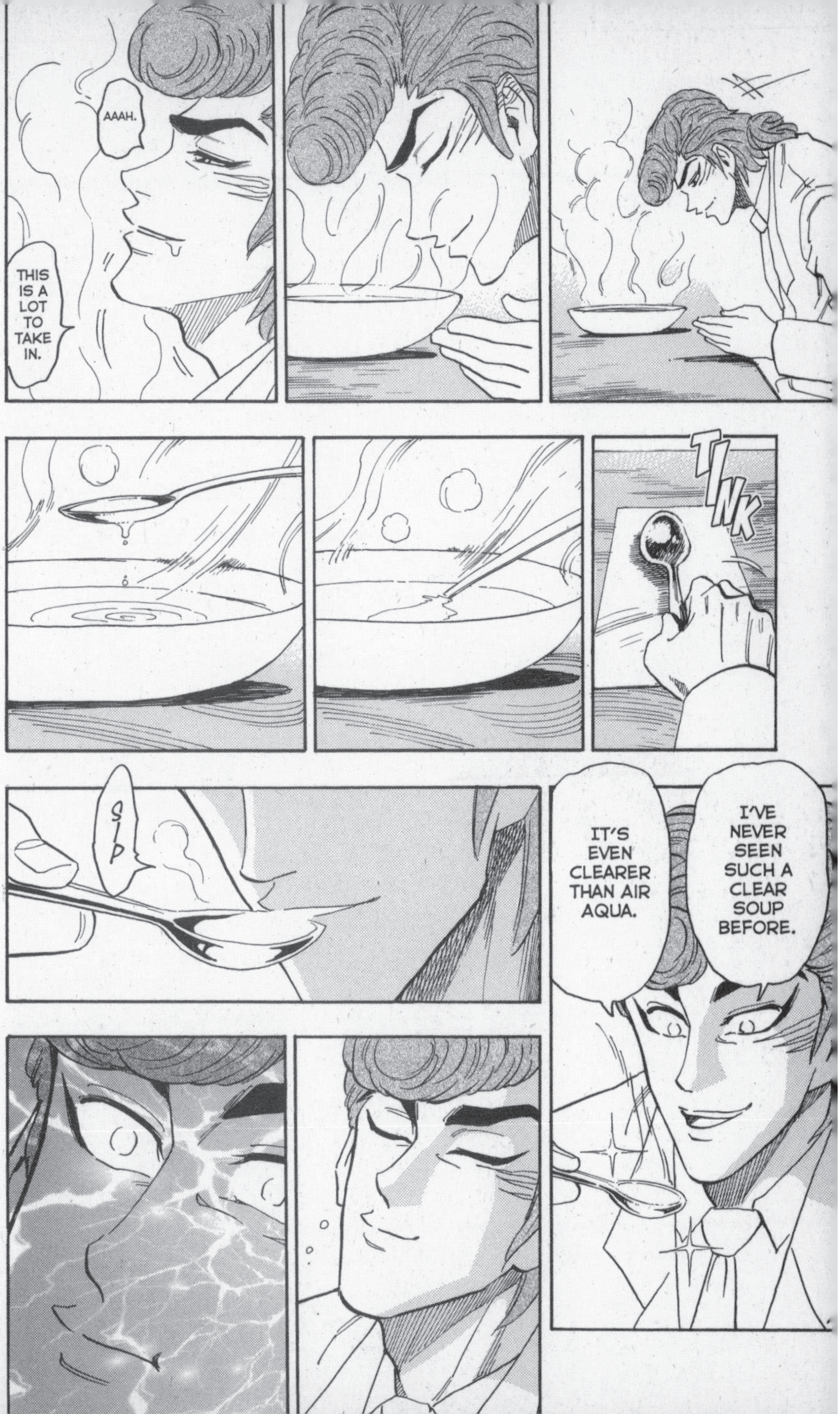
AAAH.
THIS IS A LOT TO TAKE IN.
TINK
I'VE NEVER SEEN SUCH A CLEAR SOUP BEFORE.
IT'S EVEN CLEARER THAN AIR AQUA.
SIP

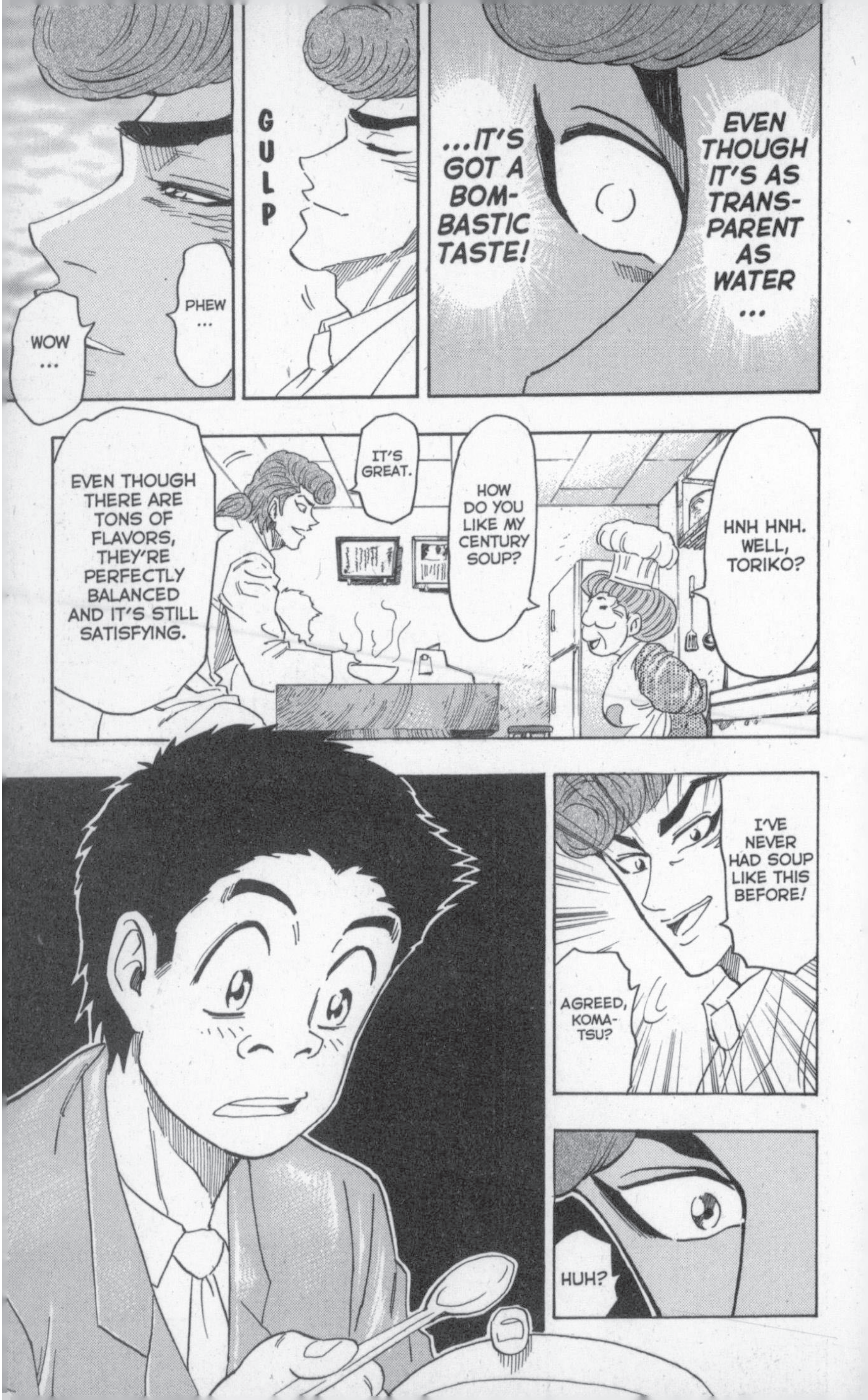
EVEN THOUGH IT'S AS TRANSPARENT AS WATER...
...IT'S GOT A BOMBASTIC TASTE!
GULP
PHEW...
WOW...
HNH HNH. WELL, TORIKO?
HOW DO YOU LIKE MY CENTURY SOUP?
IT'S GREAT.
EVEN THOUGH THERE ARE TONS OF FLAVORS, THEY'RE PERFECTLY BALANCED AND IT'S STILL SATISFYING.
I'VE NEVER HAD SOUP LIKE THIS BEFORE!
AGREED, KOMATSU?
HUH?

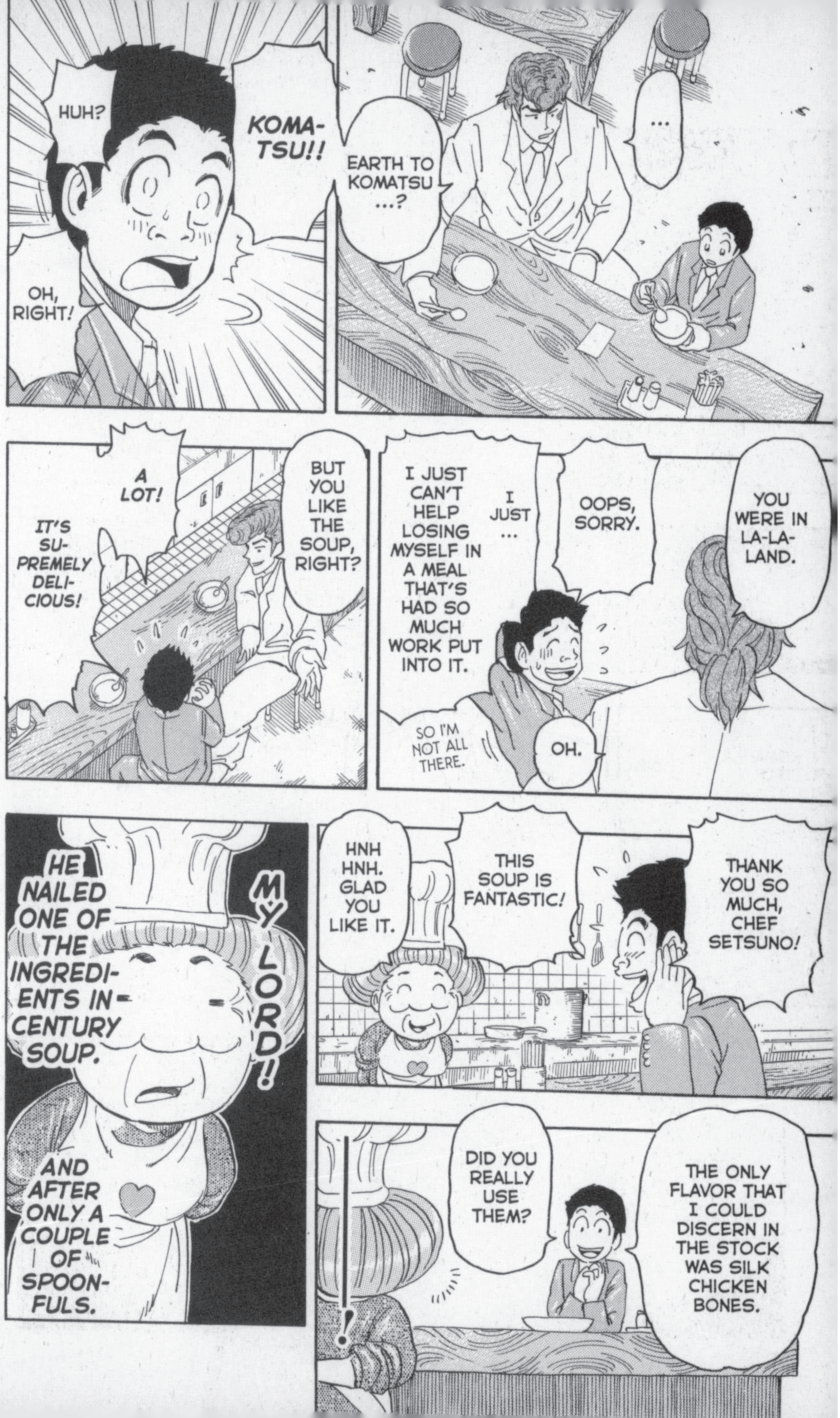
...
EARTH TO KOMATSU ...?
KOMA-TSU!!
HUH?
OH, RIGHT!
YOU WERE IN LA-LA-LAND.
OOPS, SORRY.
I JUST ...
I JUST CAN'T HELP LOSING MYSELF IN A MEAL THAT'S HAD SO MUCH WORK PUT INTO IT.
OH.
SO I'M NOT ALL THERE.
BUT YOU LIKE THE SOUP, RIGHT?
A LOT!
IT'S SU-PREMELY DELI-CIOUS!
THANK YOU SO MUCH, CHEF SETSUNO!
THIS SOUP IS FANTASTIC!
HNH HNH. GLAD YOU LIKE IT.
THE ONLY FLAVOR THAT I COULD DISCERN IN THE STOCK WAS SILK CHICKEN BONES.
DID YOU REALLY USE THEM?
!
MY LORD!
HE NAILED ONE OF THE INGREDI-ENTS IN CENTURY SOUP.
AND AFTER ONLY A COUPLE OF SPOON-FULS.

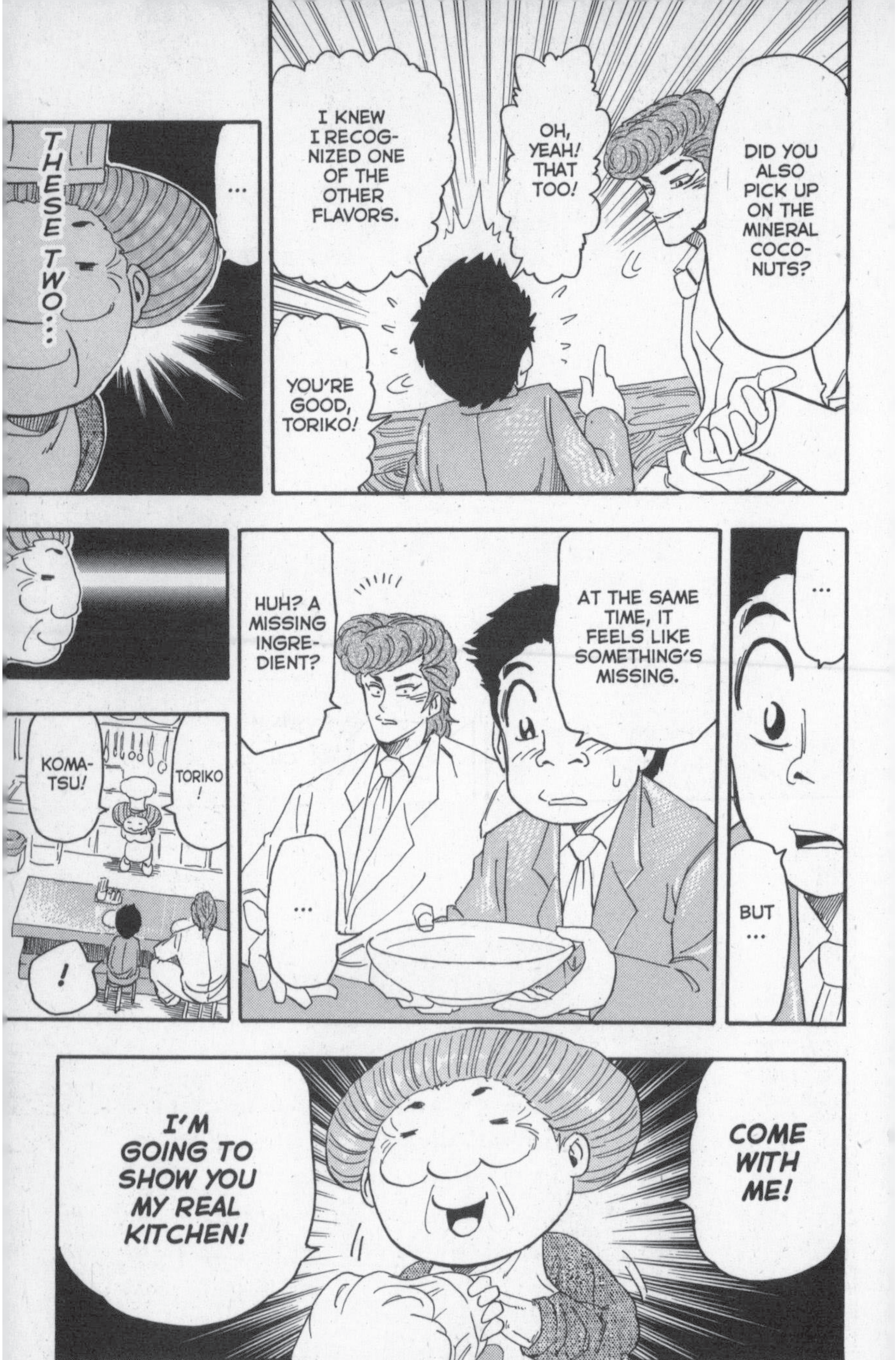
DID YOU ALSO PICK UP ON THE MINERAL COCONUTS?
OH, YEAH! THAT TOO!
I KNEW I RECOGNIZED ONE OF THE OTHER FLAVORS.
YOU'RE GOOD, TORIKO!
...
THESE TWO...
...
BUT ...
AT THE SAME TIME, IT FEELS LIKE SOMETHING'S MISSING.
HUH? A MISSING INGREDIENT?
...
TORIKO!
KOMATSU!
!
COME WITH ME!
I'M GOING TO SHOW YOU MY REAL KITCHEN!

TORIKO

GOURMET CHECKLIST

Vol. 053

 ### DEVIL CROCODILE
(REPTILE)

CAPTURE LEVEL: 21

HABITAT: SWAMPS, FORESTS, AND PLAINS.

OCCASIONALLY SEAS.

LENGTH: 21 METERS

HEIGHT: 4 METERS

WEIGHT: 16 TONS

PRICE: 1 KG OF MEAT / 120,000 YEN;

1 SQUARE METER OF HIDE / 4,000,000 YEN

SCALE

WITH A LENGTH OF 21 METERS AND WEIGHT OF 16 TONS, THIS GIANT CROC HAS BEEN THE MOST FEROCIOUS OF ITS KIND SINCE ANCIENT TIMES. IT EXCEEDS THE GARARA GATOR IN SIZE AND RIVALS THE DEVIL PYTHON IN STRENGTH. THE DEVIL CROCODILE IS VICIOUS BY NATURE AND WILL MAKE EVEN THE LARGEST BEAST ITS PREY, AND WITH JAWS THAT CAN UNLEASH EIGHT TONS OF FORCE, IT OFTEN SUCCEEDS IN THE HUNT. IT'S BEEN KNOWN TO CROSS THE SEAS AND PREY ON THE GARARA GATOR OF BARON ISLE.

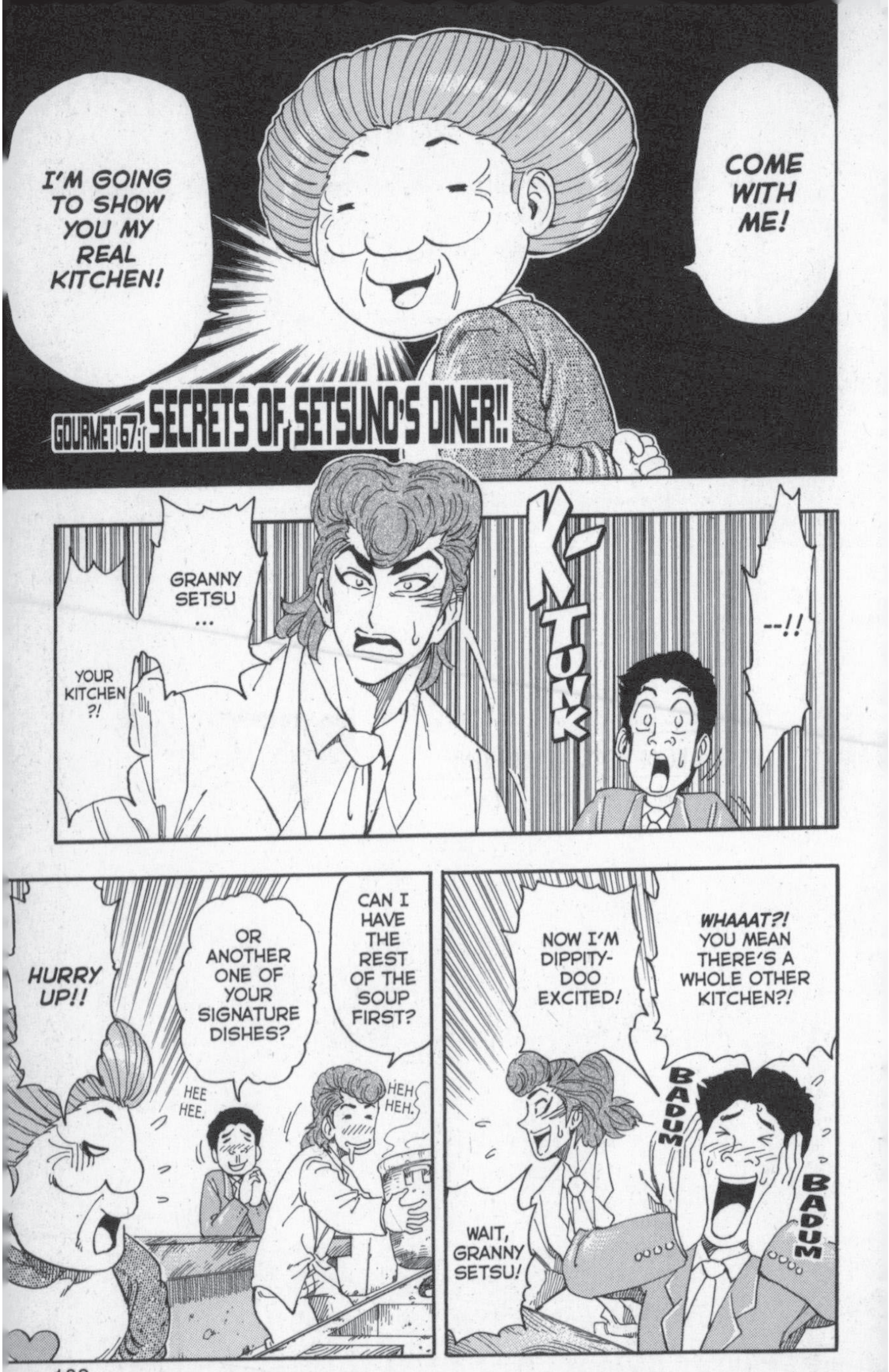
COME WITH ME!
I'M GOING TO SHOW YOU MY REAL KITCHEN!
GOURMET 67: SECRETS OF SETSUNO'S DINER!!
--!!
K-TUNK
GRANNY SETSU...
YOUR KITCHEN?!
WHAAAT?! YOU MEAN THERE'S A WHOLE OTHER KITCHEN?!
BADUM
BADUM
NOW I'M DIPPITY-DOO EXCITED!
WAIT, GRANNY SETSU!
CAN I HAVE THE REST OF THE SOUP FIRST?
HEH HEH.
OR ANOTHER ONE OF YOUR SIGNATURE DISHES?
HEE HEE.
HURRY UP!!

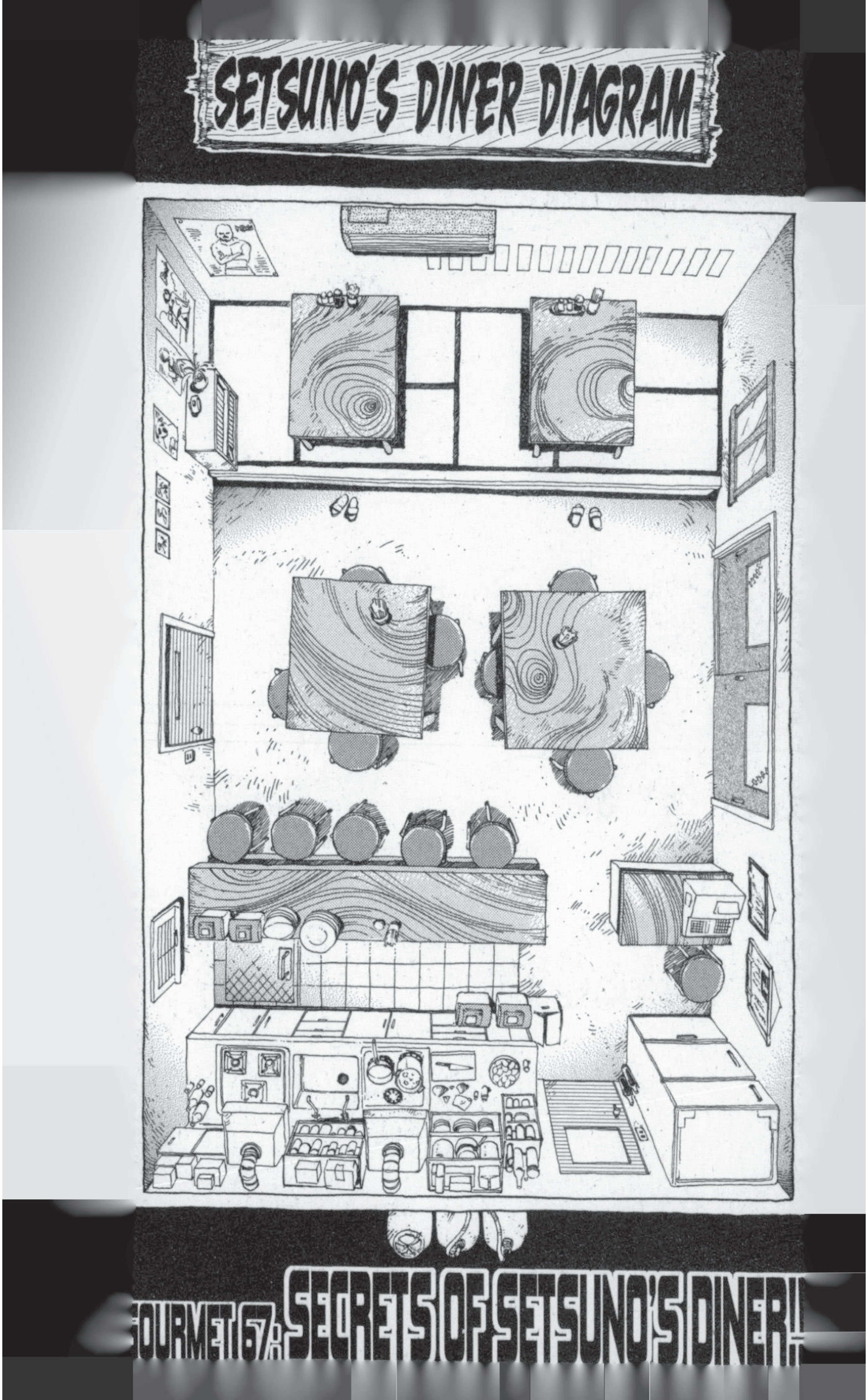
SETSUNO'S DINER DIAGRAM
OURMET 67: SECRETS OF SETSUNO'S DINER!!

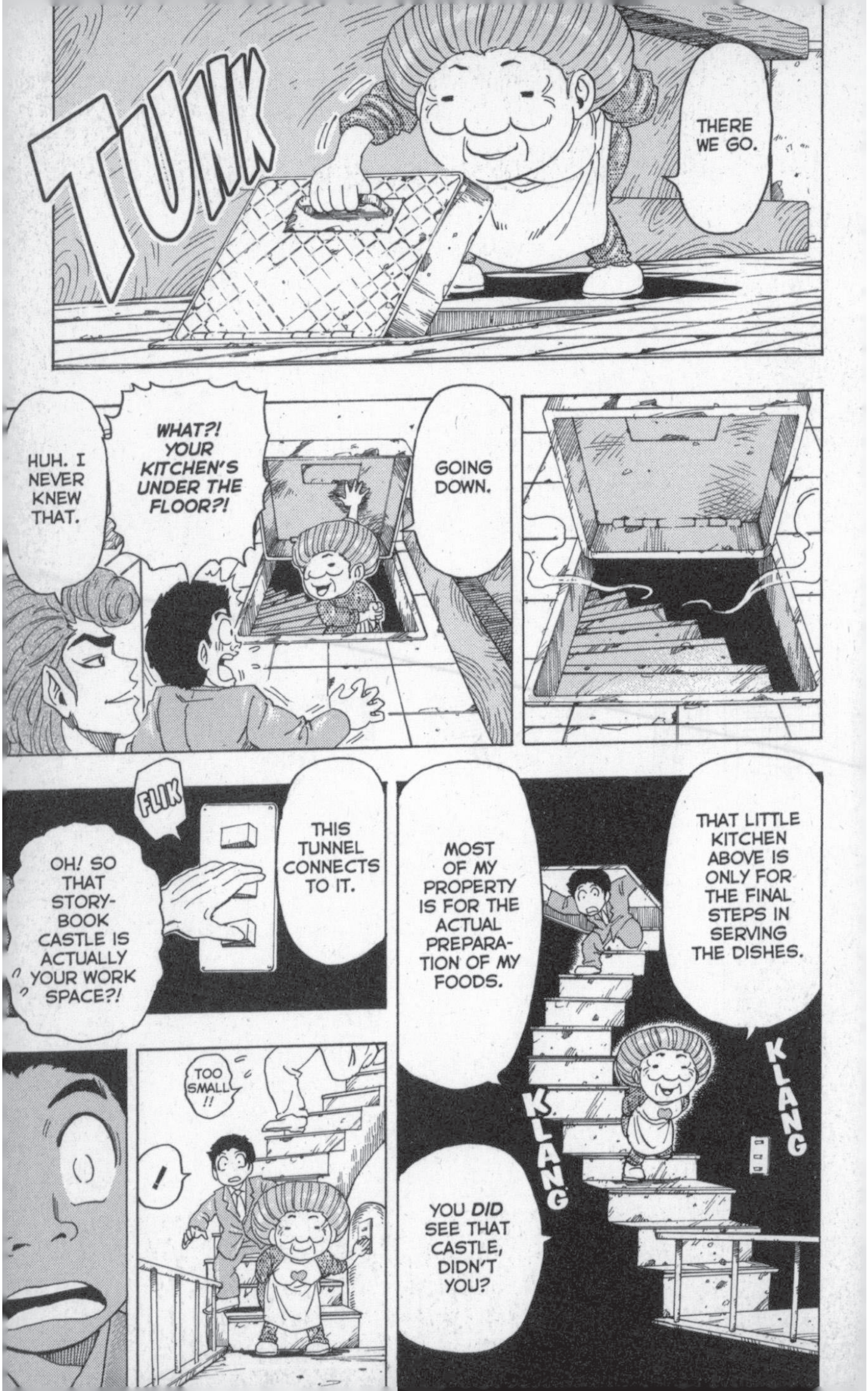
THERE WE GO.
TUNK
GOING DOWN.
WHAT?! YOUR KITCHEN'S UNDER THE FLOOR?!
HUH. I NEVER KNEW THAT.
THAT LITTLE KITCHEN ABOVE IS ONLY FOR THE FINAL STEPS IN SERVING THE DISHES.
MOST OF MY PROPERTY IS FOR THE ACTUAL PREPARATION OF MY FOODS.
KLANG
KLANG
KLANG
YOU *DID* SEE THAT CASTLE, DIDN'T YOU?
THIS TUNNEL CONNECTS TO IT.
FLIK
OH! SO THAT STORY-BOOK CASTLE IS ACTUALLY YOUR WORK SPACE?!
TOO SMALL!!
!

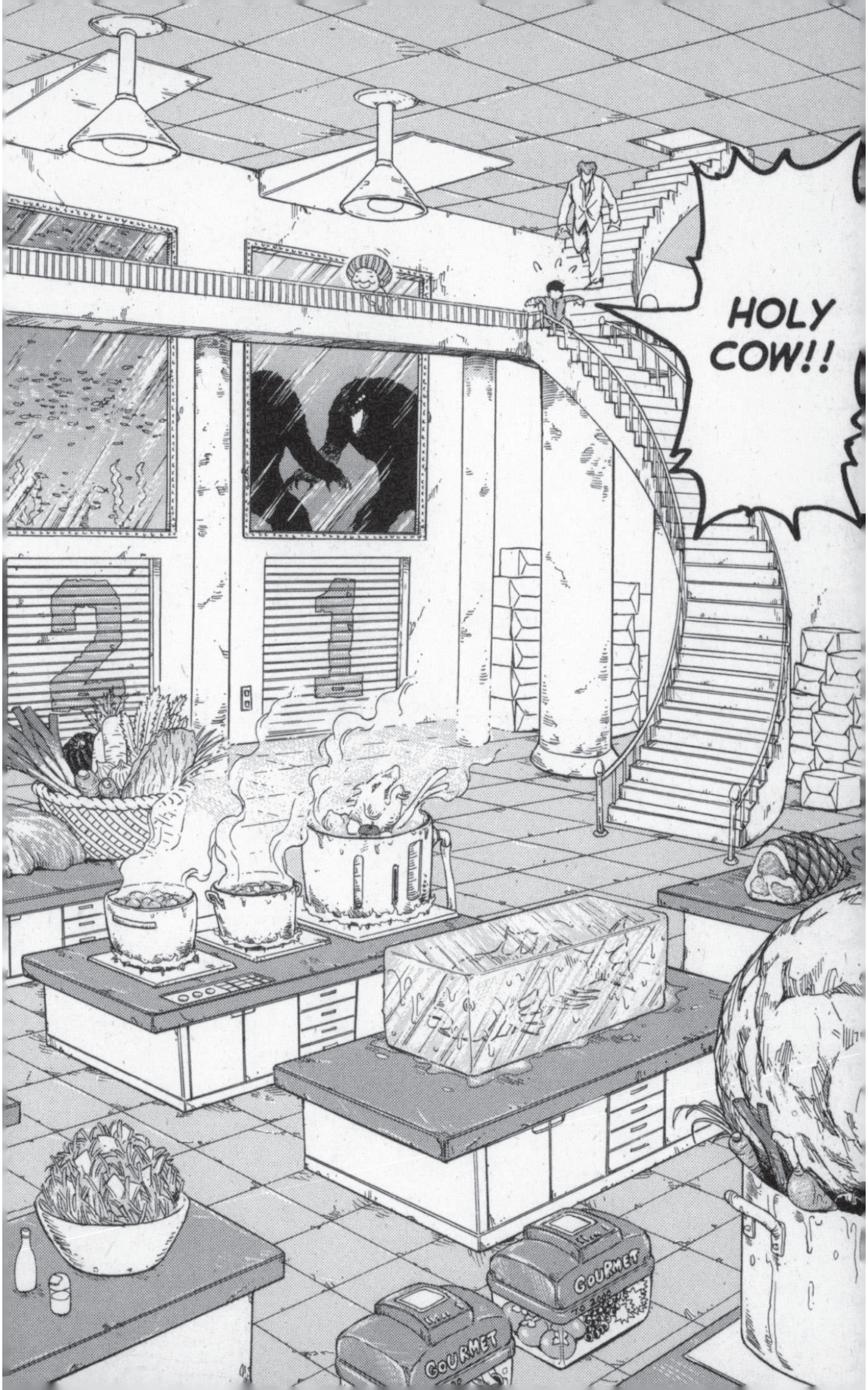
HOLY COW!!
GOURMET
GOURMET
GOURMET

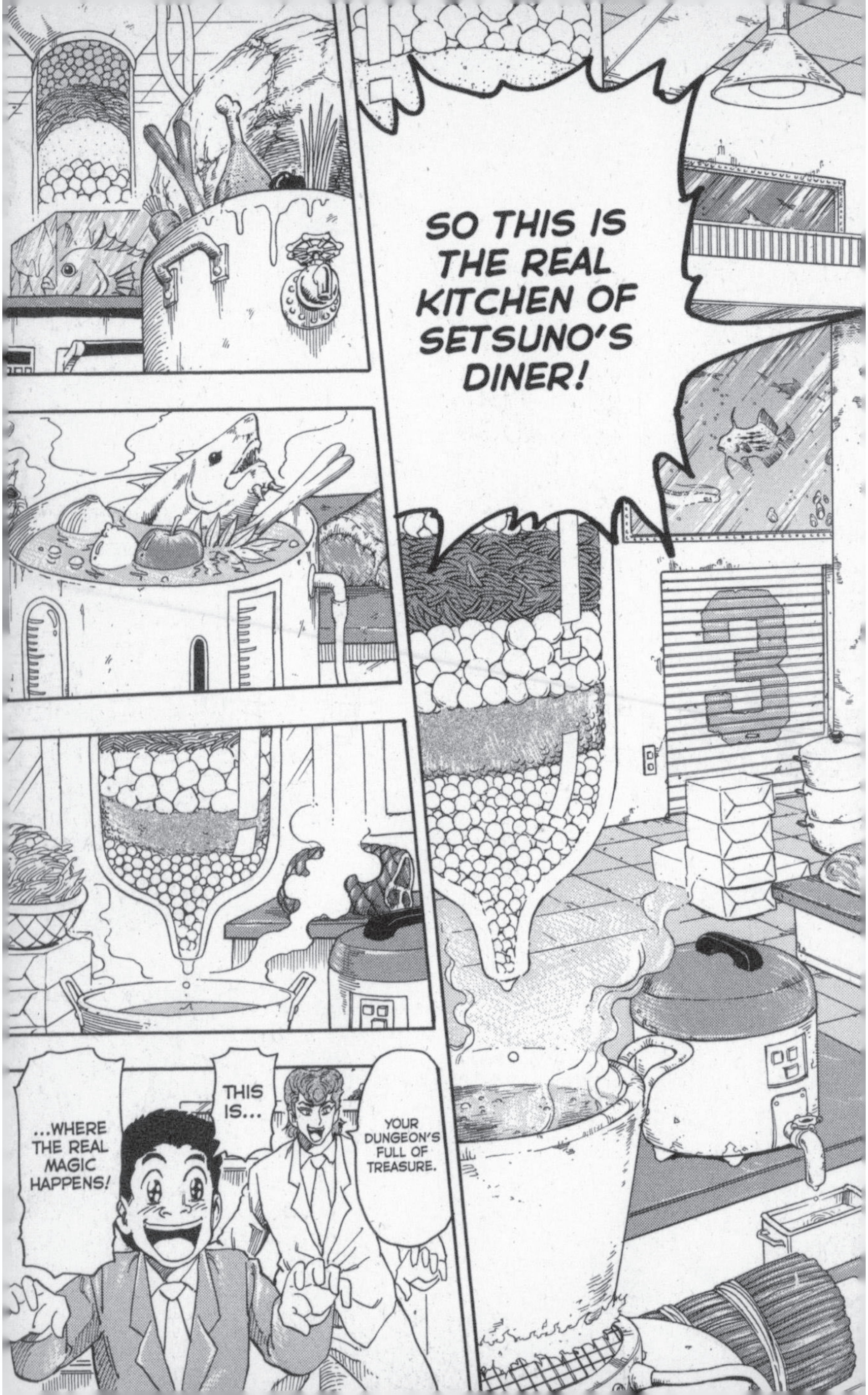
SO THIS IS THE REAL KITCHEN OF SETSUNO'S DINER!
YOUR DUNGEON'S FULL OF TREASURE.
THIS IS...
...WHERE THE REAL MAGIC HAPPENS!

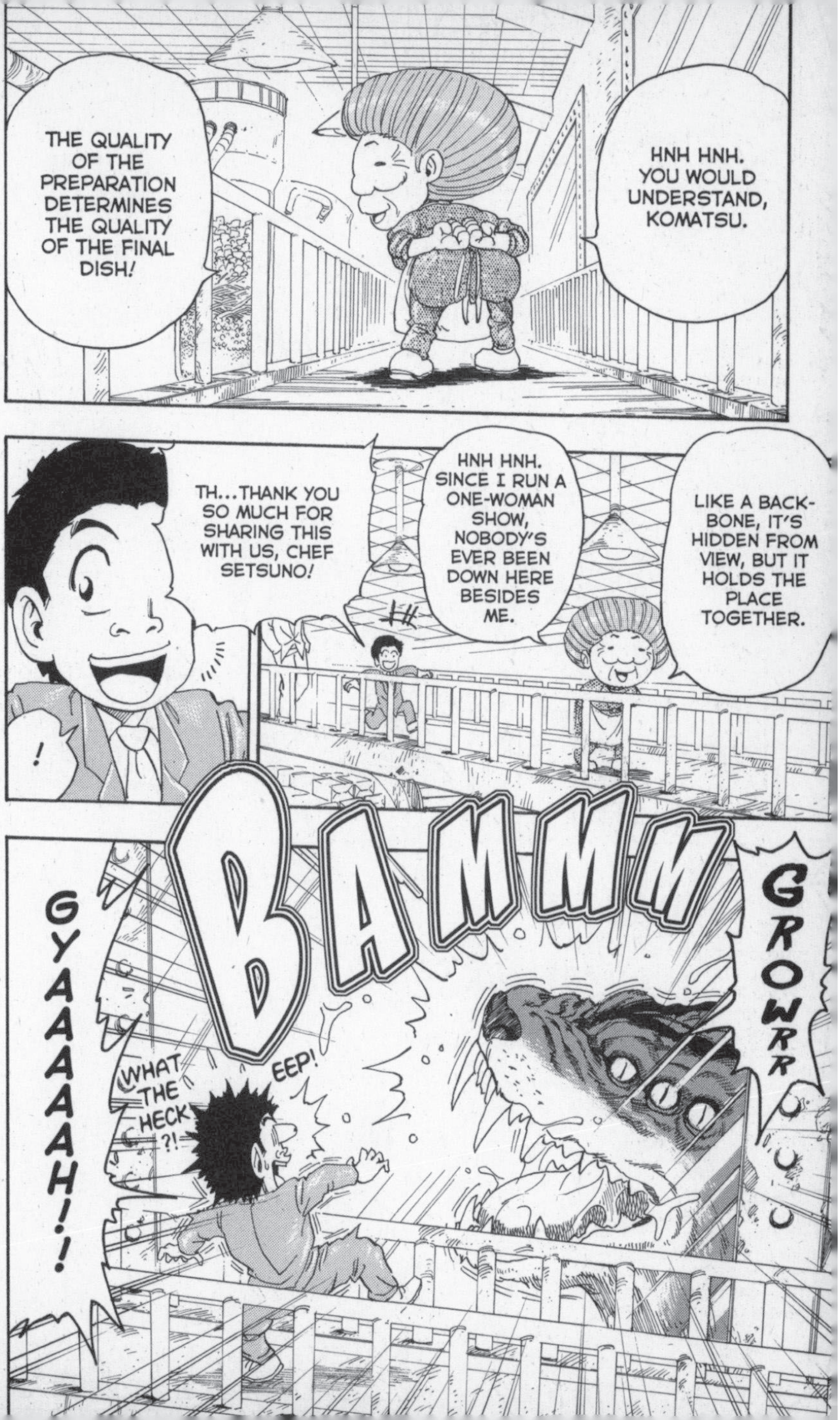
HNH HNH. YOU WOULD UNDERSTAND, KOMATSU.
THE QUALITY OF THE PREPARATION DETERMINES THE QUALITY OF THE FINAL DISH!
LIKE A BACK-BONE, IT'S HIDDEN FROM VIEW, BUT IT HOLDS THE PLACE TOGETHER.
HNH HNH. SINCE I RUN A ONE-WOMAN SHOW, NOBODY'S EVER BEEN DOWN HERE BESIDES ME.
TH...THANK YOU SO MUCH FOR SHARING THIS WITH US, CHEF SETSUNO!
!
GROWRR
BAMMMM
GYAAAAAAH!!
EEP!
WHAT THE HECK?!

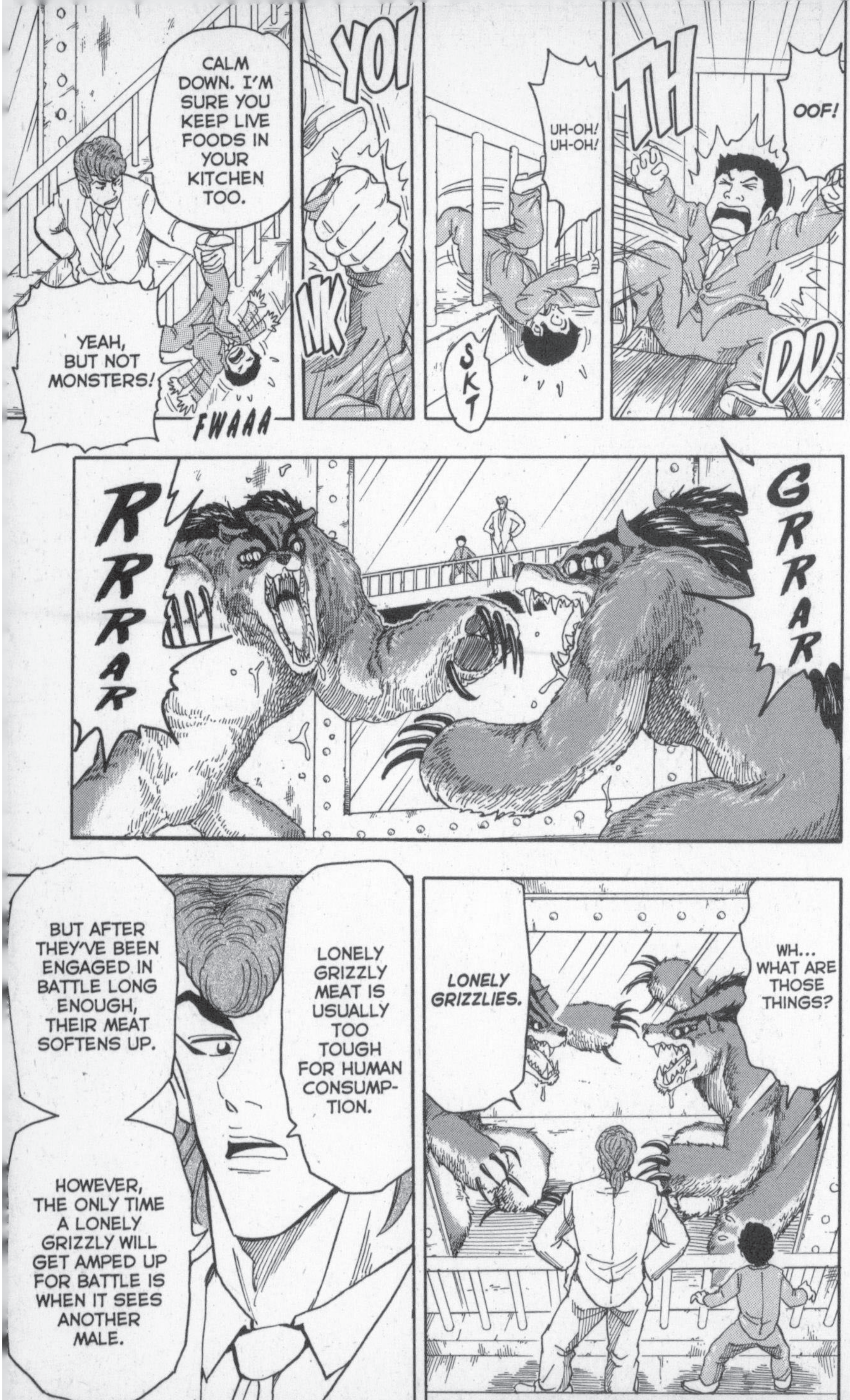
TH
OOF!
DD
UH-OH! UH-OH!
SKT
YOI
NK
CALM DOWN. I'M SURE YOU KEEP LIVE FOODS IN YOUR KITCHEN TOO.
YEAH, BUT NOT MONSTERS!
FWAAA
GRRAR
RRRRAR
WH... WHAT ARE THOSE THINGS?
LONELY GRIZZLIES.
LONELY GRIZZLY MEAT IS USUALLY TOO TOUGH FOR HUMAN CONSUMP-TION.
BUT AFTER THEY'VE BEEN ENGAGED IN BATTLE LONG ENOUGH, THEIR MEAT SOFTENS UP.
HOWEVER, THE ONLY TIME A LONELY GRIZZLY WILL GET AMPED UP FOR BATTLE IS WHEN IT SEES ANOTHER MALE.

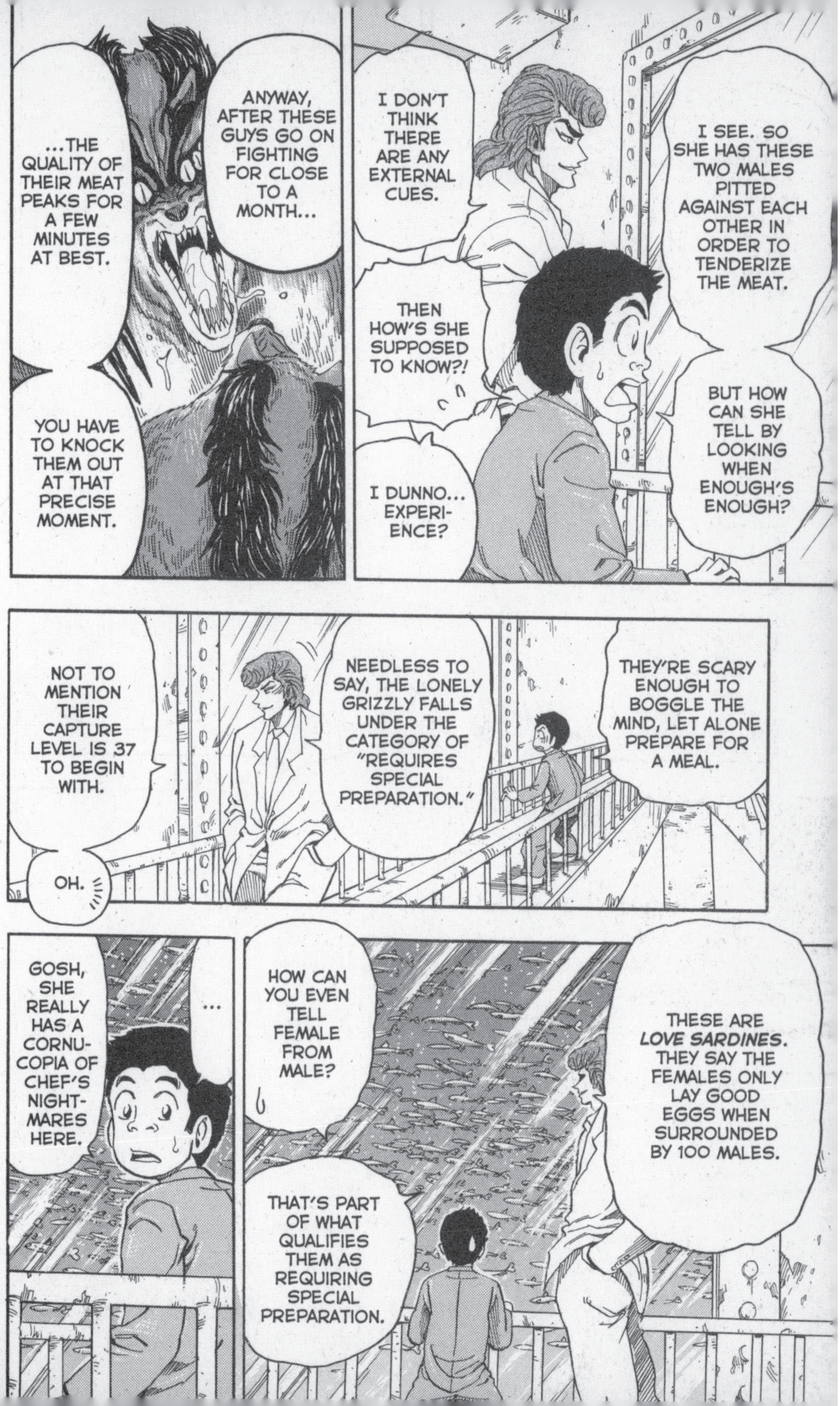
I SEE. SO SHE HAS THESE TWO MALES PITTED AGAINST EACH OTHER IN ORDER TO TENDERIZE THE MEAT.
BUT HOW CAN SHE TELL BY LOOKING WHEN ENOUGH'S ENOUGH?
I DON'T THINK THERE ARE ANY EXTERNAL CUES.
THEN HOW'S SHE SUPPOSED TO KNOW?!
I DUNNO... EXPERI-ENCE?
ANYWAY, AFTER THESE GUYS GO ON FIGHTING FOR CLOSE TO A MONTH...
...THE QUALITY OF THEIR MEAT PEAKS FOR A FEW MINUTES AT BEST.
YOU HAVE TO KNOCK THEM OUT AT THAT PRECISE MOMENT.
THEY'RE SCARY ENOUGH TO BOGGLE THE MIND, LET ALONE PREPARE FOR A MEAL.
NEEDLESS TO SAY, THE LONELY GRIZZLY FALLS UNDER THE CATEGORY OF "REQUIRES SPECIAL PREPARATION."
NOT TO MENTION THEIR CAPTURE LEVEL IS 37 TO BEGIN WITH.
OH.
THESE ARE *LOVE SARDINES*. THEY SAY THE FEMALES ONLY LAY GOOD EGGS WHEN SURROUNDED BY 100 MALES.
HOW CAN YOU EVEN TELL FEMALE FROM MALE?
...
THAT'S PART OF WHAT QUALIFIES THEM AS REQUIRING SPECIAL PREPARATION.
GOSH, SHE REALLY HAS A CORNU-COPIA OF CHEF'S NIGHT-MARES HERE.

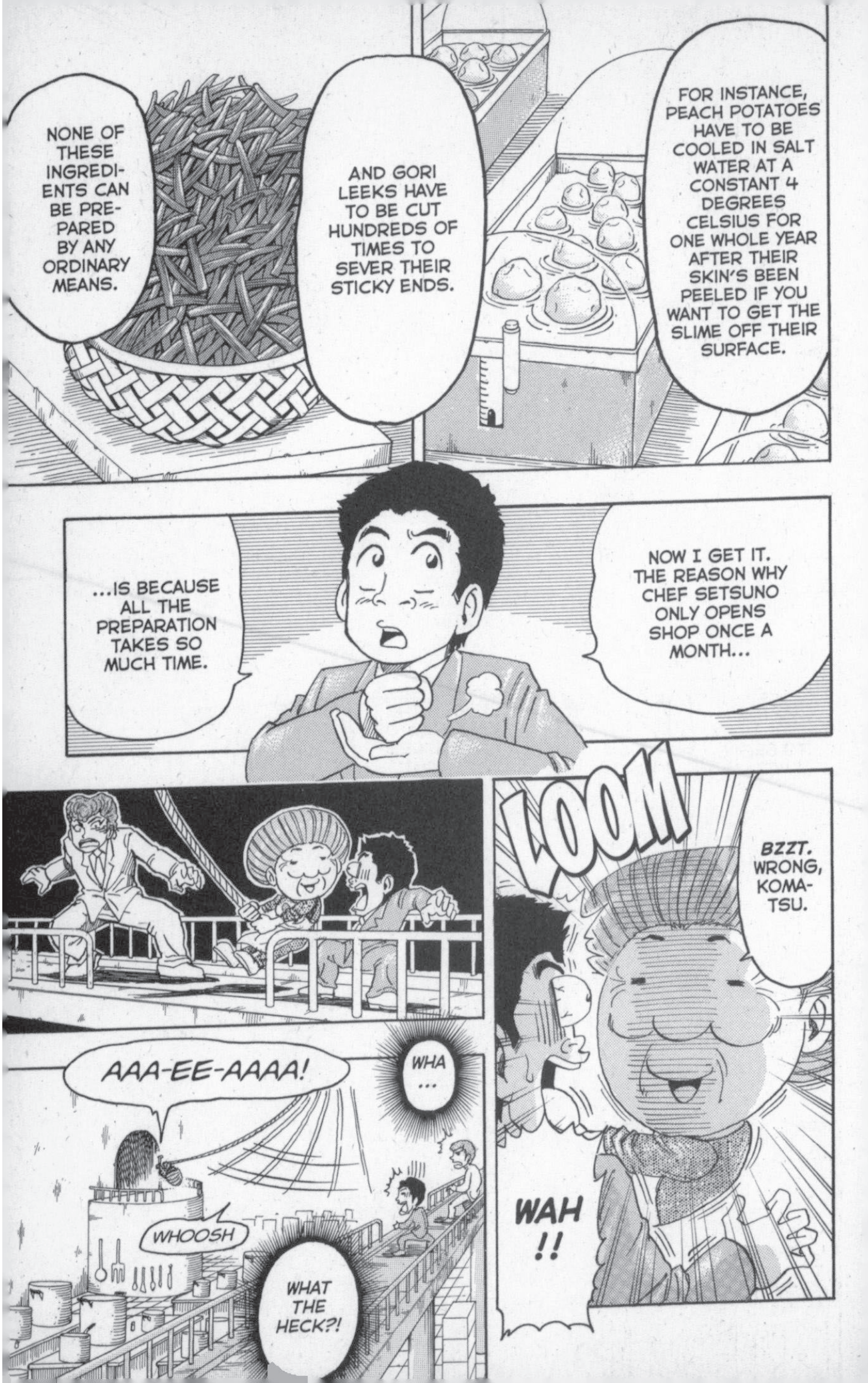

FOR INSTANCE, PEACH POTATOES HAVE TO BE COOLED IN SALT WATER AT A CONSTANT 4 DEGREES CELSIUS FOR ONE WHOLE YEAR AFTER THEIR SKIN'S BEEN PEELED IF YOU WANT TO GET THE SLIME OFF THEIR SURFACE.
AND GORI LEEKS HAVE TO BE CUT HUNDREDS OF TIMES TO SEVER THEIR STICKY ENDS.
NONE OF THESE INGREDI-ENTS CAN BE PRE-PARED BY ANY ORDINARY MEANS.
NOW I GET IT. THE REASON WHY CHEF SETSUNO ONLY OPENS SHOP ONCE A MONTH...
...IS BECAUSE ALL THE PREPARATION TAKES SO MUCH TIME.
LOOM
BZZT. WRONG, KOMA-TSU.
WAH !!
WHA ...
AAA-EE-AAAA!
WHOOSH
WHAT THE HECK?!

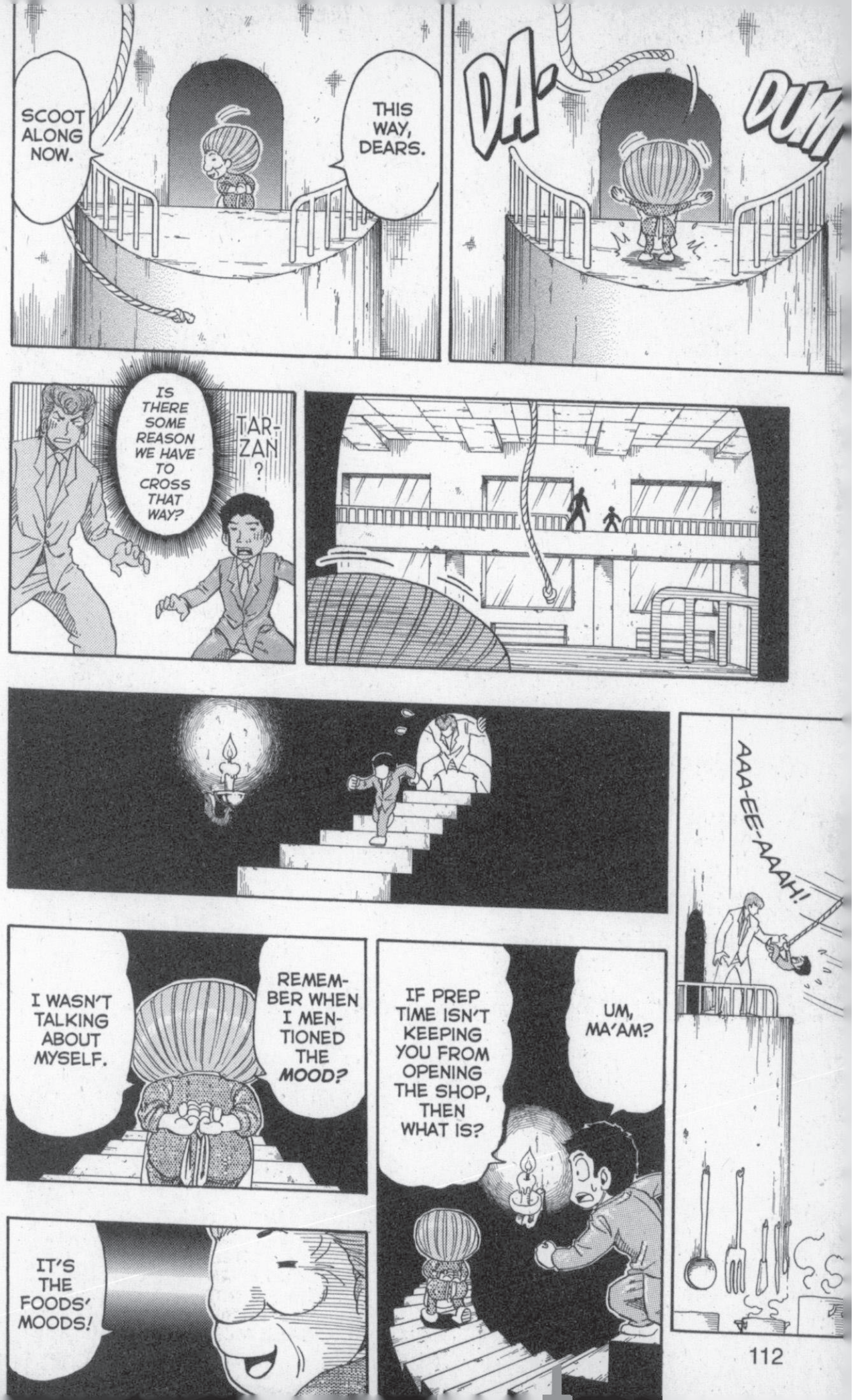
DA-DUM
THIS WAY, DEARS.
SCOOT ALONG NOW.
TAR-ZAN?
IS THERE SOME REASON WE HAVE TO CROSS THAT WAY?
AAA-EE-AAAH!
UM, MA'AM?
IF PREP TIME ISN'T KEEPING YOU FROM OPENING THE SHOP, THEN WHAT IS?
REMEMBER WHEN I MENTIONED THE *MOOD?*
I WASN'T TALKING ABOUT MYSELF.
IT'S THE FOODS' MOODS!

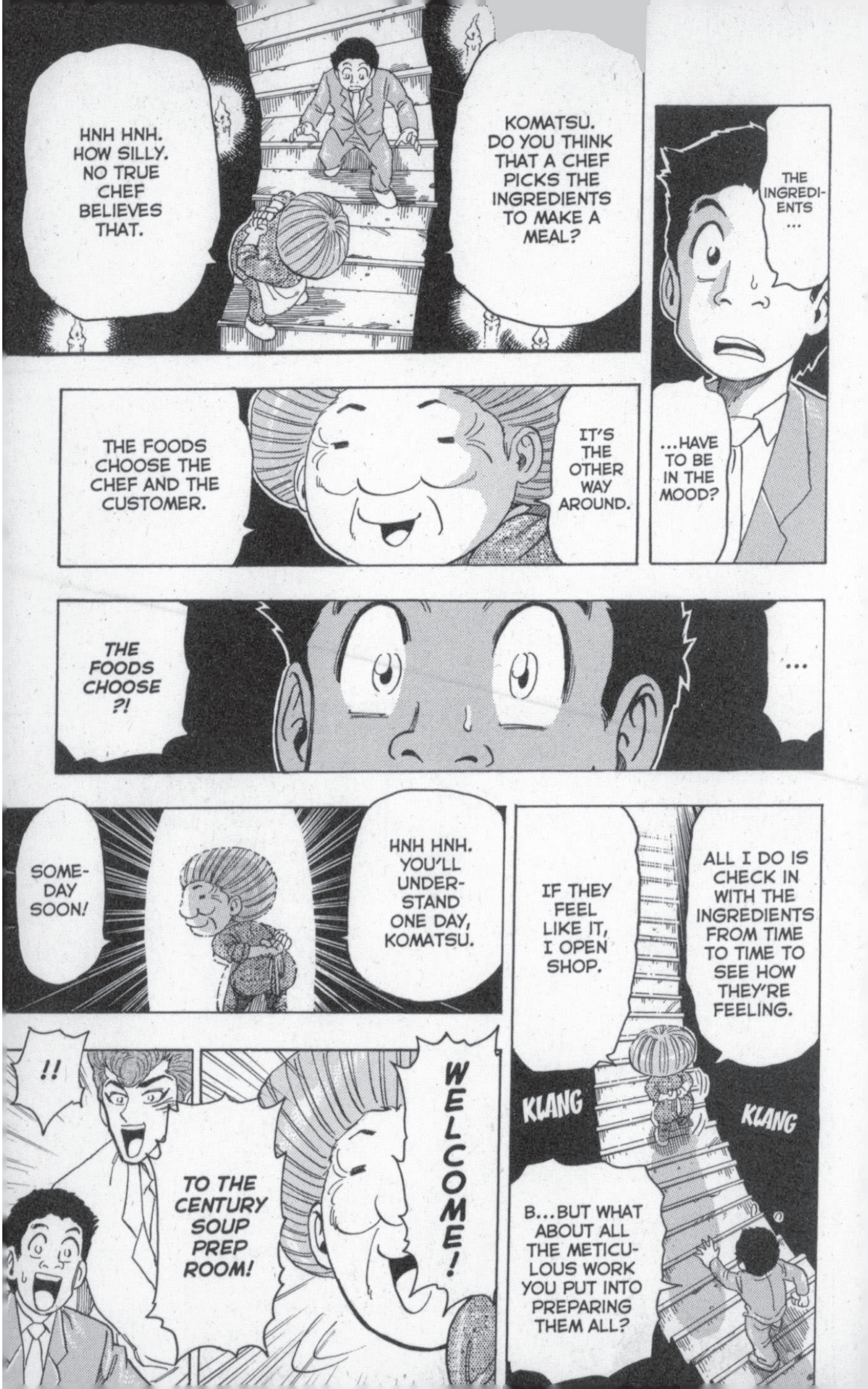
THE INGREDI-ENTS ...
...HAVE TO BE IN THE MOOD?
KOMATSU. DO YOU THINK THAT A CHEF PICKS THE INGREDIENTS TO MAKE A MEAL?
HNH HNH. HOW SILLY. NO TRUE CHEF BELIEVES THAT.
IT'S THE OTHER WAY AROUND.
THE FOODS CHOOSE THE CHEF AND THE CUSTOMER.
...
THE FOODS CHOOSE ?!
ALL I DO IS CHECK IN WITH THE INGREDIENTS FROM TIME TO TIME TO SEE HOW THEY'RE FEELING.
IF THEY FEEL LIKE IT, I OPEN SHOP.
KLANG
KLANG
B...BUT WHAT ABOUT ALL THE METICU-LOUS WORK YOU PUT INTO PREPARING THEM ALL?
HNH HNH. YOU'LL UNDER-STAND ONE DAY, KOMATSU.
SOME-DAY SOON!
WELCOME!
!!
TO THE CENTURY SOUP PREP ROOM!

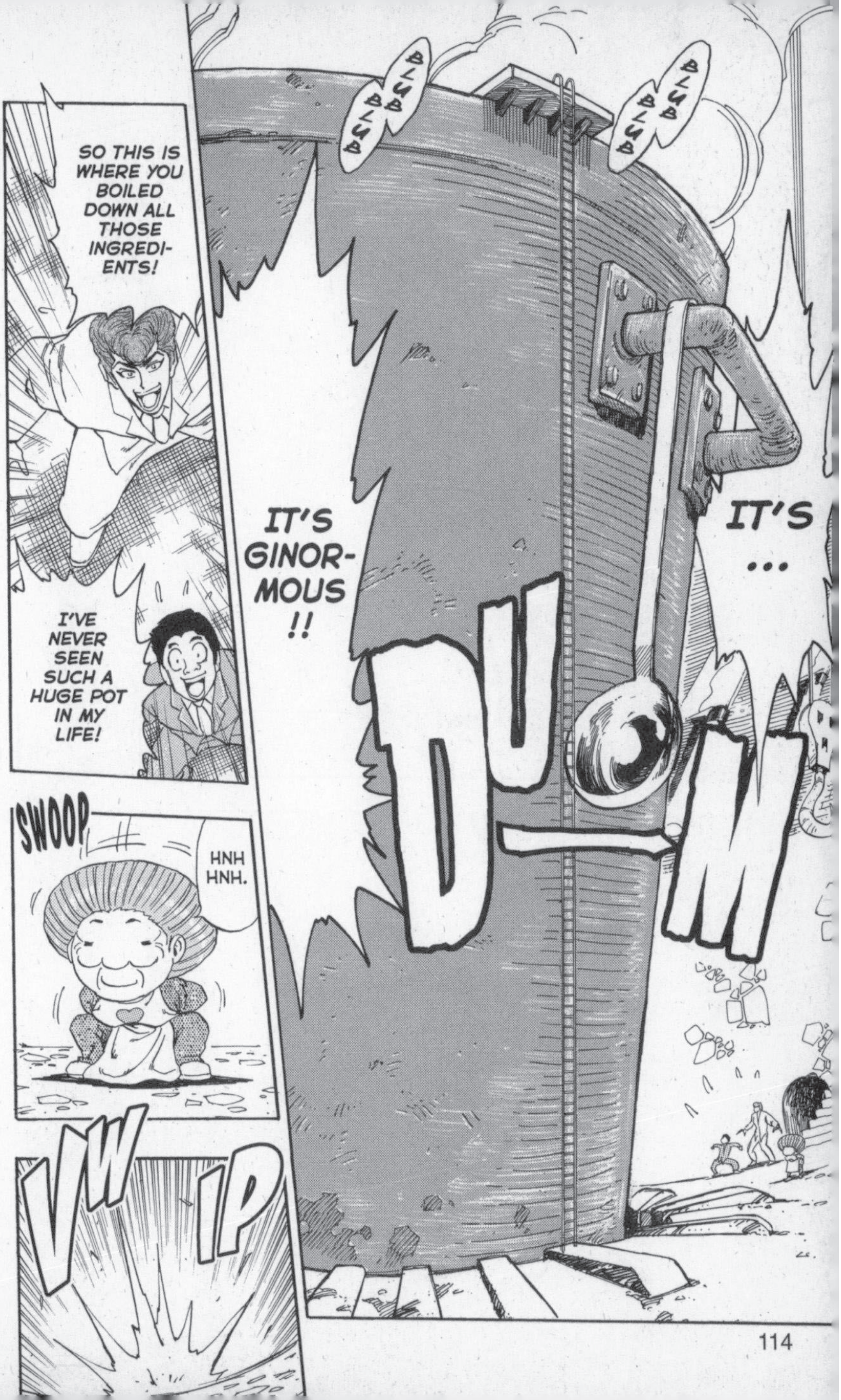
BLUB BLUB BLUB
BLUB BLUB BLUB
IT'S ...
IT'S GINORMOUS!!
DUOM
SO THIS IS WHERE YOU BOILED DOWN ALL THOSE INGREDI-ENTS!
I'VE NEVER SEEN SUCH A HUGE POT IN MY LIFE!
SWOOP
HNH HNH.
VWIP

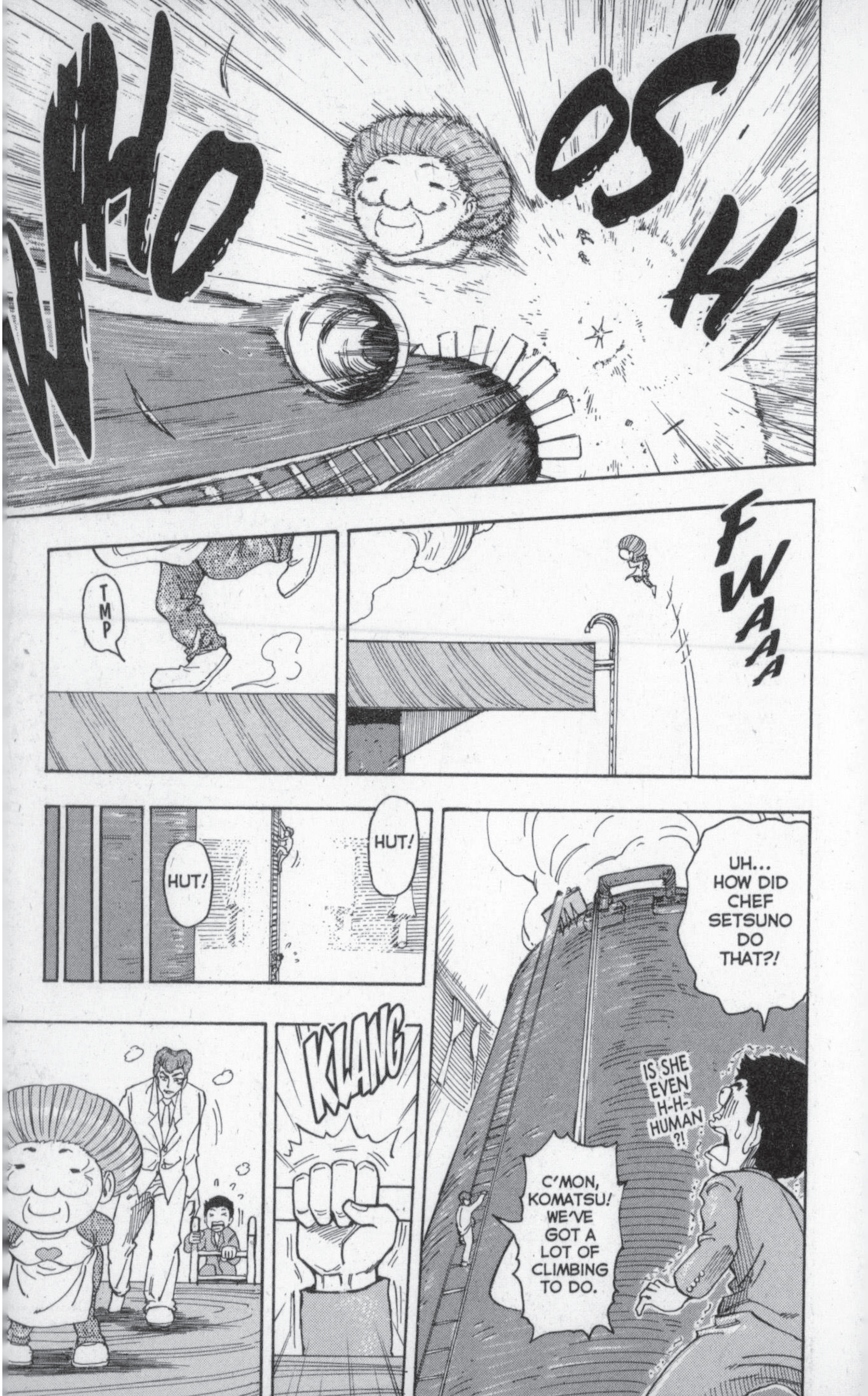
WHOOSH
FWAAA
TMP
UH... HOW DID CHEF SETSUNO DO THAT?!
IS SHE EVEN H-H-HUMAN?!
C'MON, KOMATSU! WE'VE GOT A LOT OF CLIMBING TO DO.
HUT!
HUT!
KLANG

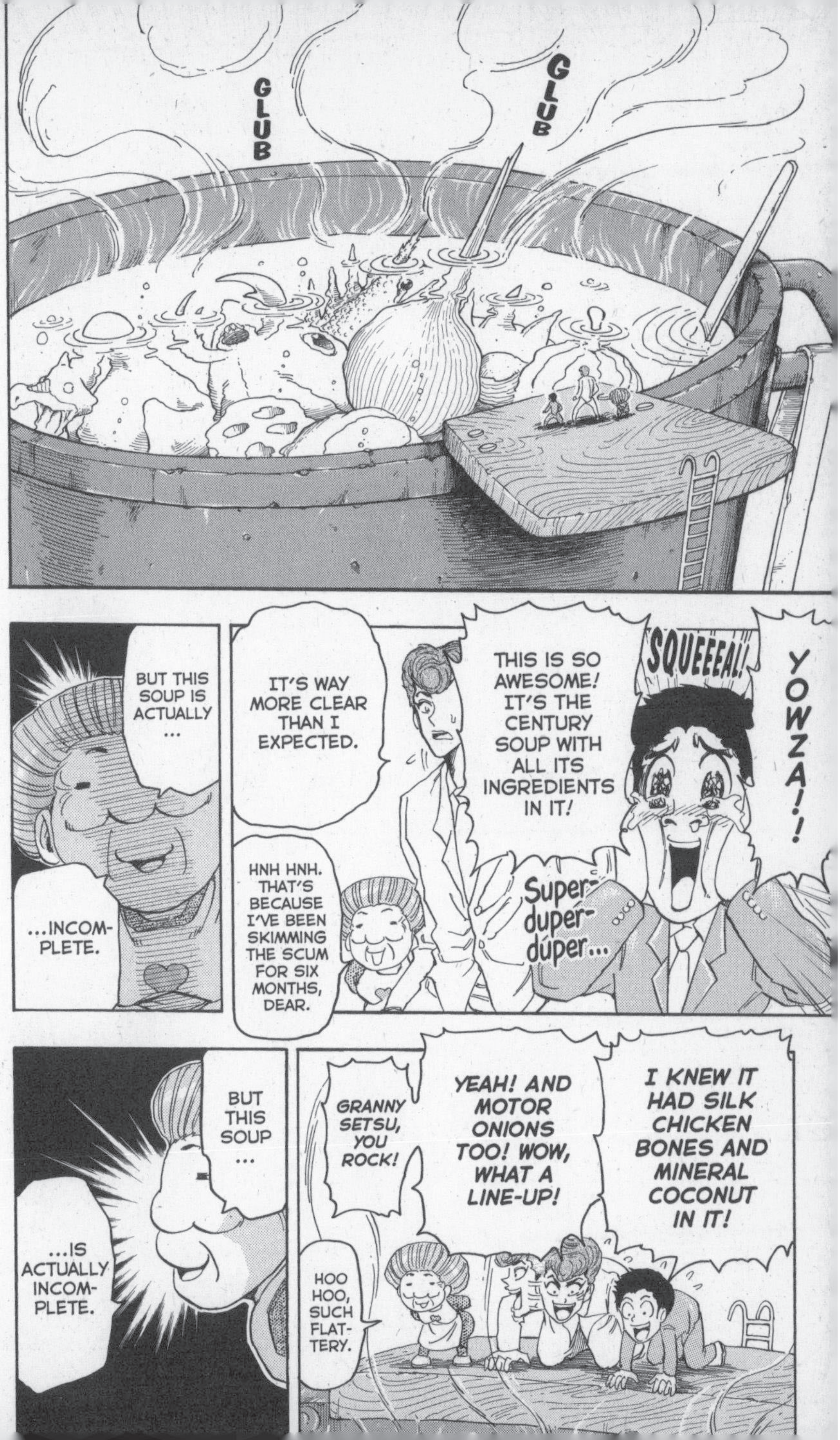
GLUB
GLUB
YOWZA!!
SQUEEEAL!
THIS IS SO AWESOME! IT'S THE CENTURY SOUP WITH ALL ITS INGREDIENTS IN IT!
Super-duper-duper...
IT'S WAY MORE CLEAR THAN I EXPECTED.
HNH HNH. THAT'S BECAUSE I'VE BEEN SKIMMING THE SCUM FOR SIX MONTHS, DEAR.
BUT THIS SOUP IS ACTUALLY ...
...INCOMPLETE.
I KNEW IT HAD SILK CHICKEN BONES AND MINERAL COCONUT IN IT!
YEAH! AND MOTOR ONIONS TOO! WOW, WHAT A LINE-UP!
GRANNY SETSU, YOU ROCK!
HOO HOO, SUCH FLATTERY.
BUT THIS SOUP ...
...IS ACTUALLY INCOMPLETE.

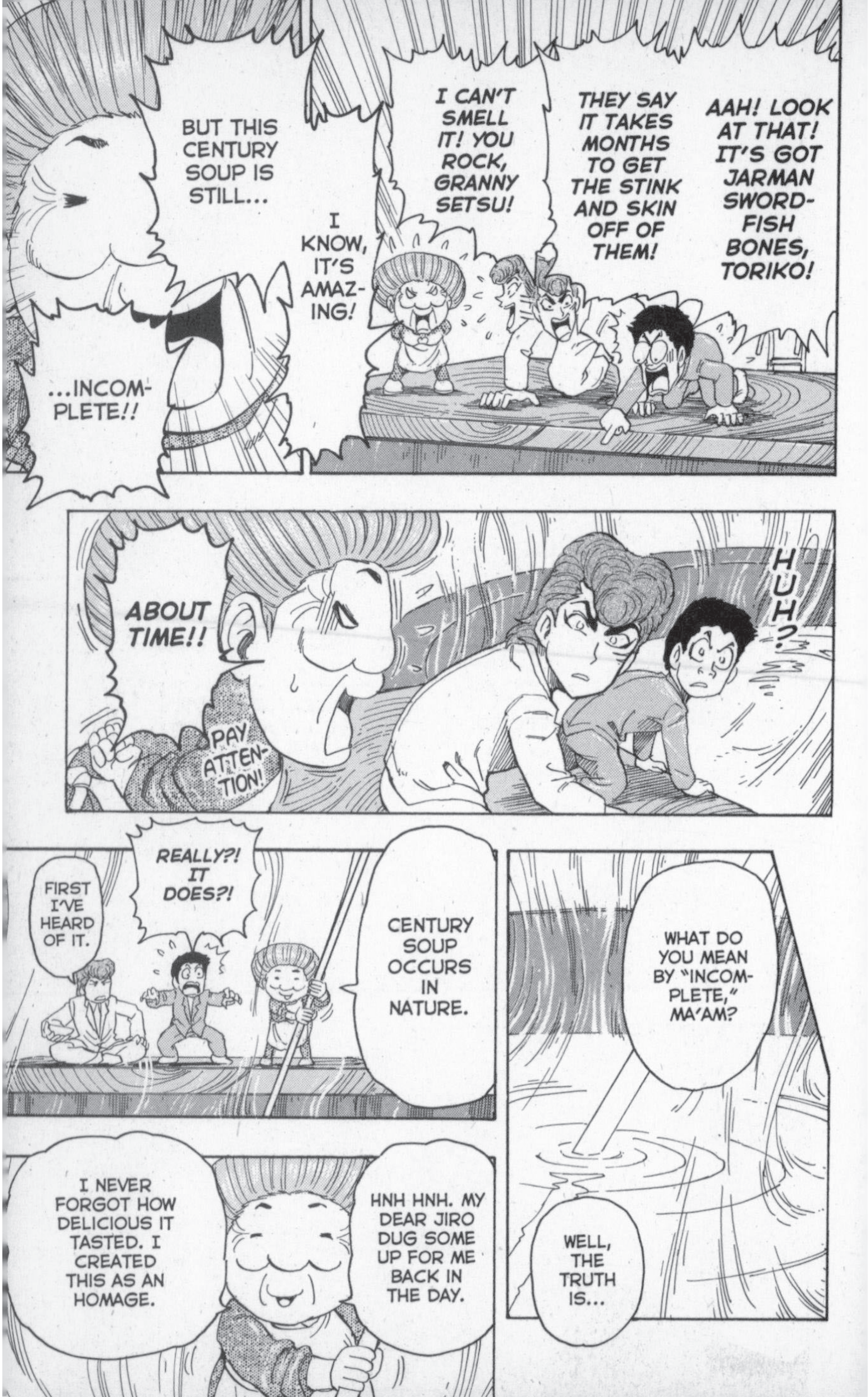
AAH! LOOK AT THAT! IT'S GOT JARMAN SWORDFISH BONES, TORIKO!
THEY SAY IT TAKES MONTHS TO GET THE STINK AND SKIN OFF OF THEM!
I CAN'T SMELL IT! YOU ROCK, GRANNY SETSU!
I KNOW, IT'S AMAZING!
BUT THIS CENTURY SOUP IS STILL...
...INCOMPLETE!!
HUH?
ABOUT TIME!!
PAY ATTENTION!
WHAT DO YOU MEAN BY "INCOMPLETE," MA'AM?
WELL, THE TRUTH IS...
CENTURY SOUP OCCURS IN NATURE.
REALLY?! IT DOES?!
FIRST I'VE HEARD OF IT.
HNH HNH. MY DEAR JIRO DUG SOME UP FOR ME BACK IN THE DAY.
I NEVER FORGOT HOW DELICIOUS IT TASTED. I CREATED THIS AS AN HOMAGE.

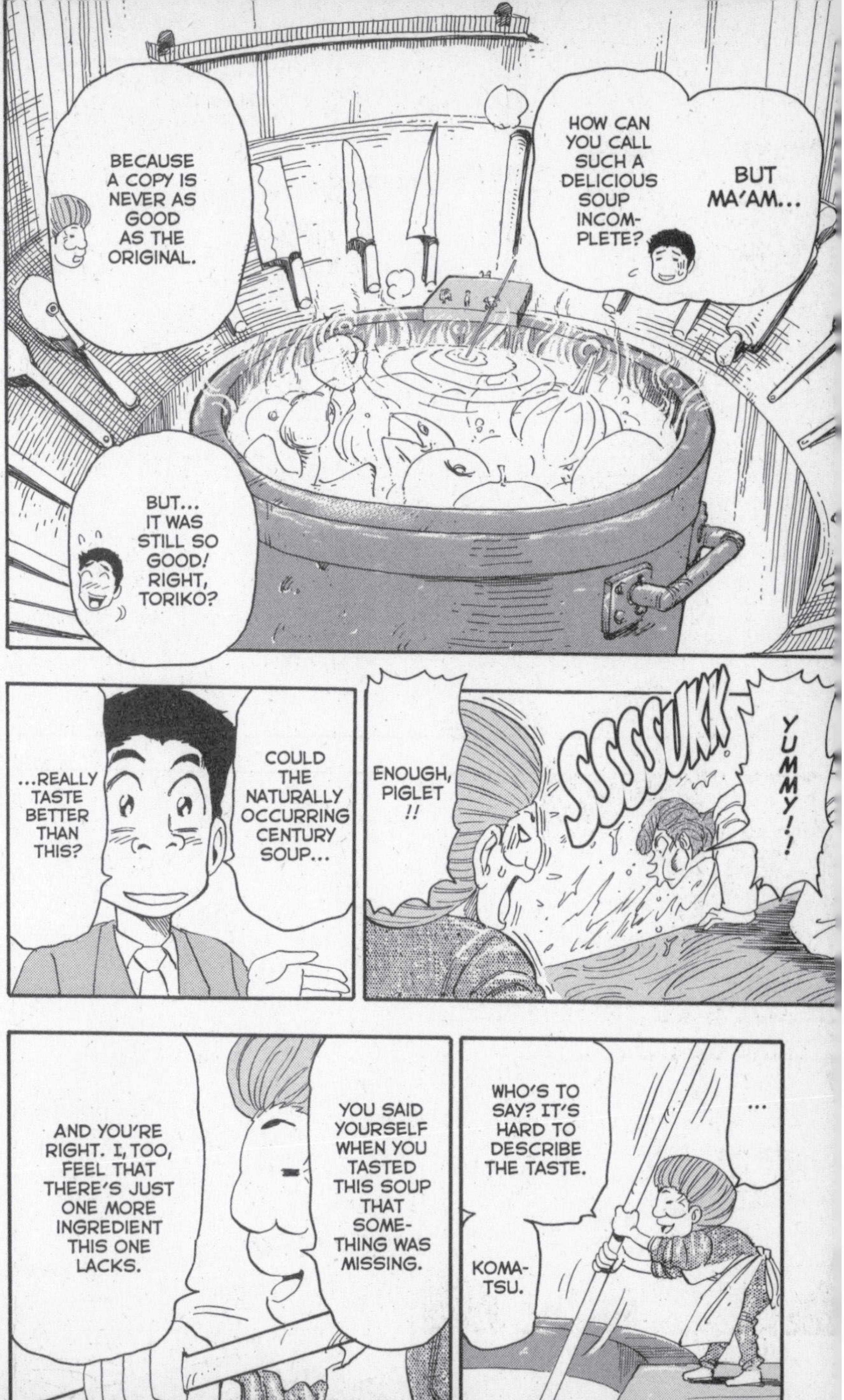
BUT MA'AM...
HOW CAN YOU CALL SUCH A DELICIOUS SOUP INCOMPLETE?
BECAUSE A COPY IS NEVER AS GOOD AS THE ORIGINAL.
BUT... IT WAS STILL SO GOOD! RIGHT, TORIKO?
YUMMY!!
SSSSUKK
ENOUGH, PIGLET!!
COULD THE NATURALLY OCCURRING CENTURY SOUP...
...REALLY TASTE BETTER THAN THIS?
...
WHO'S TO SAY? IT'S HARD TO DESCRIBE THE TASTE.
KOMATSU.
YOU SAID YOURSELF WHEN YOU TASTED THIS SOUP THAT SOMETHING WAS MISSING.
AND YOU'RE RIGHT. I, TOO, FEEL THAT THERE'S JUST ONE MORE INGREDIENT THIS ONE LACKS.

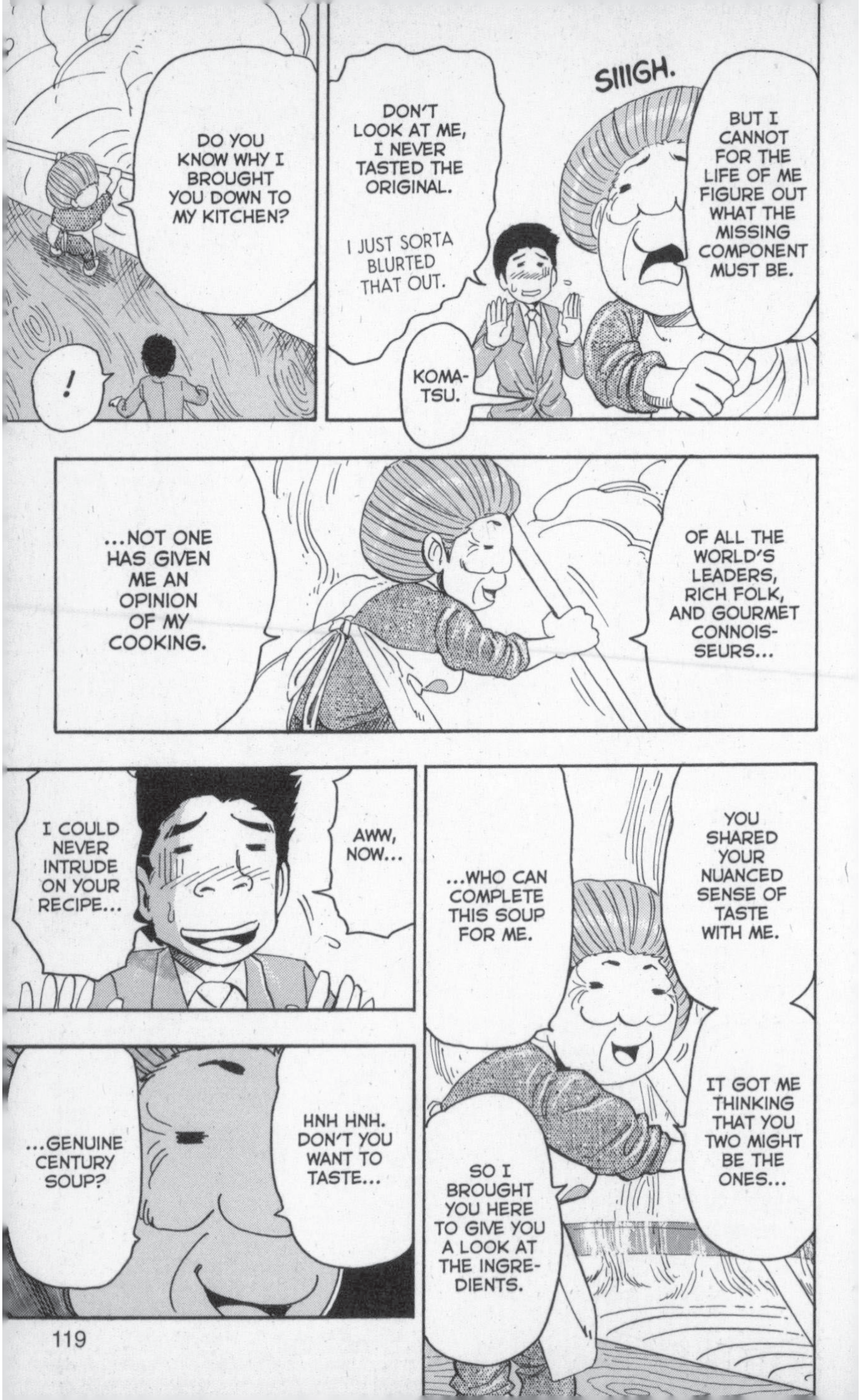
SIIIGH.
BUT I CANNOT FOR THE LIFE OF ME FIGURE OUT WHAT THE MISSING COMPONENT MUST BE.
DON'T LOOK AT ME, I NEVER TASTED THE ORIGINAL.
I JUST SORTA BLURTED THAT OUT.
KOMA-TSU.
DO YOU KNOW WHY I BROUGHT YOU DOWN TO MY KITCHEN?
!
OF ALL THE WORLD'S LEADERS, RICH FOLK, AND GOURMET CONNOIS-SEURS...
...NOT ONE HAS GIVEN ME AN OPINION OF MY COOKING.
YOU SHARED YOUR NUANCED SENSE OF TASTE WITH ME.
IT GOT ME THINKING THAT YOU TWO MIGHT BE THE ONES...
...WHO CAN COMPLETE THIS SOUP FOR ME.
SO I BROUGHT YOU HERE TO GIVE YOU A LOOK AT THE INGRE-DIENTS.
AWW, NOW...
I COULD NEVER INTRUDE ON YOUR RECIPE...
HNH HNH. DON'T YOU WANT TO TASTE...
...GENUINE CENTURY SOUP?

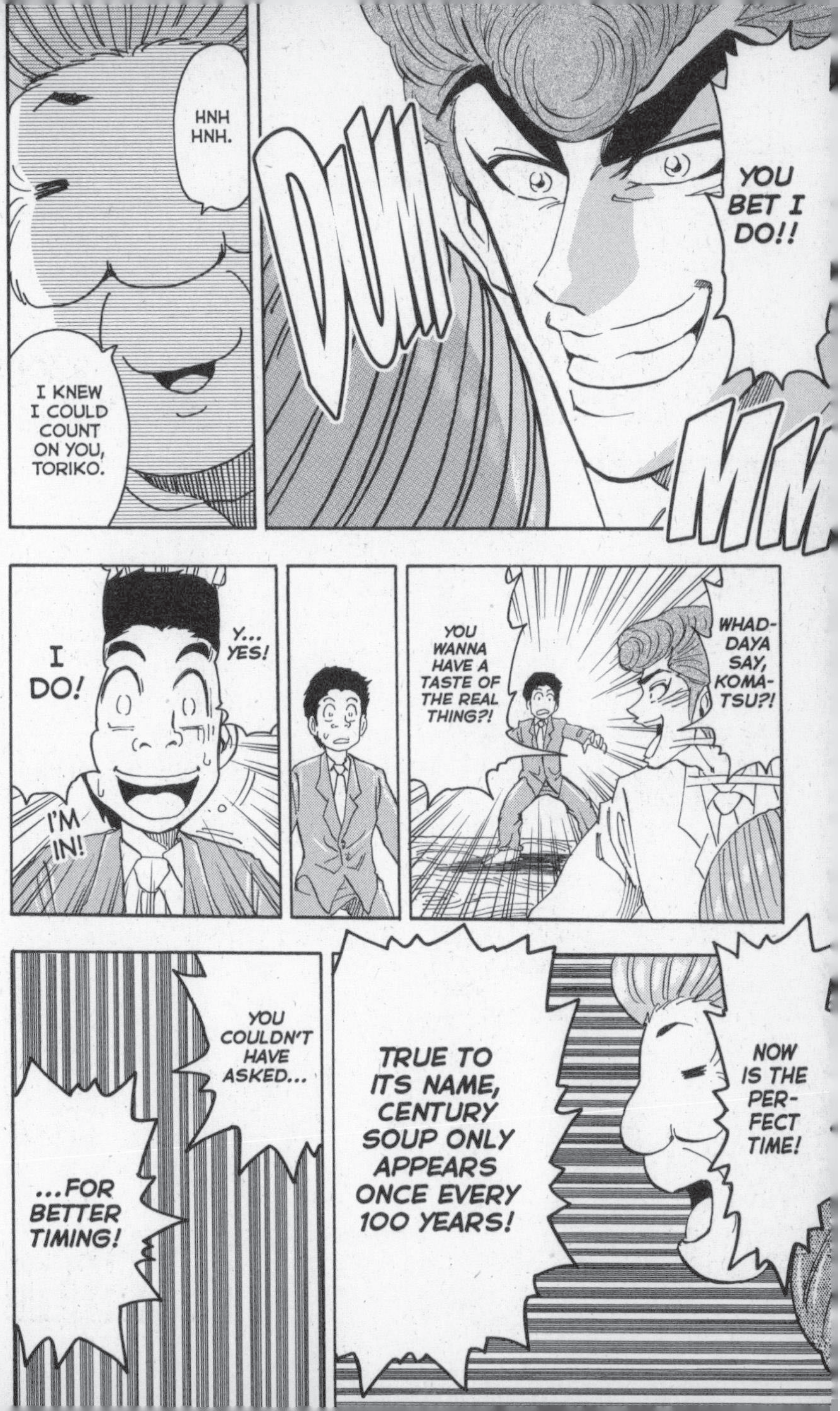
YOU BET I DO!!
DUMMM
HNH HNH.
I KNEW I COULD COUNT ON YOU, TORIKO.
WHAD-DAYA SAY, KOMA-TSU?!
YOU WANNA HAVE A TASTE OF THE REAL THING?!
Y... YES!
I DO!
I'M IN!
NOW IS THE PER-FECT TIME!
TRUE TO ITS NAME, CENTURY SOUP ONLY APPEARS ONCE EVERY 100 YEARS!
YOU COULDN'T HAVE ASKED...
...FOR BETTER TIMING!

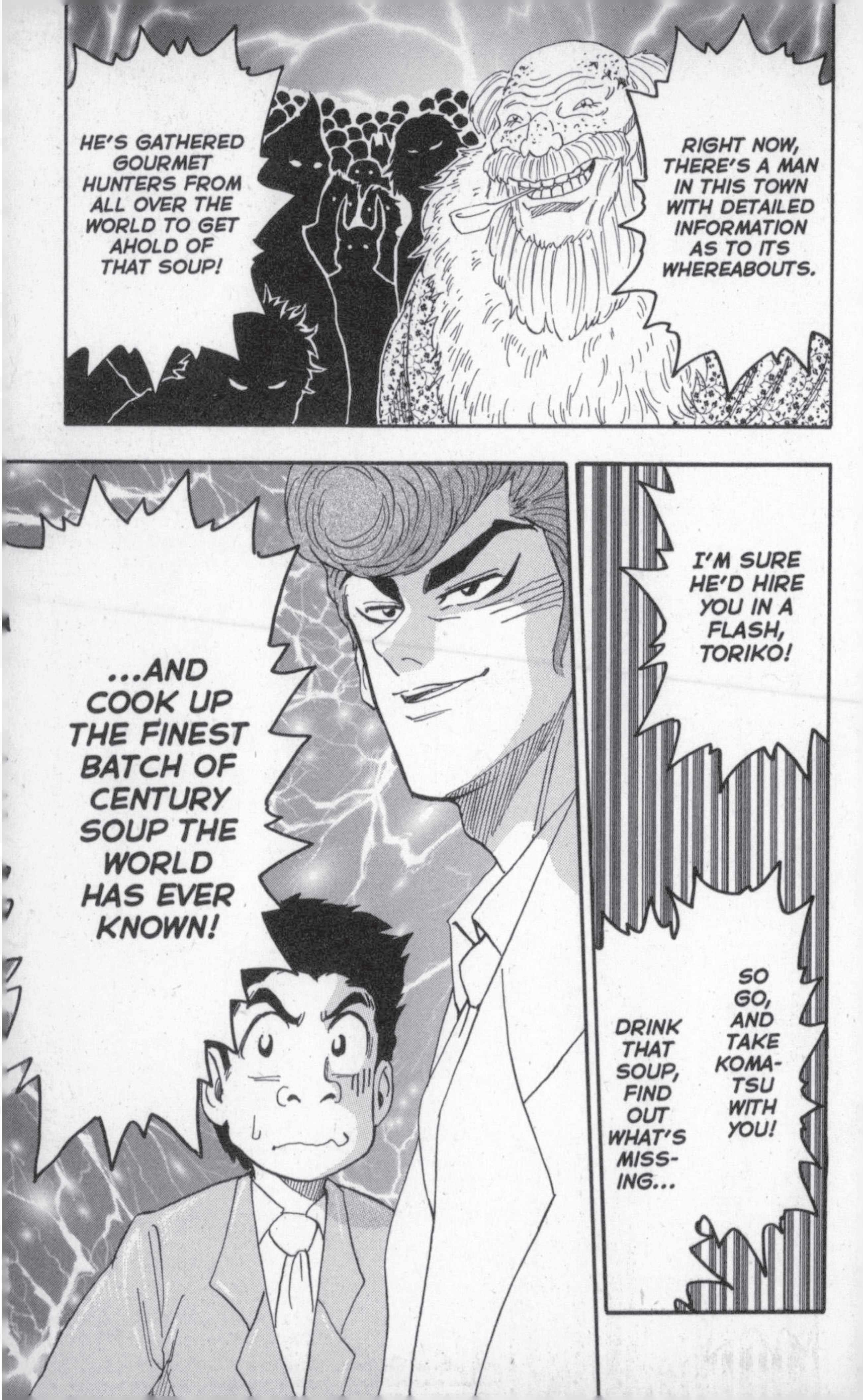
RIGHT NOW, THERE'S A MAN IN THIS TOWN WITH DETAILED INFORMATION AS TO ITS WHEREABOUTS.
HE'S GATHERED GOURMET HUNTERS FROM ALL OVER THE WORLD TO GET AHOLD OF THAT SOUP!
I'M SURE HE'D HIRE YOU IN A FLASH, TORIKO!
SO GO, AND TAKE KOMATSU WITH YOU!
DRINK THAT SOUP, FIND OUT WHAT'S MISSING...
...AND COOK UP THE FINEST BATCH OF CENTURY SOUP THE WORLD HAS EVER KNOWN!

TORIKO
GOURMET CHECKLIST
Vol. 054

PURPLE HORN
(MAMMAL)

CAPTURE LEVEL: 7

HABITAT: FORESTS AND PLAINS

LENGTH: 8.5 METERS

HEIGHT: 8 METERS

WEIGHT: 4 TONS

PRICE: MEAT IS NOT FIT FOR CONSUMPTION, BUT EACH HORN GOES FOR 800,000 YEN

SCALE

BELLIGERENT AND SAVAGE, A PURPLE HORN WILL RAMPAGE IF IT LOSES ITS PRIZED HORNS, DESTROYING EVERYTHING IN ITS PATH UNTIL ITS RAGE SUBSIDES. WHILE ON A RAMPAGE, THIS CENTAUR IS INTIMIDATING ENOUGH TO SEND EVEN CREATURES WITH CAPTURE LEVELS HIGHER THAN ITS OWN RUNNING FOR THE HILLS.

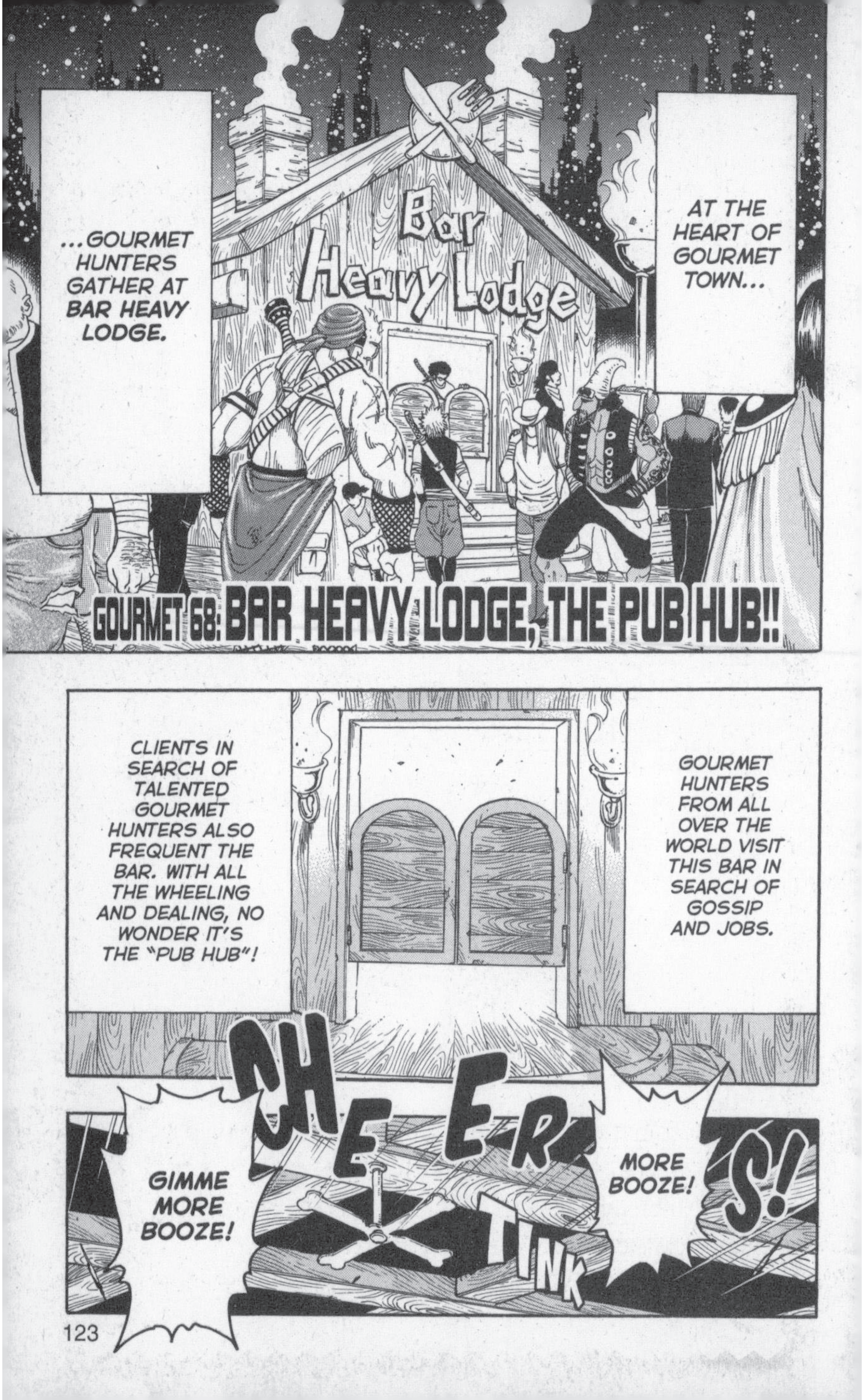
AT THE HEART OF GOURMET TOWN...
...GOURMET HUNTERS GATHER AT BAR HEAVY LODGE.
Bar Heavy Lodge
GOURMET 68: BAR HEAVY LODGE, THE PUB HUB!!
GOURMET HUNTERS FROM ALL OVER THE WORLD VISIT THIS BAR IN SEARCH OF GOSSIP AND JOBS.
CLIENTS IN SEARCH OF TALENTED GOURMET HUNTERS ALSO FREQUENT THE BAR. WITH ALL THE WHEELING AND DEALING, NO WONDER IT'S THE "PUB HUB"!
CHEERS!
MORE BOOZE!
GIMME MORE BOOZE!
TINK

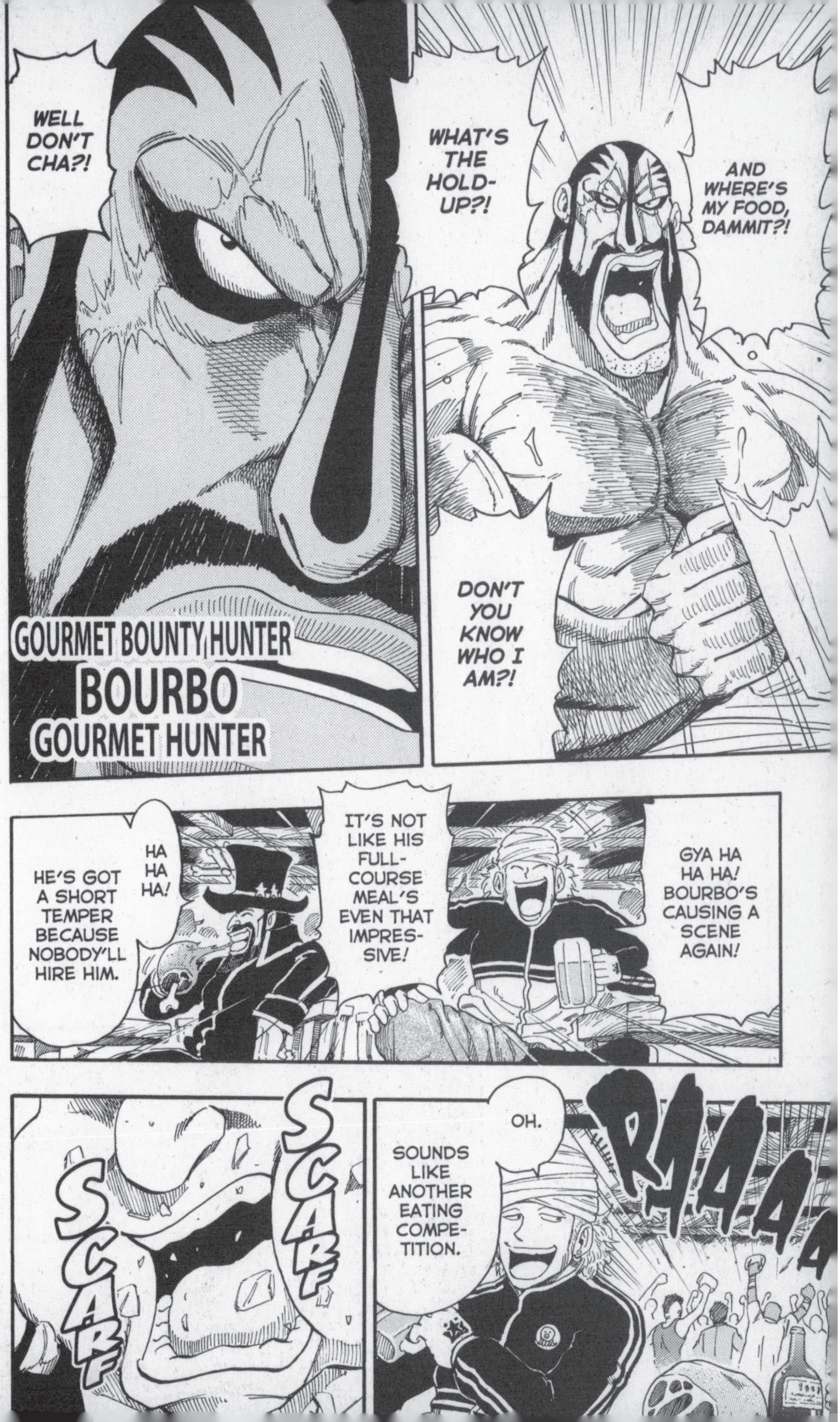
AND WHERE'S MY FOOD, DAMMIT?!
WHAT'S THE HOLD-UP?!
DON'T YOU KNOW WHO I AM?!
WELL DON'T CHA?!
GOURMET BOUNTY HUNTER
BOURBO
GOURMET HUNTER
GYA HA HA HA! BOURBO'S CAUSING A SCENE AGAIN!
IT'S NOT LIKE HIS FULL-COURSE MEAL'S EVEN THAT IMPRESSIVE!
HA HA HA!
HE'S GOT A SHORT TEMPER BECAUSE NOBODY'LL HIRE HIM.
RAAAA
OH.
SOUNDS LIKE ANOTHER EATING COMPETITION.
SCARF
SCARF
SCARF

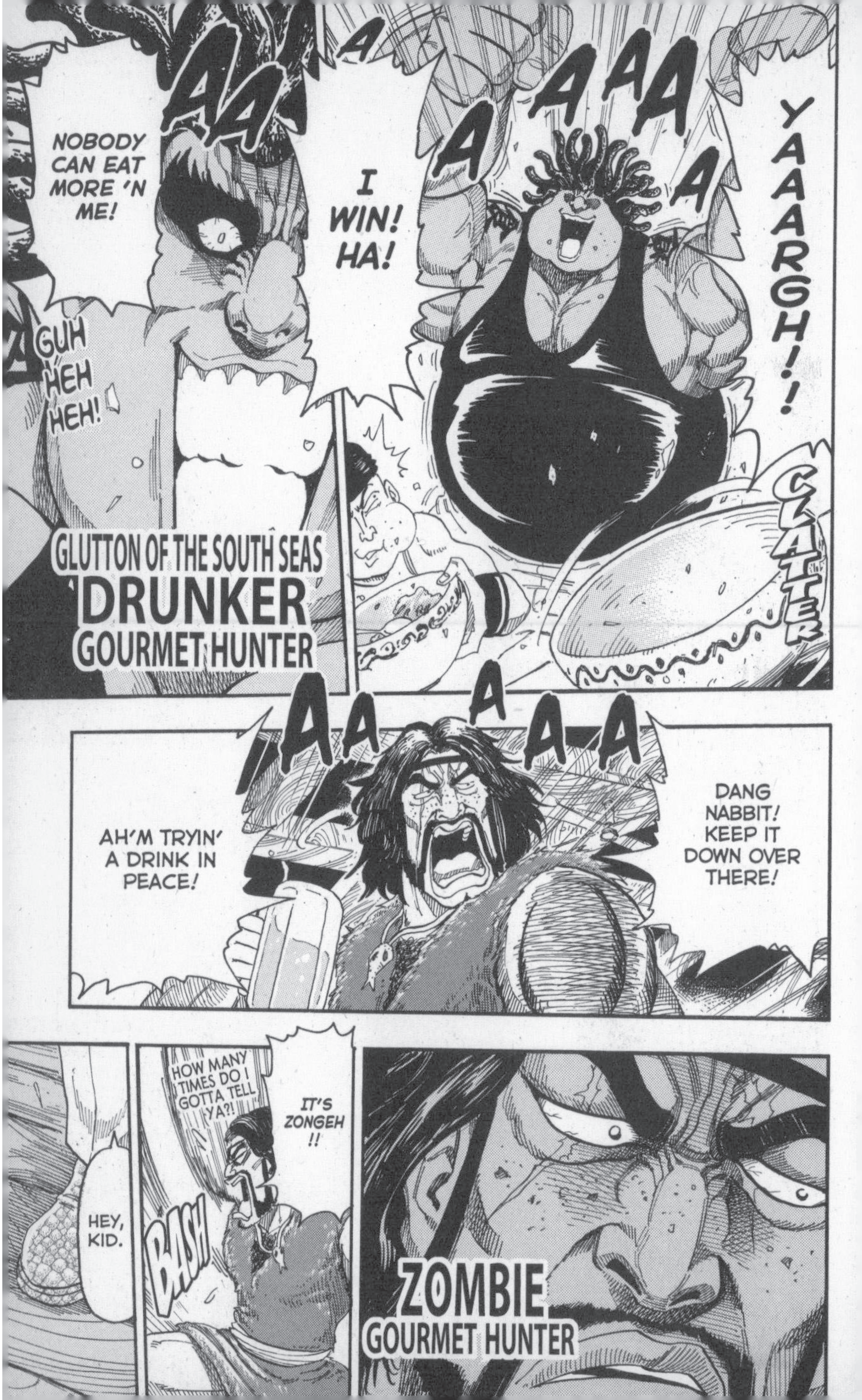
AAAAAAA
YAAARGH!!
I WIN! HA!
CLATTER
AA
NOBODY CAN EAT MORE 'N ME!
GUH HEH HEH!
GLUTTON OF THE SOUTH SEAS
DRUNKER
GOURMET HUNTER
AAAAA
DANG NABBIT! KEEP IT DOWN OVER THERE!
AH'M TRYIN' A DRINK IN PEACE!
ZOMBIE
GOURMET HUNTER
HOW MANY TIMES DO I GOTTA TELL YA?!
IT'S ZONGEH!!
BASH
HEY, KID.

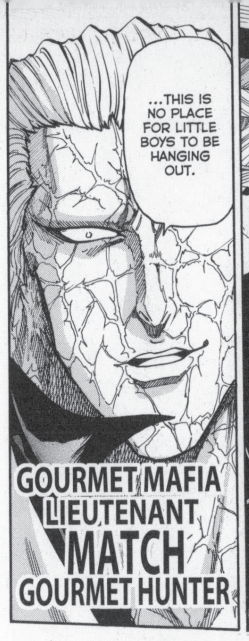

YOU MIND GIVING UP YOUR SEAT?
AFTER ALL...
...THIS IS NO PLACE FOR LITTLE BOYS TO BE HANGING OUT.
GOURMET MAFIA LIEUTENANT MATCH GOURMET HUNTER
SIP
...
I'M OLD ENOUGH TO DRINK. BUT YOU CAN HAVE THIS SEAT...
...OVER MY DEAD BODY.
GOURMET KNIGHT TAKIMARU GOURMET HUNTER

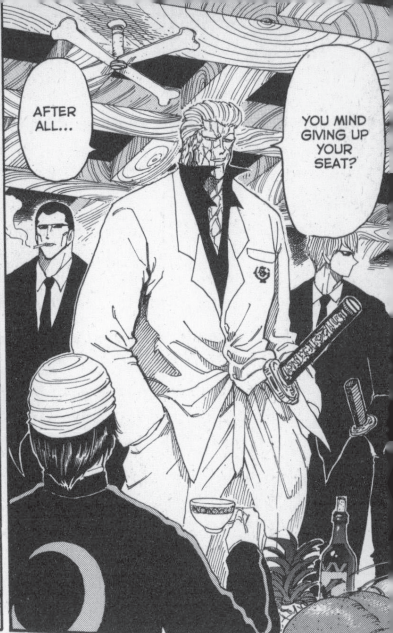

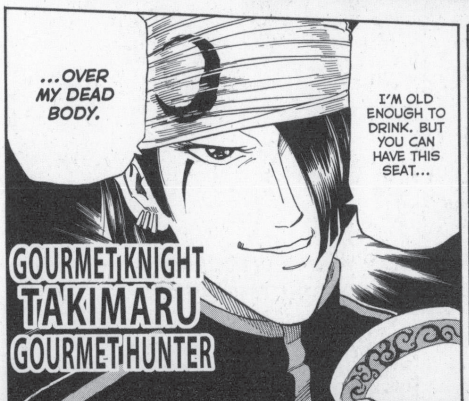

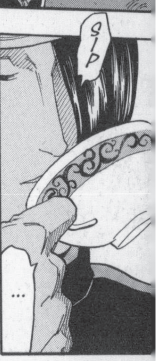

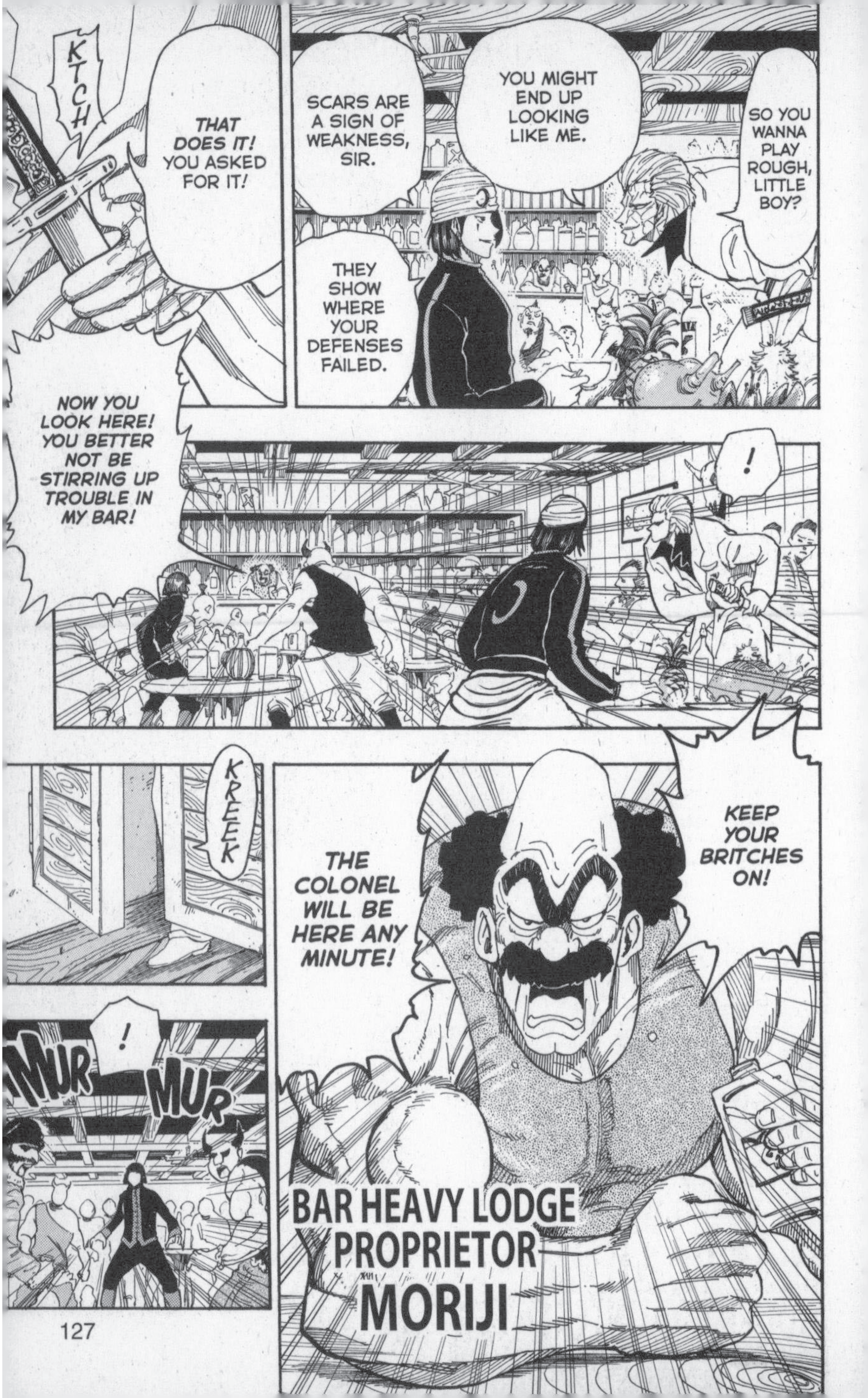

SO YOU WANNA PLAY ROUGH, LITTLE BOY?
YOU MIGHT END UP LOOKING LIKE ME.
SCARS ARE A SIGN OF WEAKNESS, SIR.
THEY SHOW WHERE YOUR DEFENSES FAILED.
KTCH
THAT DOES IT! YOU ASKED FOR IT!
!
NOW YOU LOOK HERE! YOU BETTER NOT BE STIRRING UP TROUBLE IN MY BAR!
KEEP YOUR BRITCHES ON!
THE COLONEL WILL BE HERE ANY MINUTE!
BAR HEAVY LODGE PROPRIETOR MORIJI
KREEK
!
MUR MUR

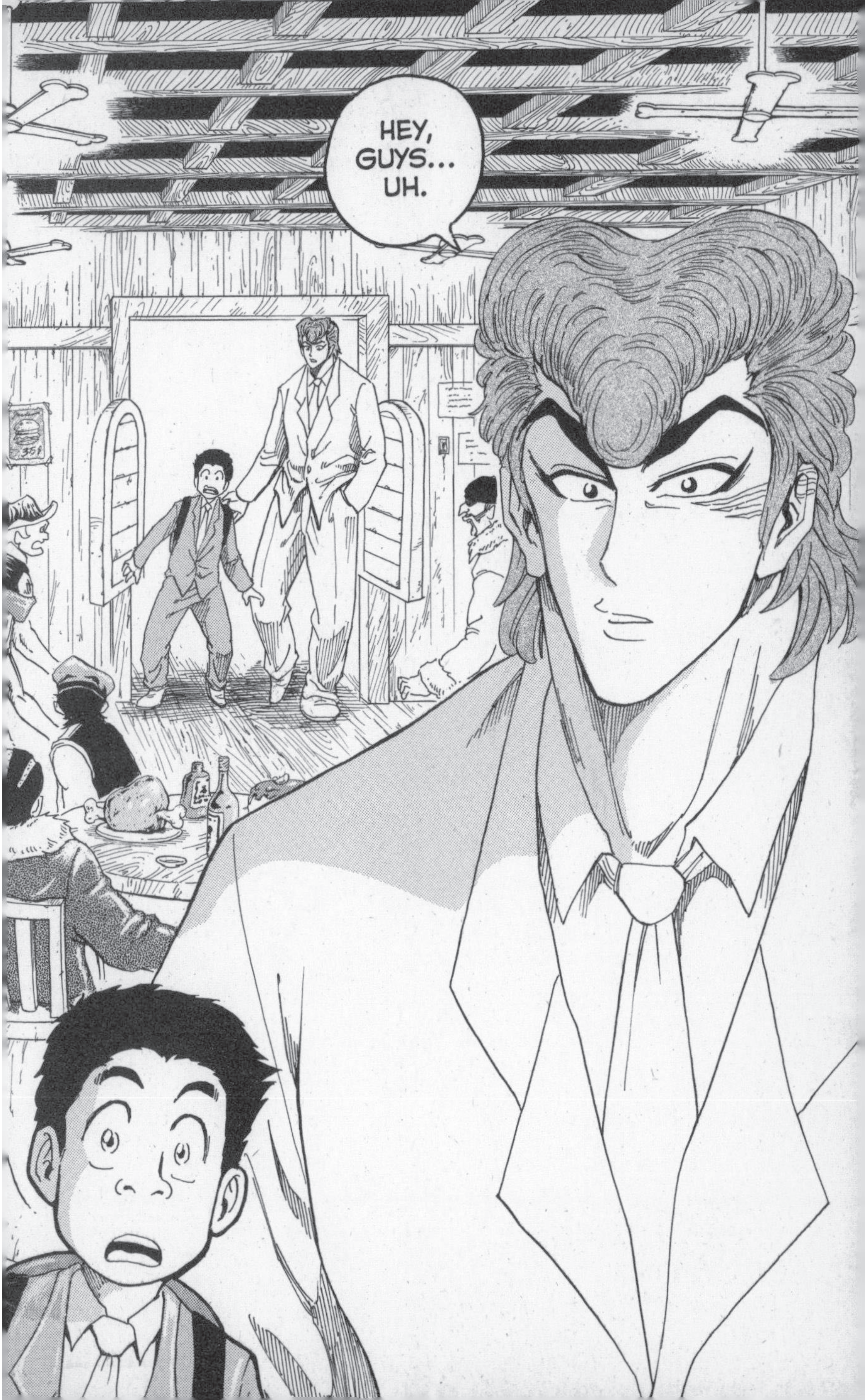
HEY, GUYS... UH.

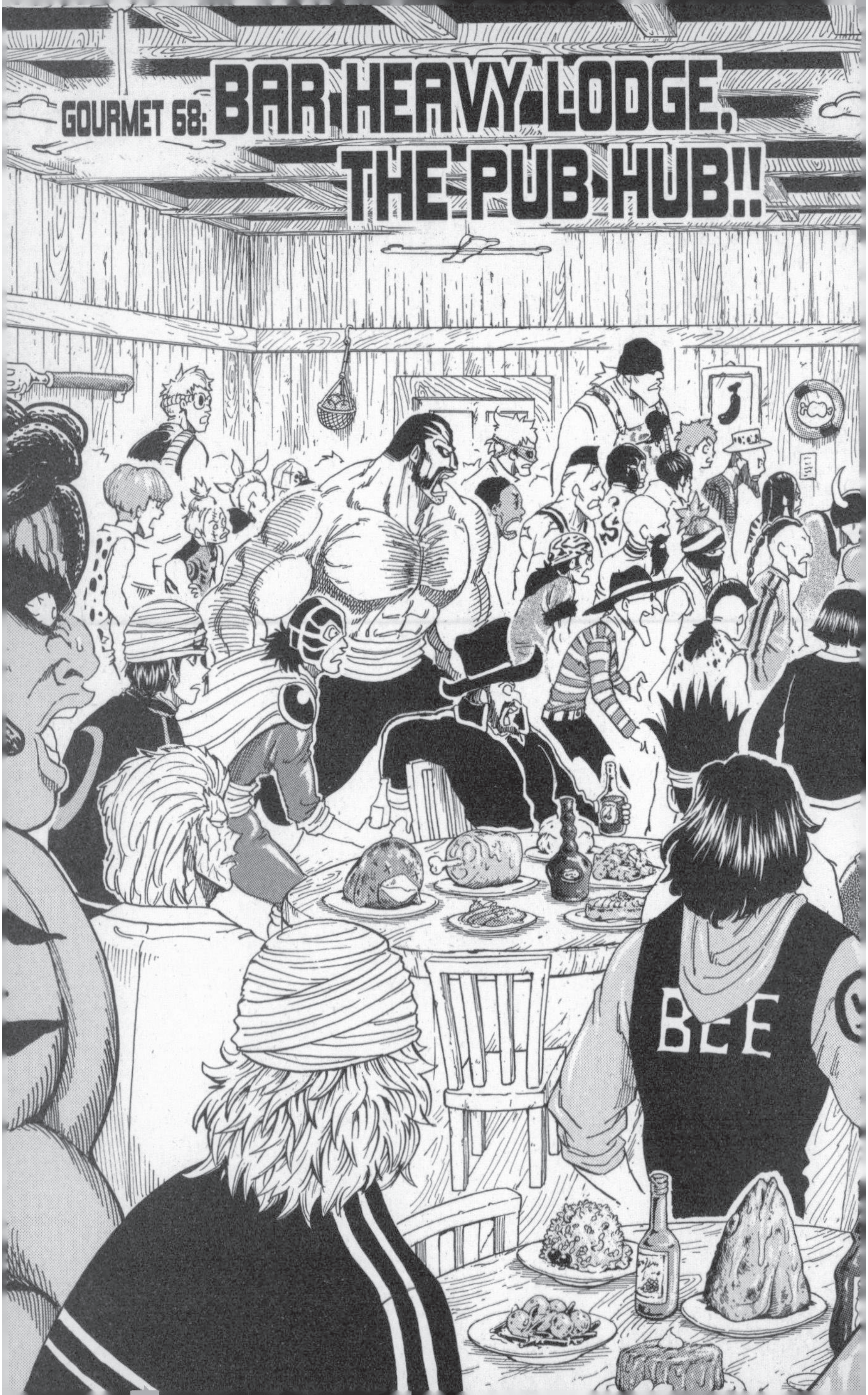
GOURMET 68: BAR HEAVY LODGE, THE PUB HUB!!
BEE

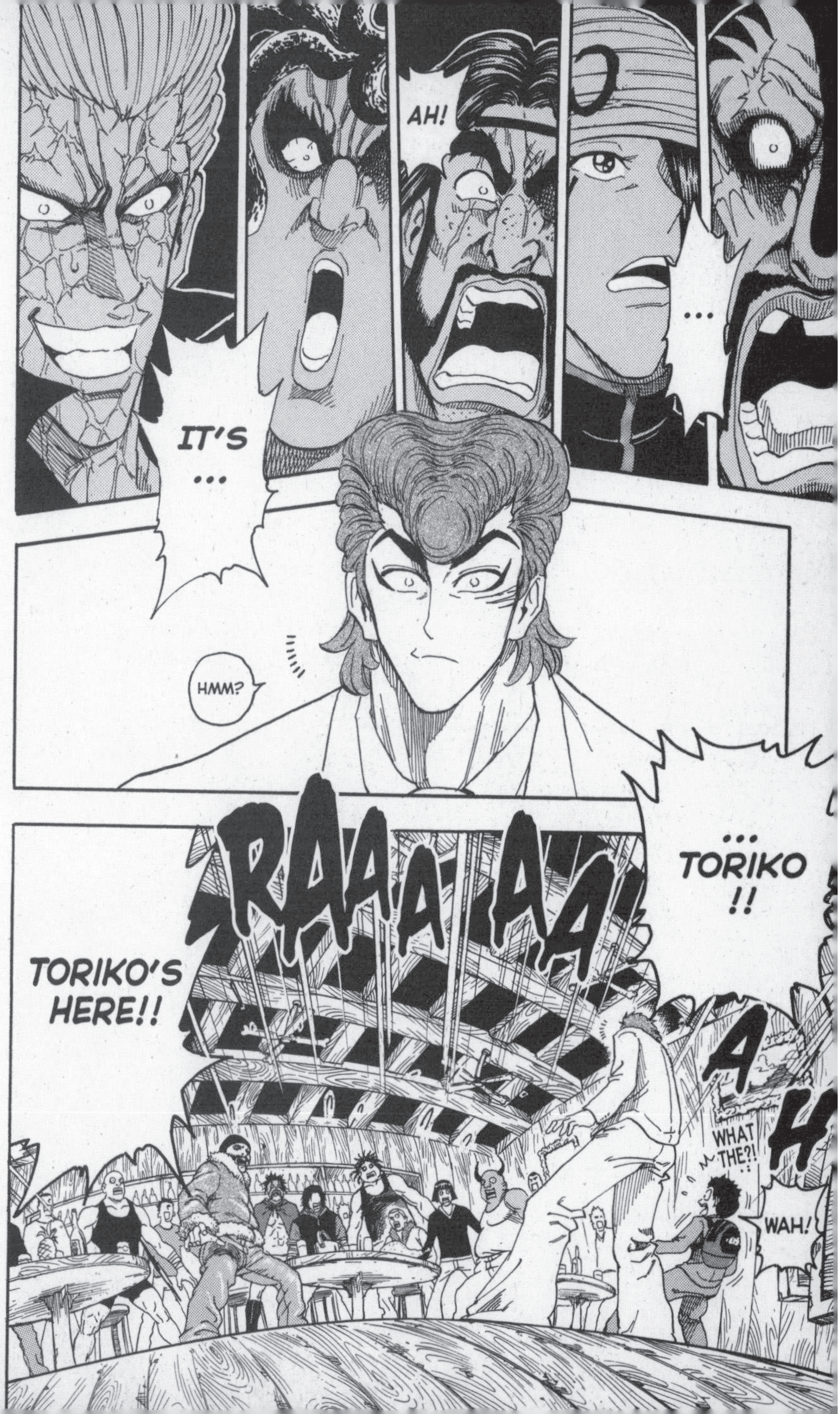
...
AH!
IT'S ...
HMM?
... TORIKO !!
RAAAAAAH
TORIKO'S HERE!!
WHAT THE?!
WAH!

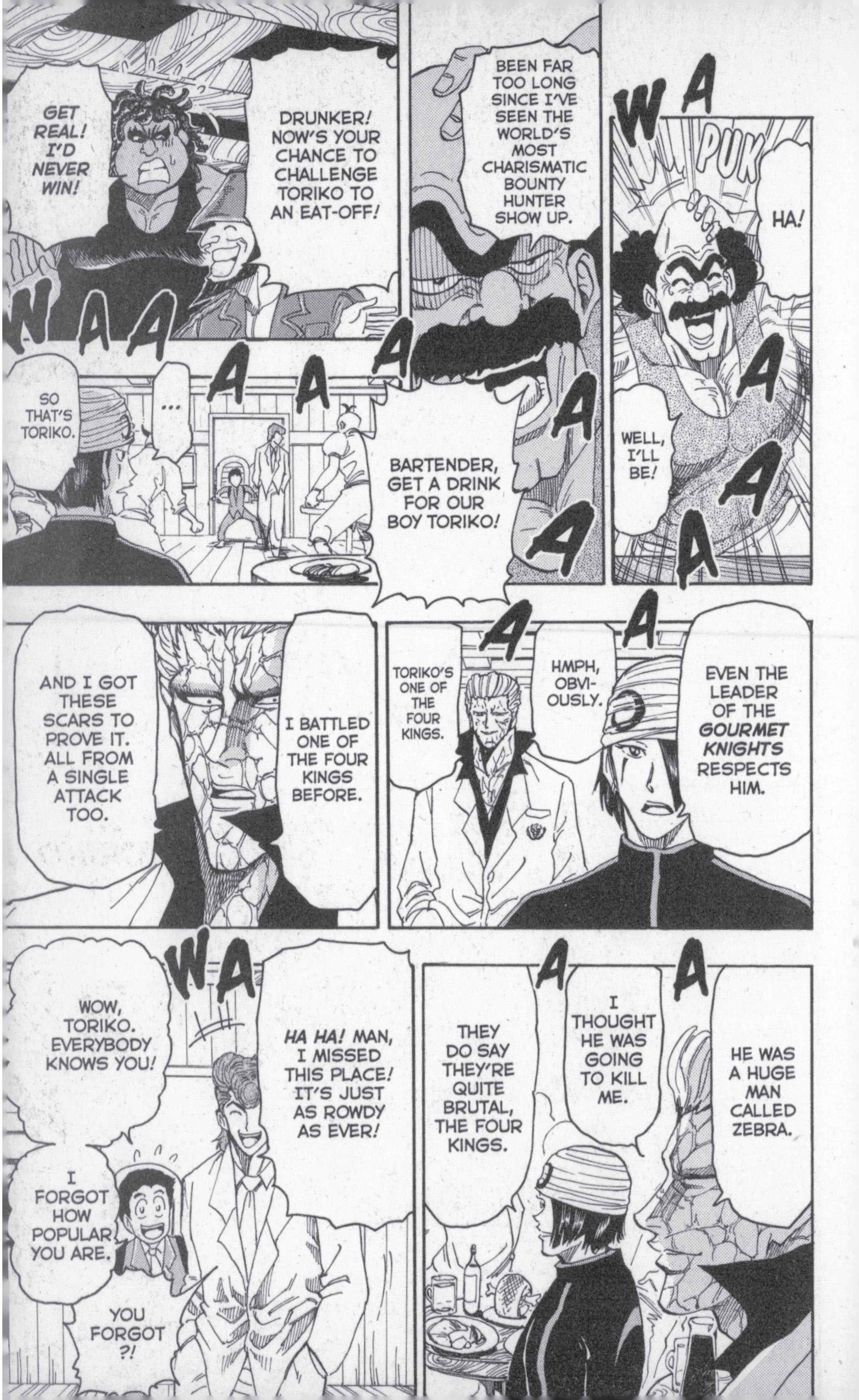
WA
PUK
HA!
WELL, I'LL BE!
BEEN FAR TOO LONG SINCE I'VE SEEN THE WORLD'S MOST CHARISMATIC BOUNTY HUNTER SHOW UP.
BARTENDER, GET A DRINK FOR OUR BOY TORIKO!
DRUNKER! NOW'S YOUR CHANCE TO CHALLENGE TORIKO TO AN EAT-OFF!
GET REAL! I'D NEVER WIN!
WAAA
…
SO THAT'S TORIKO.
EVEN THE LEADER OF THE *GOURMET KNIGHTS* RESPECTS HIM.
HMPH, OBVIOUSLY.
TORIKO'S ONE OF THE FOUR KINGS.
I BATTLED ONE OF THE FOUR KINGS BEFORE.
AND I GOT THESE SCARS TO PROVE IT. ALL FROM A SINGLE ATTACK TOO.
HE WAS A HUGE MAN CALLED ZEBRA.
I THOUGHT HE WAS GOING TO KILL ME.
THEY DO SAY THEY'RE QUITE BRUTAL, THE FOUR KINGS.
WA
HA HA! MAN, I MISSED THIS PLACE! IT'S JUST AS ROWDY AS EVER!
WOW, TORIKO. EVERYBODY KNOWS YOU!
I FORGOT HOW POPULAR YOU ARE.
YOU FORGOT?!

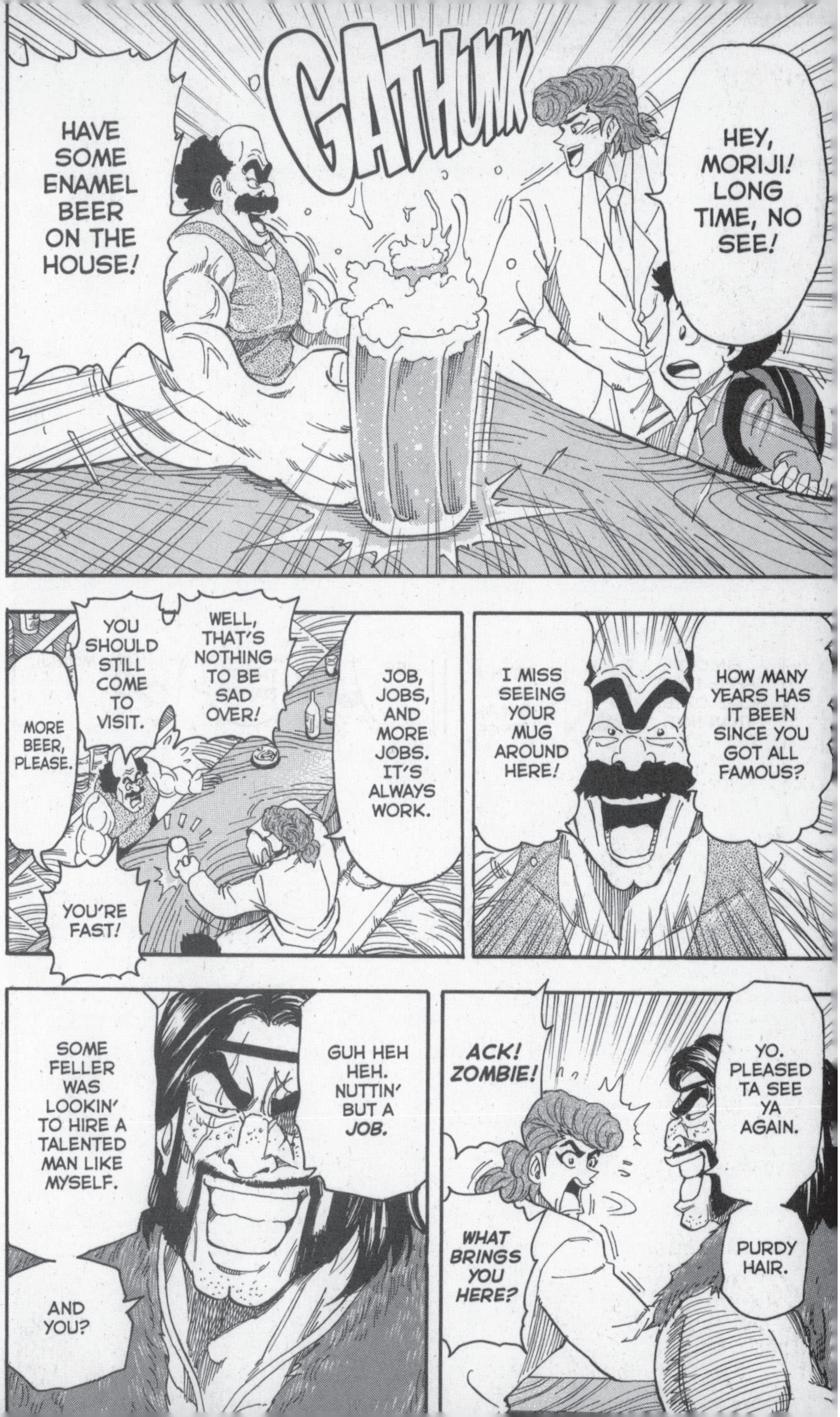
HEY, MORIJI! LONG TIME, NO SEE!
GATHUNK
HAVE SOME ENAMEL BEER ON THE HOUSE!
HOW MANY YEARS HAS IT BEEN SINCE YOU GOT ALL FAMOUS?
I MISS SEEING YOUR MUG AROUND HERE!
JOB, JOBS, AND MORE JOBS. IT'S ALWAYS WORK.
WELL, THAT'S NOTHING TO BE SAD OVER!
YOU SHOULD STILL COME TO VISIT.
MORE BEER, PLEASE.
YOU'RE FAST!
YO. PLEASED TA SEE YA AGAIN.
ACK! ZOMBIE!
PURDY HAIR.
WHAT BRINGS YOU HERE?
GUH HEH HEH. NUTTIN' BUT A JOB.
SOME FELLER WAS LOOKIN' TO HIRE A TALENTED MAN LIKE MYSELF.
AND YOU?

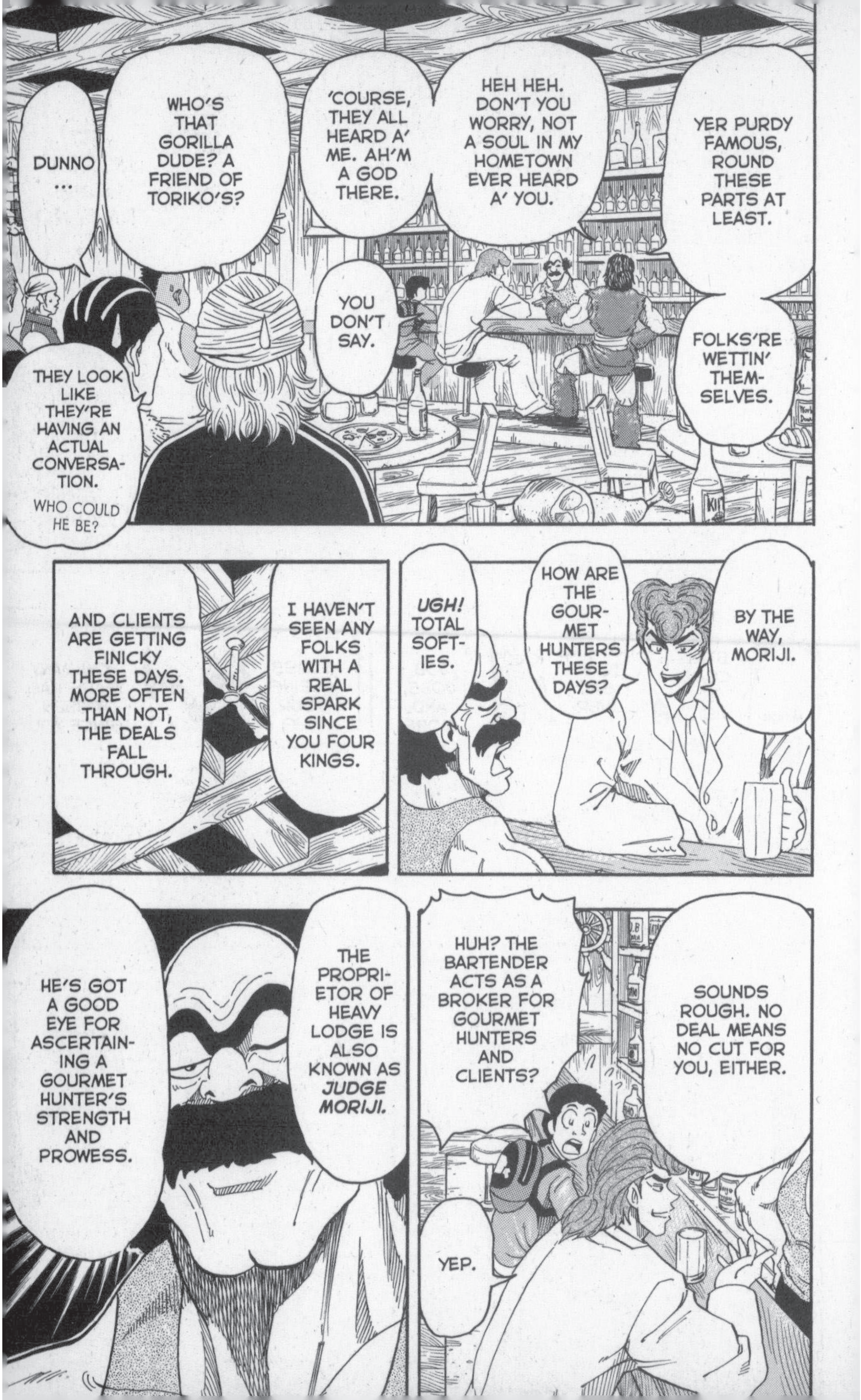
YER PURDY FAMOUS, ROUND THESE PARTS AT LEAST.
HEH HEH. DON'T YOU WORRY, NOT A SOUL IN MY HOMETOWN EVER HEARD A' YOU.
'COURSE, THEY ALL HEARD A' ME. AH'M A GOD THERE.
FOLKS'RE WETTIN' THEMSELVES.
YOU DON'T SAY.
WHO'S THAT GORILLA DUDE? A FRIEND OF TORIKO'S?
DUNNO...
THEY LOOK LIKE THEY'RE HAVING AN ACTUAL CONVERSATION.
WHO COULD HE BE?
BY THE WAY, MORIJI.
HOW ARE THE GOURMET HUNTERS THESE DAYS?
UGH! TOTAL SOFTIES.
I HAVEN'T SEEN ANY FOLKS WITH A REAL SPARK SINCE YOU FOUR KINGS.
AND CLIENTS ARE GETTING FINICKY THESE DAYS. MORE OFTEN THAN NOT, THE DEALS FALL THROUGH.
SOUNDS ROUGH. NO DEAL MEANS NO CUT FOR YOU, EITHER.
HUH? THE BARTENDER ACTS AS A BROKER FOR GOURMET HUNTERS AND CLIENTS?
YEP.
THE PROPRIETOR OF HEAVY LODGE IS ALSO KNOWN AS *JUDGE MORIJI.*
HE'S GOT A GOOD EYE FOR ASCERTAINING A GOURMET HUNTER'S STRENGTH AND PROWESS.

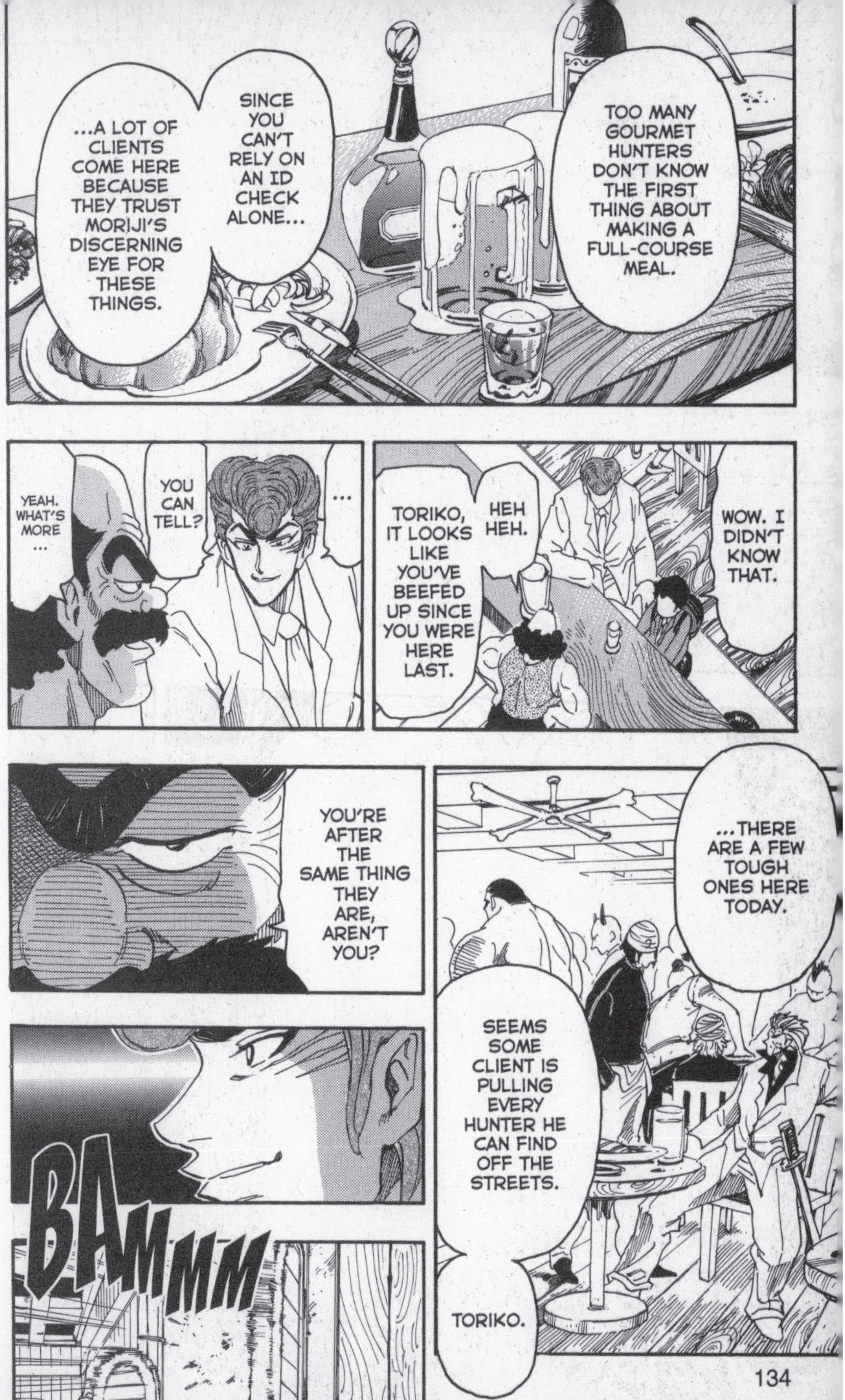
TOO MANY GOURMET HUNTERS DON'T KNOW THE FIRST THING ABOUT MAKING A FULL-COURSE MEAL.
SINCE YOU CAN'T RELY ON AN ID CHECK ALONE...
...A LOT OF CLIENTS COME HERE BECAUSE THEY TRUST MORIJI'S DISCERNING EYE FOR THESE THINGS.
WOW. I DIDN'T KNOW THAT.
HEH HEH.
TORIKO, IT LOOKS LIKE YOU'VE BEEFED UP SINCE YOU WERE HERE LAST.
...
YOU CAN TELL?
YEAH. WHAT'S MORE ...
...THERE ARE A FEW TOUGH ONES HERE TODAY.
SEEMS SOME CLIENT IS PULLING EVERY HUNTER HE CAN FIND OFF THE STREETS.
TORIKO.
YOU'RE AFTER THE SAME THING THEY ARE, AREN'T YOU?
BAMMM

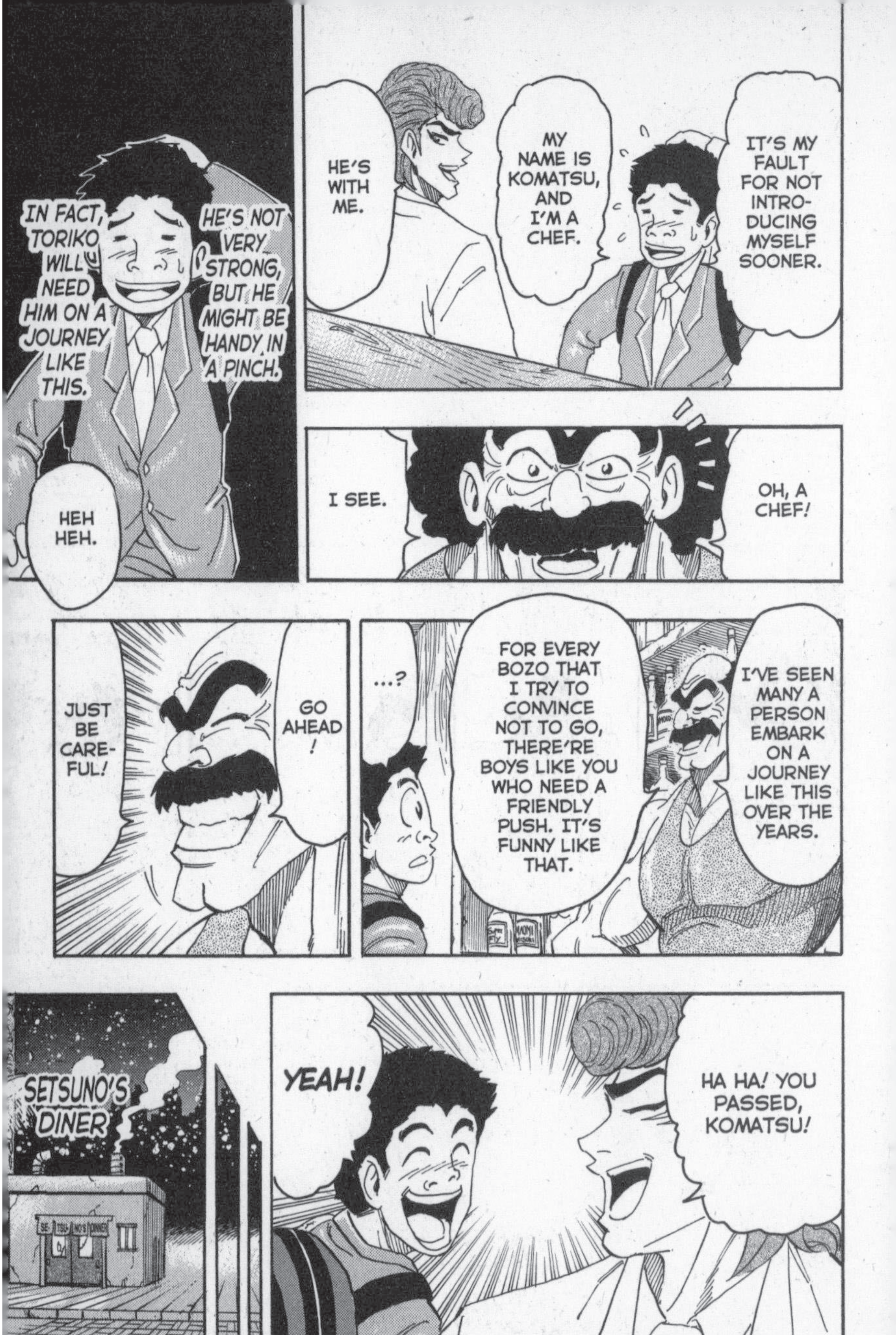
IT'S MY FAULT FOR NOT INTRODUCING MYSELF SOONER.
MY NAME IS KOMATSU, AND I'M A CHEF.
HE'S WITH ME.
OH, A CHEF!
I SEE.
HE'S NOT VERY STRONG, BUT HE MIGHT BE HANDY IN A PINCH.
IN FACT, TORIKO WILL NEED HIM ON A JOURNEY LIKE THIS.
HEH HEH.
I'VE SEEN MANY A PERSON EMBARK ON A JOURNEY LIKE THIS OVER THE YEARS.
FOR EVERY BOZO THAT I TRY TO CONVINCE NOT TO GO, THERE'RE BOYS LIKE YOU WHO NEED A FRIENDLY PUSH. IT'S FUNNY LIKE THAT.
...?
GO AHEAD!
JUST BE CAREFUL!
HA HA! YOU PASSED, KOMATSU!
YEAH!
SETSUNO'S DINER

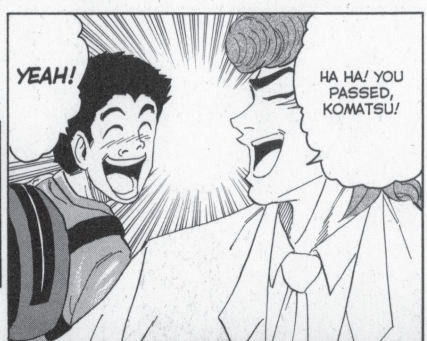

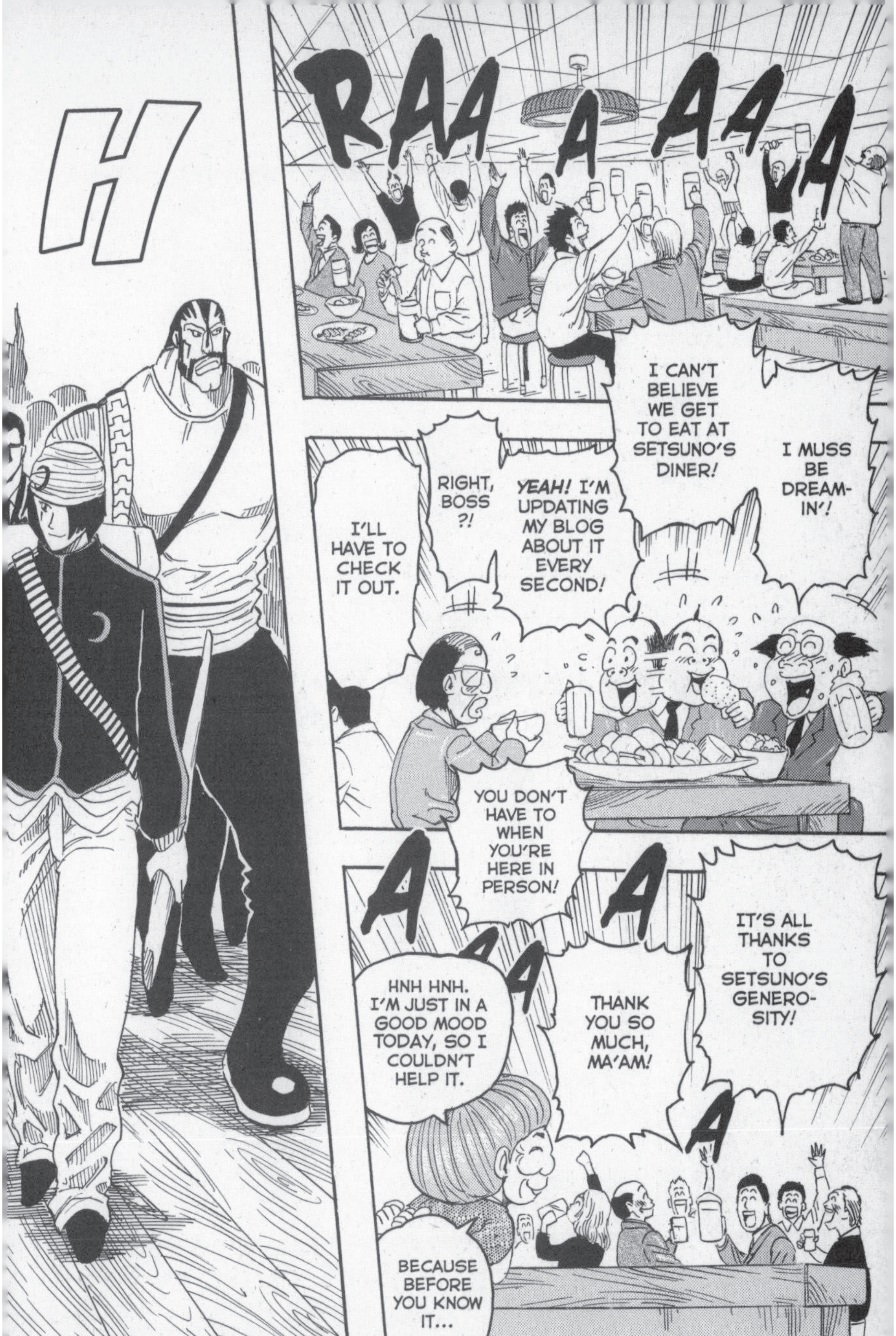

RAAAAAAA
I CAN'T BELIEVE WE GET TO EAT AT SETSUNO'S DINER!
I MUSS BE DREAMIN'!
YEAH! I'M UPDATING MY BLOG ABOUT IT EVERY SECOND!
RIGHT, BOSS?!
I'LL HAVE TO CHECK IT OUT.
YOU DON'T HAVE TO WHEN YOU'RE HERE IN PERSON!
AAAAAA
IT'S ALL THANKS TO SETSUNO'S GENEROSITY!
THANK YOU SO MUCH, MA'AM!
HNH HNH. I'M JUST IN A GOOD MOOD TODAY, SO I COULDN'T HELP IT.
BECAUSE BEFORE YOU KNOW IT...
H

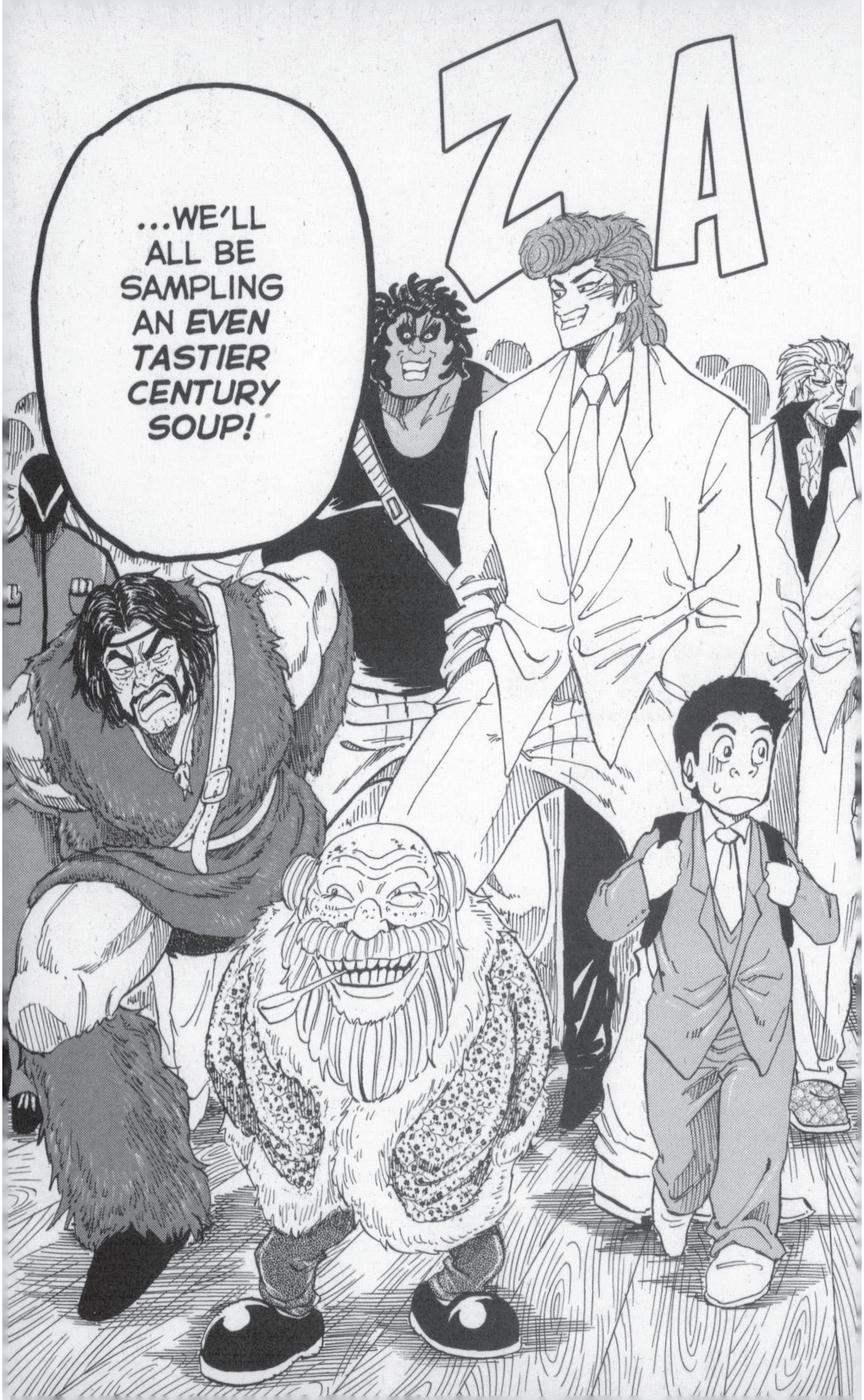
ZA
...WE'LL ALL BE SAMPLING AN EVEN TASTIER CENTURY SOUP!

TORIKO

GOURMET CHECKLIST

Vol. 055

OBASAURUS
(MAMMAL)

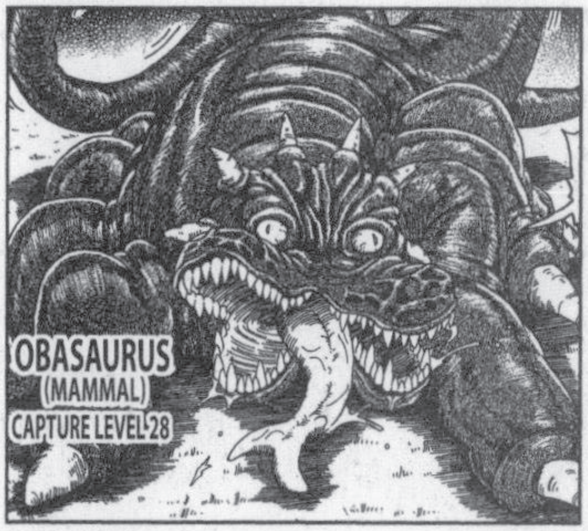

OBASAURUS
(MAMMAL)
CAPTURE LEVEL 28

CAPTURE LEVEL: 28

HABITAT: ADAPTS TO ANY ENVIRONMENT, EVEN CITIES

LENGTH: 13 METERS

HEIGHT: 2.7 METERS

WEIGHT: 6 TONS

PRICE: MEAT NOT FIT FOR HUMAN CONSUMPTION. (SALE AS A BEAST OF BURDEN IS PROHIBITED BY GOURMET LAW, BUT A BABY OBASAURUS FETCHES A HIGH PRICE ON THE BLACK MARKET.)

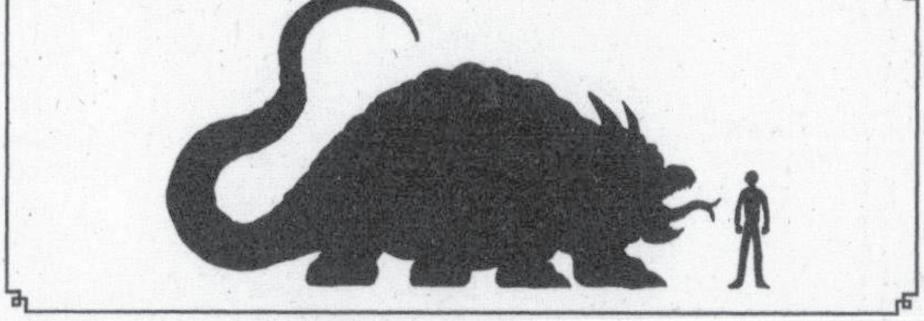

SCALE

THE OBASAURUS WILL BOW BEFORE THE WILL OF ANY CREATURE STRONGER THAN ITSELF. IT WILL GUARD THE LIFE OF ITS CHOSEN MASTER AND EVEN LET SAID MASTER RIDE ON ITS BACK...UNTIL A STRONGER MASTER SHOWS UP. AN OBASAURUS USUALLY BEGINS ITS INTENSE RELATIONSHIP WITH A MASTER BY BEING BEATEN UP, WHICH LEADS TO SPECULATION THAT OBASAURUSES ARE MASOCHISTS, BUT LITTLE IS KNOWN ABOUT THE BEHAVIOR OF THIS CREATURE IN THE WILD.

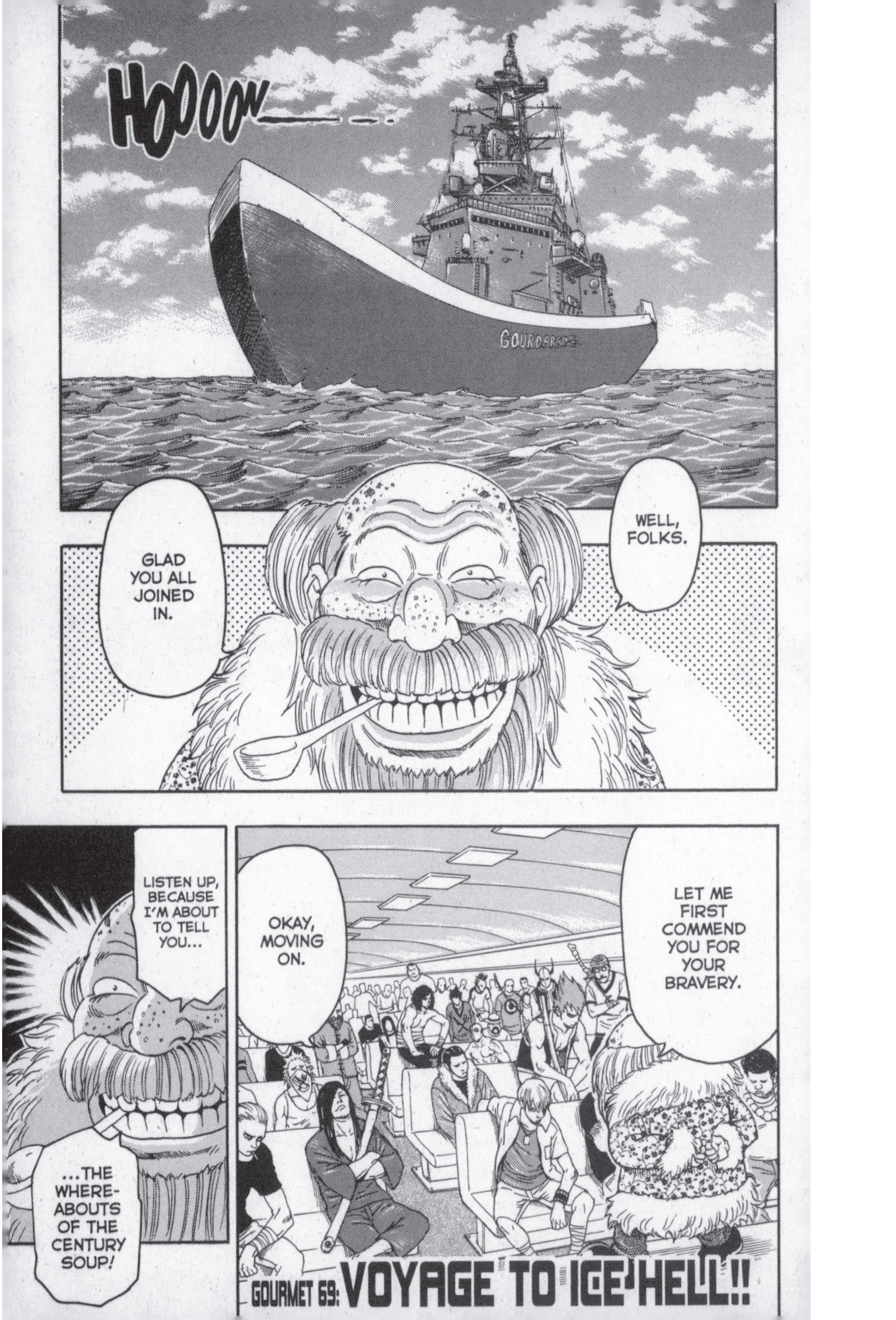
HOOOON
WELL, FOLKS.
GLAD YOU ALL JOINED IN.
LET ME FIRST COMMEND YOU FOR YOUR BRAVERY.
OKAY, MOVING ON.
LISTEN UP, BECAUSE I'M ABOUT TO TELL YOU...
...THE WHERE-ABOUTS OF THE CENTURY SOUP!

GOURMET 69: VOYAGE TO ICE HELL!!

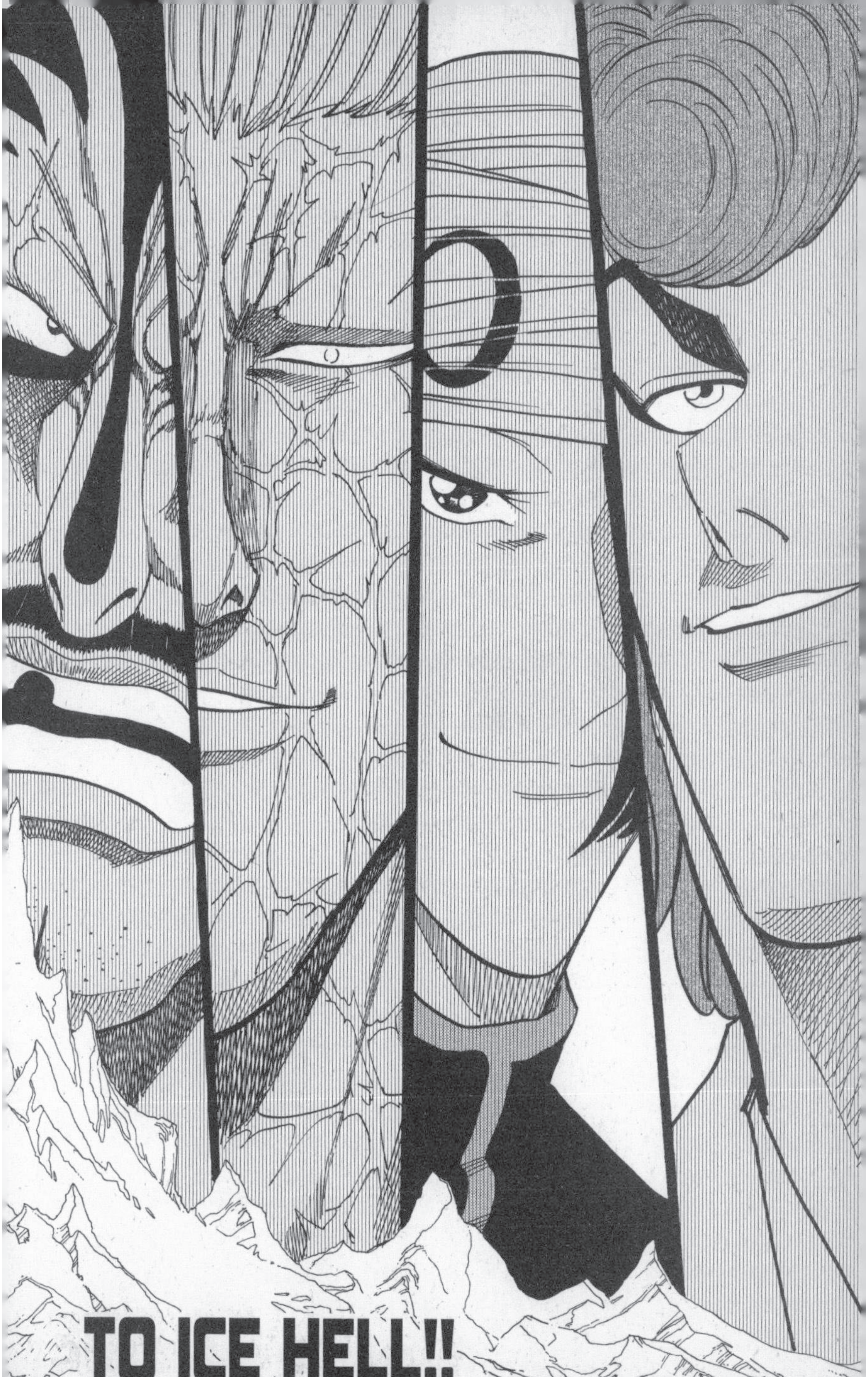
TO ICE HELL!!

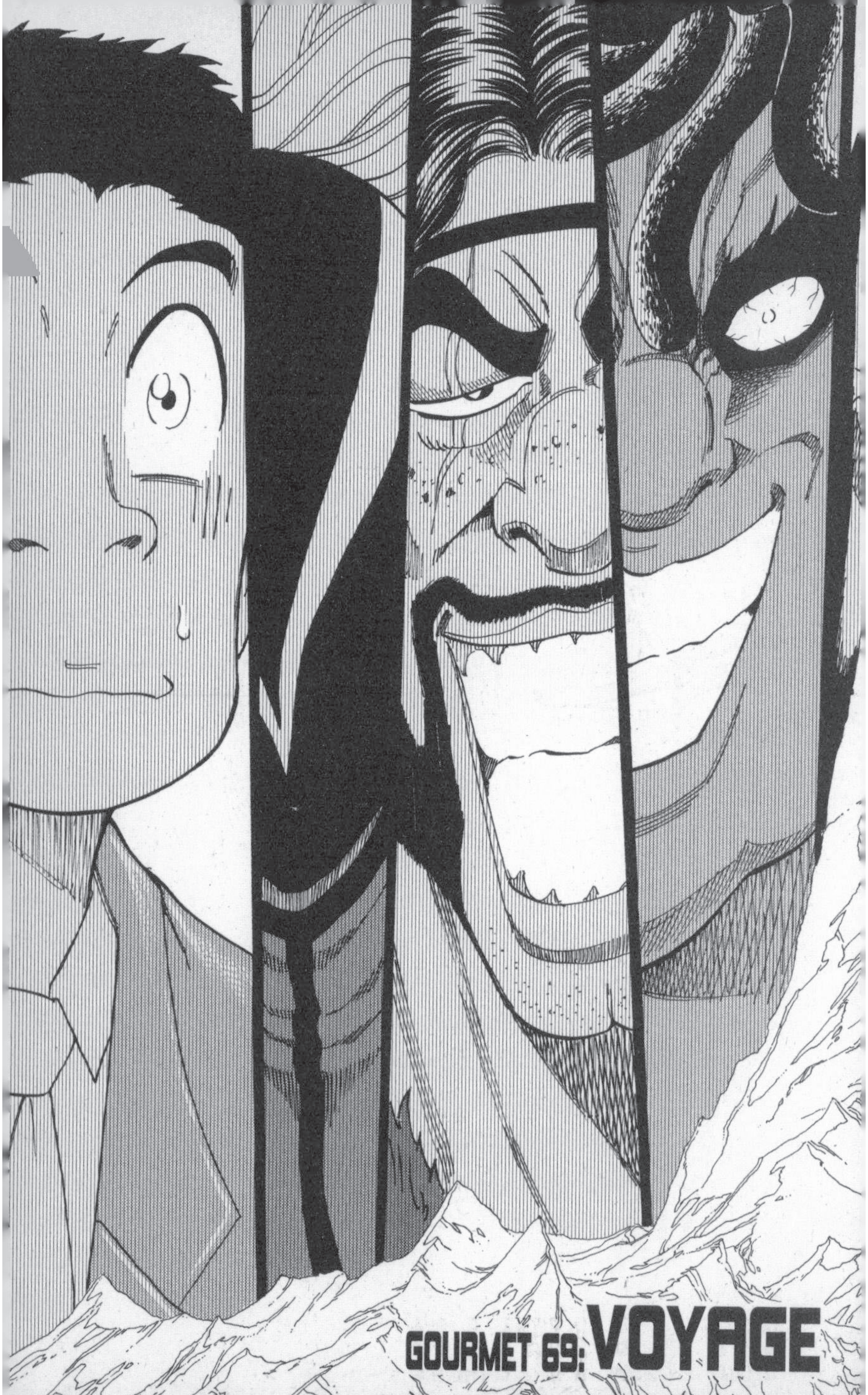
GOURMET 69: VOYAGE

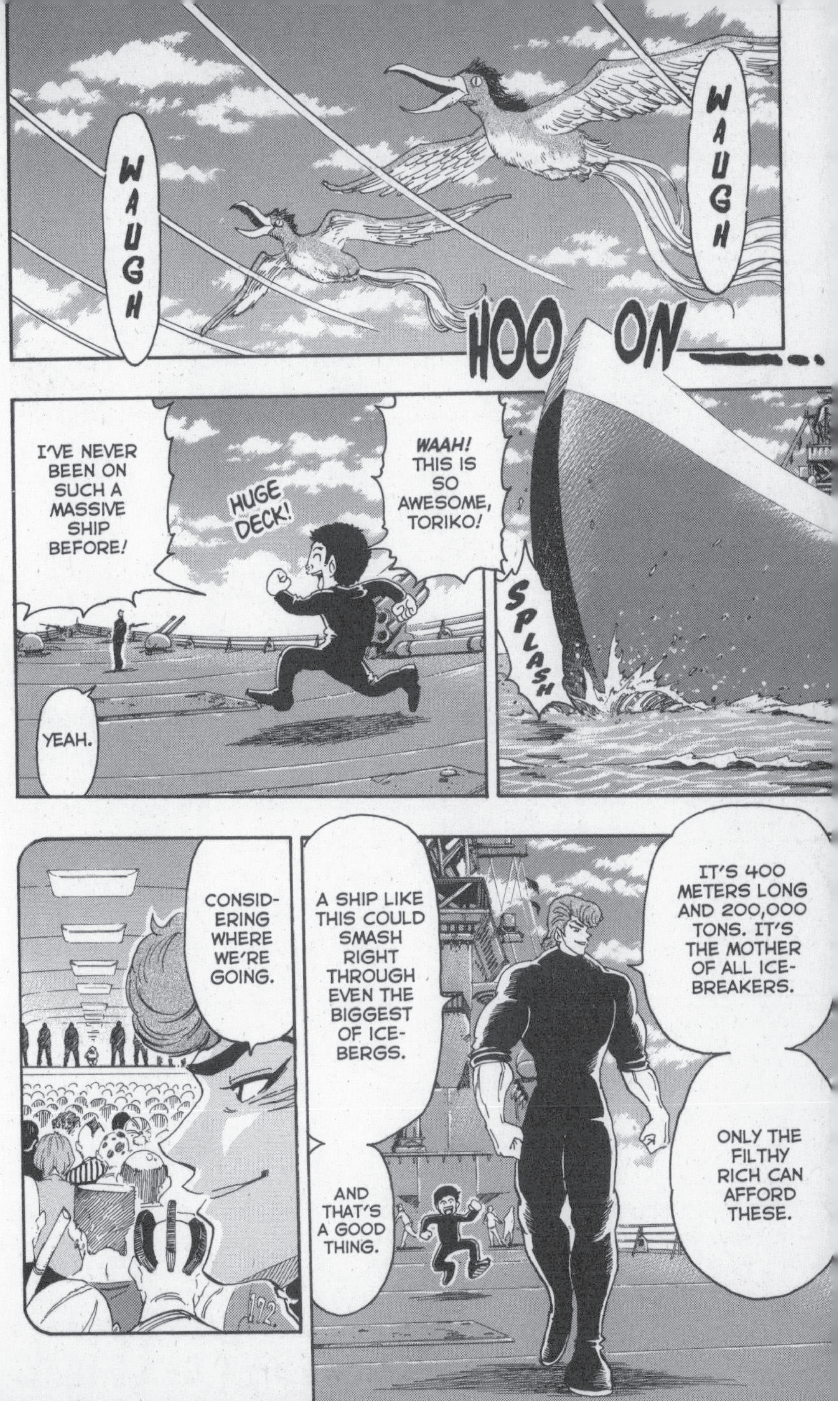
WAUGH
WAUGH
HOO ON
SPLASH
WAAH! THIS IS SO AWESOME, TORIKO!
HUGE DECK!
I'VE NEVER BEEN ON SUCH A MASSIVE SHIP BEFORE!
YEAH.
IT'S 400 METERS LONG AND 200,000 TONS. IT'S THE MOTHER OF ALL ICE-BREAKERS.
ONLY THE FILTHY RICH CAN AFFORD THESE.
A SHIP LIKE THIS COULD SMASH RIGHT THROUGH EVEN THE BIGGEST OF ICE-BERGS.
AND THAT'S A GOOD THING.
CONSID-ERING WHERE WE'RE GOING.
172

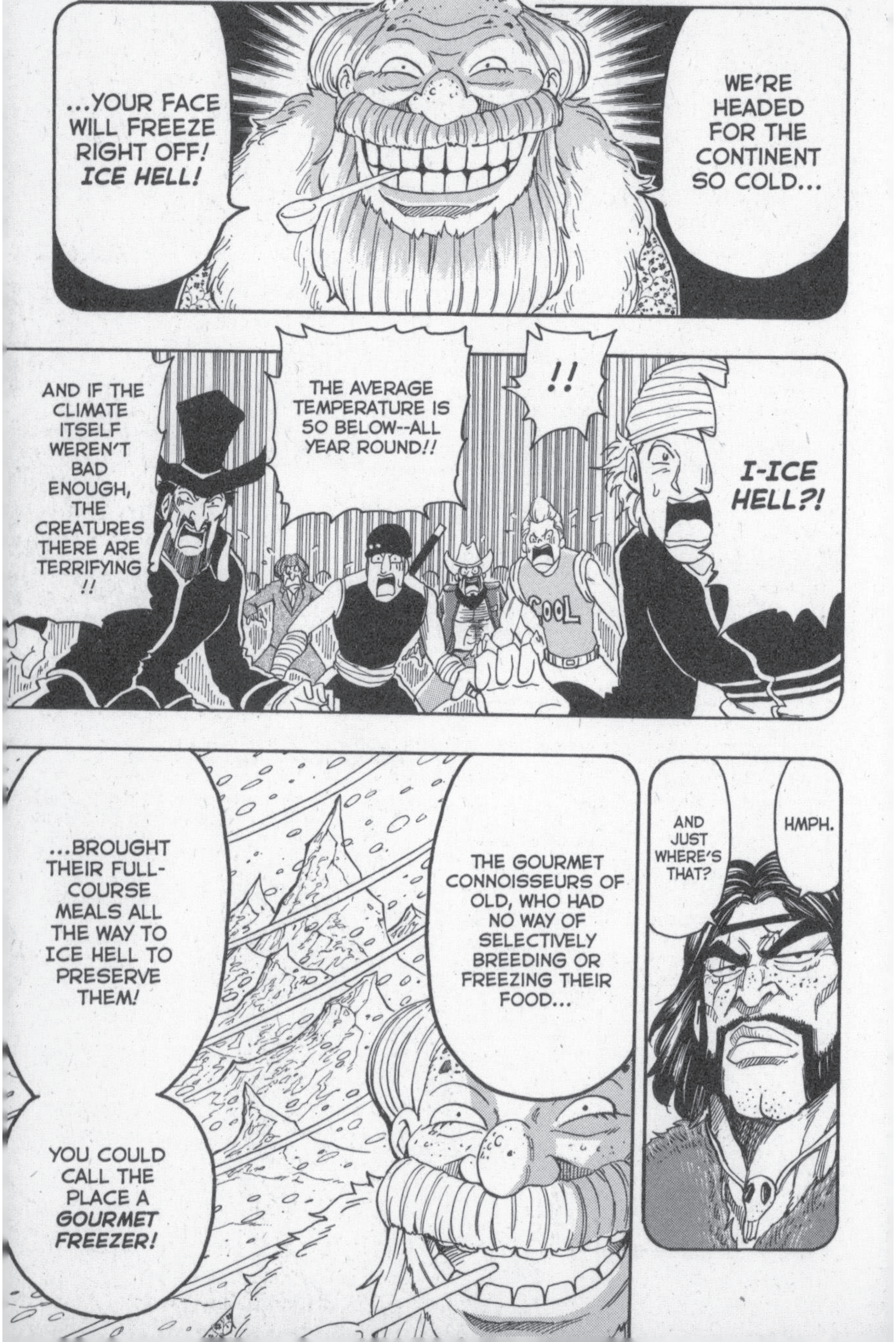
WE'RE HEADED FOR THE CONTINENT SO COLD...
...YOUR FACE WILL FREEZE RIGHT OFF! *ICE HELL!*
I-ICE HELL?!
!!
THE AVERAGE TEMPERATURE IS 50 BELOW--ALL YEAR ROUND!!
AND IF THE CLIMATE ITSELF WEREN'T BAD ENOUGH, THE CREATURES THERE ARE TERRIFYING!!
COOL
HMPH.
AND JUST WHERE'S THAT?
THE GOURMET CONNOISSEURS OF OLD, WHO HAD NO WAY OF SELECTIVELY BREEDING OR FREEZING THEIR FOOD...
...BROUGHT THEIR FULL-COURSE MEALS ALL THE WAY TO ICE HELL TO PRESERVE THEM!
YOU COULD CALL THE PLACE A *GOURMET FREEZER!*

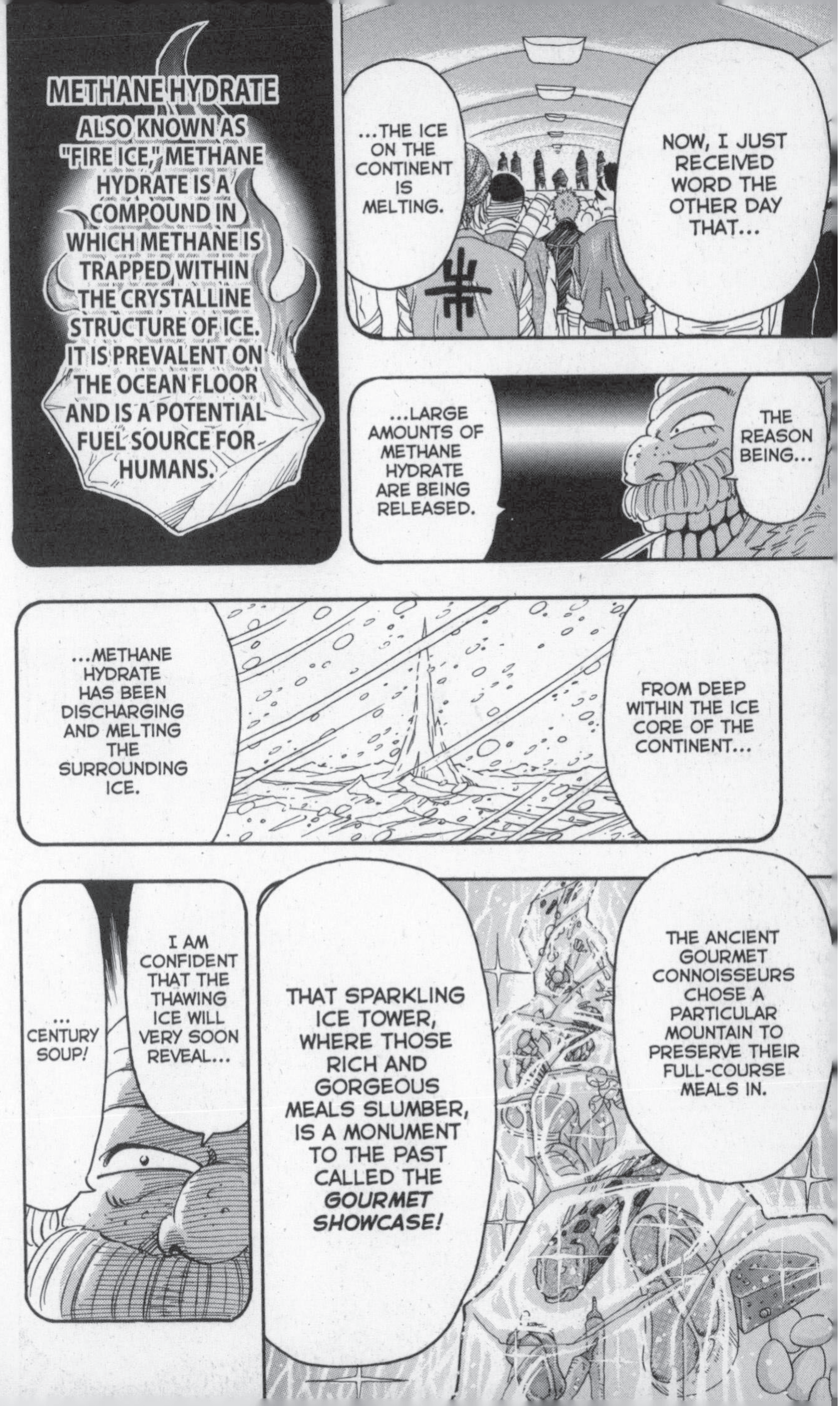
NOW, I JUST RECEIVED WORD THE OTHER DAY THAT...
...THE ICE ON THE CONTINENT IS MELTING.
THE REASON BEING...
...LARGE AMOUNTS OF METHANE HYDRATE ARE BEING RELEASED.
METHANE HYDRATE
ALSO KNOWN AS "FIRE ICE," METHANE HYDRATE IS A COMPOUND IN WHICH METHANE IS TRAPPED WITHIN THE CRYSTALLINE STRUCTURE OF ICE. IT IS PREVALENT ON THE OCEAN FLOOR AND IS A POTENTIAL FUEL SOURCE FOR HUMANS.
FROM DEEP WITHIN THE ICE CORE OF THE CONTINENT...
...METHANE HYDRATE HAS BEEN DISCHARGING AND MELTING THE SURROUNDING ICE.
THE ANCIENT GOURMET CONNOISSEURS CHOSE A PARTICULAR MOUNTAIN TO PRESERVE THEIR FULL-COURSE MEALS IN.
THAT SPARKLING ICE TOWER, WHERE THOSE RICH AND GORGEOUS MEALS SLUMBER, IS A MONUMENT TO THE PAST CALLED THE *GOURMET SHOWCASE!*
I AM CONFIDENT THAT THE THAWING ICE WILL VERY SOON REVEAL...
...CENTURY SOUP!

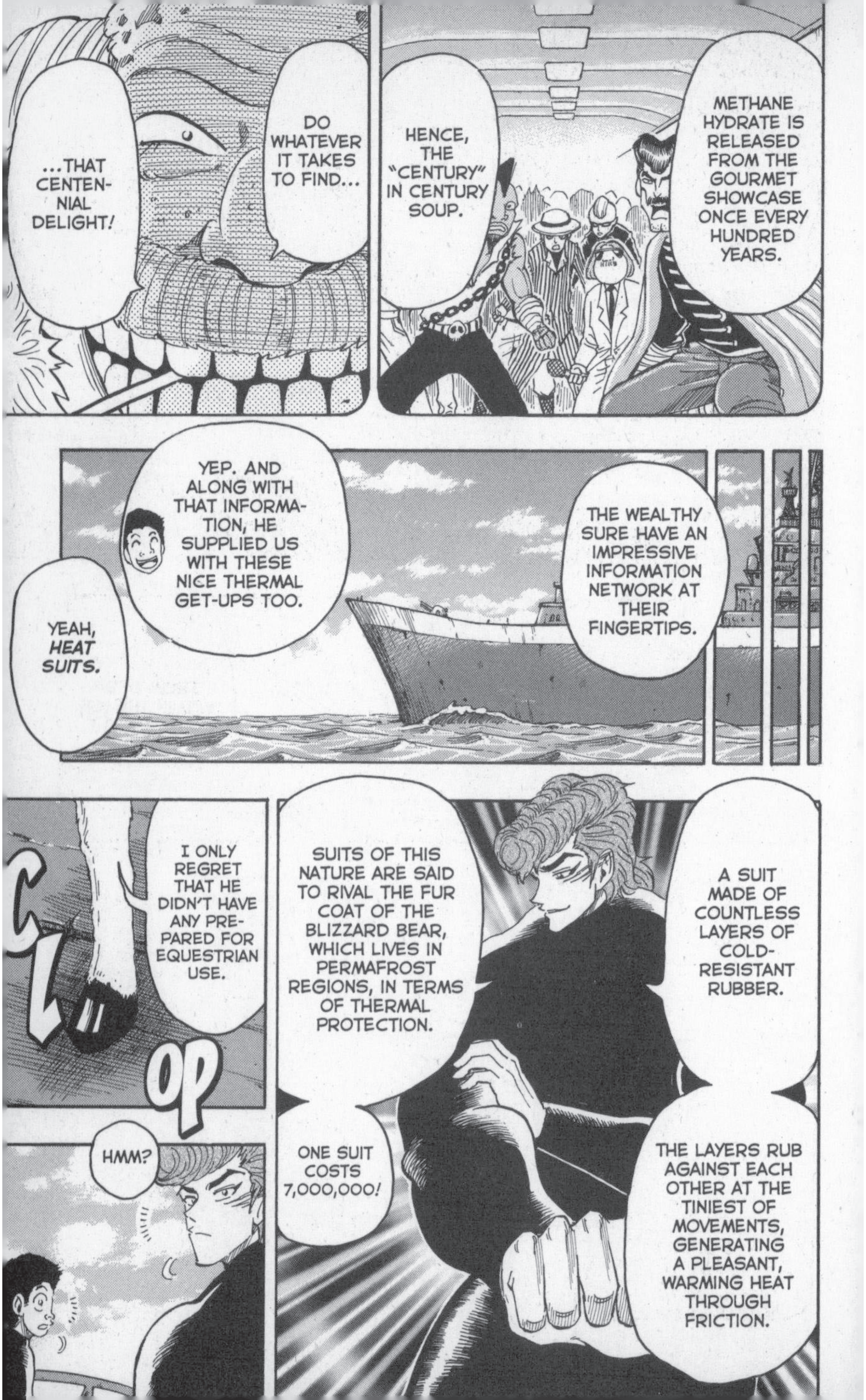
METHANE HYDRATE IS RELEASED FROM THE GOURMET SHOWCASE ONCE EVERY HUNDRED YEARS.
HENCE, THE "CENTURY" IN CENTURY SOUP.
DO WHATEVER IT TAKES TO FIND...
...THAT CENTENNIAL DELIGHT!
THE WEALTHY SURE HAVE AN IMPRESSIVE INFORMATION NETWORK AT THEIR FINGERTIPS.
YEP. AND ALONG WITH THAT INFORMATION, HE SUPPLIED US WITH THESE NICE THERMAL GET-UPS TOO.
YEAH, *HEAT SUITS.*
A SUIT MADE OF COUNTLESS LAYERS OF COLD-RESISTANT RUBBER.
SUITS OF THIS NATURE ARE SAID TO RIVAL THE FUR COAT OF THE BLIZZARD BEAR, WHICH LIVES IN PERMAFROST REGIONS, IN TERMS OF THERMAL PROTECTION.
THE LAYERS RUB AGAINST EACH OTHER AT THE TINIEST OF MOVEMENTS, GENERATING A PLEASANT, WARMING HEAT THROUGH FRICTION.
ONE SUIT COSTS 7,000,000!
I ONLY REGRET THAT HE DIDN'T HAVE ANY PREPARED FOR EQUESTRIAN USE.
CLOP
HMM?

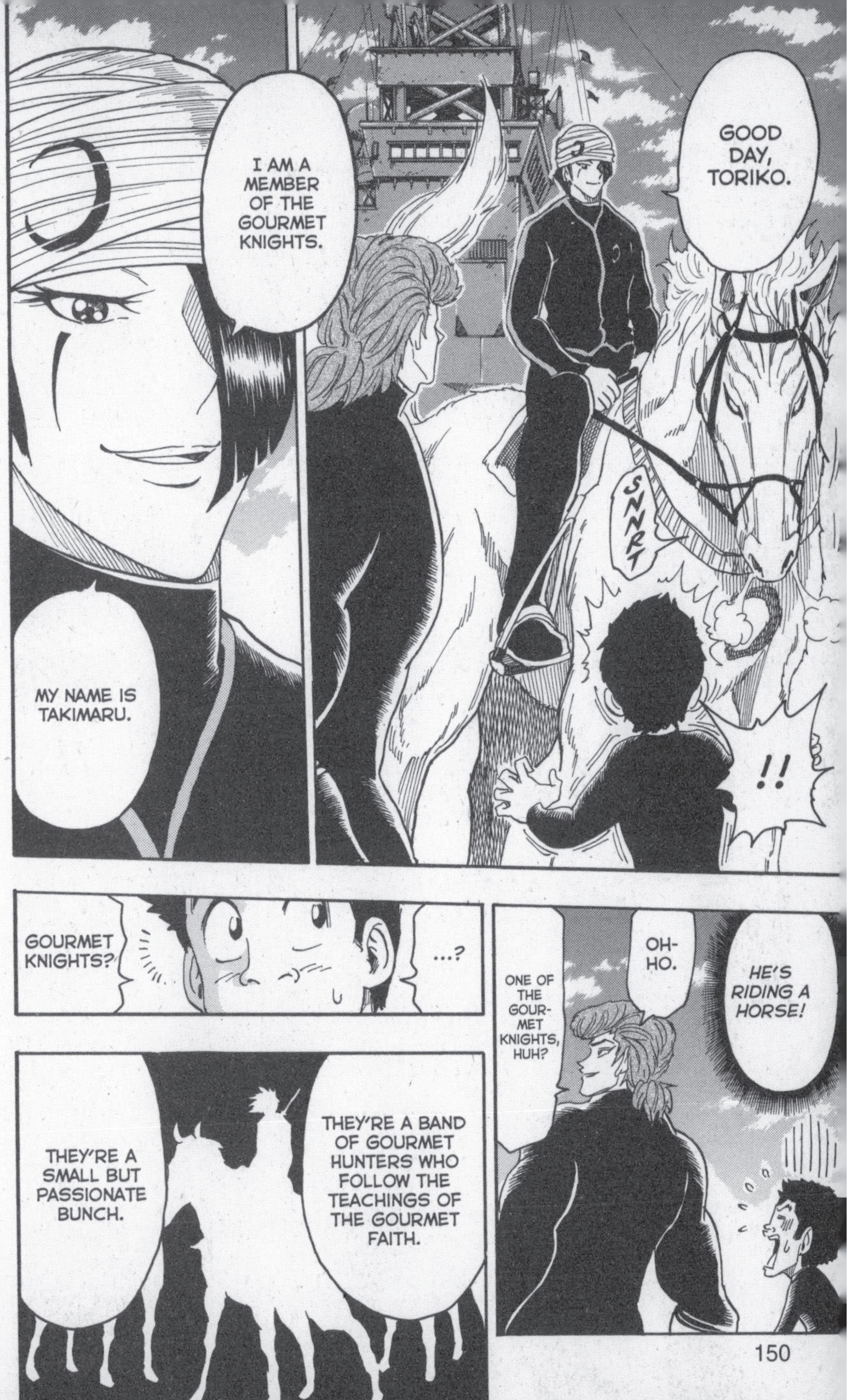
GOOD DAY, TORIKO.
SNNRT
!!
I AM A MEMBER OF THE GOURMET KNIGHTS.
MY NAME IS TAKIMARU.
HE'S RIDING A HORSE!
OH-HO.
ONE OF THE GOUR-MET KNIGHTS, HUH?
...?
GOURMET KNIGHTS?
THEY'RE A BAND OF GOURMET HUNTERS WHO FOLLOW THE TEACHINGS OF THE GOURMET FAITH.
THEY'RE A SMALL BUT PASSIONATE BUNCH.

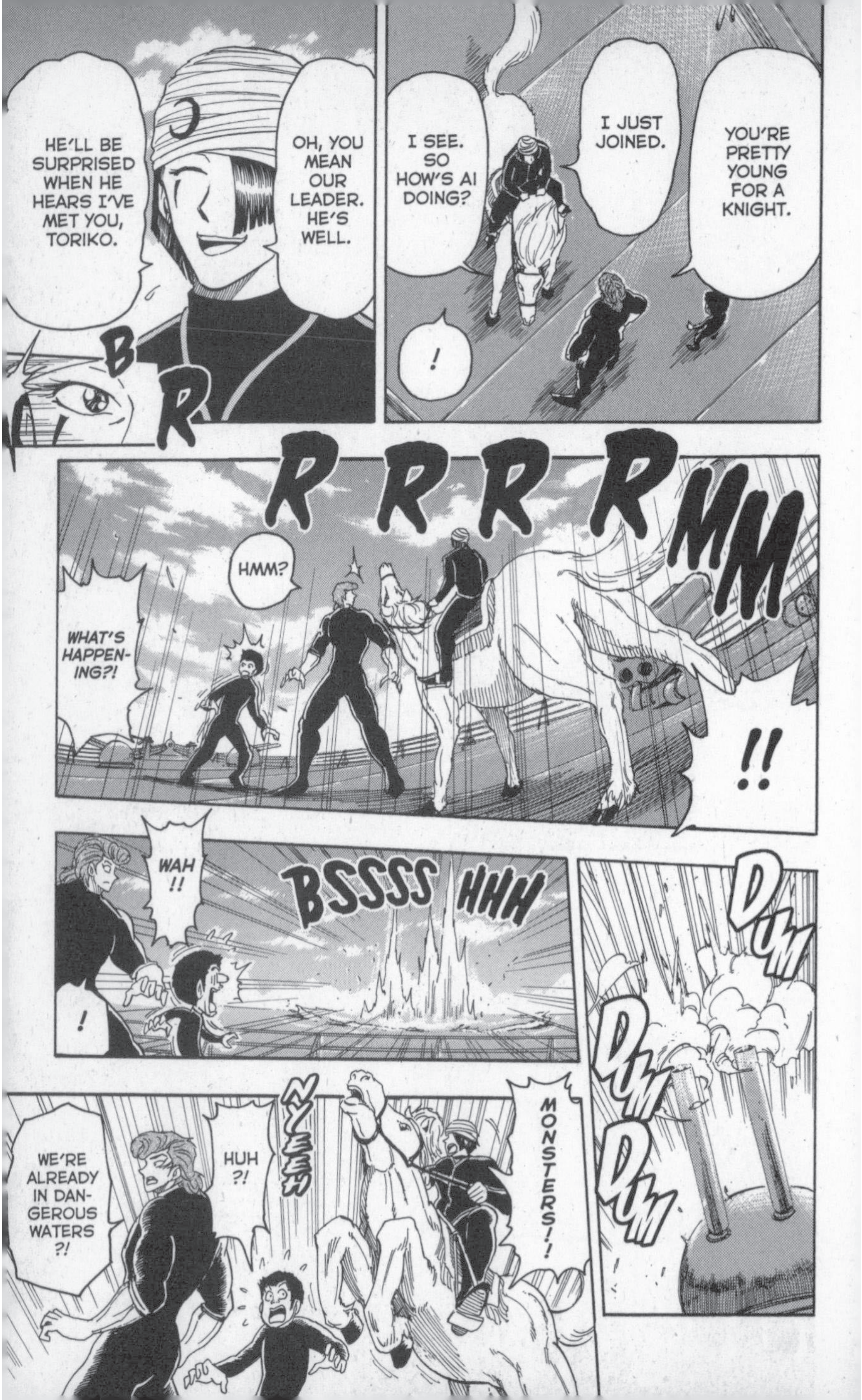
YOU'RE PRETTY YOUNG FOR A KNIGHT.
I JUST JOINED.
I SEE. SO HOW'S AI DOING?
!
OH, YOU MEAN OUR LEADER. HE'S WELL.
HE'LL BE SURPRISED WHEN HE HEARS I'VE MET YOU, TORIKO.
BRRRRRRMM
!!
HMM?
WHAT'S HAPPEN-ING?!
DUM DUM DUM DUM
WAH !!
BSSSSHHH
!
MONSTERS!!
NYEEEH
HUH ?!
WE'RE ALREADY IN DAN-GEROUS WATERS ?!

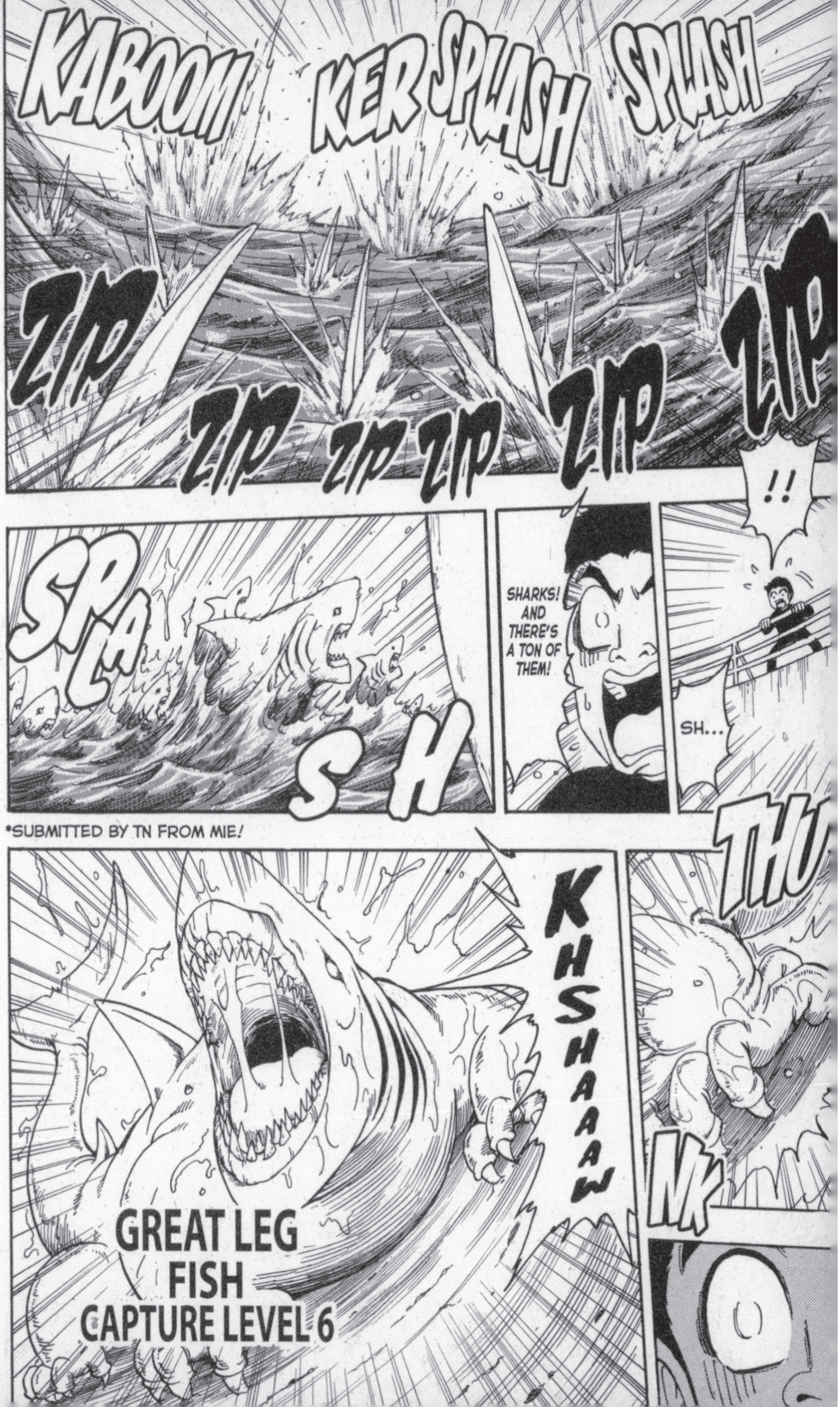

SPLASH
KERSPLASH
KABOOM
ZIP
ZIP
ZIP
ZIP
ZIP
ZIP
!!
SH...
SHARKS! AND THERE'S A TON OF THEM!
SPLASH
*SUBMITTED BY TN FROM MIE!
THUNK
KHSHAAAAW
GREAT LEG FISH
CAPTURE LEVEL 6

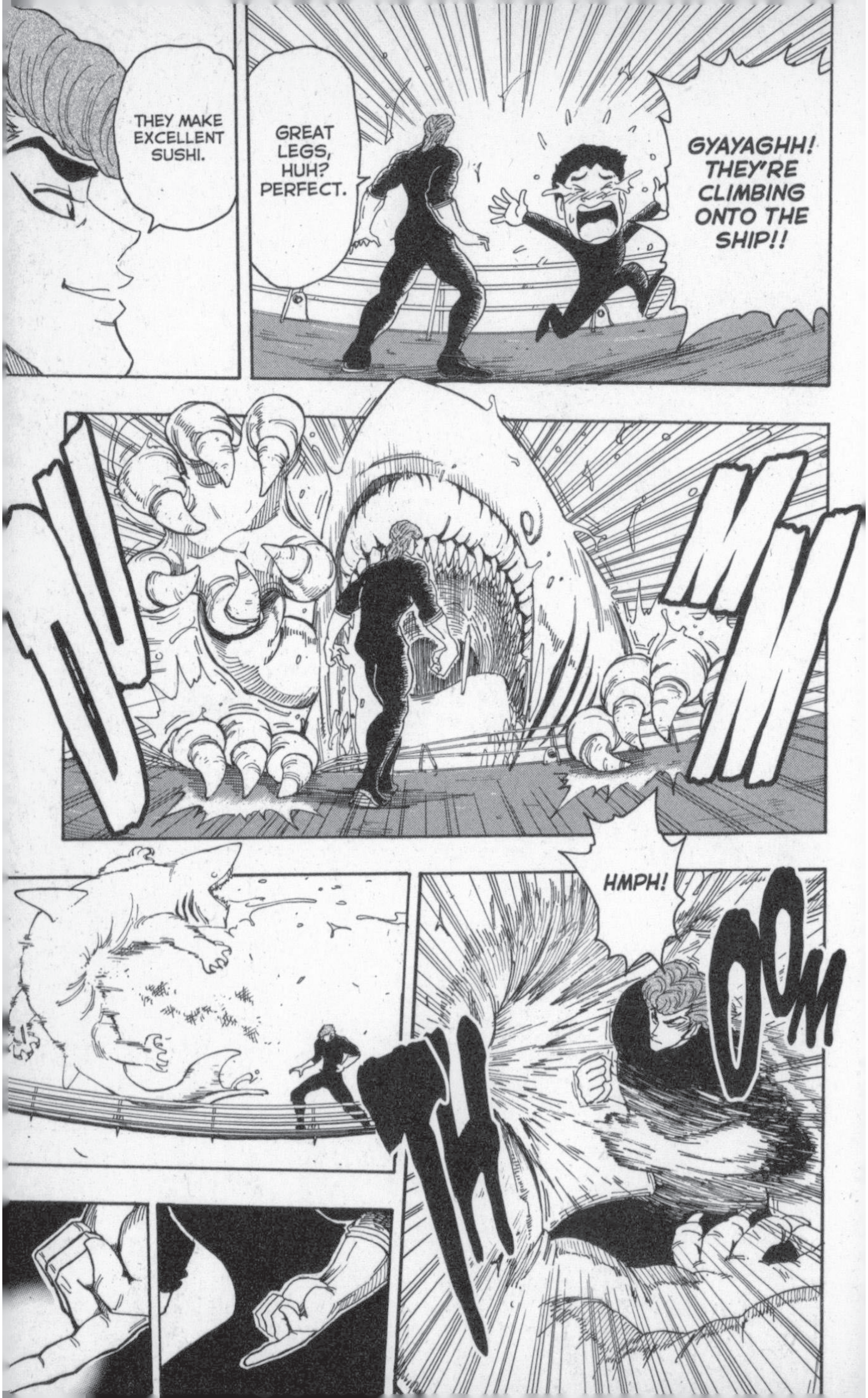
GYAYAGHH! THEY'RE CLIMBING ONTO THE SHIP!!
GREAT LEGS, HUH? PERFECT.
THEY MAKE EXCELLENT SUSHI.
HMPH!

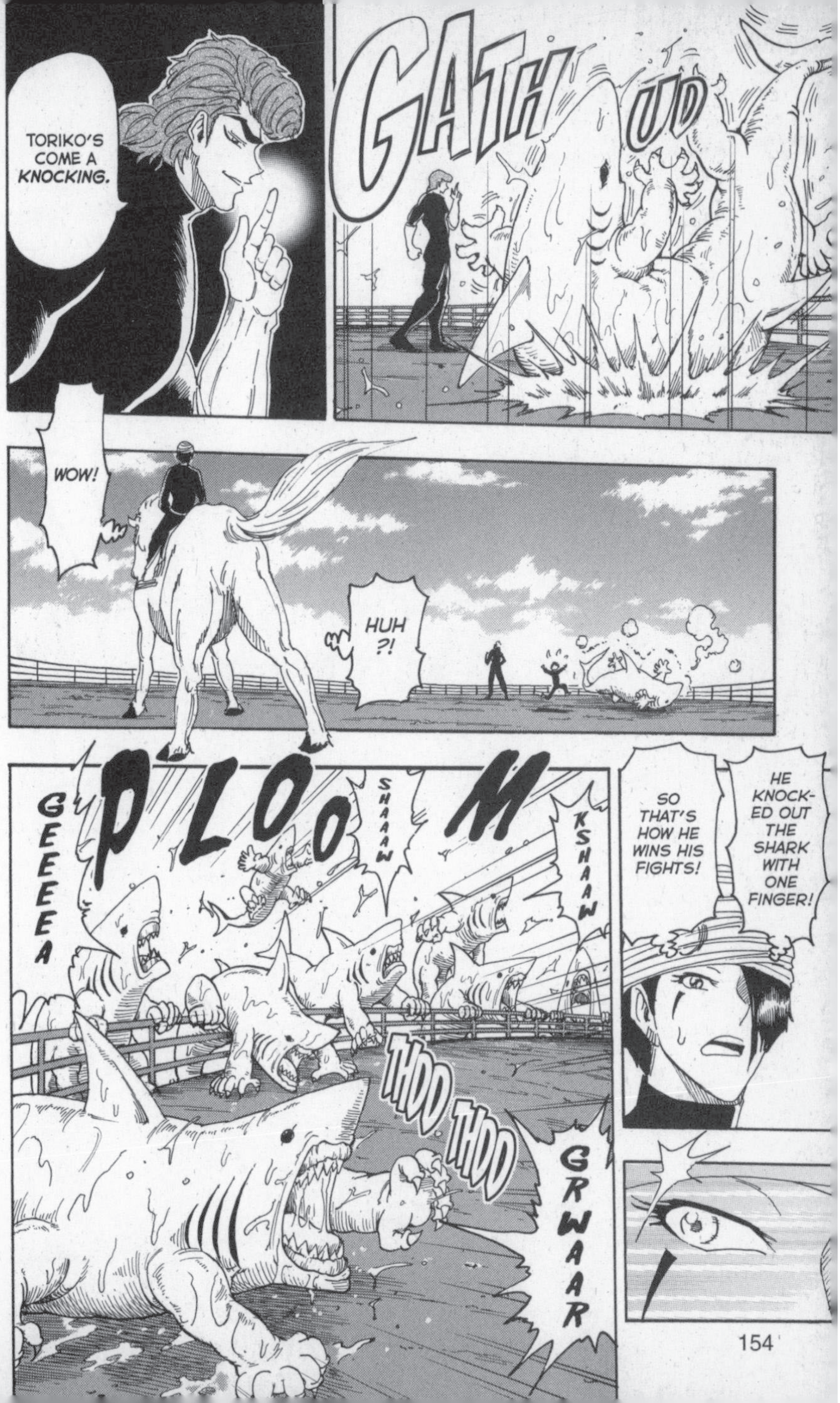
GATH
UD
TORIKO'S COME A KNOCKING.
WOW!
HUH ?!
HE KNOCKED OUT THE SHARK WITH ONE FINGER!
SO THAT'S HOW HE WINS HIS FIGHTS!
PLOOM
KSHAAAW
SHAAAAW
GEEEEEA
THOO THOO
GRWAAR

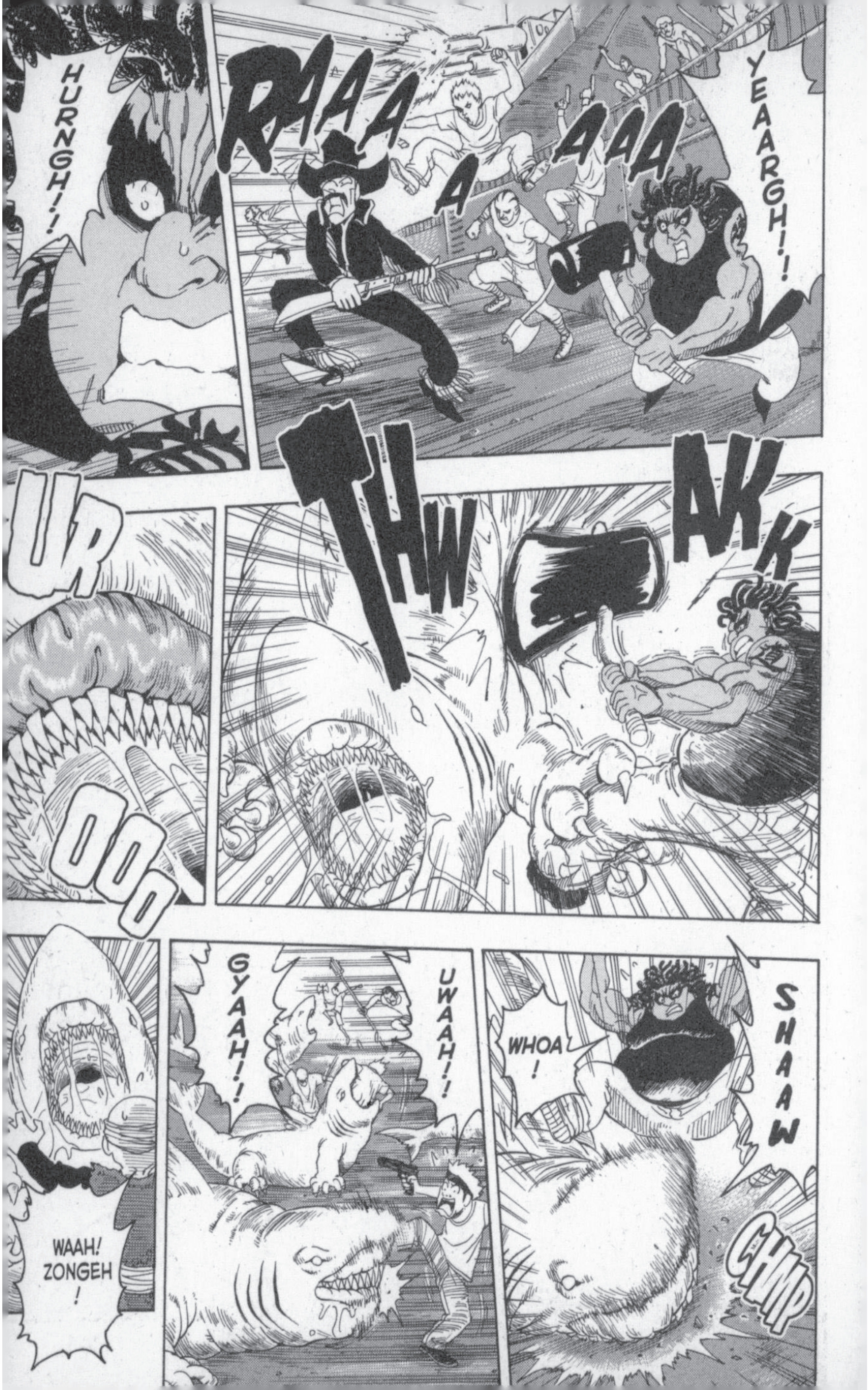
YEAARGH!!
RAAAAAAA
HURNGH!!
THWAKK
UROOO
SHAAAW
WHOA!
CHMP
UWAAAH!!
GYAAAH!!
WAAH! ZONGEH!

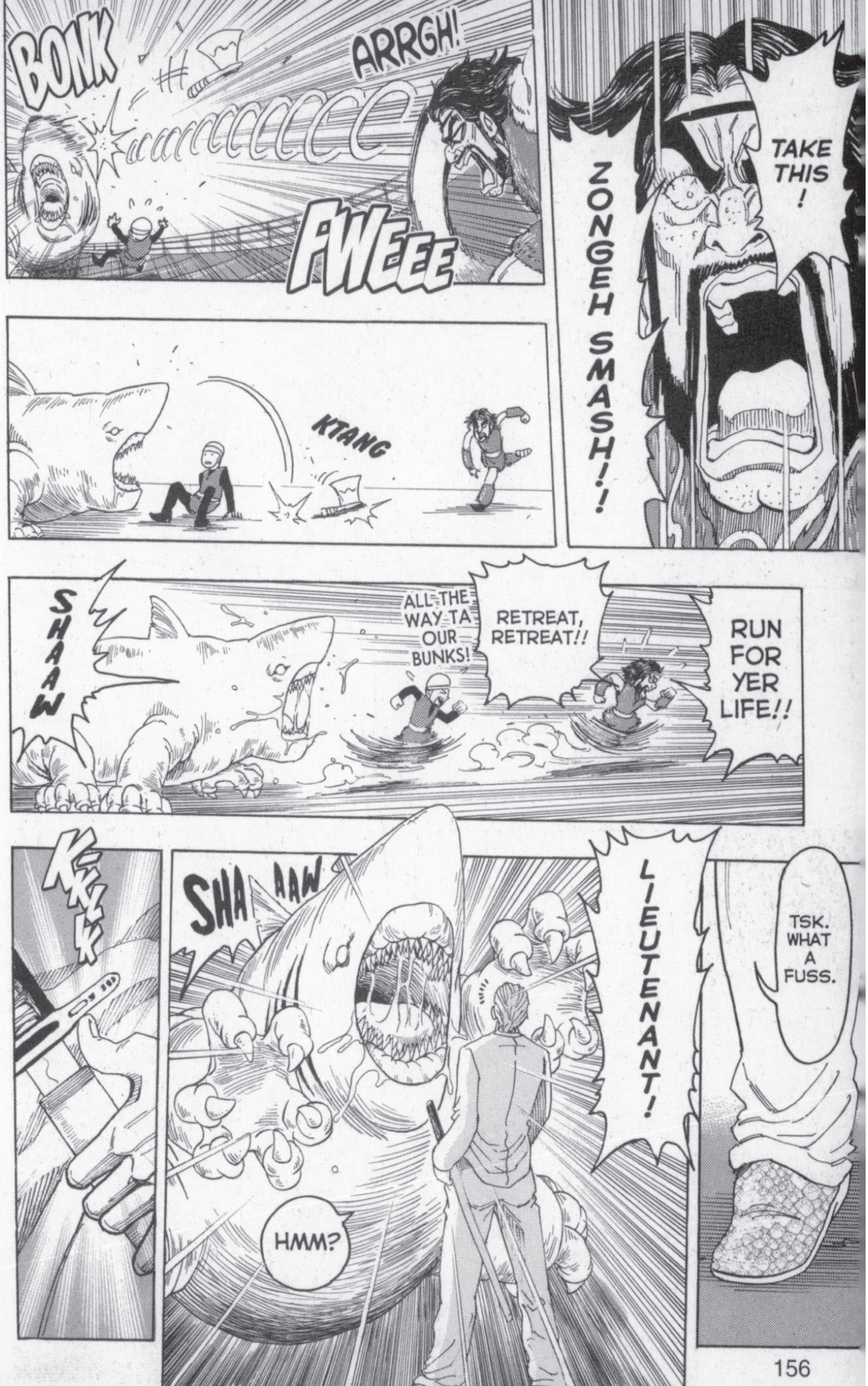
TAKE THIS!
ZONGEH SMASH!!
ARRGH!
BONK
PWEEE
KTANG
RUN FOR YER LIFE!!
RETREAT, RETREAT!!
ALL THE WAY TA OUR BUNKS!
SHAAAW
TSK. WHAT A FUSS.
LIEUTENANT!
SHA AAW
HMM?

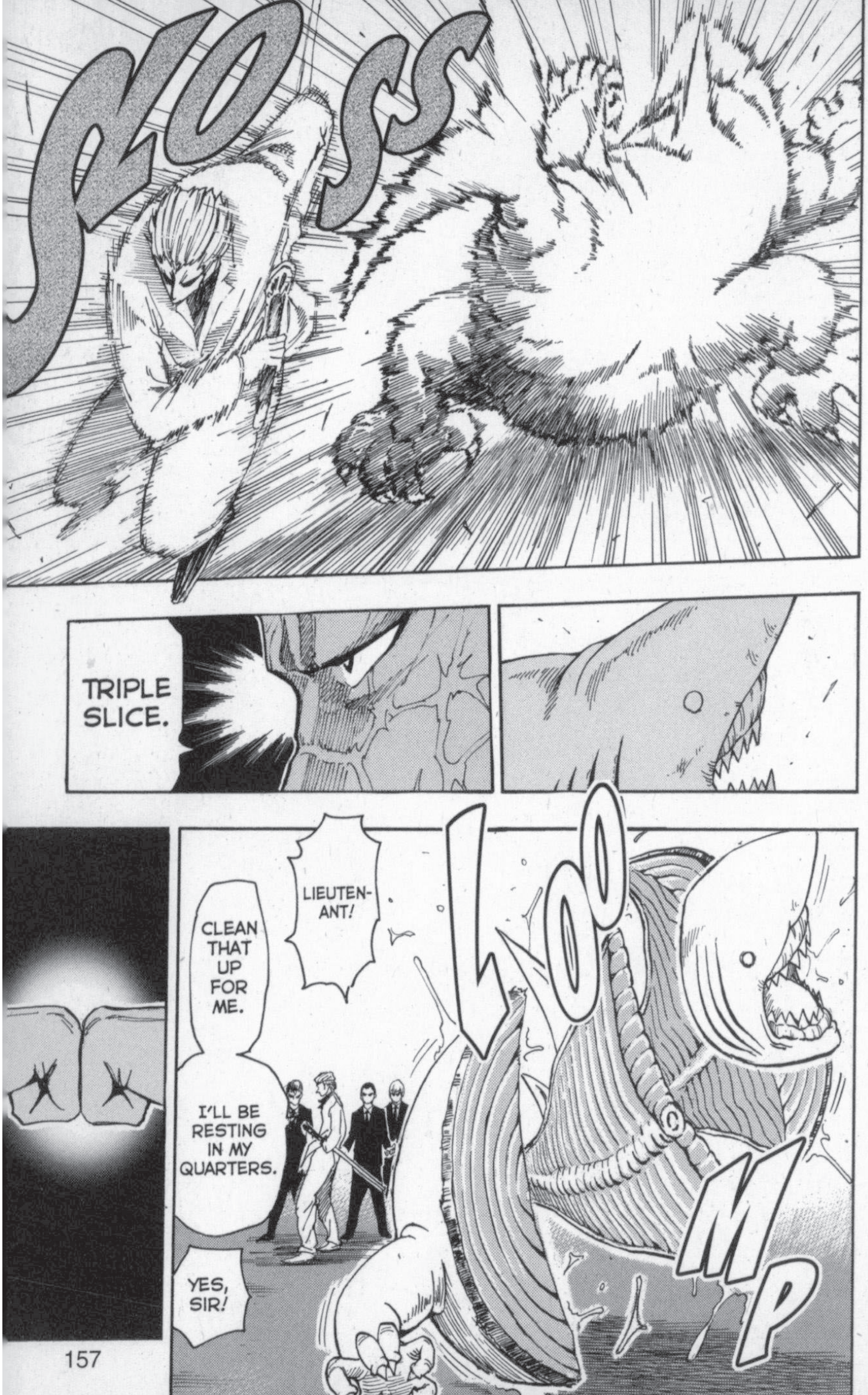
SLOSS
TRIPLE SLICE.
LOOOMP
LIEUTEN-ANT!
CLEAN THAT UP FOR ME.
I'LL BE RESTING IN MY QUARTERS.
YES, SIR!

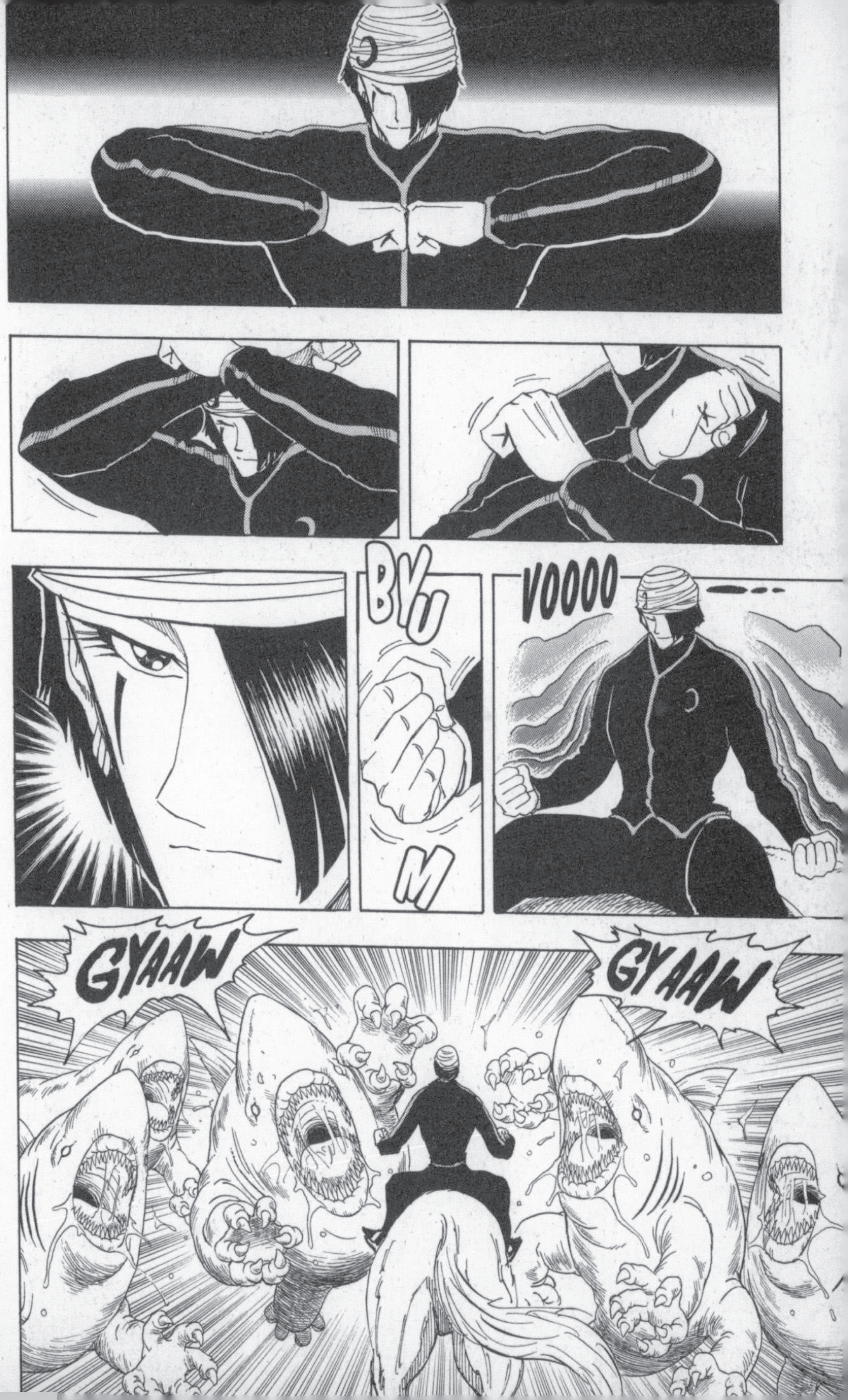
VOOOO
BYUM
GYAAW
GYAAW

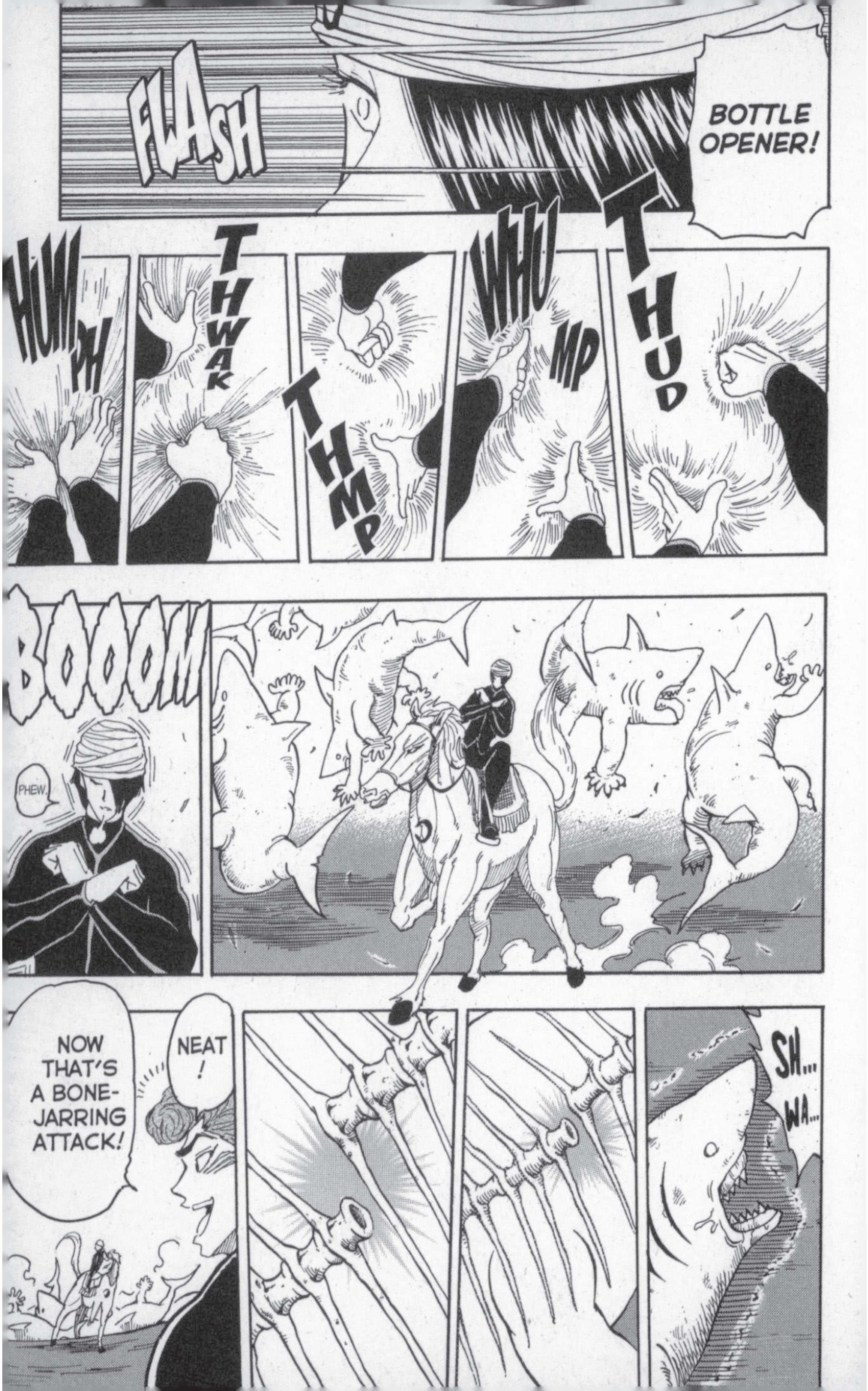
BOTTLE OPENER!
FLASH
THUD
WHUMP
THMP
THWAK
HUMPH
BOOOM
PHEW.
SH... WA...
NEAT!
NOW THAT'S A BONE-JARRING ATTACK!

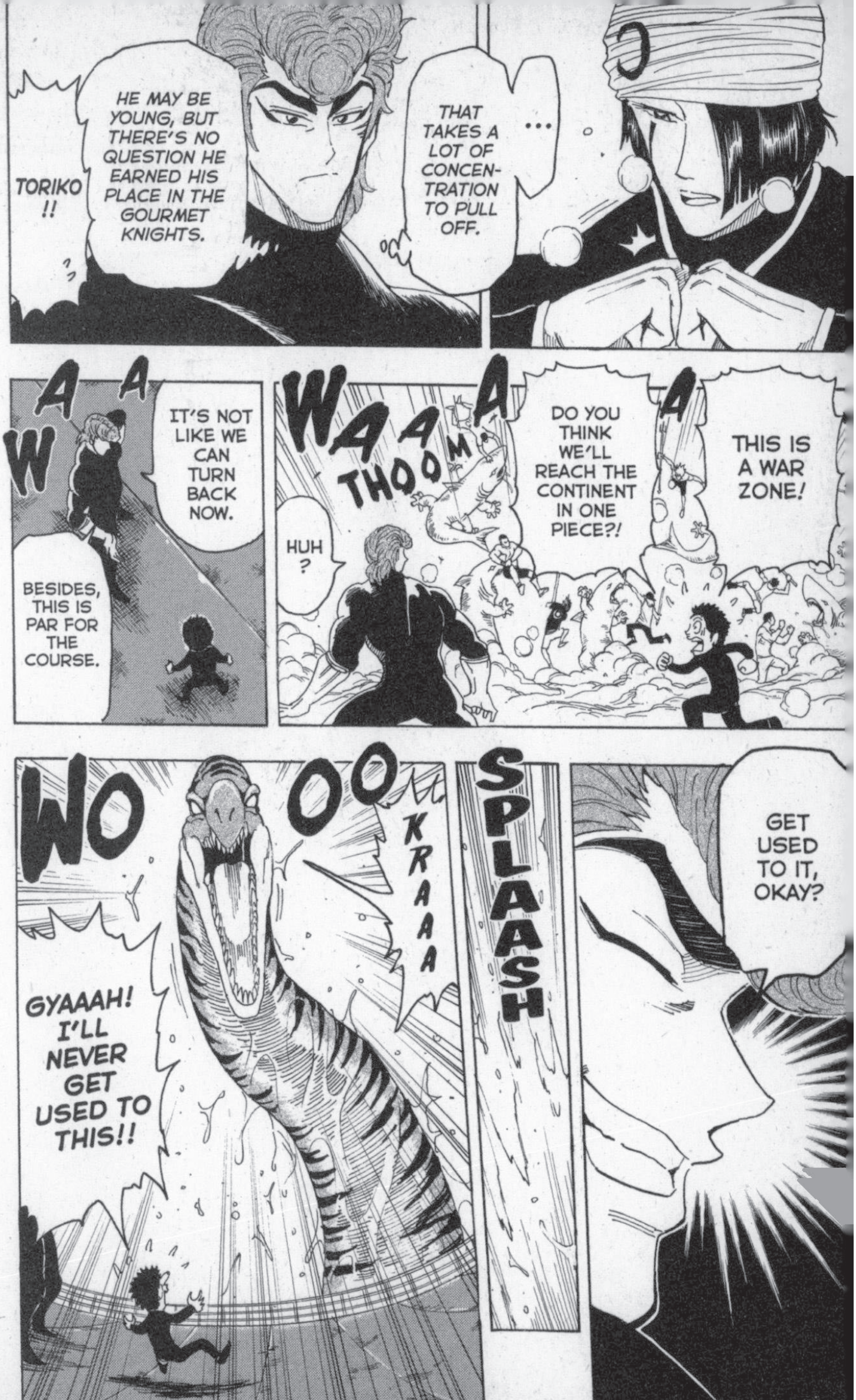

...
THAT TAKES A LOT OF CONCEN-TRATION TO PULL OFF.
HE MAY BE YOUNG, BUT THERE'S NO QUESTION HE EARNED HIS PLACE IN THE GOURMET KNIGHTS.
TORIKO !!
WAAAA
THIS IS A WAR ZONE!
DO YOU THINK WE'LL REACH THE CONTINENT IN ONE PIECE?!
THOOM
HUH ?
WAA
IT'S NOT LIKE WE CAN TURN BACK NOW.
BESIDES, THIS IS PAR FOR THE COURSE.
GET USED TO IT, OKAY?
SPLAASH
KRAAAA
WOOO
GYAAAH! I'LL NEVER GET USED TO THIS!!

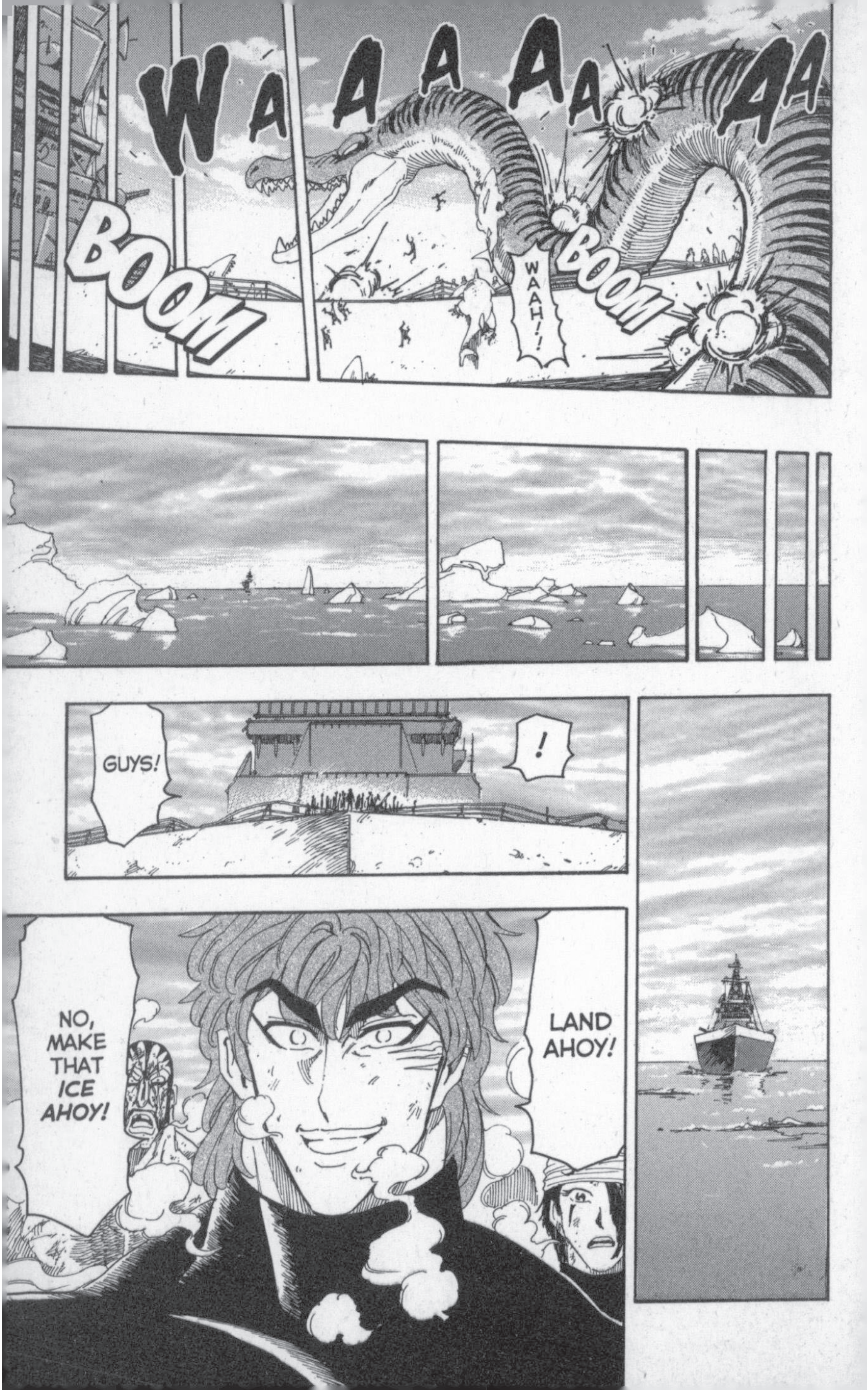
WAAAAAAA
BOOM
WAAH!!
BOOM
!
GUYS!
LAND AHOY!
NO, MAKE THAT ICE AHOY!

TORIKO

GOURMET CHECKLIST

Vol. 056

SIRLOIN MUSHROOM

(FUNGUS)

CAPTURE LEVEL: 7

HABITAT: HUMID AREAS (SUCH AS THE

MUSHROOM WOODS ON REGAL ISLE)

LENGTH: 35 CM

HEIGHT: ---

WEIGHT: 900 G

 PRICE: 50,000 YEN EACH

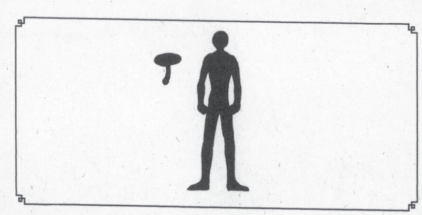

SCALE

A MUSHROOM THAT TASTES LIKE STEAK! SINCE THEY'RE SO
JUICY, SALT AND PEPPER OR EVEN SOY SAUCE MAKE GREAT
TOPPINGS. SIRLOIN SHROOMS ARE AT THEIR BEST WHEN
COOKED, SO SEAR THEM OVER AN OPEN GRILL.

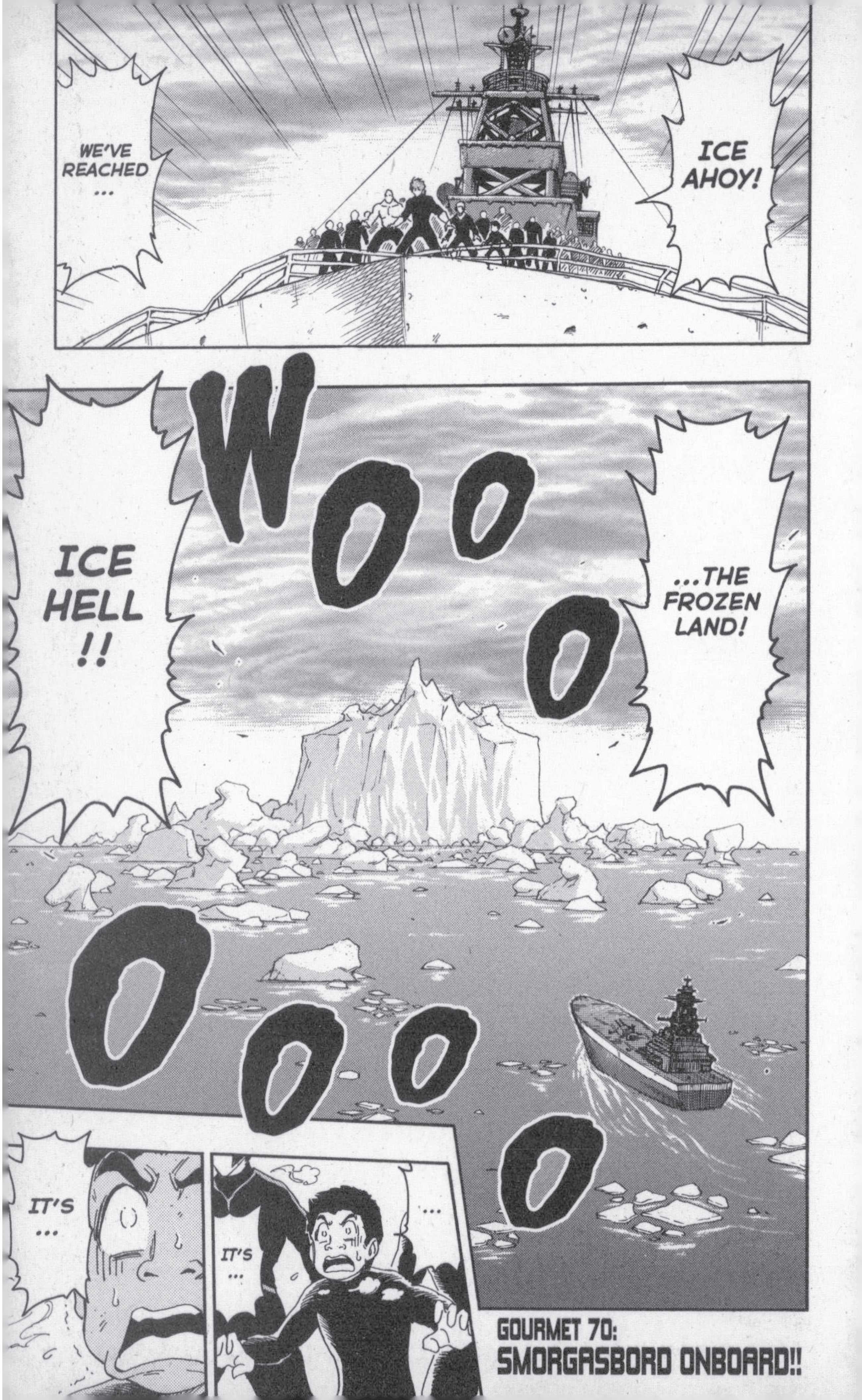
ICE AHOY!
WE'VE REACHED ...
...THE FROZEN LAND!
ICE HELL !!
WOOOOOOOOOO
...
IT'S ...
IT'S ...

GOURMET 70: SMORGASBORD ONBOARD!!

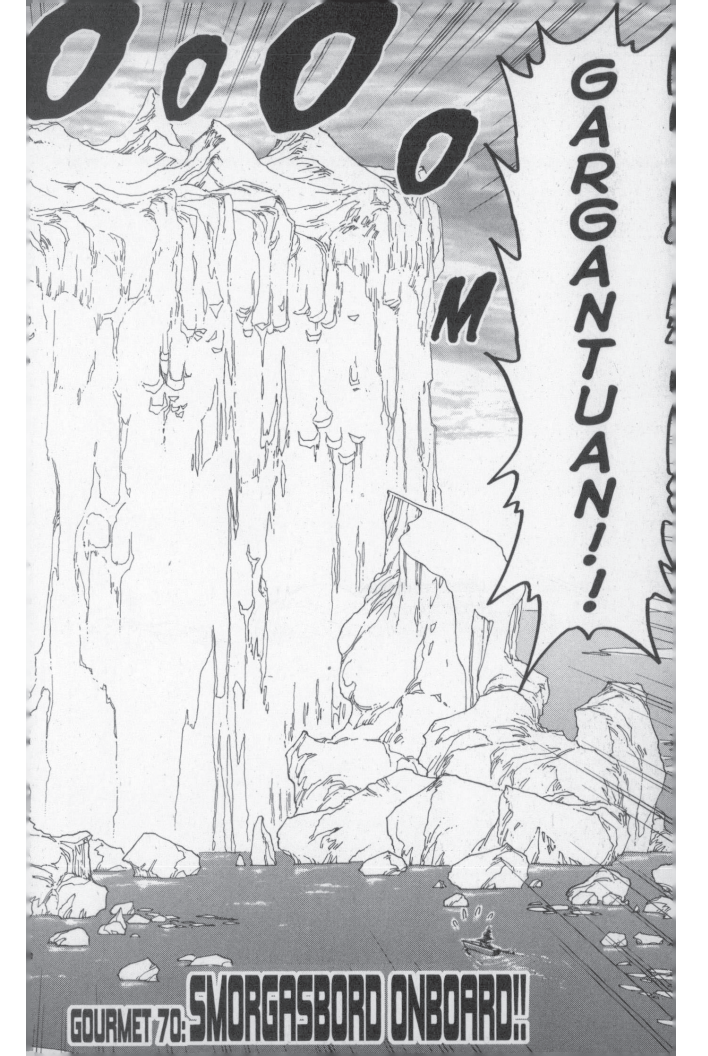

GOURMET 70: SMORGASBORD ONBOARD!!

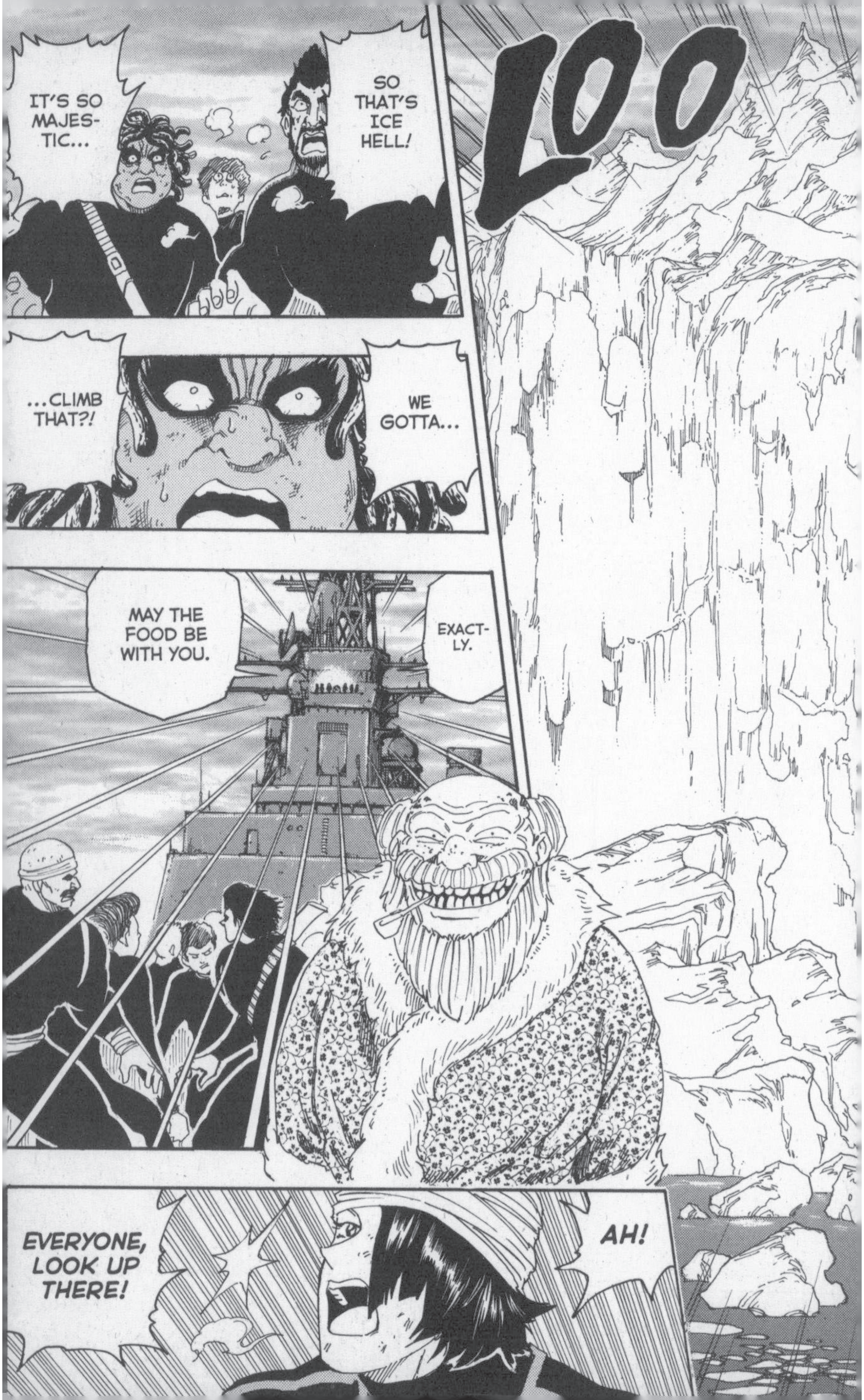
LOO
SO THAT'S ICE HELL!
IT'S SO MAJES-TIC...
WE GOTTA...
...CLIMB THAT?!
EXACT-LY.
MAY THE FOOD BE WITH YOU.
AH!
EVERYONE, LOOK UP THERE!

PLOO

SLUP!!

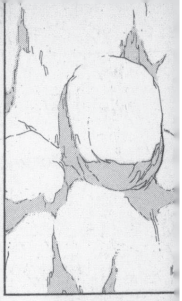

THE ICE IS FALLING !!

YEEEE!!

WHOOOSH

TATTA TATTA

OTRA

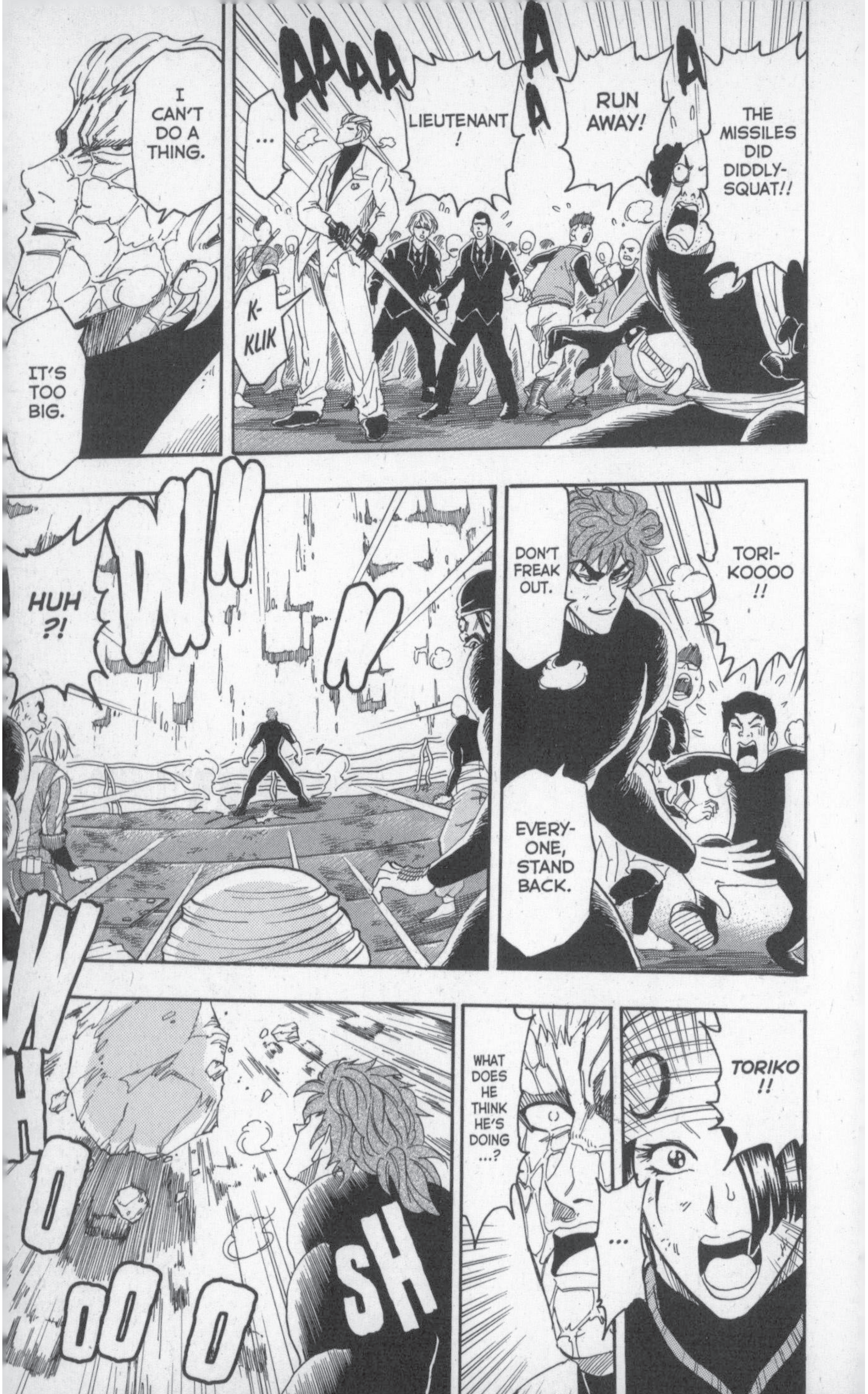
THE MISSILES DID DIDDLY-SQUAT!!
A
RUN AWAY!
AAA
LIEUTENANT!
AAAA
...
K-KLIK
I CAN'T DO A THING.
IT'S TOO BIG.
TORI-KOOOO!!
DON'T FREAK OUT.
EVERY-ONE, STAND BACK.
DUN N
HUH?!
TORIKO!!
WHAT DOES HE THINK HE'S DOING...?
...
WHOOOOOOSH

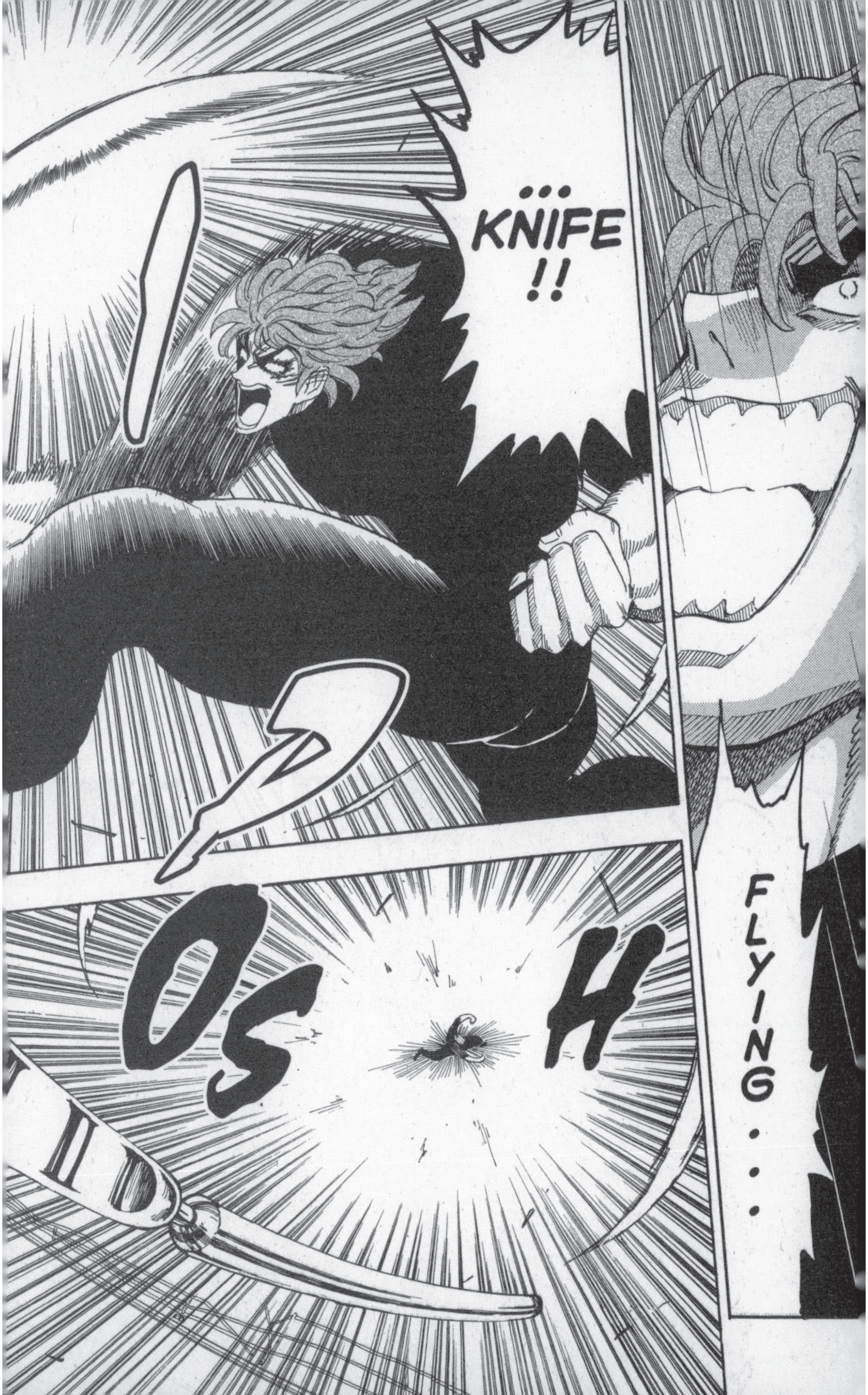
FLYING...
...KNIFE !!
OSH

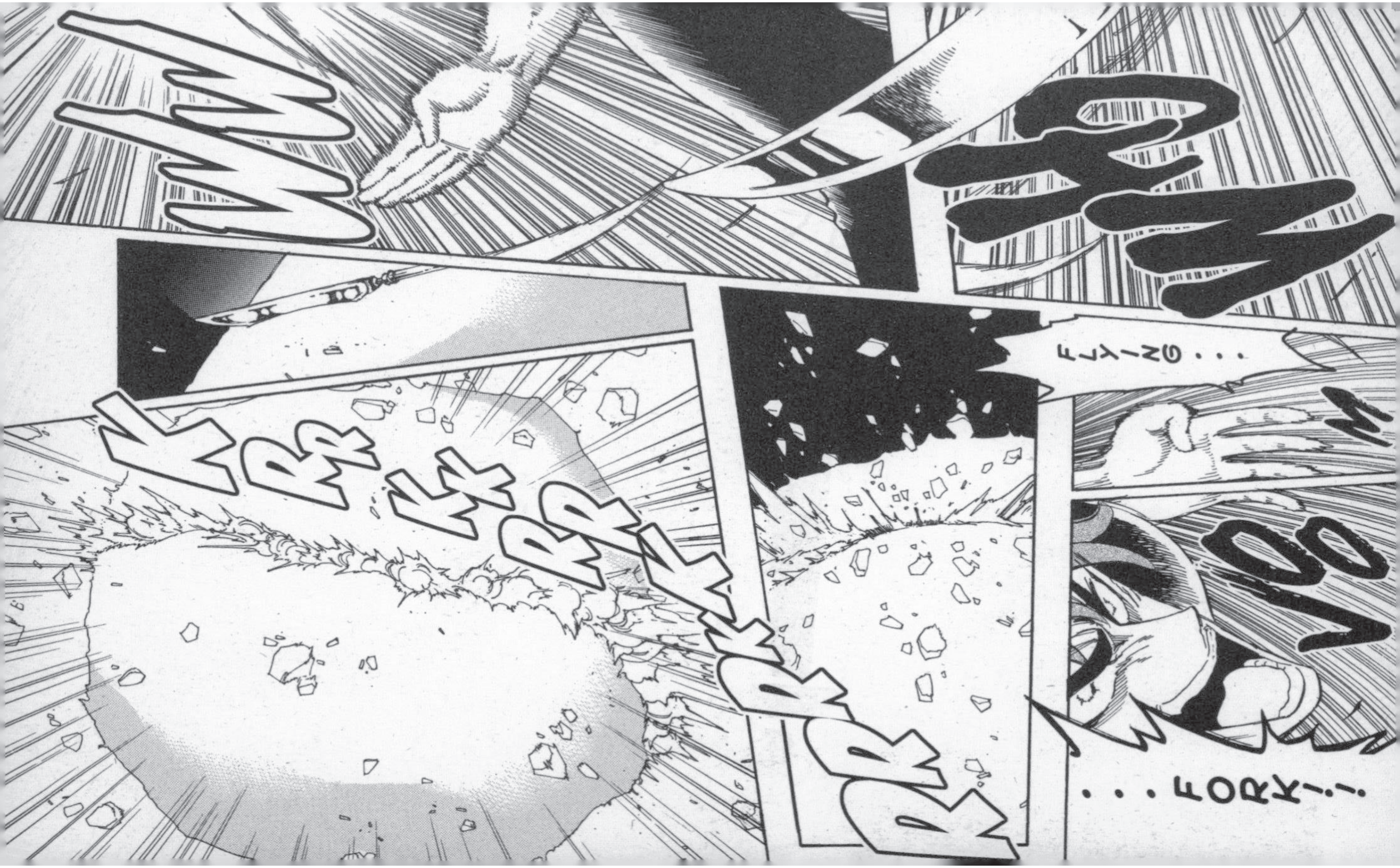
FLYING...
...FORK!!

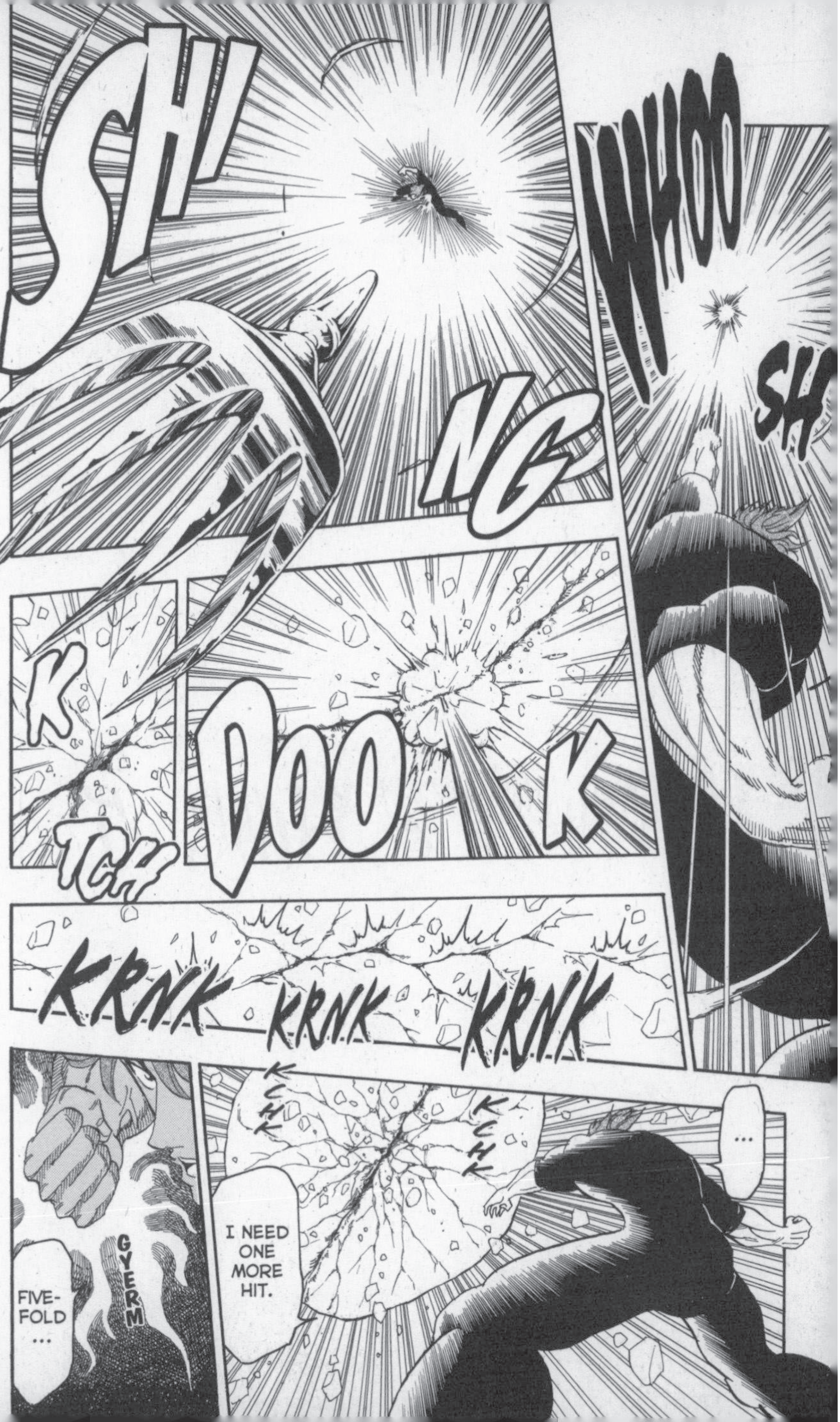
WHOO
SH
SHI
NG
DOO K
K TCH
KRNK KRNK KRNK
...
KCHK
KCHK
I NEED ONE MORE HIT.
GYERM
FIVE-FOLD ...

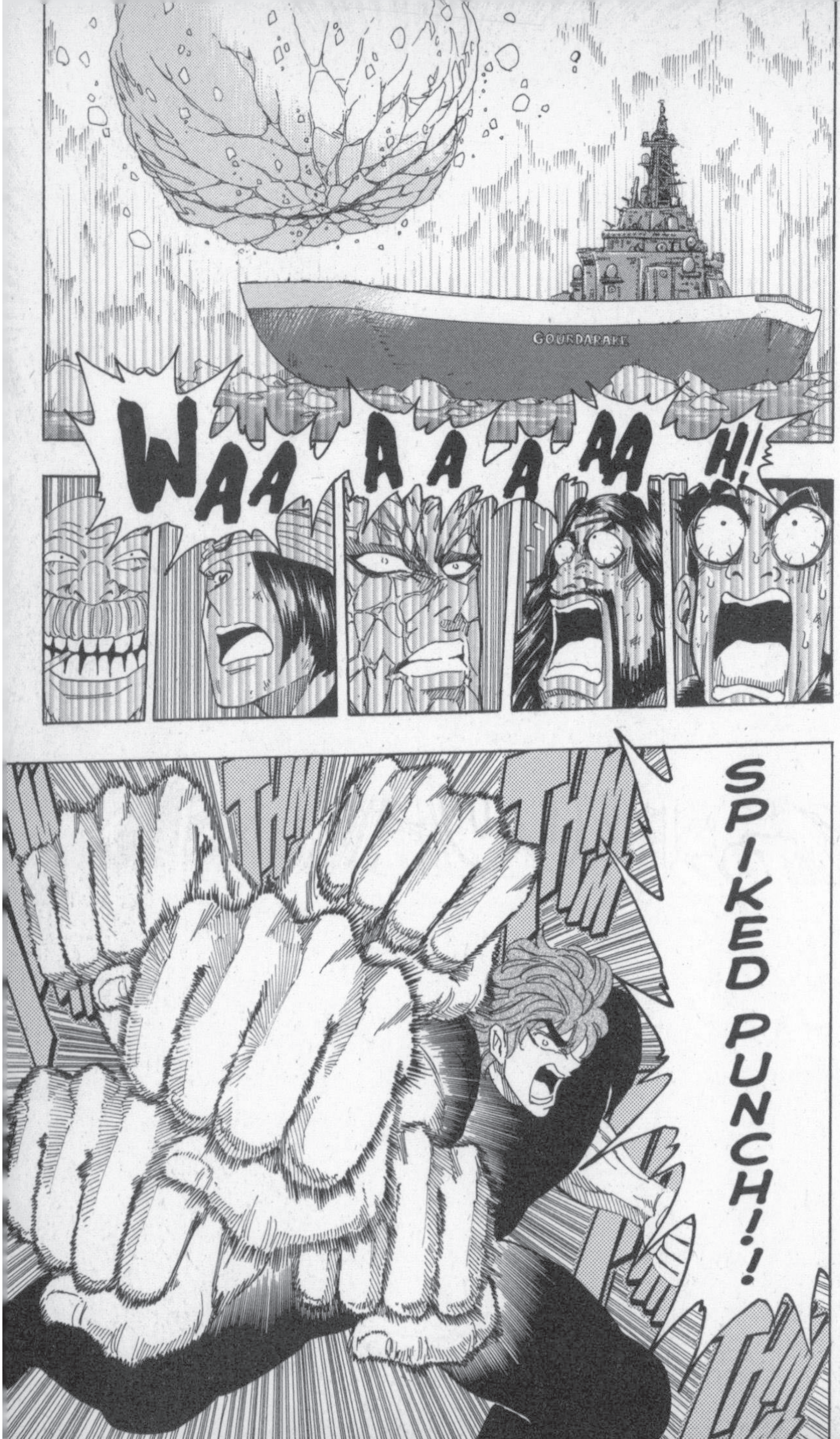
GOURDARAKE
WAAAAAAAH!
SPIKED PUNCH!!

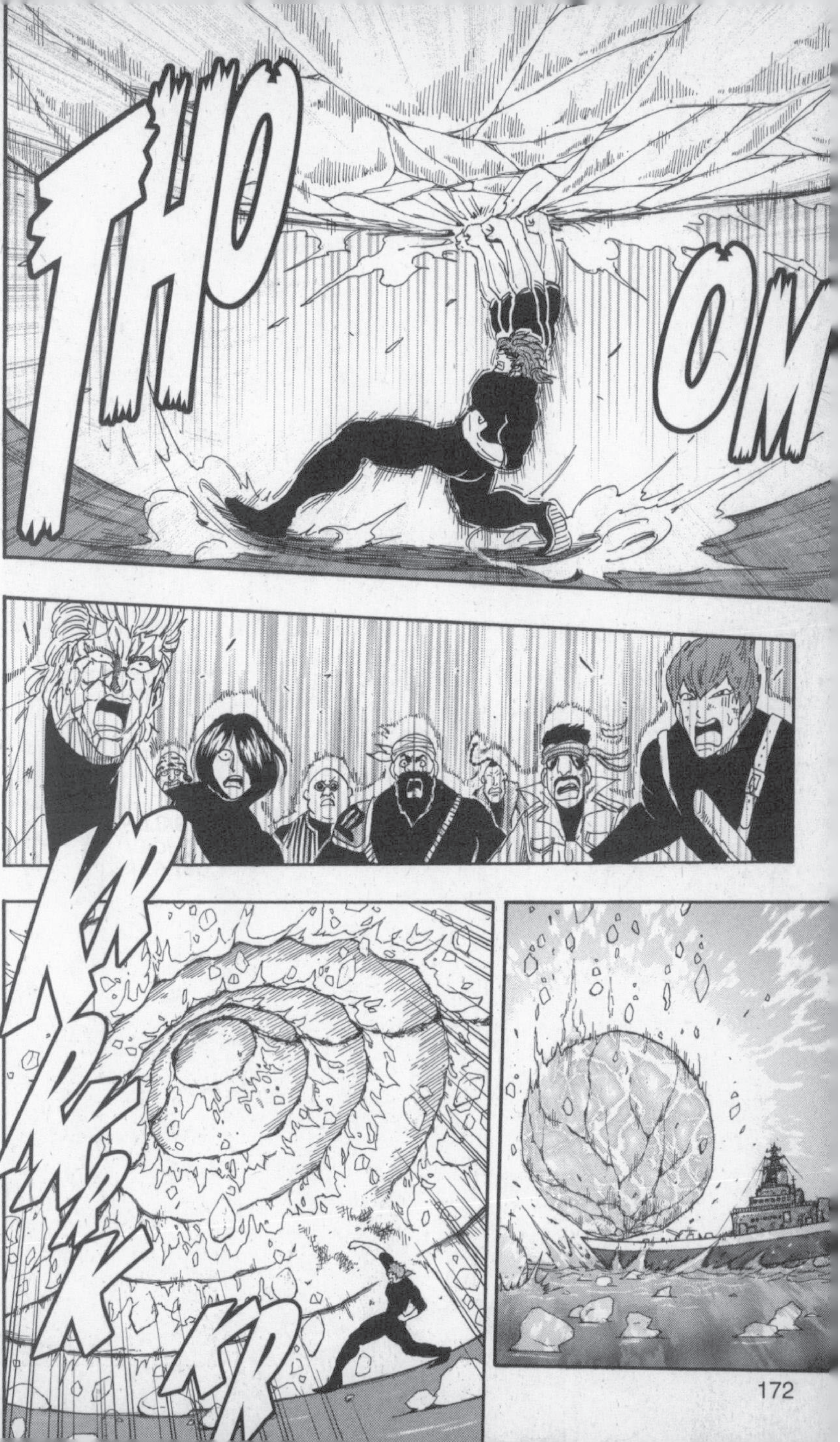
THOOM
KRRRK KR

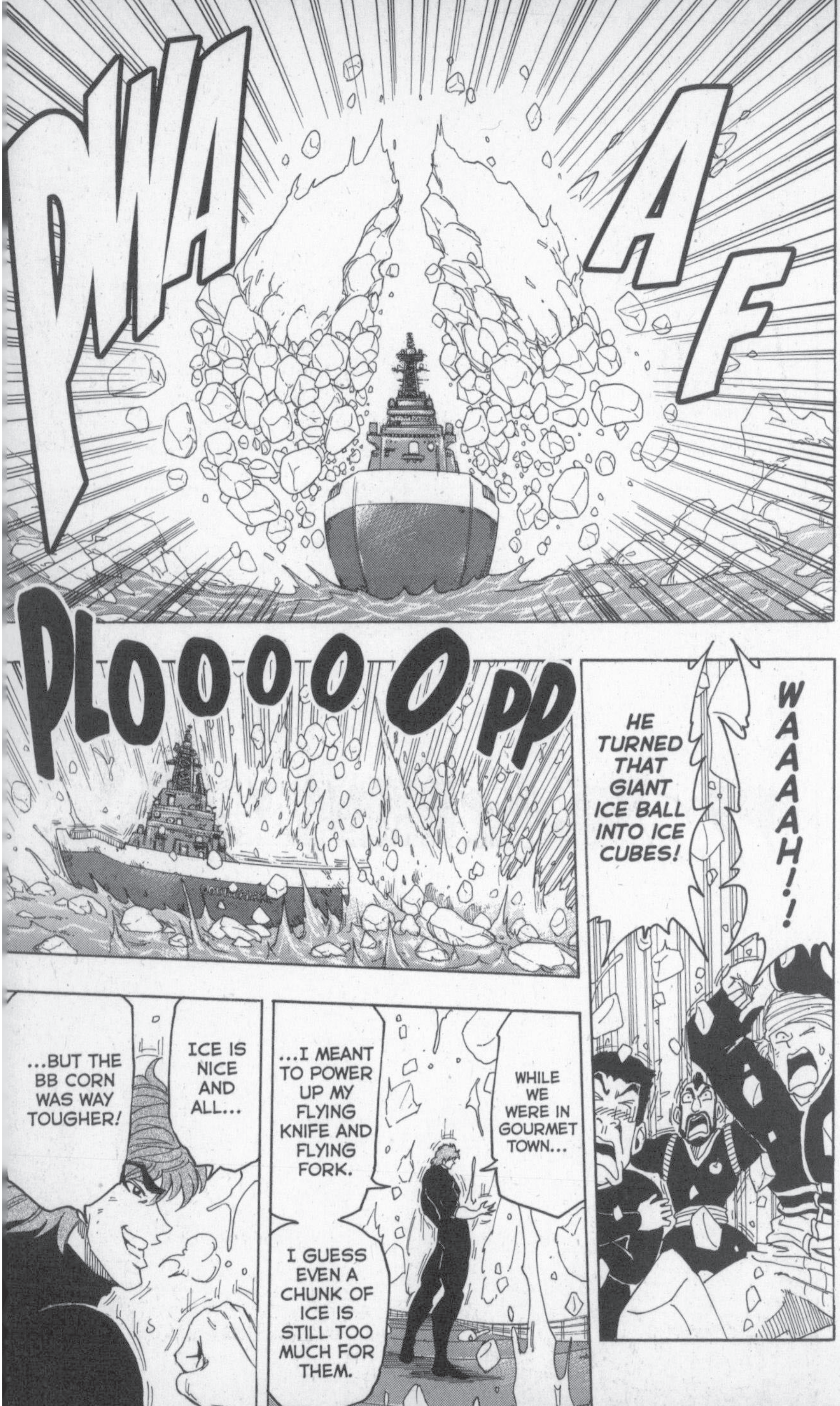
DWAAF
WAAAAH!!
HE TURNED THAT GIANT ICE BALL INTO ICE CUBES!
PLOOOOOPP
WHILE WE WERE IN GOURMET TOWN...
...I MEANT TO POWER UP MY FLYING KNIFE AND FLYING FORK.
I GUESS EVEN A CHUNK OF ICE IS STILL TOO MUCH FOR THEM.
ICE IS NICE AND ALL...
...BUT THE BB CORN WAS WAY TOUGHER!

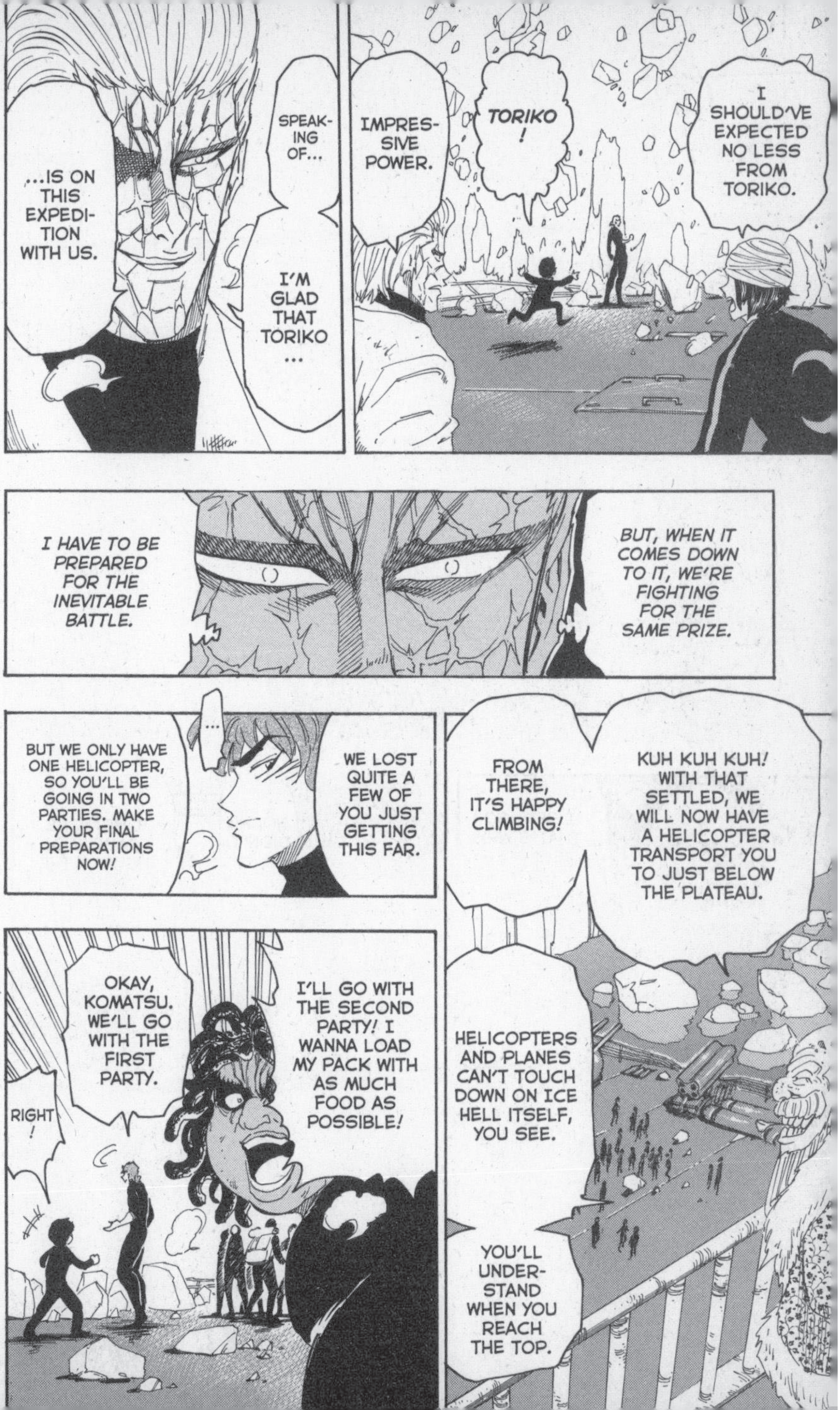
I SHOULD'VE EXPECTED NO LESS FROM TORIKO.
TORIKO!
IMPRESSIVE POWER.
SPEAKING OF...
I'M GLAD THAT TORIKO...
...IS ON THIS EXPEDITION WITH US.
BUT, WHEN IT COMES DOWN TO IT, WE'RE FIGHTING FOR THE SAME PRIZE.
I HAVE TO BE PREPARED FOR THE INEVITABLE BATTLE.
KUH KUH KUH! WITH THAT SETTLED, WE WILL NOW HAVE A HELICOPTER TRANSPORT YOU TO JUST BELOW THE PLATEAU.
FROM THERE, IT'S HAPPY CLIMBING!
HELICOPTERS AND PLANES CAN'T TOUCH DOWN ON ICE HELL ITSELF, YOU SEE.
YOU'LL UNDERSTAND WHEN YOU REACH THE TOP.
WE LOST QUITE A FEW OF YOU JUST GETTING THIS FAR.
...
BUT WE ONLY HAVE ONE HELICOPTER, SO YOU'LL BE GOING IN TWO PARTIES. MAKE YOUR FINAL PREPARATIONS NOW!
I'LL GO WITH THE SECOND PARTY! I WANNA LOAD MY PACK WITH AS MUCH FOOD AS POSSIBLE!
OKAY, KOMATSU. WE'LL GO WITH THE FIRST PARTY.
RIGHT!

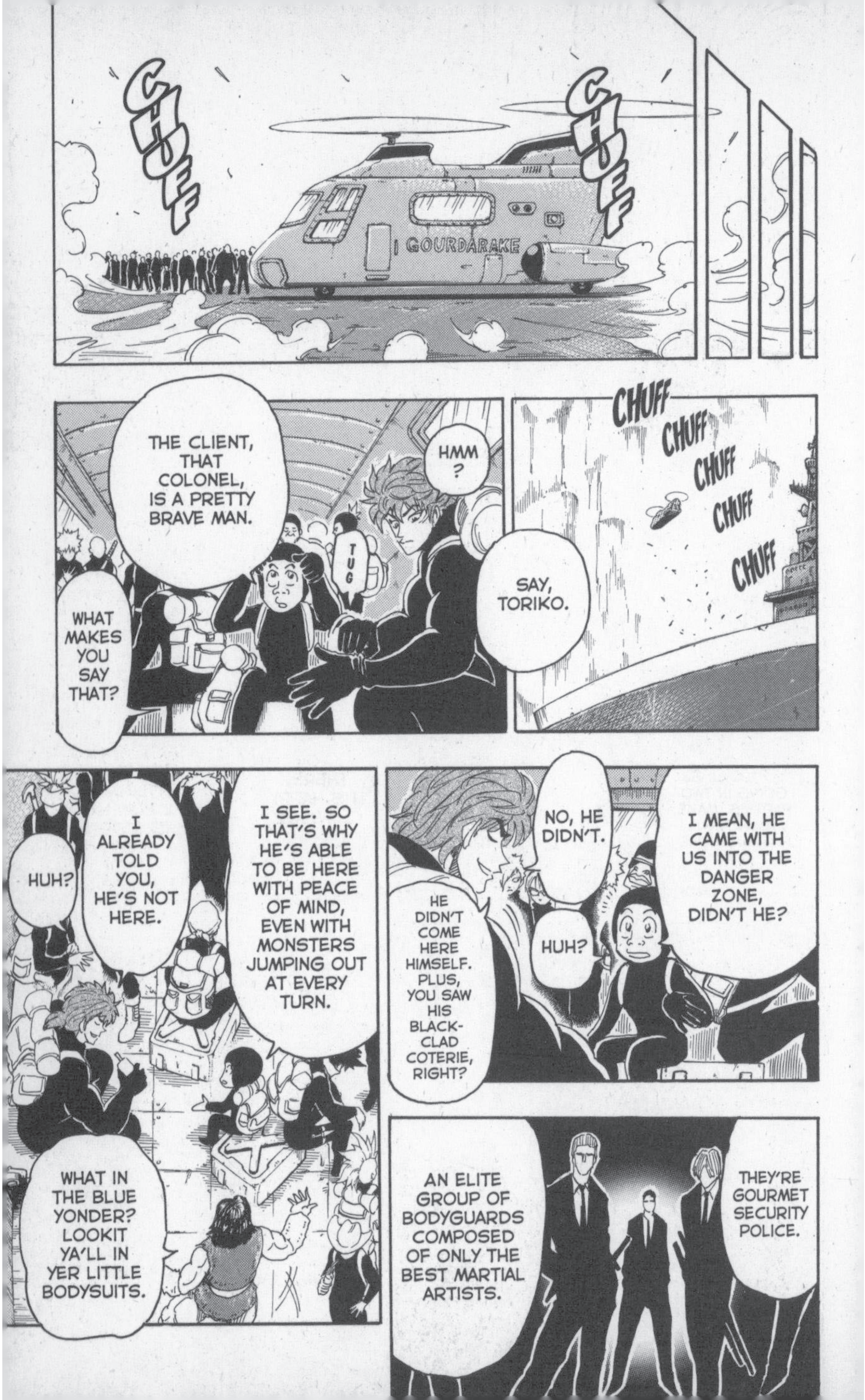
CHUFF
GOURDARAKE
CHUFF
CHUFF CHUFF CHUFF CHUFF CHUFF
SAY, TORIKO.
HMM?
THE CLIENT, THAT COLONEL, IS A PRETTY BRAVE MAN.
TUG
WHAT MAKES YOU SAY THAT?
I MEAN, HE CAME WITH US INTO THE DANGER ZONE, DIDN'T HE?
NO, HE DIDN'T.
HUH?
HE DIDN'T COME HERE HIMSELF. PLUS, YOU SAW HIS BLACK-CLAD COTERIE, RIGHT?
THEY'RE GOURMET SECURITY POLICE.
AN ELITE GROUP OF BODYGUARDS COMPOSED OF ONLY THE BEST MARTIAL ARTISTS.
I SEE. SO THAT'S WHY HE'S ABLE TO BE HERE WITH PEACE OF MIND, EVEN WITH MONSTERS JUMPING OUT AT EVERY TURN.
I ALREADY TOLD YOU, HE'S NOT HERE.
HUH?
WHAT IN THE BLUE YONDER? LOOKIT YA'LL IN YER LITTLE BODYSUITS.

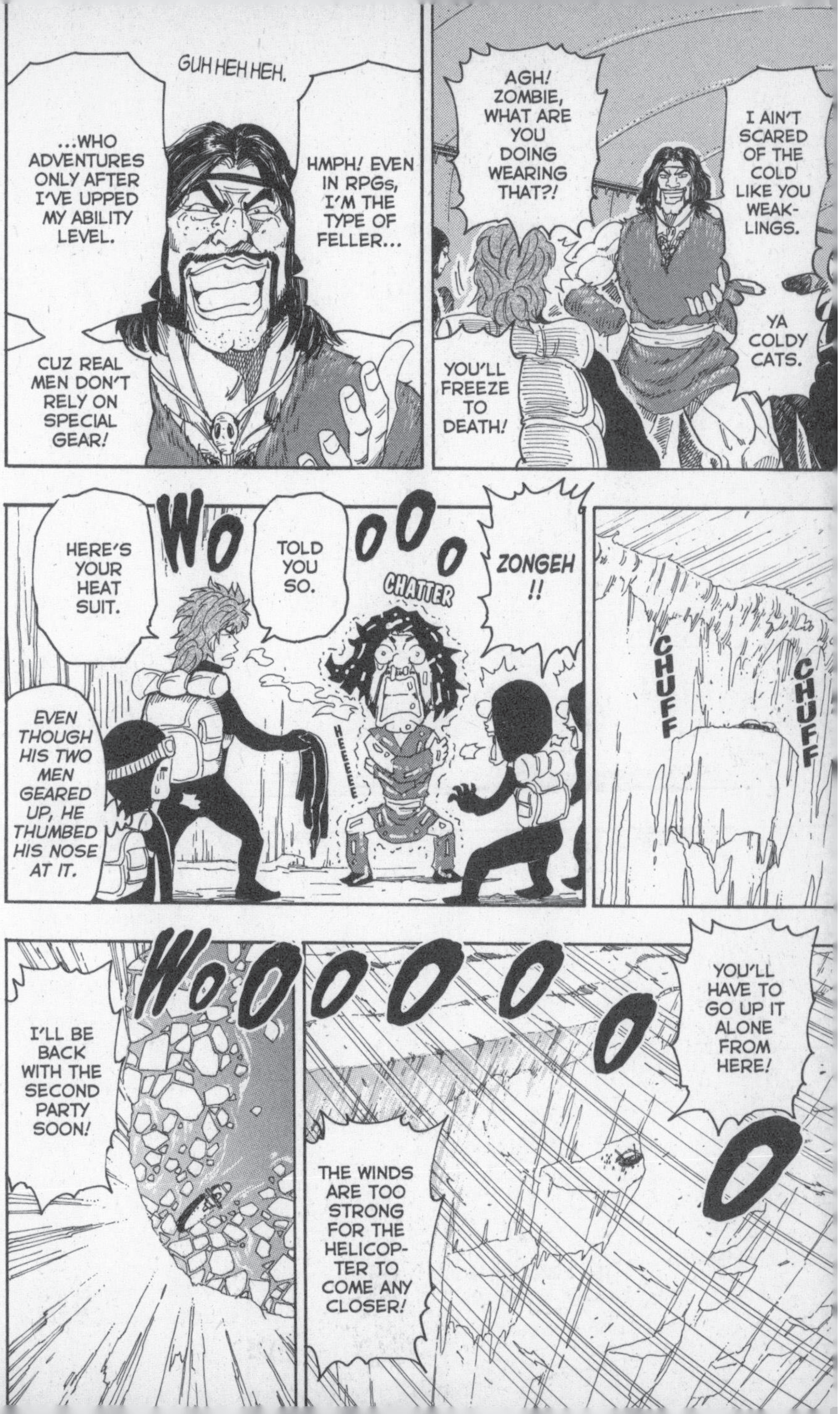
AGH! ZOMBIE, WHAT ARE YOU DOING WEARING THAT?!
I AIN'T SCARED OF THE COLD LIKE YOU WEAKLINGS.
YOU'LL FREEZE TO DEATH!
YA COLDY CATS.
GUH HEH HEH.
HMPH! EVEN IN RPGs, I'M THE TYPE OF FELLER...
...WHO ADVENTURES ONLY AFTER I'VE UPPED MY ABILITY LEVEL.
CUZ REAL MEN DON'T RELY ON SPECIAL GEAR!
CHUFF
CHUFF
ZONGEH !!
WOOOO
CHATTER
TOLD YOU SO.
HERE'S YOUR HEAT SUIT.
HEEEEE
EVEN THOUGH HIS TWO MEN GEARED UP, HE THUMBED HIS NOSE AT IT.
YOU'LL HAVE TO GO UP IT ALONE FROM HERE!
WOOOOOOOO
THE WINDS ARE TOO STRONG FOR THE HELICOPTER TO COME ANY CLOSER!
I'LL BE BACK WITH THE SECOND PARTY SOON!

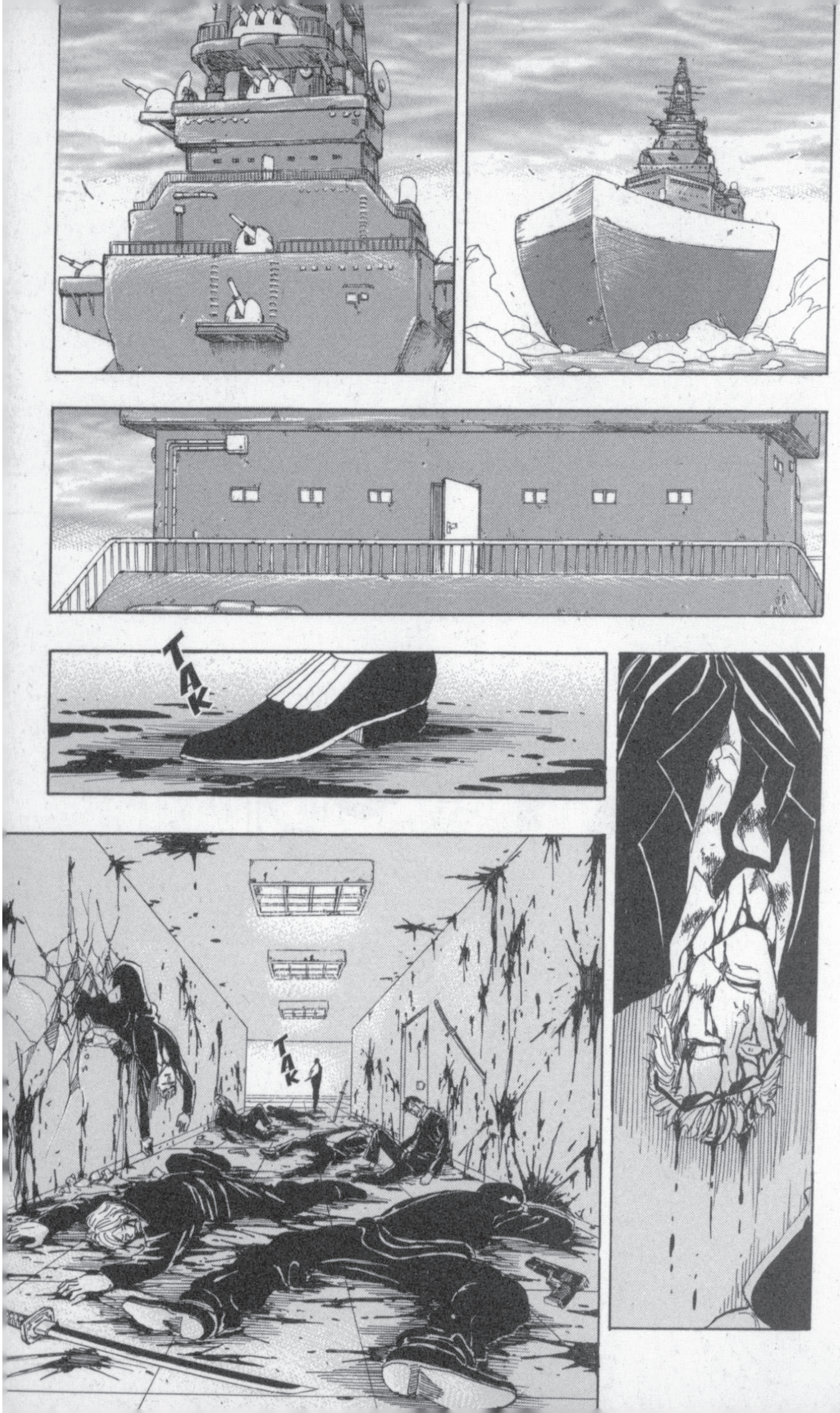
TAK
TAK

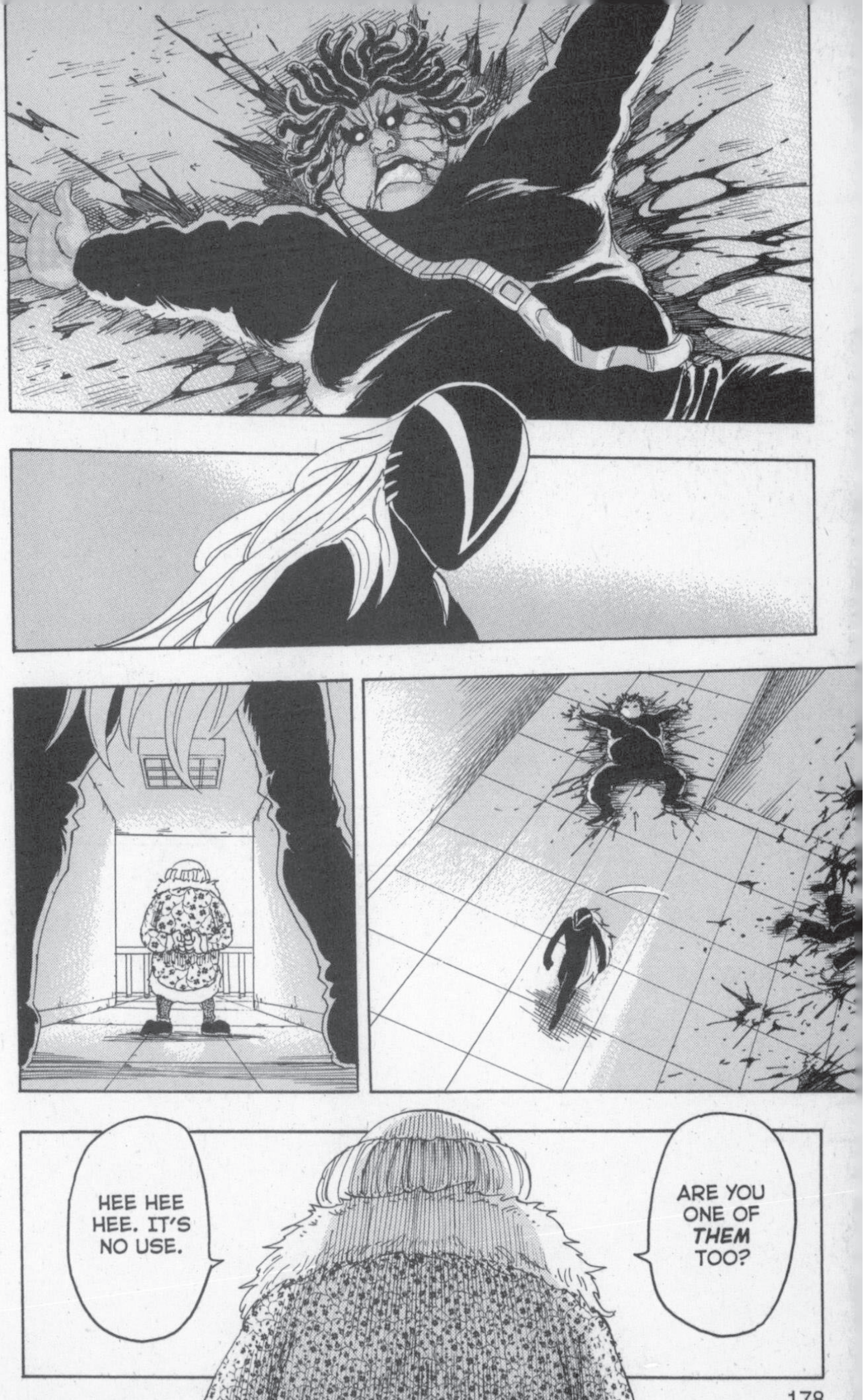
ARE YOU ONE OF *THEM* TOO?
HEE HEE HEE. IT'S NO USE.

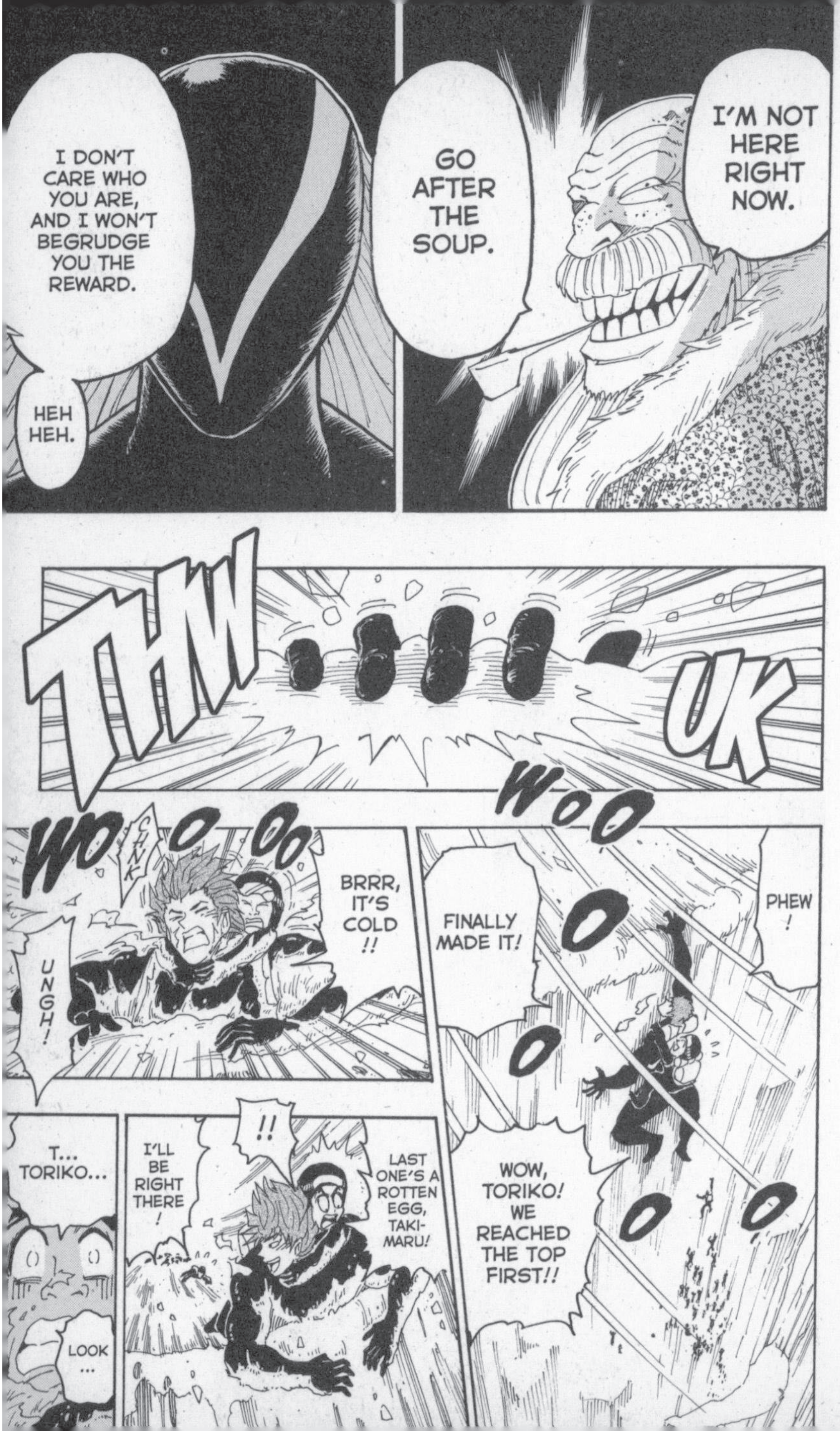
I'M NOT HERE RIGHT NOW.
GO AFTER THE SOUP.
I DON'T CARE WHO YOU ARE, AND I WON'T BEGRUDGE YOU THE REWARD.
HEH HEH.
THW
UK
WOOOOOO
PHEW!
FINALLY MADE IT!
WOW, TORIKO! WE REACHED THE TOP FIRST!!
WOOOO
CHNK
BRRR, IT'S COLD!!
UNGH!
!!
LAST ONE'S A ROTTEN EGG, TAKI-MARU!
I'LL BE RIGHT THERE!
T... TORIKO...
LOOK...

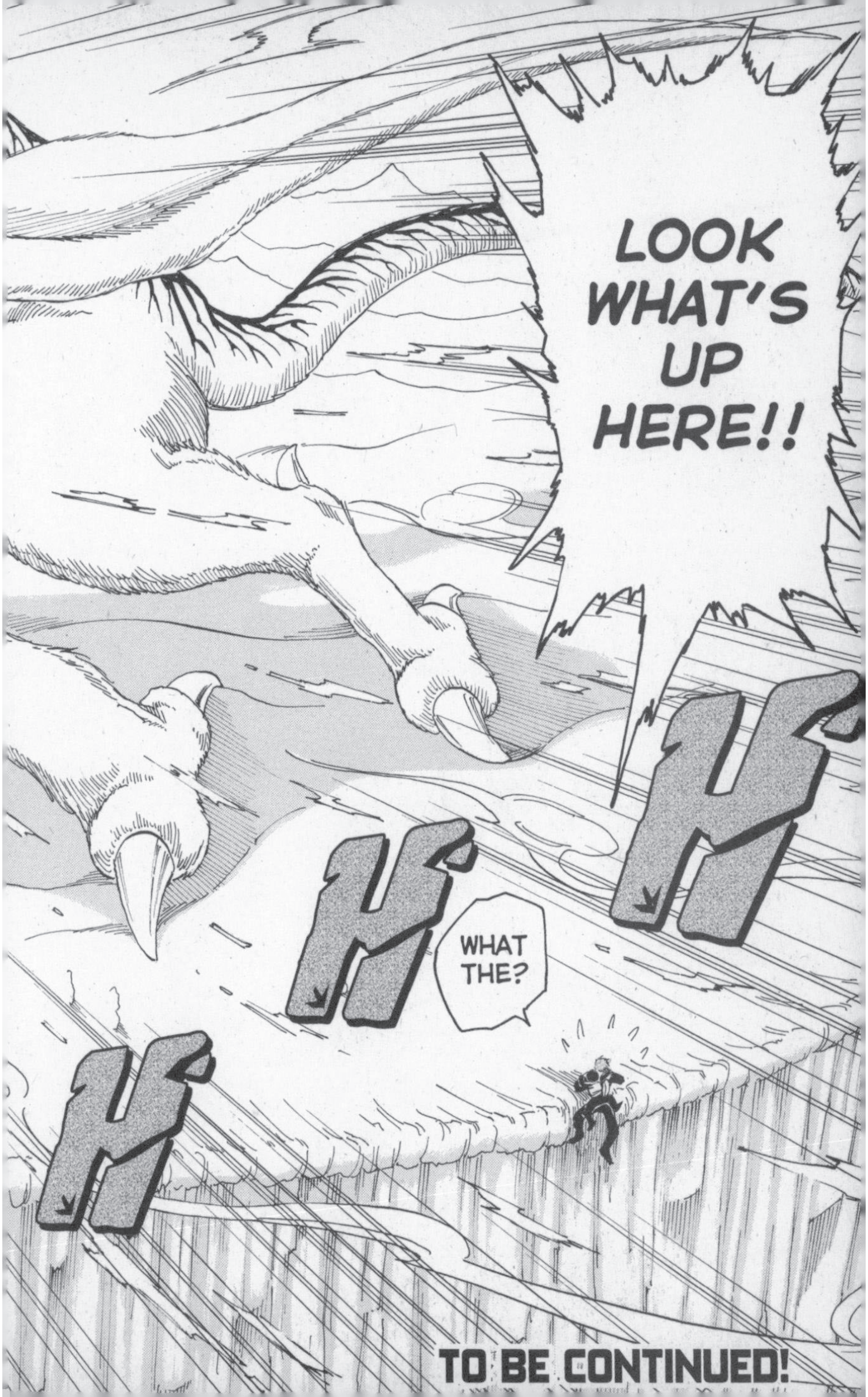
LOOK WHAT'S UP HERE!!
H
H
H
WHAT THE?
TO BE CONTINUED!

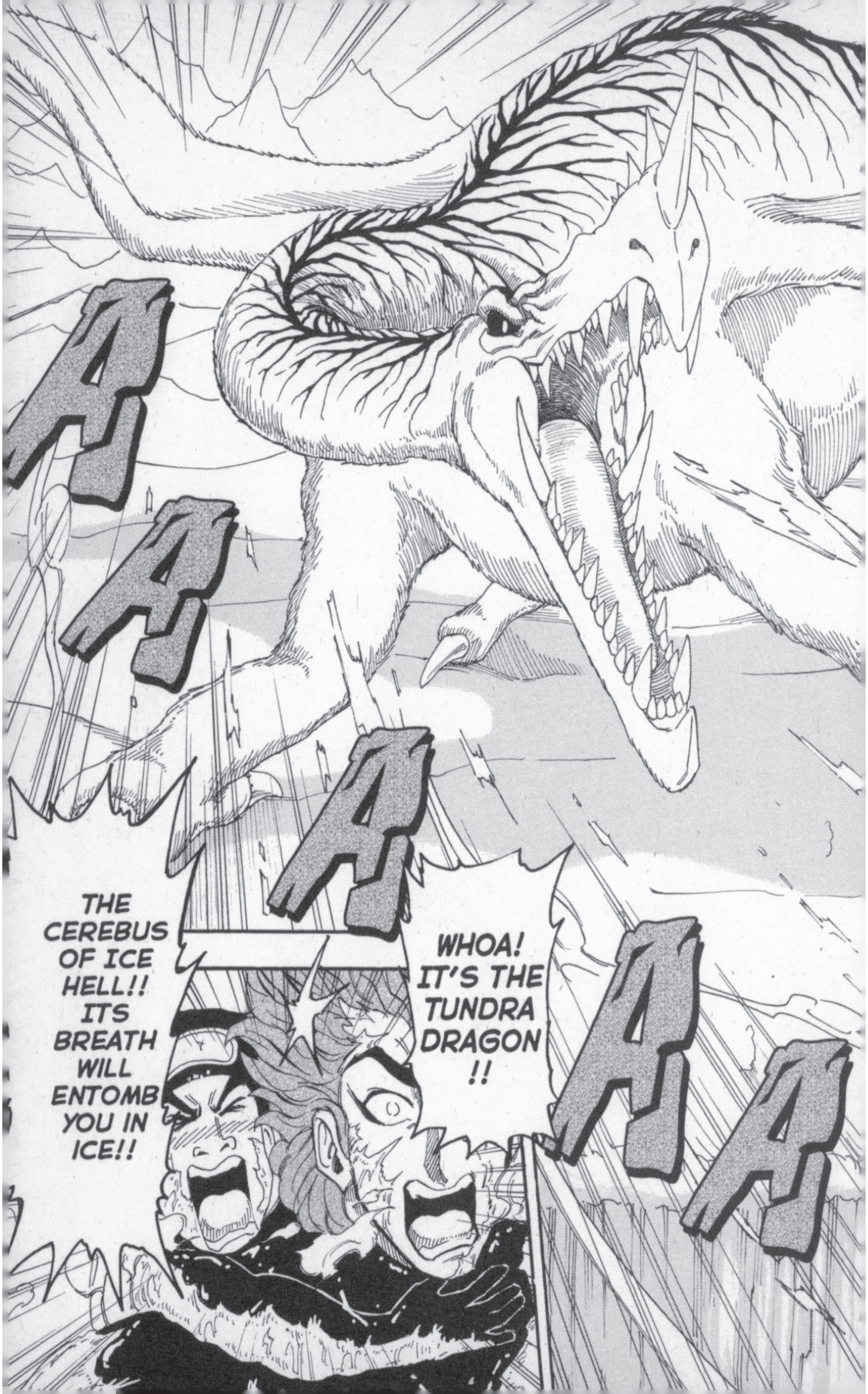
AAAAA
WHOA! IT'S THE TUNDRA DRAGON!!
THE CEREBUS OF ICE HELL!! ITS BREATH WILL ENTOMB YOU IN ICE!!

TORIKO

GOURMET CHECKLIST

Vol. 057

SWAMP EEL

(FISH)

CAPTURE LEVEL: 18

HABITAT: RICH SWAMPS

LENGTH: 29 METERS

HEIGHT: ---

WEIGHT: 7.5 TONS

PRICE: 100 G / 4,900 YEN

SWAMP EEL
(FISH)
CAPTURE LEVEL: 18

SCALE

THIS EEL-LIKE CREATURE LIVES IN SWAMPS AND UTILIZES ITS LONG NECK AND SHARP FANGS TO SNATCH PREY FROM THE LAND AND SKY. IT'S THE BIGGEST BADDIE IN YOUR TYPICAL SWAMP, BUT IN THE PREHISTORIC MARSH, IT'S ACTUALLY ONE OF THE LOWEST ANIMALS ON THE FOOD CHAIN.

TORIKO

GOURMET CHECKLIST

Vol. 058
EIGHT-HEADED SNAIL
(MOLLUSK)

HABITAT: REGAL ISLE

LENGTH: 15 METERS

HEIGHT: 9 METERS

WEIGHT: 14 TONS

PRICE: 1 KG / 90,000 YEN

EIGHT-HEADED SNAIL
(MOLLUSK)
CAPTURE LEVEL 23

SCALE

WITH ITS EIGHT HEADS, THIS IS ONE FEROCIOUS SNAIL. IT EXCRETES A SLIME THAT CAN MELT MOST NEAR ANYTHING. IT HAS A HUGE SHELL THAT IT HIDES IN IF EVER IN DANGER. THE SHELL IS VERY TOUGH AND MOST HUMAN WEAPONS ARE COMPLETELY POWERLESS AGAINST IT. CATCHING THIS MEGA SNAIL IS PRETTY TOUGH, BUT IT'S A BAYOU DELICACY!

TORIKO

GOURMET CHECKLIST

Vol. 059

GATOR SHARK
(FISH-BEAST)

CAPTURE LEVEL: 27

HABITAT: ANY LARGE BODY OF WATER

LENGTH: 43 METERS

HEIGHT: ---

WEIGHT: 27 TONS

PRICE: 100 G / 47,000 YEN

GATOR SHARK
(FISH-BEAST)
CAPTURE LEVEL: 27

SCALE

THIS GIANT FISH CAN POP OPEN ITS JAWS A FULL 180 DEGREES. ITS BITE HAS THE SAME FORCE AS AN ALLIGATOR'S, MEANING MOST PREY IS DOOMED ONCE IT'S BEEN NABBED. THE GATOR SHARK'S CAPTURE LEVEL MAKES IT THE TOP OF THE FOOD CHAIN IN THE PREHISTORIC MARSH. ITS MEAT IS SUPERB, AND CAN BE EATEN RAW.

TORIKO

GOURMET CHECKLIST

Vol. 060

 ## MONSTER BIRD RUBANDA
(BIRD)

CAPTURE LEVEL: 30

HABITAT: DEVIL ATHLETIC ON REGAL ISLE

LENGTH: ---

HEIGHT: 4 METERS

WEIGHT: 1 TON

PRICE: MEAT NOT FIT FOR HUMAN
CONSUMPTION

MONSTER BIRD
RUBANDA
(BIRD)
CAPTURE LEVEL 30

SCALE

THIS QUIXOTIC BIRD IS CAPABLE OF A NUMBER OF UNUSUAL FEATS
RANGING FROM CAUSING HALLUCINATIONS WITH ITS BEWITCHING
BREATH TO CREATING VISUAL ISOLATION EFFECTS. IT ONLY LIVES IN
THE DEVIL ATHLETIC, BUT IT DOES QUITE WELL THERE WITH ITS
CUNNING AND COLD-BLOODED NATURE. JUST LOOKING AT IT IS
REPULSIVE ENOUGH THAT MOST GOURMET HUNTERS DESPISE IT.

TORIKO

GOURMET CHECKLIST

Vol. 061

HEAVY CLIFF
(MAMMAL)

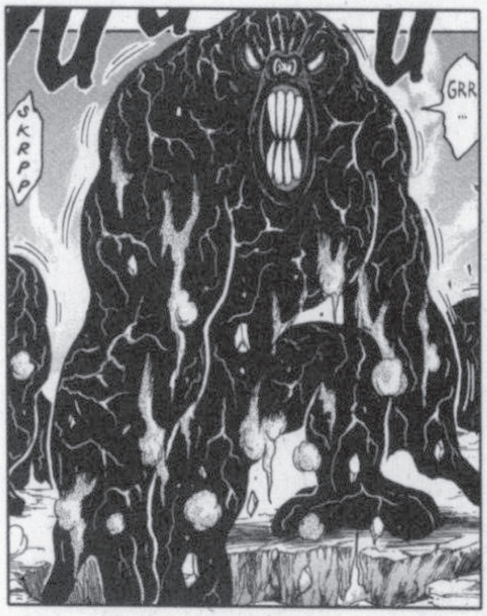
GRR ...
SKRPP

CAPTURE LEVEL: 30

HABITAT: REGAL WALL ON REGAL ISLE

LENGTH: ---

HEIGHT: 12 METERS

WEIGHT: 10 TONS

PRICE: MEAT NOT FIT FOR HUMAN CONSUMPTION

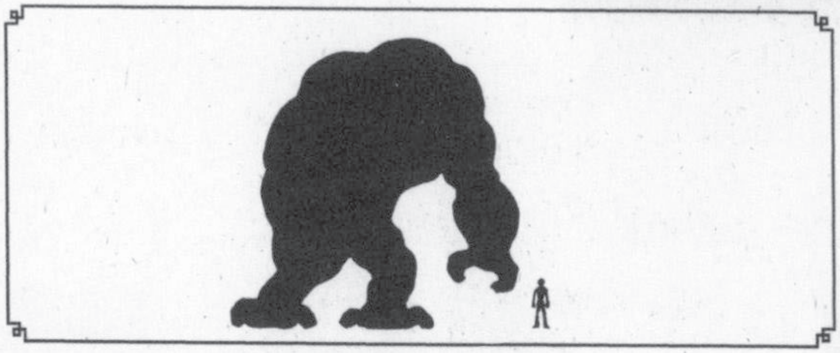

SCALE

THIS MASSIVE RODENT SPECIES RESIDES WITHIN THE REGAL WALL AT THE ENTRANCE TO THE REGAL HIGHLANDS. THEY WON'T ATTACK UNLESS THREATENED, BUT THE MOMENT THEY SENSE DANGER, THEY'LL SWARM EN MASSE. A HEAVY CLIFF'S BODY IS HIGHLY MALLEABLE, ALLOWING IT TO HARDEN ITS FLESH, AND IT WILL IMPLEMENT SUCH TRICKS WHILE FIGHTING. EVEN ON AN ISLAND LIKE REGAL ISLE, FULL OF FORMIDABLE BEASTS, THEY SAY A HEAVY CLIFF CAN HOLD ITS OWN.

CHARACTER PROFILE

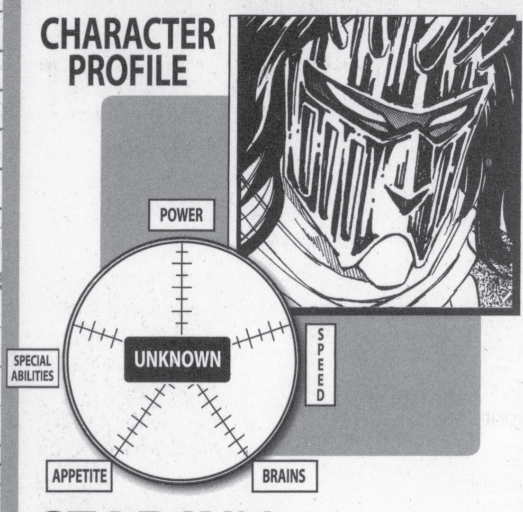

POWER

SPECIAL ABILITIES

UNKNOWN

SPEED

APPETITE

BRAINS

STARJUN

AGE	UNKNOWN	**BIRTHDAY:**	UNKNOWN
BLOOD TYPE	UNKNOWN	**SIGN:**	UNKNOWN
HEIGHT	232 CM	**WEIGHT:**	307 KG
EYESIGHT	20/2.6	**SHOE SIZE:**	48 CM

SPECIAL MOVES/ABILITIES

● **Unknown**

All that is known about him is that he's one of three Vice-Chefs at Gourmet Corp. From the battle on Regal Isle, it's clear he can see Toriko's massive potential and is watching his growth intently.

CHARACTER PROFILE

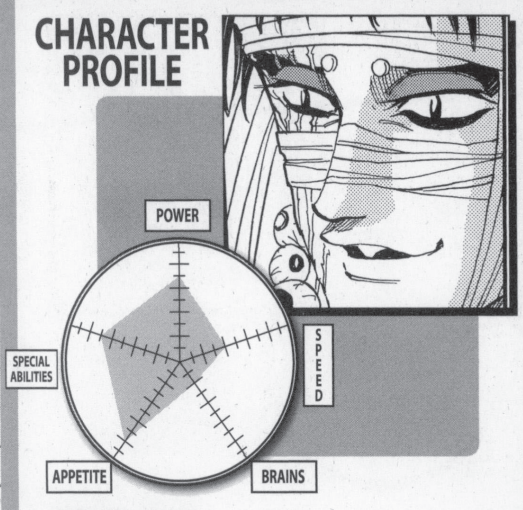

POWER

SPECIAL ABILITIES

SPEED

APPETITE

BRAINS

CEDRE

AGE	24	**BIRTHDAY:**	JUNE 3
BLOOD TYPE	B	**SIGN:**	GEMINI
HEIGHT	178 CM	**WEIGHT:**	80 KG
EYESIGHT	20/100	**SHOE SIZE:**	28 CM

SPECIAL MOVES/ABILITIES

● **Unknown**

Culinary Head of Gourmet Corp.'s Branch #6. He's in charge of supplying the provisions for all Gourmet Corp. operations. He lost to Sunny on Regal Isle, and now hankers for a rematch outside of his GT Robot. He's a strange guy with a creepy hobby of collecting critters' eyeballs.

CHARACTER PROFILE

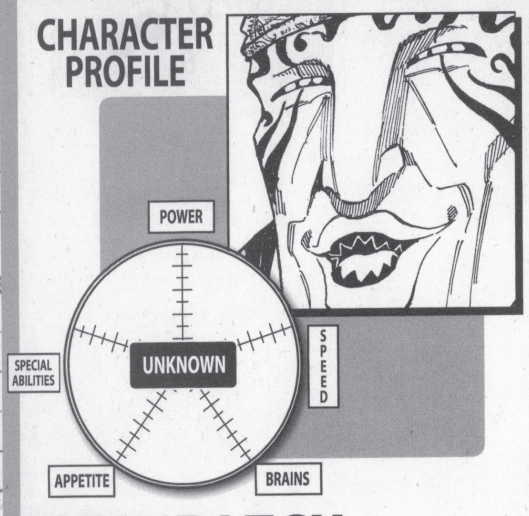

POWER

SPECIAL ABILITIES

SPEED

UNKNOWN

APPETITE

BRAINS

GRINPATCH

AGE	UNKNOWN	**BIRTHDAY:**	UNKNOWN
BLOOD TYPE	UNKNOWN	**SIGN:**	UNKNOWN
HEIGHT	240 CM	**WEIGHT:**	290 KG
EYESIGHT	20/4	**SHOE SIZE:**	50 CM

SPECIAL MOVES/ABILITIES

● **Breath Gun, Breath Bazooka, Breath Missile**

One of the Gourmet Corp.'s Vice-Chefs. His lung capacity far exceeds a normal human's, and he has three pupils and four arms. Not only is he an oddity in body, his mind's pretty out there too. His attacks involve propelling his own breath, and he's quite proud of his unrivaled long-range attacks.

COMING NEXT VOLUME

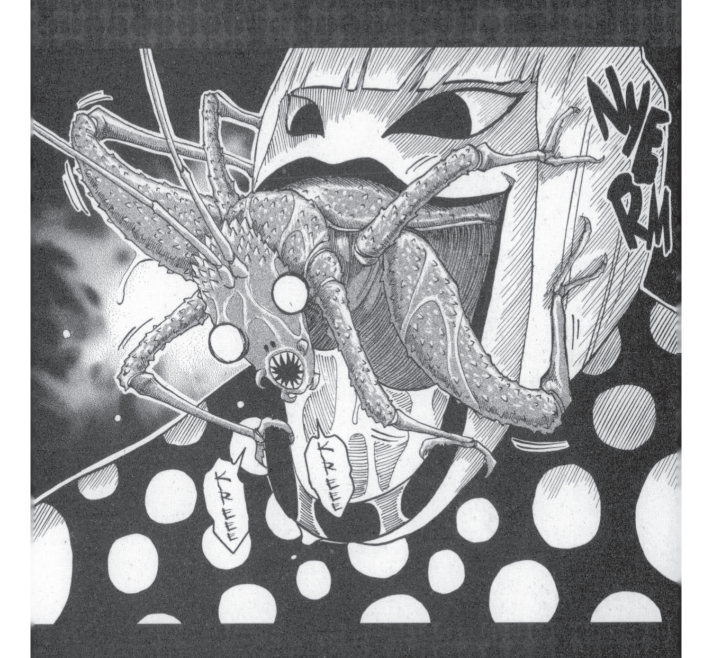

HELL FROZEN OVER

Toriko and the other gourmet hunters finally reach the freezing continent of Ice Hell. Here they will face the toughest environmental challenges of their lives. And unfortunately, they aren't the only ones there in search of the legendary Century Soup.

AVAILABLE APRIL 2012!

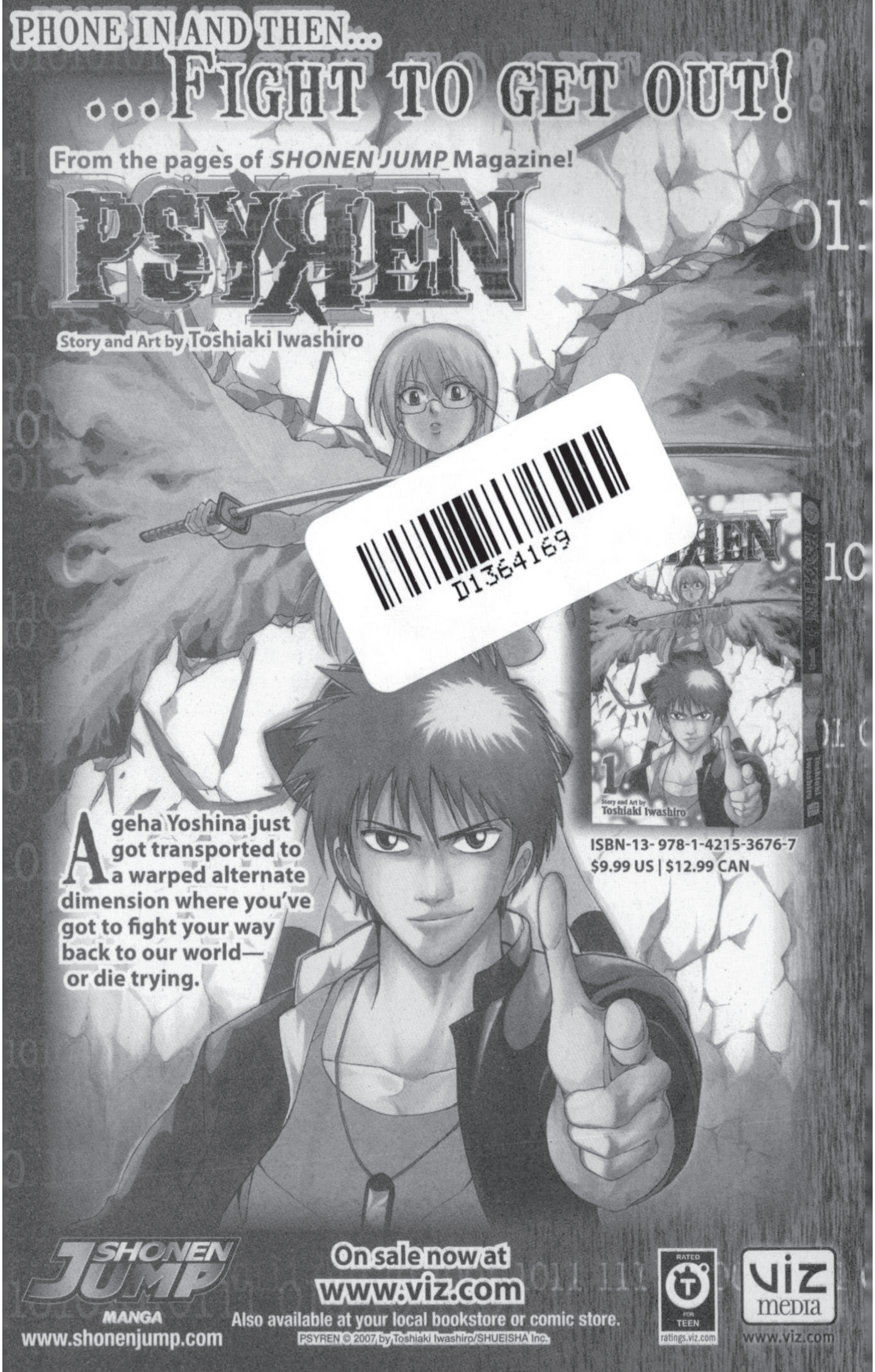
PHONE IN AND THEN...
...FIGHT TO GET OUT!
From the pages of SHONEN JUMP Magazine!
PSYREN
Story and Art by Toshiaki Iwashiro
D1364169
A geha Yoshina just got transported to a warped alternate dimension where you've got to fight your way back to our world—or die trying.
PSYREN 1
Story and Art by Toshiaki Iwashiro
ISBN-13- 978-1-4215-3676-7
$9.99 US | $12.99 CAN
SHONEN JUMP MANGA
www.shonenjump.com
On sale now at www.viz.com
Also available at your local bookstore or comic store.
PSYREN © 2007 by Toshiaki Iwashiro/SHUEISHA Inc.
RATED T FOR TEEN
ratings.viz.com
VIZ media
www.viz.com